The Holy Grail on Film

The Holy Grail on Film

Essays on the Cinematic Quest

Edited by
KEVIN J. HARTY

McFarland & Company, Inc., Publishers
Jefferson, North Carolina

ALSO BY KEVIN J. HARTY

*The Reel Middle Ages: American, Western and Eastern European,
Middle Eastern and Asian Films
About Medieval Europe* (1999; paper 2006)

EDITED BY KEVIN J. HARTY

The Vikings on Film: Essays on Depictions of the Nordic Middle Ages (2011)

Cinema Arthuriana: Twenty Essays, rev. ed. (2002; paper 2010)

King Arthur on Film: New Essays on Arthurian Cinema (1999)

ALL FROM MCFARLAND

Frontispiece: A replica of the *santo caliz* in Valencia
Cathedral claimed by some to be the Holy Grail.

Photographs are, unless otherwise indicated, from the collection of the editor.

ISBN 978-0-7864-7785-2 (softcover : acid free paper) ∞
ISBN 978-1-4766-2053-4 (ebook)

LIBRARY OF CONGRESS CATALOGUING DATA ARE AVAILABLE

BRITISH LIBRARY CATALOGUING DATA ARE AVAILABLE

On the cover: Harrison Ford, Sean Connery and John Rhys-Davies
in *Indiana Jones and the Last Crusade*, 1989 (Paramount Pictures/
Photofest); foreground cup (Photos.com/Thinkstock)

Printed in the United States of America

*McFarland & Company, Inc., Publishers
Box 611, Jefferson, North Carolina 28640
www.mcfarlandpub.com*

For Norris J. Lacy
with continued gratitude

En lui fu Nature si large
que trestot mist en une charge,
si li dona quanque ele ot.
—Chrétien de Troyes, *Cligés*

Table of Contents

Acknowledgments

This collection of essays would never have been published without the kindness and generous help of many, many people. I owe debts of thanks to the contributors who, like the members of the cast of the Broadway musical *Spamalot*, each set out to find his or her own Grail by agreeing to write the essays that I commissioned them to write.

The true heroes of any research in the many areas of film studies are the staffs at university, research and film libraries and archives world-wide, and I want especially to thank specifically the following for their multiple—and, in many cases, continuing—kindnesses. (Blanche DuBois was only half correct; film researchers and scholars, I have found, always rely upon the kindness of friends and strangers!) I am as always indebted to the staff of the Library, Special Collections Division, Stills Archive, and Viewing Services at the British Film Institute in London—whose devotion to preserving the history and scholarship of film for students of the genre like me is unflagging. I owe thanks as well to Rosemary Hanes at the Library of Congress in Washington, D.C., and to Nancy Goldman at the Pacific Film Archive in Berkeley.

At La Salle University, I am indebted to John Baky, Director of the Connelly Library, and to the members of his often overworked (and always underappreciated) staff, especially Eithne Bearden, Stephen Breedlove, Carol Brigham, Bernetta Doane, Marian Golden, Rebecca Goldman, Chris Kibler, and Martha Tarlue; and to my colleagues in La Salle's Department of English who offered advice, suggestions, and encouragement: Eileen Barrett, John Beatty, Jacob Bennett, Phyllis Betz, Claire Busse, Jim Butler, Craig Franson, Kevin Grauke, Andrew Hibschman, Jamie Jesson, Liz Langemak, Br. Emery Mollenhauer FSC, Judith Musser, Bryan Narendorf, Megan Schoen, and Steve Smith. My own research on Grail films has been supported in part by generous summer subventions from the Committee on Leaves and Grants and from the Office of the Provost at La Salle University.

Any number of friends offered me their support and advice as I was putting together this collection of essays, some of whom, having put me up, then had to put up with me as they sat through repeated screenings of many of the Grail films discussed in this volume: Charlie Wilson and Matt McCabe, Richard Meiss and Peter Rudy, Kathleen Harty, Barbara Tepa and Alan Lupack, Olwen and Gordon Terris, Rick Fisher and Marcus Tozini, David Barrable and Simon Cunniffe, Sheena Napier, Judith Greenwood, Jeffrey Richards, Norris J. Lacy, Debra Mancoff, Don Hoffman, Rick Tempone, Donald Burns and Bob Parker, Jeff Petraco, Linda Merians, and Helena White.

For all these kind folk, I wish the blessings and rejuvenation promised to everyone who seeks the Holy Grail.

Introduction

Tante sainte chose est li graals
[Such a holy thing is the Grail].
—*Chrétien de Troyes*

"The Holy Grail is Jesus' juice glass."
—*Mercedes Ruehl as Anne Napolitano in Terry Gilliam's* The Fisher King

"Raising taxes is the Holy Grail of liberalism."
—*Mitch McConnell, then U.S. Senate Minority Leader (R–Kentucky)*

"Repealing the Affordable Care Act is the Republicans' Holy Grail."
—*President Barack Obama*

"The Grail is an empty signifier!"
—*Martin B. Shichtman*

In the Metropolitan Cathedral-Basilica of the Assumption of Our Lady of Valencia (also known, in Valencian, as Església Catedral-Basílica Metropolitana de l'Assumpció de la Nostra Senyora de València, and, in Spanish, as Iglesia Catedral-Basílica Metropolitana de la Asunción de Nuestra Señora de Valencia), inside the main doors and to the right is a dimly lit smaller chapel. Pilgrims enter reverently, some dropping to their knees, others prostrating themselves on the worn marble floors, before an illuminated altar atop of which, behind glass in a slightly elevated golden reliquary, rests a vessel, Valencia's so-called "santo caliz" (Holy Chalice), claimed by some to be the Holy Grail, the cup used by Jesus at the Last Supper, which subsequently caught the blood dripping from His pierced side as He hung on the Cross on Calvary.

The pedigree of the Holy Chalice of Valencia—other cities such as Jerusalem, Antioch, and Genoa have, at one time or another, also claimed to own the cup from the Last Supper—and the complicated relationship between that Chalice and the Holy Grail are beyond the scope of this introduction, or even this volume, which focuses instead solely on the Quest for the Holy Grail (or any Grail) in one genre: film. Those interested in larger issues related to the Grail—the word itself ("graal") a neologism coined by the Old French writer Chrétien de Troyes in the late twelfth century—would be well served to consult Richard Barber's excellent study, *The Holy Grail: Imagination and Belief*, published by Harvard University Press in 2004, and Dhira B. Mahoney's invaluable edited collection of essays, *The Grail: A Casebook*, reprinted by Routledge in 2014.

In the last quarter century, the serious study of "medieval film"—cinema medievalia—has become a fair field full of folk. And scholarly studies in the field, general and more focused, in book and collected and individual essay form, continue to be published. *The Holy Grail on Film* shares an aim with earlier collections of essays on medieval film that I have edited—*Cinema Arthuriana: Essays on Arthurian Film*; *King Arthur on Film*; *Cinema Arthuriana: Twenty Essays*; and *The Vikings on Film*. This volume, like its predecessors, brings together scholars from both sides of the Atlantic with varying backgrounds and areas of expertise to discuss a subgenre of cinema medievalia: films about the Quest for the Grail (Holy and otherwise). The essays that follow look at the Grails in films both expected and unexpected, all offering fresh perspectives on one of the enduring myths of the Arthurian world and of Western culture.

The Holy Grail on Film begins with my essay on Grail films made before the advent of the talkies, most notably Thomas Edison's *Parsifal* (1904) and his *Knights of the Square Table* (1917), Clarence Brown's *The Light in the Dark* (1922), and Arnold Fanck's *Der Heilige Berg* (1926). The 1917 film is a ringing endorsement of the merits of Scouting, made, not surprisingly, with the blessing and endorsement of the Boy Scouts of America, while the specter of National Socialism hangs, to one degree or another, over the other three.

K. S. Whetter's essay on Victor Saville's *The Silver Chalice* (1954) discusses the pre-medieval Grail. In the film and in its source, the 1952 novel of the same title by the best-selling novelist Thomas B. Costain, the eponymous vessel is to contain the cup used by Christ at the Last Supper and is the first-century handiwork of one Basil the Silversmith, played by Paul Newman in a role he later disavowed as an embarrassment. Whetter argues that both the novel and the film, by providing the prequel to the medieval story of the Grail, focus on the object itself, rather than on the medieval Quest for the by-then-lost object, thereby providing a possible backstory to the complicated and often conflicting medieval (and post-medieval) accounts of knights worthy (and not) questing for the Holy Grail. Both the novel and the film prophesize the return of the Grail, lost at the separate conclusions of their accounts, a prophesy that continues to inspire Grail questors even in the twenty-first century. At the same time, both the novel and film suggest that the Grail is not only a physical object but also a series of ideas that reinforce the revolutionary message that the New Testament offers.

If *The Silver Chalice* is an exercise in "Hollywood-does-the Grail," with all the strengths and weaknesses that such a characterization affords, Robert Bresson's *Lancelot du lac* (1974), with its conscious use of the medieval story of the Quest for its source, is, as Joan Tasker Grimbert shows, a decidedly different kind of film. In its dark view of the Arthurian world, a world from which the Grail is conspicuously absent, Bresson's film offers not a cinema without symbols, but a cinema with symbols emptied of all their symbolism.

Alan Baragona also looks at avant-garde European cinematic Quests—two somewhat expected, Rohmer's *Perceval* (1978) and Blank's made-for-German-television *Parzival* (1980), with their decidedly different sources and approaches—and a third somewhat unexpected, von Trier's *Breaking the Waves* (1996). All three, Baragona argues, underscore the continuing appeal of the original Grail Knight, whose innocence is a symbol of a deeply flawed humanity that requires him to try again and again to achieve his goal—in a pattern perhaps emulated by the avant-garde filmmakers themselves.

Jon Sherman shifts attention from flawed Grail Knight to flawed Grail Maiden in an essay re-examining the role Kundry plays in Hans-Jürgen Syberberg's epic film adaptation of Wagner's *Parsifal* (1982). Sherman finds, as with almost every facet of his complex film, that Syberberg both reinforces as well as undercuts Wagner in his characterization of Kundry. Syberberg's Kundry is at times more maternal, less seductive, than Wagner's—but, ultimately, she becomes a conflation of her characterization by Wagner and those by his medieval sources and predecessors.

In what may seem at first like a shift from the sublime to the ridiculous, Christine M. Neufeld next discusses what may arguably be the best-known (and most beloved) Grail film, *Monty Python and the Holy Grail* (1975). But comedy is always serious stuff, and Neufeld argues that a film about a Quest predicated on questions both asked and unasked leaves us not with a neat, pat set of answers, but rather with a whole new set of questions.

Raeleen Chai-Elsholz and Jean-Marc Elsholz focus on John Boorman's *Excalibur* (1981), specifically in terms of the way the concept of light reinforces the narrative. *Excalibur* has previously been discussed in terms of its mythopoeia and its use of the elements of fire, water, and earth. Here the authors apply medieval and cinematic theories of light literally to illuminate what is at work in the film's reinterpretation of the Arthurian Quest narrative, whether based on Malory or as interpolated by its screenwriter and its director. *Excalibur*, they argue, ends on a note of "liquid light" that underscores the legendary promised Arthurian return.

The post-medieval Quest is found perhaps nowhere more quintessentially than in the endless, multi-faceted circus surrounding Dan Brown's *Da Vinci Code* franchise. Susan Aronstein charts the backstories to the novel and the 2006 film, the legal battles over copyright infringement that surrounded the release of the film, the relationship between the novel and the film, the Catholic Church's reaction to the book and the film, and the delicate balancing act that Ron Howard attempted when he directed the film. Aronstein argues that Howard's film seems to want to have it both ways: It wants to exploit the popularity of Brown's novel and the conspiracy theories that it gave new life to, while also affirming the necessity of traditional faith. Whether Howard succeeded in so doing is something that the viewer will have to decide.

America, the New World, for all its attempt to throw off the Old World continues to be fascinated with it. The continuing American embrace of the world of Arthur is especially noteworthy—e.g., Twain, Hemingway, Faulkner, Fitzgerald, and Steinbeck, just for starters— and James Jesson, in an essay on Barry Levinson's film adaptation of Bernard Malamud's novel, *The Natural* (1984), suggests how, in the film, the mythology surrounding the American national pastime mediates the Arthurian quest. The film offers a conscious conflation of mythologies, Cooperstown's and Camelot's, that reflects the continuing reworking, on page and screen, of the non-democratic narratives of the European Old World into the more egalitarian narratives of the American New World.

Cory James Rushton examines another New World Grail sighting in an essay on Terry Gilliam's *The Fisher King* (1991). Rushton finds that, in its depiction of the Grail Quest as played out on the streets of twentieth-century Manhattan, the film shares common ground with other Gilliam films in which an eccentric struggles to survive in an oppressive society, a society here marked by the ever-widening disparity between the haves and the have-nots. As such, *The Fisher King* not only remaps the Grail Quest but also holds a mirror to contemporary New York as a modern reincarnation of the Wasteland in need of healing.

Just who is and who is not a Grail Knight, and what a Grail Knight might indeed be seeking, are the subject of Joseph M. Sullivan's reading of the Lucas-Spielberg film *Indiana Jones and the Last Crusade* (1989). Ultimately, the film, Sullivan argues, is less about the Quest for Grail and more about the Quest of a son for his father. As such, the film is a "prequel" that turns the now four-film *Indiana Jones* franchise into a true narrative adventure cycle.

Earlier in this introduction, I indicated that the Grail films discussed in this collection of essays would include both the so-called usual suspects, and some that were not. The last four essays here discuss the "nots." Paul B. Sturtevant first asks two important questions: What makes a Grail film a Grail film? Does it need a Grail? After all, Joan Tasker Grimbert's earlier essay here discusses a Bresson film in which the Grail is nowhere to be found. Sturtevant's concern is specifically with George Miller's *The Road Warrior* (1982)—the second installment in the director's *Mad Max* cinematic trilogy. His conclusion is simple enough: Grails can be found in films when we want to find them. But such a simple conclusion belies the multiple ways of reading and approaching *The Road Warrior* that Sturtevant uses in his essay, each based on the director's own recognition that his Max is a reflection of a larger collective unconsciousness that sees the film's main character as "a kind of weird Australian" mythological figure who has universal resonance.

Andrew B. R. Elliott turns his attention to Russian director Andrei Tarkovsky's *Stalker* (1979)—I should note in passing that the idea that Tarkovsky's film might indeed be a Grail film was first suggested to me by the always generous and collegial late Austrian Arthurian scholar Ulrich Müller in a discussion we had over glasses of beer a number of years ago at one of the annual Medieval Congresses at Western Michigan University in Kalamazoo. Elliott first considers a number of possible generic approaches for discussing a film whose director vehemently dismissed all critical attempts to classify any of his films. He concludes that here, as in a number of other films discussed in this volume, what is sought is less important than the actual seeking. The very act of questing is an affirmation of what it means to be human.

Laurie A. Finke and Martin B. Shichtman—the latter of whom caused more than a critical ruckus when he emphatically announced at another Kalamazoo Medieval Congress, "The Grail is an empty signifier!"—discuss the Grail and Quest intertexts in Frank Coraci's comedy *The Waterboy* (1998) starring Adam Sandler as an admittedly unlikely Grail Knight—but then aren't all Grail Knights, by definition, unlikely? Finke and Shichtman argue that Sandler makes fun of the linked myths of the Quest for the Holy Grail and American masculinity though, ironically by, in the final analysis, reinscribing the very myths it seeks to undermine.

David W. Marshall completes this collection of essays by framing it with another discussion of a group of Grail films—not silent Grail films as in my first essay—but four recent B-films that show that ultimately nothing is sacred, here because all four films—*Code of the Templars, Cup of My Blood, The Librarian: Curse of the Judas Chalice,* and *Rosencrantz and Guildenstern Are Undead*—emphasize the potentially destructive nature of the Grail, a theme touched upon by a number of earlier essays in this volume. What the essays in this volume attest to is a continuing fascination with myth on the part of filmmakers, specifically the primal myth of the Quest as it has been enlivened by the specific Quest for the Holy (and, at times, not-so-Holy) Grail. Martin B. Shichtman is correct: *The Grail has become an empty signifier!* One need simply turn to the World Wide Web and Google "Holy Grail of" to produce millions of hits. The Grail is, of course, still a symbol, but it has become a symbol for whatever the signifier chooses it to be—and the films discussed in this collection of essays are only one small manifestation of this phenomenon.

Holy Grail, Silent Grail

Kevin J. Harty

The popular cultural phenomenon that I first in 1987 called "cinema Arthuriana"[1] had its beginnings in America with the story of the Quest for the Holy Grail. No less an internationally recognized genius than Thomas A. Edison in 1904 commissioned Edwin S. Porter, his principal director and cameraman, to attempt a screen version of Wagner's *Parsifal*. Both Edison and Porter were interested in capitalizing on the success of the 1903 live production in German of Wagner's Grail opera that had opened at New York's Metropolitan Opera House on Christmas Eve. German Wagnerians and other purists may have shuddered at the thought of this, or of any other, production of the Meister's work on any stage but that for which it had been designed, the Bayreuth Festspielhaus, but opera buffs and critics on this side of the Atlantic were more than eager to see, hear, and show their appreciation for *Parsifal*. Quickly dubbed the highlight of the New York opera season, a second production of Wagner's *Parsifal*, in English, opened in October 1904 in Boston, before moving to New York and then going on a national tour.[2]

The Edison-Porter film is an interesting artistic failure, hampered by the fact that technology did not yet, and would not for quite some time, exist to synchronize phonographic recordings with frames on the screen (Bush 607–608). And Edison soon ran into additional difficulties, once the film was released, when the owner of the copyright to the Met production successfully sued him for using the script of the opera without permission in a far-reaching legal case that established the right of authors and others to withhold a work from being turned into a film, thereby forcing Edison to withdraw his film from distribution (Niver, *The First Twenty Years* 74; Spears 336). In 1990, the film was remastered and began to be shown at festivals in Europe and in the United States.[3]

The Edison-Porter film consists of eight sections, each with a separate title and an individual copyright, varying in length from 2 to 282 feet (Niver, *The First Twenty Years* 74), and each introduced by intertitles (Spears 336):

Parsifal Ascends the Throne
Ruins of a Magic Graden
Exterior of Klingson's [*sic*] Castle
Magic Garden
Interior of the Temple

Scene outside the Temple
Return of Parsifal
In the Woods [Niver, *Motion Pictures* 207].

An advertisement in the Edison Catalogue offering the film for screening and distribution promised "the greatest religious subject that has been produced in motion pictures ... [given the] amount of time, labor and money ... [that have] been expended producing this picture" ("Parsifal" 50). According to Niver, the film was indeed the "most ambitious and costly" made by Edison and Porter during their collaboration (*The First Twenty Years* 74).

While the film's production values may seem primitive by today' standards, the Edison-Porter *Parsifal* did manage to record a fairly elaborate version of Wagner's opera. Porter positioned his camera so that all shots are from the audience's point of view, and the acting style is highly exaggerated to suggest that the actors are singing as they stand and move about the set, which consists of large painted backdrops that often blow in the wind (Niver, *Motion Pictures* 207).

The film opens after the founding of the Grail society by Titurel who has entrusted the care of the sacred vessel to his son, Amfortas. When Klingsor is refused membership in the Grail society—he has previously led a selfish and an impure life—he renounces good and embraces a personification of Evil, from whom he receives both magical powers and a company of false Grail maidens to lure knights away from the true fellowship of the Grail. Kundry is the first among the false Grail maidens, having been Evil's faithful handmaiden for more than a millennium, even going so far as to have mocked Christ as He carried his Cross up Calvary. Condemned as a result to wander the Earth for her sin, Kundry longs to meet the Holy Knight who will not spurn her advances, thus enabling her redemption. Meanwhile, Parsifal is spirited away by his mother Herzeloid, intent on preventing her son's death in defense of the Grail since his father died in just that way. Kundry returns to interrupt the enthronement of Amfortas as Grail King, plunging the Sacred Spear into his side and then making off with it. Titurel then announces that the wound will not heal until the true Grail Knight appears, spear in hand, to make both Amfortas and the Grail kingdom whole again.

Fifteen years pass, during which Amfortas continues to suffer without remedy. Gurnemanz and the Grail knights then appear, dragging behind them a young man who has just killed a swan with his bow and arrow. The young man, soon revealed to be Parisfal, claims not to know that it is wrong to kill a swan, admitting that he does not even know his own name. Kundry and Gurnemanz both come to the conclusion that Parsifal may well be the long-awaited guileless fool, but Parsifal views the Grail ceremony without any reaction and is driven into exile.

An unspecified period of time then passes, and Parsifal appears at the court of Klingsor, defeats his guards, and prepares to do battle with Evil, who summons his handmaidens and Kundry to tempt the knight. At first Parsifal succumbs to Kundry's wiles, but her kiss produces an unexpected effect: overwhelmed initially by a lust that pierces his heart just as the Sacred Spear pierced Amfortas's side, Parisfal falls to the ground and calls upon Christ for salvation. His plea is heard as Parsifal is granted a vision of the Grail and an understanding of all that has happened at Amfortas's castle.

The Hall of the Grail King in the 1904 Edison-Porter *Parsifal* (Library of Congress).

Prodded by Evil, Kundry tries again to tempt Parsifal, who rebuffs her. Klingsor then appears with the Sacred Spear and hurls it at Parsifal, only to have it fall harmlessly at the now Grail Knight's feet. Parsifal grasps the Spear and uses it to make the Sign of the Cross, as Klingsor falls dead and his castle crumbles—only Kundry survives. Again years pass, and a knight clad in black emerges from a forest seeking Amfortas. The knight is, of course, Parsifal, who has brought the Sacred Spear to heal the king. Gurnemanz and the now-repentant Kundry anoint Parsifal and prepare him for the Grail ceremony. As Parsifal heals Amfortas, a white dove appears, Kundry sinks to the ground, and a chorus of voices chant: "Wondrous work of mercy; / Redemption to the Redeemer."[4]

The technical and legal problems that plagued Edison's attempt to stage Wagner's *Parsifal* did not dissuade other directors from attempting to film, or even to create original productions of, operas for the screen. Italian directors, not surprisingly, filmed operas by Donizetti and Verdi for the screen throughout the teens, despite continuing technical problems in synchronizing sound to film, but Wagner too remained popular as the subject for filmed opera: there were a 1909 French film version of his *Tristan* and a 1912 Italian version of *Parsifal*, which featured more elaborate sets and an even more detailed screen scenario than Porter's had.[5]

Two American films from 1914 and 1915 suggest that the cinematic Grail had already come to signify more than simply the sacred vessel from the Last Supper and the Crucifixion. The first, *Sir Galahad of Twilight*, sets a love triangle on Twilight Mountain, where two rivals for the hand of a young girl try to prove who is her true Galahad. The second, *The Grail*, tells the story of an embezzling banker who blames the fiancé of his own daughter for his crime. When the daughter and her father are stranded in the wastelands of a dessert, the fiancé comes to their rescue in a series of scenes that draw clear parallels to the story, medieval in its origins, of Galahad's Quest for the Holy Grail.[6] In 1916, D. W. Griffith announced plans for a spectacle, *The Quest for the Holy Grail*, to be based on the famous series of fifteen murals by Edwin Austin Abbey that decorate the Book Delivery Room in the Boston Public Library.[7] Griffith had been studying the murals while attending the Boston Premiere of *The Birth of a Nation* (Wagenknecht and Slide 259). But, after obtaining the rights from Abbey's widow to use the murals in a film project, Griffith abandoned the project, initially because of pressures from his financial backers to return to projects such as *Intolerance* already in production on the West Coast, and finally, after World War I broke out, when public interest and demand turned to more contemporary screen scenarios (Stern 7–8).

Edison would return to the story of the Grail in his 1917 film, *The Knights of the Square Table*, a film that linked the Scouting Movement with the Quest for the Holy Grail. The National Headquarters of the Boy Scouts of America endorsed the film, whose working title was *The Grail* (Hanson 493), and James Austin Wilder, National Field Scout Commissioner, wrote the screenplay for and played the role of the Scoutmaster in the film.[8] Links between the Scouting Movement and Arthurian tradition predate the film as far back as the origins of Baden-Powell's scheme for that Movement.[9] While the intent and the chronology of some of the events in the earliest days of the Scouting Movement remain the subject of historical discussion and disagreement,[10] it is clear that Baden-Powell had mapped out his scheme for the Scouting Movement as early 1904 when he delivered a lecture on "Soldiering" to Eton College on 26 November and sent a follow-up letter published on 22 December in the Eton College *Chronicle* (Rosenthal, "Knight" 604). Clearly reflecting the jingoistic attitudes peculiar to his times, the letter (text in Rosenthal, "Knight" 604) provides the first mention in print of Baden-Powell's notion that the Scouts are modern-day equivalents of the Knights of the Middle Ages.

Subsequent publications by Baden-Powell produce variations on the code of knightly behavior to which he favorably compares the laws of Scouting. In *Scouting for Boys* (1908), Baden-Powell writes "In the old days the knights were the scouts of Britain, and their rules were very much the same as the scout law which we have now" (117). Chapter VII of the same book, offering hints to Scouting instructors and would-be Scoutmasters, discusses the chivalry of the knights that "was started in England some 1500 years ago by King Arthur" (209), provides a brief summary of the story of Arthur and the Knights of the Round Table, and enumerates the principles of the knightly code linking the preparedness of knights and of Scouts (209–210). In *Yarns for Boy Scouts* (1910), Baden-Powell retells the story of Arthur in full, designating him as "the founder of British Scouts, since he first started the Knights of England" (117), and declaring his Scouts nothing short of Knights seeking the Holy Grail (142–143)—though the Victorian Baden-Powell's admiration for the code of chivalry was not for the code as it may (or may not) have existed in medieval times but rather as it had been recreated by nineteenth-century antiquarians (see Jeal 422).

The Knights of the Square Table successfully balances two parallel but interrelated plots: the misadventures of a gang of delinquent boys, the Wharfrats-Motherless-Knights-Erring-of-the-Square-Table, and the events that lead up to their transformation into a Boy Scout Troop. As the film is little known, a detailed plot summary may be in order.[11] The central character is Richard Haddon, better known as "Pug," whose prize possession is a copy of Howard Pyle's *The Story of King Arthur and His Knights* (first published in 1903), which was presented to him by his mother on her deathbed with the injunction that he be brave and honest. Pug's father is a thief who has no time for Pug's fantasies about Arthur and his knights.

As the film opens, Pug imagines a scene from the court of King Arthur in which yet another cinematic Grail Knight, Sir Launfal, kisses King Arthur's ring as he sets out on a Quest for the Holy Grail. Arthur is shown in a stylized chamber standing before a throne flanked by two Grail-shaped *torchères*. Next, the camera cuts to a warehouse where a deadly gun battle between Pug's father and Police Detective Boyle takes place. Boyle shoots and kills Pug's father.

Back home, Pug tells his friend Chick that he is going to start a new kind of gang:

It's gonna be like King Arthur and his knights.
Every guy that belongs has gotter be brave an' he's gotter do bloody and desprit deeds, an' he's gotter stick to the rest of the gang till death.

By starting such a gang, Pug says:

Some day we might see this here Grail.
I tell you one thing we ain't going to have in this gang—that's stealing!
I'll tell you something else, too—you haven't got a mother, have you?
We won't have any guys into this gang that has mothers. It ain't fair to the rest of us. They can have fathers if they want, but—.

Pug is interrupted by the arrival of Detective Boyle who tells him what has happened to his father. Pug and Boyle struggle briefly. Boyle points out that right not might is what counts, but Pug vows to fight Boyle and everything he represents for the rest of his life. Pug's friend, Chick, pledges to do the same, as Boyle leaves and Pug consults his book on Arthur—"Winning of Knighthood. Duties of a true knight: to fear God; to love the smiling land wherein he dwells with all his heart and strength; to..."—the intertitles break off as a weeping Pug collapses on top of the book.

The film then introduces a second group of boys, a Troop of Boy Scouts, and juxtaposes scenes from the initiation rituals of both groups of boys—the gang's violent, the Scouts' uplifting. The Boy Scouts are under the direction of their Scoutmaster and troop leader David Scudder, better known as "Scud." Pug's gang soon spies another boy, Billy, who is rewarded with an apple by his mother after he rakes the front yard of his house. Billy wants to join Pug's gang, but he is immediately denied membership because he has a mother. Pug's gang next comes across Scud's Scout Troop and verbally harasses them. The two groups confront each other over a bridge. Scud asks Pug to let the Scouts pass, and a fight breaks out in which Billy, who has been following Pug and his gang, is accidentally knocked from the bridge into the water.

Pug's gang seems confused about what to do, but the Scouts quickly spring into action, pulling Billy from the water, wrapping him in a blanket, and telephoning for a doctor and an ambulance—the film's pro–Scouting agenda is less than subtle. Pug and his gang, fearing that the Scouts have also summoned the police, "beat it," though not before Chick says of the Scouts, "For a bunch o' sissies them fellers ain't so bad, hey, Pug?"

That evening, the Boy Scouts meet around a campfire, as the Scoutmaster tells them the story of "a very haughty man called Sir Launfal. In the pride of his youth, like many other knights, he set out to try and find the Grail." While the story continues, the camera cuts to a scene in which two thieves case a jewelry store. They decide to force a "kid" to go through the window and hand the jewelry out to them, pressing an unwilling Billy into service. Pug comes upon the scene and, after flashing back to the scene in which Billy's mother kisses him and gives him an apple for doing his chores, agrees to take Billy's place.

In breaking the window, Pug cuts his arm and begins to bleed profusely. He also remembers his own mother's deathbed injunction not to steal. On the counter in the jewelry store, he sees a loving cup which he takes to be the Grail, as the film cuts back to the Scoutmaster who concludes his story of Sir Launfal with the knight finally finding the Grail. The scene returns again to the jewelry store where Pug is warned not to "blab." In panic, he cries out: "An'—now—I won't never—see—the Grail," as he collapses from the loss of blood.

The next morning, Detective Boyle inspects the scene of the robbery and notices that the loving cup is covered with a boy's fingerprints. The scene switches back to the warehouse where Pug's gang holds an emergency meeting to decide what to do about Pug's wounds—"It just keeps bleeding. He'll die if we don't do something." The gang seeks out Billy, initiates him into the club, and decides to send him out to find the Scouts to come to the aid of Pug.

Boyle arrives unexpectedly looking for Pug as part of his investigation of the jewelry store robbery, and Billy tells him the story of how Pug saved him during the robbery. Pug confronts the policeman—"You're the guy that killed my father"—but collapses from weakness. As Boyle tries to give Pug something to drink, the glass turns into a loving-cup shaped Grail held by Sir Galahad. Pug drinks from the glass-now-turned-Grail, as the Scouts arrive, remove a shard of glass from his arm, and bind up his wound. Pug immediately recovers, and he and his gang become Boy Scouts, having learned as Sir Launfal did in the Scoutmaster's story that pride has no place in their lives. "So you see, boys, the Grail had been right at home all the time—only he didn't know it" because Sir Launfal was too proud—this version of the Grail Quest is clearly indebted to that contained in James Russell Lowell's 1849 poem *The Vision of Sir Launfal*.

When it was released, *The Knights of the Square Table* was well received critically.[12] Not surprisingly, the Boy Scouts of America embraced the film whole-heartedly. *Scouting*, the official publication of the Boy Scouts of America, saw the film as combining human interest with solid boy-rearing psychology:

> Action, human interest, real life, tears, laughs and thrills abound and through it all runs the story of the development of the motherless wharf rats, with their mixture of good and evil, into a Boy Scout troop. What Booth Tarkington has done in "Penrod" and "Seventeen" to interpret the adolescent boy, Mr. Wilder has done for "the gang" in "Knights of the Square Table" ["Knights" 11].

The film's appeal further lies in its attempt to address the problem of how boys should be properly reared. Indeed, in its review of the film, *Wid's Independent Review of Feature Films*, a leading trade publication, suggested that the proper box office angle was to concentrate on the boy problem:

> Every community, no matter how big or small, has on its hands the "boy problem." Some boys are too "sissified," and some too rough. Every parent is anxious to hit the happy medium. This picture shows intelligently why many boys are members of roughneck gangs, and at the same time gives intelligent reasons why boys should join the Boy Scout movement. At the finish it also registers very definitely the fact that no man is "too busy" to give some attention to the training of the boys of his country ["Very Pleasing Boy Stuff" 474].

This last comment, of course, echoes any number of statements made by Baden-Powell himself about the importance of proper training for the boys of England, and the film affords two occasions when Pug's gang does not know what to do in contrast to the ever-prepared Scouts—Bill's near drowning and Pug's profusely bleeding wound.

Interestingly, this early cinematic Grail Quest contains a noteworthy, though obviously unplanned, connection to a more recent Grail film, Terry Gilliam's *The Fisher King* (1991).[13] In both films, someone mistakes a loving cup for the Holy Grail. But, more importantly, *The Knights of the Square Table* continues the association of the Boy Scouts—both in England and abroad—with the matter of Arthur. Baden-Powell's writings clearly document that he carefully thought through the traditions upon which he founded the Scouting Movement, and the matter of Arthur in general and the Quest for the Holy Grail in particular were essential parts of those traditions. Finally, the film reflects a general movement in the late nineteenth and early twentieth centuries, especially in America, to address the problem of the proper education of boys. This movement often had links to the Arthurian tradition and the Quest for the Holy Grail not only because of the Scouting Movement but also because of various competing programs for boys, of which the largest in the United States was William Byron Forbush's Order of the Knights of King Arthur.[14] Clearly, *The Knights of the Square Table* has both educational and entertainment value and attests to the long-standing and continuing adaptability of the Grail legend to different times, different genres, and different purposes.

The corrective, as well as the healing, powers of the Holy Grail and the Quest are demonstrated in another silent film in which the Grail itself shows up in early twentieth-century New York, Clarence Brown's 1922 film *The Light in the Dark*, starring Lon Chaney, from a screenplay by William Dudley Pelley. In the film, a wealthy playboy finds the Sacred Cup, which a film title and a shot of a newspaper article refer to as "Tennyson's Grail," in the ruins of an English church and brings it home. Once in New York, the Grail mysteriously appears several times to heal the playboy's critically-ill, now-jilted fiancée and to reform a down-on-his-luck ne'er-do-well, played by Chaney. In a dream sequence in the middle of the film, the playboy and his fiancée are transformed into a medieval Grail Knight and Grail Maiden who re-enact an elaborate religious ceremony in which the Grail heals the faithful of a variety of ailments and infirmities.[15] The film's inspirational message proved so popular that *The Light in the Dark* was rereleased in a shorter version entitled *The Light of Faith*, which was shown in churches and schools across America in the 1920s.[16]

Undeniably, the history of the legends associated with the Holy Grail has had some darker chapters, thanks especially to the Nazi fascination with and attempt to co-opt those legends. The first Grail film, Edison's 1904 unsuccessful attempt to transfer from stage to screen Wagner's *Parsifal*, is at least tangentially one of those darker chapters, given both the Nazi embrace of Wagner and their eagerness to find the Grail itself.[17] A similar tangential note of National Socialist sympathy taints *The Light in the Dark*. The author of the screenplay and the short story on which it was based, William Dudley Pelley, was a notorious anti–Semite and Hitler sympathizer who would later founded the first American National Socialist Party, the Silver Legion, whose paramilitary group, the Silver Shirts, emulated Hitler's SS.[18] Nazi ideology contemporary with the rise of the National Socialists to power in the late 1920s would more directly influence the last Grail film to be made in the silent era, a film that serves as a clear example of the National Socialist appropriation of the sacred to support an ideology that was anything but sacred.

The online catalog of the British Film Institute offers the following synopsis of Arnold Fanck's 1926 film *Der Heilige Berg*: "a mountain story of Diotima, the dancer and her lover ... wandering through smoky halls in search of the Holy Grail."[19] While that synopsis is succinct enough, it does not accurately reflect the plot of the film. *Der Heilige Berg* was in its time well known thanks to a wide release throughout Germany, England, and the United States—though under various titles.[20] But, truth to tell, *Der Heilige Berg* is not by any objective standard a good film; nonetheless, the film is notable for a number of reasons, not the least of which being its association with the Nazi version of the Legend of and Quest for the Holy Grail.[21] On the surface, *Der Heilige Berg* is a mountain film (*Bergfilm*), a cinematic genre which Fanck introduced,[22] that remained popular in Germany from the days of the Weimar Republic until well into the 1950s, but which found special favor under the Nazis because it so clearly and so early reflected National Socialist ideology and mythology. Typically, such films are set in an idealized mountain setting in which the natural is glorified, if not deified, and against which a battle plays out that tests the character of the main characters, who are usually personifications of the ideals of German masculinity.

Der Heilige Berg, Fanck's second mountain film after his 1924 film *Der Berg des Schicksals* (*The Mountaineers*), grafts a documentary onto a melodrama about a love triangle involving a dancer and two mountain climbers, one younger and one older. The film opens with a prelude in which the dancer Diotima, "whose life is dance," performs a free form (almost comical) hymn to the sea, whose waves her very movements seem to control. As much as Diotima is associated with the sea, she is at the same time drawn to the mountains, where she hopes "to satiate all her desires" with a man atop a holy mountain, whom she has only seen in her dreams.

The end of the prelude finds Diotima performing on stage at the Grand Hotel situated at the foot of a range of mountains capped by the most unscalable of peaks known simply as the Santo. As Diotima performs her dance of desire to a packed hotel ballroom crowd, she catches the attention of two mountaineers, Vigo, a young medical student, and his older companion, simply referred to throughout the film as "the Friend." Both men fall in love with Diotima at first sight, with Vigo following her around like some Alpine "stage-door Johnny," and the Friend retreating to the mountains to savor alone what he has seen.

Diotima's preference is clearly for the Friend, but Vigo misinterprets her many acts of kindness to him as something more than they are intended to be. When Vigo wins several Alpine skiing competitions, inspired by Diotima, her innocent embrace of the victor is witnessed and misinterpreted by the Friend, who had thought that he and Diotima were to marry, thus uniting sea and mountain. Furious, the Friend challenges Vigo to join him in a suicidal attempt to climb the north face of the Santo.

The two set off in the most horrific weather conditions, and halfway through their night-time climb, Vigo slips and is left dangling by a rope off a cliff. So steep is the precipice that the Friend cannot anchor the rope to pull Vigo up to the ledge on which the Friend is standing, but somehow the Friend musters the strength to hold on to the rope so that Vigo does not plunge to his death, the mountaineer code of loyalty and friendship trumping his earlier jealousy. The Friend's efforts are in vain, however, as both freeze to death before a rescue party can reach them the next morning. As the night passes, the Friend slips into a dream-like trance, in which he envisions Diotima and himself entering a Cathedral of Ice. The film's final frames return to the sea, above which the intertitles indicate looms "the holy mountain, a symbol of the greatest values that humanity can embrace—fidelity—truth—loyalty—faith."

Fanck indicated that the film's scenario, which he called "a drama poem with scenes from nature," was based on events that had occurred in the Alps over a period of several years. More importantly, Fanck wrote the screenplay with one person in mind for the role of Diotima, Leni Riefenstahl, who made her screen acting debut in the film, and performed her "Dance of the Sea" live at the film's opening on 17 December 1926 and before each evening performance for several nights thereafter, generally to enthusiastic audience response and critical acclaim in the press (Salkeld 37). And it is clear that her role as Diotima in *Der Heilige Berg* launched her career in the film industry; previously she had been a little known dancer. Riefenstahl would soon enough, of course, find a more powerful patron, Adolph Hitler, who in 1932 during one of their meetings declared that the "most beautiful thing I have ever seen in a film was Riefenstahl's dance on the sea in *The Holy Mountain*" (quoted in Bach 91).

The relationship of the *Bergfilm* genre to Nazi ideology was all but cemented by *Der Heilige Berg* and by Riefenstahl's role in the film. Two of the film's harshest critics have made this point from different perspectives. Siegfried Kracauer, writing first as a contemporary reviewer of the film and then subsequently with hindsight in his book-length study of National Socialist film, initially was one of the lone dissenting critics of the film when it opened. In his review for the *Frankfurter Zeitung*, Kracauer complained that *Der Heilige Berg* was a "masterpiece for small youth groups that attempt to counter everything that they call mechanization by means of an overrun nature worship [and] panic-stricken flight into the foggy brew of vague sentimentality."[23]

Subsequently, Kracauer linked *Der Heilige Berg* and other Fanck mountain films directly to Riefenstahl's 1935 unapologetically Nazi film vehicle *The Triumph of the Will* (*From Caligari* 257–258). According to Kracauer, the kind of heroism displayed in *Der Heilige Berg* "was rooted in a mentality kindred to the Nazi spirit. Immaturity and mountain enthusiasm were one.... [T]he idolatry of glaciers and rocks was symptomatic of an antirationalism on

The Cathedral of Ice and its Grail-laden altar in Arnold Fanck's 1926 film *Der Heilige Berg* (British Film Institute).

which the Nazis would capitalize" (*From Caligari to Hitler* 112). Susan Sontag would later expand upon Kracauer's criticism:

> Fanck's pop–Wagnerian vehicles for Riefenstahl were not just "intensely romantic." No doubt thought of as apolitical when they were made, these films now seem in retrospect, as Siegfried Kracauer has pointed out, to be an anthology of proto–Nazi sentiments. Mountain climbing in Fanck's films was a visually irresistible metaphor for unlimited aspiration toward the high mystic goal, both beautiful and terrifying, which was later to become concrete in Führer worship [76].

Nowhere does the Nazi link to *Der Heilige Berg* become clearer than in the Friend's dream vision of Diotima and himself in the Cathedral of Ice whose center point is clearly a Grail bearing altar. An intertitle labels the scene "His World." When the Friend—a proto–Nazi Everyman figure—concentrates on holding on to the rope bearing the now dead body of Vigo as the frozen corpse dangles over the side of the mountain, the camera zooms in for a close-up of his face, and that image quickly dissolves into a scene of Diotima and the Friend walking hand in hand in a more hospitable world of ice, a gigantic Gothic Cathedral formed from glaciers. As they enter this clearly holy place, they are drawn to the central altar, which bears a Grail. As the couple mounts the altar steps, the Grail, which first starts to give off smoke or steam, begins to shatter, as does the Friend's reverie. The now ruined

Cathedral, with its shattered Grail, becomes also a symbol for the now dead Friend. The scene in the Cathedral of Ice dissolves into a second close up of what is the face of a man who has also frozen to death. The Nazi ideal has been realized by the Friend, but only very, very briefly.

Nazi ideology and mythology are nothing if not bizarre, and as Kevin Sim's 1999 documentary for British television, *Hitler's Search for the Holy Grail*,[24] makes abundantly (and embarrassingly) clear, the number of academics and holders of Ph.D.s who rushed to join the Nazi Party and even the ranks of the SS for personal advancement only gave a patina of pseudo-credibility to that ideology and mythology when it came to the Holy Grail. Officially, the cult of the Holy Grail—and that of the associated Holy Spear or Lance—were seen as having Aryan pre–Christian origins until they were appropriated by the Jews (Kater passim).

The mystical origins of Nazism were, moreover, older than any theories advanced by, or based on, Wagner and Nietzsche. Rather, they were based on a view of spiritualism that privileged the soul over the body, and that saw the Aryan past as the first and most "genuine manifestation" of the soul's inner force—which in turn alone could "penetrate [life's true] secret mysteries" (Morse 81–96). The key icon for those mysteries was the Holy Grail, hence the Nazi fascination with finding it—a search so well-known even long after the end of World War II that it could without any explanation form the basis of Steven Spielberg's 1989 film *Indiana Jones and the Last Crusade*—of course, in an earlier installment of the Indiana Jones franchise, *Raiders of the Lost Ark*, the Nazis were intent upon finding Noah's Arc.

And, for the Nazis, the new twentieth-century keepers of the Grail were none other than the brotherhood of the SS and the *Ahnenerbe*, whom Heinrich Himmler dubbed a new society of Grail knights modeled on the Knights of Arthur's Round Table and who met for Grail-associated rituals at his triangular castle of Wewelsburg in Westphalia (Kater passim). Fanck's *Der Heilige Berg* anticipates and is one with Nazi's efforts to find the Grail.[25] Early responses to the film at home and abroad saw *Der Heilige Berg* as surpassing in "point of sheer visual beauty" anything that the Germans have yet done in the cinema (Gerstein 297), and as giving expression to a "blend of sport, sensation and mysticism" that spoke to the German notion of "ennoblement" (Carter 269)—all Nazi code words and phrases.

While Fanck's film certainly reflects the Nazi fascination with and quest for the Grail, it had in turn its own influence on later Nazi aesthetics. Carsten Strathausen quotes a comment made by Britain's pre-war ambassador to Nazi Germany to Albert Speer, Hitler's chief architect, that the *Lichtdom* ("Cathedral of Light") that Speer had constructed in Nüremberg was "solemn and beautiful at the same time, as if one stood in an overwhelming cathedral of pure ice" (182). The cinematic prototype of Speer's work was, of course, the Cathedral of Ice in Fanck's *Der Heilige Berg,* an earlier reliquary for the Nazi image of the Holy Grail. And, in yet another unintended link between silent and later Grail films, the image of the Grail Chapel at the conclusion of Hans-Jürgen Syberberg's 1982 film of Wagner's *Parsifal* is almost eerily the same as the close-up of the Grail on the altar of the Cathedral of Ice in *Der Heilege Berg*—surely Syberberg cannot have had this image from Fanck's film in mind![26]

The Nazi imprint on German film from 1933 until the end of the Second World War is well-documented. But Fanck's *Der Heilige Berg* clearly shows that German cinema had, through the genre of the mountain film, readily embraced Nazi ideology before Hitler totally solidified his position by becoming chancellor, and again Wagner is a link here. Hamann details the pro–Nazi spirit apparent at Bayreuth at a time coincidental with the production and release of Fanck's film (89–121). And part of National Socialist ideology was the appropriation of what many would argue was among Christianity's most sacred icons and relics, the Holy Grail from which Christ supposedly drank at the Last Supper and which may have subsequently, according to yet other legends, caught the blood flowing from His side when it was pierced during the final moments of the Crucifixion. The silent cinematic Quest for the Holy Grail then offers a rich and varied legacy with an unintended, and more than unfortunate frame: the seeds and eventual imprint of the National Socialist agenda.

Notes

1. In the Spring 1987 issue of *Quondam et futurus,* which would go through a number of editorial transformations and expansions before eventually becoming, in 1994, *Arthuriana,* the quarterly scholarly journal of the North American Branch of the International Arthurian Society.

2. Details about the New York and touring Boston productions of Wagner's *Parsifal* can be found in the *New York Times* 27 December 1903: 12; 28 August 1904: 13; 13 September 1904: 9; 18 October 1904: 6; 23 October 1904: 4. 6; and 30 October 1904: 4. 3.

3. The film has never gone into more general release on either VHS tape or DVD. I have viewed the copy of the film on deposit at the Library of Congress in Washington, D.C. A 1993 screening at Washington's National Gallery of Art included a slide show of scenes from the original New York production of the opera, along with an illustrated lecture about Wagner's life, the opera, and the story of Parsifal. See the *National Gallery of Art Film Calendar* (September 1993).

4. For a more-detailed plot summary of the Edison-Porter *Parsifal,* see the description in the *Edison Film Catalogue* (50–53).

5. See *Moving Picture World* 28 December 1912: 1307–1308.

6. The identify of the Grail Knight has varied from version to version of the legend since medieval times. For further details about *Sir Galahad of Twilight,* see *Moving Picture World* 7 November 1914: 789 and *Bioscope* 3 December 1914: Supplement i. For further details on *The Grail,* see *Moving Picture World* 3 July 1915: 66 and *Bioscope* 2 September 1915: Supplement i. Despite its title, the 1923 film *The Grail* about a highly-principled Texas Ranger has no connection, other than titular, to the Holy Grail or the Quest.

7. On the murals, see Lupack and Lupack 279–280.

8. According to his obituary in *Scouting* (17), Wilder, who died on 4 July 1934, was one of the most influential and successful organizers that the early Scouting Movement had in America. Artist, author, musician and lawyer, Wilder organized the Sea Scout Program and the Pine Tree Patrol method of camping on the move. See also Wilder's obituary in the *New York Times* (17).

9. Robert Stephenson Smyth, First Baron Baden-Powell (1857–1941), founded both the Boy Scouts in 1908 and the Girl Guides in 1909 after a distinguished military career. See the entry on Baden Powell by E. E. Reynolds in the *DNB 1941–1950*: 34–38.

10. Cf. the accounts in Jeal's biography of Baden-Powell and in Rosenthal's history of the Scouting Movement.

11. Nothing further has been written about the film since my essay in the Winter 1994 issue of *Arthuriana* (313–323). Again the film has never been made available on VHS tape or DVD, and I have viewed the copy of the film on deposit at the Library of Congress in Washington, D.C.

12. See the reviews in *Moving Picture World, Scouting,* and *Wid's,* along with an article ("Boy Scouts' Endorsement") in the *New York Dramatic Mirror.*

13. For a fuller discussion of Gilliam's *The Fisher King,* see the essay by Cory James Rushton later in this volume.

14. Forbush founded his group in 1893. It went on to become the largest Christian fraternity of boys, eventually numbering 130,000 members by 1922. See the entry on Forbush (1868–1927) in the *National*

Cyclopædia of American Biography (1933; rpt. Ann Arbor: University Microfilms, 1967): 23: 346–347, and Lupack and Lupack 60–70.

15. The review of the film in *Moving Picture World* 9 September 1922: 138 identifies them as Lancelot and Elaine from Tennyson's "story" of the Holy Grail.

16. The shorter version was released on both VHS tape and DVD. The longer version has recently been remastered and screened at the Eastman Kodak House in Rochester, New York (http://dryden.eastmanhouse.org/films/2013/10/the-light-in-the-dark). For a complete synopsis of the film's plot, see O'Dell 289–291.

17. The complicated relationship between Nazi ideology and several generations of the Wagner family has been the subject of two very interesting (and damning) recent studies. See Carr, especially pp. 172–191, and Hamann, especially pp. 89–121.

18. On Pelley's anti–Semitism and admiration of Hitler—and his subsequent imprisonment for sedition during the Second World War—see Mathis 71–75 and Pelley's obituary in the *New York Times* 2 July 1965: 27. Whether those who sponsored the frequent screenings of the shorter version of the film throughout the 1920s were aware of, or simply turned a blind idea to, Pelley's extremist views is unclear—the reviews of the film when it was first released certainly do not comment on them, though Pelley himself would complain that the Jews of Hollywood had ruined his film by changing its emphasis to the character of the fiancée (played by Hope Hampton) from Chaney's ne're do-well and then denied him a chance to do a final edit to right this wrong—see Mathis 73–74.

19. http://www.bfi.org.uk.

20. In England, the film was released in 1927 under the title *The Wrath of the Gods*. In the United States, the film was also released in 1927, but under the title *Peaks of Destiny*. The film is also variously referred to as *The Holy Mountain* and *The Sacred Mountain* in a number of discussions. Representative reviews sometimes suggest variations in, or misunderstandings of, the film's scenario as it was released more widely. For reviews of the German release, see *Berliner Morgenpost* 16 December 1927: n.p. and *Die Weltbühne* 11 January 1927: 64–65. For reviews of the British release, see *Bioscope* 8 June 1927: 28; *Sunday Times* [London] 29 May 1927: 6; and *Westminster Gazette* 28 May 1927: 7. For reviews of the American release, see *Chicago Daily Tribune* 21 December 1927: 33; *Harrison's Reports* 10 (1928): 34; *Motion Picture News* 21 January 1928: 213; *New York Times* 29 November 1927: 31; *Pathéscope Monthly* June-July 1933: 8–9; and *Variety* 30 November 1927: 19. UFA, the film's production company and soon to be arm of the Nazi Party, also published a two-page press sheet to accompany the American release of the film; a copy of that press sheet can be found in the Film Library at the Museum of Modern Art in New York.

21. For two very different views of the Nazi quest for the Grail, see Sinclair 246–253 and Pennick 162–167. For a more recent discussion, with implications for the cinematic tradition of the Quest for the Holy Grail, see Finke and Shichtman 184–214.

22. For a quick overview of the mountain film as genre, see Vincendau, 202–203. For a fuller discussion of the mountain film and Arnold Fanck's contribution to this film genre, see Horak, passim.

23. *Frankfurter Zeitung* 4 March 1927: 1—English translation as found in Bach 47.

24. For details on the documentary, see *Bristol Evening Post* 19 August 1999: 27; *Independent* 22 August 1999: Features 9; and *Radio Times* 14–20 August 1999: 90 and 93.

25. For further discussion of Fanck's *Der Heilige Berg*, see my essay in the *Festschift* in honor of Dhira B. Mahoney 223–233.

26. In an essay later in this volume, Jon Sherman discusses Syberberg's *Parisfal* film at length.

Works Cited

Bach, Steven. *Leni: The Life and Work of Leni Riefenstahl*. New York: Knopf, 2007.
Baden-Powell, Sir R. S. S. *Scouting for Boys*. Rev. ed. London: C. Arthur Pearson, 1910.
_____. *Yarns for Boy Scouts*. London: C. Arthur Pearson, 1910.
"Boy Scouts' Endorsement." *New York Dramatic Mirror* 25 August 1917: 26.
Bush, W. Stephen. "The Possibilities of Synchronization." *Motion Picture World* 2 September 1911: 607–608.
Carr, Jonathan. *The Wagner Clan*. New York: Atlantic Monthly Press, 2007.
Carter, Huntly. *The New Spirit in the Cinema*. London: Harold Shaylor, 1930.
Finke, Laurie A., and Martin B. Shichtman. *King Arthur and the Myth of History*. Gainesville: University Press of Florida, 2004.

Gerstein, Evelyn. "Four Films of New Types." *Theatre Arts Monthly* 11 (1927): 29.

Hamann, Brigitte. *Winifred Wagner, A Life at the Heart of Hitler's Bayreuth.* Trans. Alan Bance. 2002; Orlando: Harcourt, 2005.

Hanson, Patricia King, ed. *The American Film Institute Catalog of Motion Pictures Produced in the United States, Feature Films, 1911–1920.* Berkeley: University of California Press, 1988.

Harty, Kevin J. "Arnold Fanck's 1926 Film *Der Heilige Berg* and the Nazi Quest for the Holy Grail." In *Romance and Rhetoric: Essays in Honour of Dhira B. Mahoney.* Ed. Georgiana Donavin and Anita Obermeier. Turnhout, Belgium: Brepols, 2010.

_____. "Cinema Arthuriana: A Filmography." *Quondam et futurus* 7 (Spring 1987): 5–8.

_____. "*The Knights of the Square Table*: The Boy Scouts and Thomas Edison Make an Arthurian Film." *Arthuriana* 4 (Winter 1994): 313–323.

Horak, Jan-Christopher, ed. *Berge, Licht und Traum: Dr. Arnold Fanck und der deutsche Bergfilm.* Munich: Bruckmann, 1997.

"James Austin Wilder." *Scouting* 32 (September 1934): 17.

"Jas. A. Wilder Dies." *New York Times* 6 July 1934: 17.

Jeal, Tim. *The Boy-Man: The Life of Lord Baden-Powell.* New York: William Morrow, 1990.

Kater, Michael H. *Das "Ahnenerbe" der SS 1935–1945: Ein Beitrag zur Kulturpolitik des Dritten Reiches.* Stuttgart: Deutsche Verlags-Anstalt, 1974.

"Knights of the Square Table." *Scouting* 5 (15 July 1917): 11.

Kracauer, Siegfried. *From Caligari to Hitler: A Psychological History of the German Film.* Princeton: Princeton University Press, 1947.

Lupack, Alan, and Barbara Tepa Lupack. *King Arthur in America.* Cambridge, Eng.: D. S. Brewer, 1999.

Mathis, Andrew E. *The King Arthur Myth in Modern American* Literature. Jefferson, NC: McFarland, 2002.

Morse, G. L. "The Mythical Origins of National Socialism." *Journal of the History of Ideas* 22 (1961): 81–96.

Niver, Kemp R. *The First Twenty Years: A Segment of Film History.* Los Angeles: Locare Research Group, 1968.

_____. *Motion Pictures from The Library of Congress Paper Print Collection, 1894–1912.* Berkeley: University of California Press, 1967.

O'Dell, Scott. *Representative Photoplays Analyzed.* Hollywood: Palmer Institute of Authorship, 1924.

"Parsifal." *Edison Film Catalogue* ([to] July 1906): 50–53.

Pennick, Nigel. *Hitler's Secret Sciences.* Suffolk: Neville Spearmann, 1981.

Review of *Knights of the Square Table. Moving Picture World* 11 August 1917: 955–956.

Rosenthal, Michael. *The Character Factory: Baden-Powell's Boy Scouts and the Imperative of Empire.* New York: Pantheon, 1986.

_____. "Knights and Retainers: The Earliest Version of Baden-Powell's Boy Scout Scheme." *Journal of Contemporary History* 15 (October 1968): 603–617.

Salkeld, Audrey. *A Portrait of Leni Riefenstahl.* London: Pimlico, 1997.

Sinclair, Andrew. *The Discovery of the Grail.* New York: Carol and Graf, 1998.

Sontag, Susan. *Under the Sign of Saturn.* New York: Farrar, Straus and Giroux, 1980.

Spears, Jack. "Edwin S. Porter." *Films in Review* 21 (June-July 1970): 327–354.

Stern, Seymour. "An Index to the Creative Work of David Wark Griffith." [Special Supplement to] *Sight and Sound* 7 (August 1946).

Strathausen, Carsten. "The Image as Abyss: The Mountain Film and the Cinematic Sublime." In *Peripheral Visions: The Hidden Stages of Weimar Cinema.* Ed. Kenneth S. Calhoon. Detroit: Wayne State University Press, 2001.

"Very Pleasing Boy Stuff Quite Humanly Presented." *Wid's Independent Review of Feature Films* 29 July 1917: 474.

Vincendau, Ginette, ed. *The Encyclopedia of European Cinema.* New York: Facts on File, 1995.

Wagenknecht, Edward, and Anthony Slide. *The Films of D. W. Griffith.* New York: Crown, 1975.

The Silver Chalice:
The Once and Future Grail

K. S. Whetter

Victor Saville's 1954 film *The Silver Chalice* (Warner Brothers), adapted from Thomas B. Costain's historical novel of the same name, stars Pier Angeli (as Deborra), Lorne Greene (as Peter), Walter Hampden (as Joseph of Arimathea), E. G. Marshall (as Ignatius), Virginia Mayo (as Helena), Paul Newman (as Basil), Jack Palance (as Simon the Magician), and Alexander Scourby (as Luke). The film marks Newman's first major motion picture role, though the twenty-nine-year-old Newman gained prominence (much to Newman's annoyance) as much for looking like Marlon Brando as anything else (Quirk, *Films of Paul Newman* 11 and 18).[1] Natalie Wood also makes a very brief appearance as the young Helena early in the picture, but, when the slightly older Helena reappears later in the film, she is thereafter played by Mayo. Costain's novel, first published in 1952 and reprinted within one year with an author's foreword outlining some sources (to be discussed below), was quite successful.

The film has had a more checkered history.[2] One of the earliest and most damaging responses appeared with John McCarten's January 1955 review for *The New Yorker*, where McCarten denounces everything about the film's plot, acting, and sets (66). Newman himself apparently hated the movie, and, when it was scheduled for American television broadcast in the mid-sixties, he went so far as to take out apologetic ads in the Hollywood trade papers; he also regularly derided it as one of the worst motion pictures of the 1950s (Quirk, *Films of Paul Newman* 17; O'Brien 22, 26). In the late seventies, Newman once screened the film in his home for friends with the expectation that they would all laugh at it—but Newman, at least, did not enjoy the experience, being soon overcome by what he called "the awfulness of the thing" (O'Brien 26).

Newman's biographers, no doubt influenced by Newman's own well-known sentiments, tend to echo the actor's assessment. Thus Lawrence J. Quirk, in the first biography of Newman, dismisses *The Silver Chalice* as a "turgid costume drama" presented "in ponderous, statuesque style by usually competent character actors," including, it should be said, Newman himself (*Films of Paul Newman* 17 and 40). Newman's most recent biographer agrees, styling the film "a disastrous ... début," a "risible biblical epic," "a bad start in Hollywood," and a "famously awful" movie entirely deserving of its reputation (O'Brien xi, 24)! Certainly many of the exterior sets are indeed laughable, making even the original *Star Trek* look high-tech—

though one of the worst parts of the set, the rooftop domes over which Deborra and Basil flee after Deborra starts a riot defending Jesus' reputation against the machinations of Simon the Magician, is perhaps meant to be an anachronistic reflection of the Dome of Jerusalem. Anachronistic or not, *The Silver Chalice* certainly lacks the grandeur of Mankiewicz's *Cleopatra* (1963) or Reed's *The Agony and the Ecstasy* (1965). It also frequently falls short of the general quality and occasional excellence of other well-known 1950s Biblical or period dramas epitomized by *The Ten Commandments* (1956) or *Ben-Hur* (1959). Nor does the film or acting compare entirely favorably with the pictures that would soon make Newman famous: *Cat on a Hot Tin Roof* (1958), *The Hustler* (1961), or *Hud* (1963).

It is said that Warner Brothers hoped in *The Silver Chalice* to cash in on—and emulate—the success of *The Robe*, released in 1953 by rival studio 20th Century Fox (O'Brien 23). *The Robe* was the first picture filmed in CinemaScope, "an ultra-wide format intended to lure audiences away from their television sets" (O'Brien 23). According to *Screen Archives Entertainment*, "The early CinemaScope era was replete with biblical epics designed to appeal to 1950s audiences with religious subject matter and colorful widescreen cinematography. *The Silver Chalice* was unusual in that director Victor Saville opted for an interior, moody approach utilizing spare, almost abstract Art Deco sets rather than the customary panoramas of the genre" (screenarchives.com; accessed 19 December 2012).

It is easy, in retrospect, to castigate this decision as a remarkably bad experiment, but it should be noted that the costumes, acting, and interior sets are much of the period, no worse or better than many of the more average contemporary pictures. *The Silver Chalice* is hardly a great example of movie-making at its finest, nor is the movie Newman's finest hour; but both the film and Newman have their moments. According to Virginia Mayo, the film and the sets were "supposed to be highly stylized," something audiences and reviewers failed to understand (quoted in Quirk, *Paul Newman* 53; for one such misunderstanding, see McCarten 66). Quirk himself, perhaps now influenced by Mayo, markedly altered his original assessment of the picture when he returned to the subject of Newman in a second biography written twenty-five years after his original study. This time round, Quirk notes— perhaps rightly—that "*The Silver Chalice* is not that bad a picture and Newman isn't that bad in it," repeating a few pages later that "Newman's performance was perfectly adequate and the movie reasonably entertaining" (*Paul Newman* 49 and 53).

Newman *is* visibly awkward in places, but part of Newman's awkwardness may have stemmed from transitioning from stage to screen. It may also be that Joanne Woodward's claims that the screen never completely or adequately captured the intensity Newman possessed on the stage are accurate (on Woodward, see O'Brien 109, 302). It is also argued that his character Basil is a remarkably static protagonist, involved in only one fight scene and thus hardly the typical epic, or Biblical, hero (Quirk, *Paul Newman* 52; cf. O'Brien 23), but it is noteworthy that the fight scene is given prominence by both its length and its appearance at roughly the middle of the picture; not only does it involve sword-fights and wrestling, but the major battle sequence begins when Basil and his companion, riding camels and couching their spears like lances, charge four members of the Brotherhood; given this camel-back jousting, the adventure gains in uniqueness what it loses in traditional war-gear or machismo! In addition to this fight, Basil rescues Deborra from soldiers early in the movie before they flee across the (admittedly curious) domed roofs, and he rushes into a larger and more violent mob to hunt for the stolen Grail at the picture's end. So Newman's Basil is not as passive as he first appears. Nevertheless, Newman does spend much of his time brooding or sculpting or drawing. Such a role is thus not necessarily the kind of charismatic, adventurous, or sexual hero a young actor would get noticed for portraying.

Newman may also have had concerns with public perceptions of his sexuality: this was mid-fifties America, after all. Virginia Mayo recalls how Newman disparagingly referred to the toga he had to wear for much of the film as "his cocktail dress" (Quirk, *Paul Newman* 49), a sentiment echoed by Joanne Woodward (O'Brien 25). Newman's friend Gore Vidal recounts a similar "cocktail dress" complaint when Vidal had to inform MGM executive Sam Zimbalist that Newman would never agree to star in the studio's remake of *Ben-Hur* (Vidal 301–302).[3] Newman's dress and sexuality concerns were seemingly exacerbated when his friend James Dean propositioned him on set. According to Quirk, Newman did not much mind Dean's "proclivities," but he did "fear ... guilt by association" (*Paul Newman* 51–52). Regardless of whether or not these anecdotes explain Newman's reaction to the picture, *The Silver Chalice*, nonetheless, has considerable interest as a Grail narrative.

The Grail story has its origins in medieval Europe, but there exists even in the Middle Ages quite a diverse array of Grail narratives and nearly as wide an array of different types of Grails: a dish, a cup, a platter, Christ's cup from the Last Supper, a stone, a bloody head.[4] Nor is the Arthurian legend to which the Grail became so firmly attached any less diverse. While it may go too far to claim, as do Elizabeth S. Sklar and Donald L. Hoffman, that "the Matter of Britain may be seen as an empty receptacle" (6), the Arthurian legend even in the Middle Ages clearly already existed as the kind (or kinds) of narrative which Tolkien would later and somewhat individualistically classify under the wide umbrella of "Faërie." Tolkien famously compares faërian narratives to a large "Pot of Soup" or "Cauldron of Story" (44–47), and in the case of the Arthurian legend, the size of the cauldron and the variety of its ingredients—both already large to begin with—have only grown over the centuries. Far from being empty, then, the Arthurian receptacle is so capacious and full as to allow each new storyteller to add his or her own ingredients and flavor things accordingly. This multiplicity of Grails is equally as true of medieval as of modern storytellers (literary or cinematic). I shall return to this variety of Arthurian and Grail traditions later; for now, it is sufficient to observe that notwithstanding the equally diverse imaginings of the Grail in modern stories and cinema, it is safe to say that, in modern popular culture, the Holy Grail is most typically associated with the cup of Christ. Such is the case, for instance, in the successful and popular *Indiana Jones and the Last Crusade* (1989).[5]

As I hope to show, there are in fact an impressive variety of Grails and Grail quests in *The Silver Chalice*, but this Christian Grail expectation is certainly fulfilled when Basil is commissioned by Joseph of Arimathea to sculpt a chalice which will house the cup used by Christ at the Last Supper. In this sense, although certain European modernist film "directors mock our desire for origin" with their Grail pictures (Finke and Shichtman 286), Saville's *The Silver Chalice* offers an explicitly etiological account of the Holy Grail and the early rise of Christianity. As the brief account of the cast given at the outset of my paper indicates, there are no Arthurian characters or even allegorical Arthurian types in *The Silver Chalice*.

There is likewise no explicit Wasteland and no obvious Fisher King—though John B. Marino argues that "Nero's persecution of the early Church" creates a sort of social and spiritual unrest signifying waste (66–67). Marino's claim, however, is only partly convincing since whatever feelings of persecution the Christians may have in the story are manifestly and repeatedly superseded by the joy created in Christ's flock by Christ's teachings, by Christ's disciples, and—for a select few—by Christ's cup. At the crucial moment, moreover, Simon the Magician spectacularly fails to outperform Christ. Given that Simon's aerial attempt to disprove Christ's powers is sanctioned by Nero and given that Simon plummets to his death in a tower constructed in Nero's gardens, the viewer is thus encouraged to believe that, just as Christ's reputation and religion survive Simon's machinations, so too will they survive the threats of Nero or other political enemies. The true Waste Land of *The Silver Chalice* does not in fact appear in the film (or novel); rather, it is instead prophesied by Peter as coming in a later day when the social, spiritual, and technologically-derived evils of the modern industrial and war-riven world demand the resurfacing of the Chalice. And the point, for Peter (and Basil and Deborra and the audience, to whom he is collectively declaiming at the picture's end), is the surety that the Chalice *will* reappear in such an age—for instance, the modern world post–Second World War—and that it will inspire faith and healing.

For the most part, then, the focus in the film (as in its novel source) is on the Grail and connecting the Grail to biblical history. Unlike more famous Grail films like *Monty Python and the Holy Grail* or *Excalibur*, this film is not a story about which Arthurian knights might seek for the Grail and why, or about which Grail knight might heal the wounded king, but rather about how the Grail came to be. The separation of Arthurian and Grail narratives in *The Silver Chalice* reminds us that, initially, these two legends were quite distinct.

The novel on which the film is based was successful enough to warrant reprinting within its first eight months, and for this reprinting Costain added an Author's Note in which he explicitly classifies the work as a piece "of [historical] fiction" inspired by the early twentieth-century discovery and analysis of the Chalice of Antioch. As Costain notes, this Chalice was purchased by New York's Metropolitan Museum of Art in 1950, where it remains to this day. There is a drawing of a chalice on the title page of the novel that is heavily indebted to the Antioch Chalice, and the Silver Chalice of the film likewise seems closely modeled on the Antioch Chalice.[6] Antioch itself—now Antakya in modern Turkey—was one of the largest cities in the Roman Empire, cosmopolitan home to (inter alia) Greeks, Syrians, and Jews. Founded by one of Alexander the Great's generals, Antioch by Romano-Christian times "ranked with Rome, Alexandria, and Constantinople as one of the four great cities of the Roman and Early Christian world" (Kondoleon 3). Both Peter and Paul were said to have preached there, and—after a series of sixth-century disasters, subsequent Roman rebuilding, and a prolonged period as an Arab state—Antioch in the twelfth century became a Crusader principality.

According to Acts of the Apostles 11.26, the term "Christian" actually originated in Antioch as a label, perhaps derogatory, for the disciples of Jesus.[7] The Antiochian origin of the word "Christian" is explicitly acknowledged in the novel—though not in the film—when Luke and the others arrive back in Antioch as part of the interwoven quests of protecting the Church, protecting the Cup and Chalice, and protecting Deborra's future, and

Luke remarks that "it was here that the name 'Christian' was conceived and first used" (Costain 287). Regardless of the exact origins and connotations of the term "Christian," the fact that St. Ignatius of Antioch was traditionally accounted the city's third bishop may well explain the name of Basil's foster-father Ignatius in both the literary and cinematic versions of *The Silver Chalice*. The film does not acknowledge the origins of the word "Christian," but it does emphasize Antioch's importance through an opening monologue and map that situate Antioch as a great city of trade not far from Jerusalem. This monologue also notes that, at the time of the story's setting, most of Antioch's citizens are ignorant of Christ and his teachings. In this sense, the very rise of Christianity is another Grail in *The Silver Chalice*.

The real Antioch Chalice was discovered during the digging of a well in 1910 when "[a]t a depth of many metres the excavators came upon underground chambers, in which the treasure [the chalice and other objects] was discovered" (Eisen, "Preliminary Report" 426). Gustavus A. Eisen, whose work is cited in Costain's Author's Note, initially dated the chalice "with certainty ... to the second half of the first century AD [CE]" and proposes that it once formed part of the treasure of a cathedral supposedly built in Antioch by Constantine the Great ("Preliminary Report" 426–27). Eisen subsequently modified his *terminus ante quem* to allow that the general shape of the chalice *might* extend as far back as the second century BCE; Eisen remained adamant, however, that the inner cup predated the outer chalice, and that despite the general similarities to slightly earlier work, the decorations on the chalice (and likely the chalice itself) were no later than the close of the first century CE ("Date"). In his definitive two-volume study Eisen adamantly defends this mid–first century date. On the basis of artistic style, "form and proportions" and decorative features, Eisen insists that the chalice belongs to the decade "between 60 and 70 AD" and is accordingly "the earliest artistic Christian object known" (*Great Chalice*, I: 181–183; cf. 145–146).

Broadly speaking, the chalice comprises two parts: an older and plainer inner cup; and an elaborate outer shell, silver, measuring 7½ × 5⅞ inches (or 19 × 15 cm), carved with vines, birds, animals, and twelve human figures, two of which are thought to represent Christ and the other ten of which may—and for Eisen *did*—depict most of the Apostles.[8] Indeed, in his longer study, Eisen suggested that the images of the Apostles "were made ... when most of the personages represented were yet alive" (*Great Chalice*, I: 181; cf. vii). This outer shell in turn houses a smaller and plainer silver bowl or cup; the inner cup is older than the chalice and "was once identified as that used by Christ at the Last Supper" (Evans 21). Consequently, the Antioch Chalice was touted by its first post-discovery owner as *the* Holy Grail, and it appeared as such at the World's Fair in Chicago in 1933–1934.

The Holy Grail has long had its own identity and history, whether it be in popular culture and modern media allegories or in literary and cinematic traditions, but Juliette Wood is no doubt correct in observing that the associations of the Antioch Chalice with both the medieval Crusades and modern archaeology considerably strengthened speculation about its status as *the* Grail ("Great Chalice" 1). The bipartite nature of the Antioch Chalice is also reflected in the novel and film where Christ's cup is venerated but plain, "with the hastiest workmanship and no attempt whatever at ornamentation" (Costain 94). Joseph himself suggests that the sculpted frame or larger chalice that Basil will create "should be of openwork so the Cup will show through, [with] perhaps a scroll of leaves around the figure of Jesus and those who were closest to him" (Costain 95). Paul agrees, but adds that the "frame must be of the finest workmanship," positing further that the appropriately "beautiful receptacle" might "become the chief symbol of the Christian faith" (95). Although less explicit in the film, these sentiments are nonetheless clearly present, as is the physical resemblance between the Antioch Chalice and the representation of the Silver Chalice on screen. The film's Joseph explicitly instructs Basil to carve the face of Jesus and those who were closest to him onto the Chalice, and Luke and Deborra equally explicitly add (in contrast to Eisen's conclusions) that one such face should belong to Joseph himself. It is partly through such scenes and sentiments as these that *The Silver Chalice* offers a story of the Grail's origins.[9]

Eisen was "a colourful but respected antiquary" (Wood, *Eternal Chalice* 24). Although the identification of the Antioch Chalice as the Holy Grail was eventually discredited, and although current scholarly opinion considers the erstwhile Chalice to be in actuality a sixth-century standing lamp and not a chalice at all, such was not the only view in the mid-twentieth century. For that matter, even as recently as 2008–2009, when the Antioch Chalice was loaned to the Royal Academy of Arts in London for an exhibition of Byzantine Art, the identification of the Chalice as the Grail re-appeared, albeit in very qualified terms (see Wood, "Great Chalice" and references therein; see also Wood, *Eternal Chalice* 24). We must, therefore, briefly reacquaint ourselves with Eisen's principal conclusions, especially since Costain in his Author's Note explicitly acknowledges the Antioch Chalice and Eisen's investigations as his main inspiration. Having established further connections between the Antioch Chalice and the Silver Chalice, I shall then turn to the sundry ways in which the Holy Grail and the Arthurian Quest for the Grail manifest themselves in the cinematic version of *The Silver Chalice*.

According to Eisen, the Chalice has "three distinct parts: (A) an inner bowl of plain silver (B) an outer covering or shell of 'chased-applied' ornaments, soldered on to the inner bowl, and (C) the stand and foot, turned out of a solid block of silver."[10] Parts of the outer shell are further decorated with red and yellow "heavy gold leaf." In shape, the Chalice is larger at top than at bottom, forming a "large truncate-ovoid bowl on a remarkably short and slender stem" with a "very narrow foot disk." In contrast to the crudely-worked inner bowl, the outer shell or Chalice proper still "show[s] the touch of a master hand, unfailing in steadiness and delicacy"; even the sculptures reveal "consummate skill and taste and ... beauty." Given the marked discrepancy in workmanship between the inner bowl and its outer chalice, Eisen makes a good case for the bowl being "a sacred object which it would have been sacrilege to alter." It is statements such as this which presumably inspired Juliette Wood's pithy—but incorrect—assessment that Eisen "rather masterfully made it clear that he thought the object was the cup of the Last Supper without ever actually saying so" ("Great Chalice" 4).[11] Equally pertinent to the film is Eisen's conclusion that the "delicacy and extreme minuteness of the design and execution of details in the portraits suggest the probability that the artist reduced his work after large and fully elaborated models were sculptured or drawn" (*Great Chalice*, I: 178), which is precisely how we see Basil create the chalice in the film. At one point he even explains to Deborra (and the audience) how, having made the

**Paul Newman as Basil the silversmith (center) and Alexander Scourby as Luke (right) present the epony-
mous cup to Walter Hampden as Joseph of Arimathea in Victor Saville's 1954 film *The Silver Chalice*.**

undecorated outer chalice, he next "model[s] the heads in wax" before molding these wax
faces onto smaller silver pellets, which he would then "fuse ... around the [larger] chalice."

Like the actual physical appearance of the Antioch Chalice, Eisen's emphasis on the
quality of the Antioch Chalice's artist is carried over into the novel and the film. The opening
scenes of *The Silver Chalice* regularly emphasize Basil's skills in all areas of art, from carving
in wood to drawing to sculpting to silversmithing. He is described by the narrator of the
novel as having an "artistic soul" (Costain 9), and the film reflects this characterization in
various shots of the young Basil carving, drawing, or sculpting. Giving Newman and Saville
the benefit of the doubt, perhaps even some of Newman's brooding or awkward poses in
the film are meant to be reflective of the stereotypical turmoil of the struggling artist. More
certainly, it is explicit in the novel and implicit in the film that Ignatius adopts Basil as
opposed to one of Basil's older brothers precisely because the boy is a dreamer and a talented
artisan. Ignatius thus quests not only for an heir, but also to reclaim Greece's artistic heritage.
Ignatius believes that, with his wealth and Basil's talent, this goal can be achieved. Unfortu-
nately, Ignatius dies before the fulfillment of this quest, and Basil is illegally but nonetheless
effectively disinherited and sold as a slave to a silversmith and his wife.

Basil's skills as a smith are—of course—infinitely greater than those of his master and
mistress, and the fame of the shop and its worker quickly travels, soon reaching Jerusalem.

This plot detail is evident in the film when the character of Luke arrives and insists on buying Basil's freedom so that Basil can accompany Luke back to Jerusalem to enshrine some sort of (initially unspecified) "sacred" Christian artifact in a suitably splendid silver housing. Once in Jerusalem, Basil is introduced to Joseph of Arimathea and the cup of Christ, already an object of veneration among Christ's most devoted and devout followers. Joseph has long kept the existence of the cup a secret, but the cup's associations with Christ and the hope it brings to his followers render it one prominent type of Grail in the story. This aspect of Costain and Saville's Grail again—consciously or not—has medieval parallels, for, as P. J. C. Field points out, in the most famous Grail story in English, Sir Thomas Malory's *Le Morte Darthur* (completed 1469–1470), the Grail functions much like a medieval relic (Field 150). As for Joseph's relic in *The Silver Chalice*, faced with his own approaching death and Basil's fame as an artist, it is now Joseph's wish that Basil create an appropriate vessel to house the cup, and it is this twofold chalice that becomes the Silver Chalice of the story's title and the Holy Grail of popular imagination. The Silver Chalice is consequently the most obvious Grail icon in the film; but it is not the only such icon.

As noted above, there exist in the Middle Ages a diverse range of literary conceptions of what precisely is the Holy Grail, and there are equally diverse scholarly interpretations. A. T. Hatto, in a standard translation of the very early thirteenth-century Middle High German *Parzival*, emphasizes that "there never was a Story of *the* Grail, and never could be. On the other hand there were stories of as many different Grails as there were writers or syndicates exploiting the potent name" (Hatto 7). Alfred Nutt long ago divided the medieval Grail narratives into two broad types, "Quest Versions" focusing primarily on the human quester or questers, and "Early History Versions" focusing primarily on the talismanic object or objects (Nutt 5). Dhira B. Mahoney, meanwhile, in her more recent and authoritative survey of Grail matters, argues for a triptych of traditional medieval narratives which she categorizes as "the Perceval strain, the Joseph of Arimathea strain, and the *Queste* strain" (Mahoney 2). She likewise outlines the traditional etiological triptych of scholarly explications of the Grail myth, "the Christian, the Ritualist, and the Celtic" (Mahoney, "Introduction" 8; see further Goetinck 117–47). Mahoney notes further that occasionally the quest for the Grail is itself as important as the Grail (1), something which is in fact true of many quest narratives, Grail or otherwise. Significantly, there are elements of each of these themes and ideas scattered throughout *The Silver Chalice*.

As is frequently remarked, the first extant medieval narrative to mention the Grail is Chrétien de Troyes' French verse romance of about 1180–1190 CE, *Le Conte du Graal,* or *Roman de Perceval*. Etymologically, the Old French word *graal* (from the Latin *gradale/ gradalis* or perhaps *garalis*) means either a large serving vessel or dish, or a specific course or dish in a large multi-course meal.[12] It is possible that as early as the twelfth century there were already diverging types of Grails at large, for Chrétien famously introduces the object of Perceval's failed quest as "I [or sometimes "Un"] graal": *a* Grail, not *the* Grail (v. 3220). Significantly for the conflicting etymologies, Chrétien also tells us that this unspecified Grail re-appears "at the serving of every dish" throughout the course of the lavish meal which he shares with the Fisher King. Later in the narrative, the poet offers a more specific and more Christian description in which the old king is sustained by a Mass wafer carried in the Grail, or "une sole oiste ... Que l'en en cel graal li porte" (6422–23). Unlike Chrétien's initial presentation of "I graal," the second appearance of this mysterious object has clear Christian overtones in its Eucharistic properties and in the manner in which it sustains the Fisher King's father.

Certainly, Chrétien in *Le Conte du Graal* instigates an important tradition of Grail narratives and raises more questions than he answers about what exactly this Grail might be. These answers were soon provided by the many writers who came in Chrétien's wake and explicitly evoked or continued his work. One such set of followers devoted themselves to the Grail Quest. Most obviously these authors include the Continuators of *Le Conte du Graal*, but for our purposes the most important post–Chrétien authors are Robert de Boron (writing in verse around 1200 but whose work is more fully preserved by his prose adaptors) and the authors of the Vulgate or *Lancelot-Graal Cycle* (c. 1215–1230).[13] With both Robert and the *Lancelot-Graal*, we see an attempt not only to complete Chrétien's unfinished Grail Quest, but, equally significantly, to define the Grail and provide origins. Robert's Grail is thus explicitly the "veissel" ("vessel") used by Christ at the Last Supper (verse 395). Modern scholars contradict one another in variously styling this "vessel" a wine-cup or a serving dish, but it is Robert who clearly links this "vessel" first to Christ and the Last Supper, and then to Joseph of Arimathea, into whose possession the "vessel" falls and who uses this vessel to catch the blood that still flows from the wounds of the crucified Christ when Joseph removes the body from the Cross (see vv. 395–96 and 562–72). Then, in the Prose *Lancelot*, the Grail becomes a (holy) chalice, used to hold the wine of the Eucharist. And in the *Queste del Saint Graal*, the original middle section of the *Lancelot-Graal Cycle*, the Grail is again an "escuele" ("dish") from the Last Supper, but is ultimately more notable less for whatever object it might be than for the Christian visions and grace granted to those select knights predestined to achieve (in varying degrees of success) the Quest.[14] This duality is partly continued by Malory, but Malory is also quite explicit that the Grail is "a vessell of golde" and "the holy dysshe wherein [Christ] ete the lambe on Estir Day."[15]

The confusion of even religious Grails in medieval narrative is reflected in the equally diverse depictions of the Grail in medieval art (see Meuwese). *The Silver Chalice* likewise possesses a plurality of Grails: most obviously Christ's Cup and Basil's Chalice, but also freedom, love, and selfish desires. This last option is obviously a false Grail, but it is nevertheless the one consistently pursued by Simon and his evil allies. Saville's (and obviously Costain's) association of the Grail with Christ's Cup and with Joseph of Arimathea, as well as with both literal and figural Grails, may well owe something to both Robert de Boron and the *Lancelot-Graal Cycle*.

The diversity of medieval Grails is echoed in modern cinematic accounts of the Grail, where we have everything from the symbolic fertility Grail of Boorman's *Excalibur* to the wooden cup of a carpenter in *Indiana Jones and the Last Crusade* to gasoline-as-Grail in the Mad Max movies.[16] Here, too, Monty Python encapsulate the spirit of the matter by having the French knights taunt Arthur and the Round Table knights by telling them that the French already have a Grail (*Monty Python and the Holy Grail*)![17] Whether or not Costain or Saville and screenwriter Lesser Samuels knew what they were doing, the Grail-savvy viewer can see a number of Grails and quests at work in *The Silver Chalice*, some literal, some figural. Mention has already been made of the Chalice itself and the ways in which it is meant to support the Antioch Chalice's candidacy as the Holy Grail, but an early figural Grail appears in the story's recurring theme of freedom from slavery. This theme is given even greater prominence in the film than it has in the novel. One of the adopted Basil's first actions in the house of his foster-father Ignatius, for instance, is to assist the young Helena to escape from slavery: not only does Basil not hinder or report her, he assists her egress from a window and gives her a large purse of money to aid her in her quest for freedom. Helena herself, in another cinematic addition to the story, exclaims quite explicitly that she is running away because she hates the feeling of slavery. When Basil and Helena are reunited a few scenes, but some years later, and he is now a slave in the silversmith's shop, Basil demands that he be set free, threatens to escape again, and chases his owners away by crying, "Freedom, freedom! Now!" and pretending to destroy the shop. This Grail-as-freedom theme is further emphasized when Luke arrives and offers to make the dream of freedom a reality for Basil.

Freedom is thus associated with Christ through Luke's intercession, but, throughout Luke's visit, there are also repeated verbal and visual reminders that Basil was "bought" and is now kept in chains. In light of the explicitly Christian associations of the chalice–Grail in *The Silver Chalice* and the preservation and expansion of Christianity itself in the film (and novel), we are perhaps meant to see in this scene an echo of the Harrowing of Hell. Luke ascends rather than descends to Basil's cell, and he is met by a knife-wielding Basil, who, having been warned by Helena that Linus plots his death, is prepared to fight any strangers. Luke, however, is nonplussed, reassuring Basil by offering him hammer and chisel, gently exclaiming: "Here, I've come to set you free." Luke and Basil then escape out of the window as Linus and his soldiers arrive in the street. The combination of the emphasis on chains and freedom, on Basil's concerns with his own and others' freedom, and especially Luke's status as a cipher for Christ who offers and secures Basil's release all suggest the Harrowing. At the same time, there is also a variation on established medieval romance or Grail Quest traditions, for like many a questing knight, Basil is initially known to others, including even Joseph and Luke, for his deeds (as a smith) rather than because if his actual identity as dispossessed heir. And just as Perceval learns his name and identity in the course of his adventures in Chrétien's *Conte du Graal*, so Basil accompanies Luke to Jerusalem in part to secure his true identity while concomitantly securing revenge on the greedy uncle who cast him out—though the revenge element is somewhat downplayed in the film.

The idea of the Grail as freedom is emphasized all the more by its equal ability to motivate the villains of the story: Mijamin and the Brotherhood desire freedom from the Romans and hire Simon to help fulfill this quest by destroying Christ's reputation and teachings, teachings that Mijamin thinks have unmanned the Jews. Simon, meanwhile, is happy to comply not only because of his own ambitions, but also for "the glory of revenge"; he wishes to get back at Peter for an old slight when Simon tried to buy his way into Christianity and Peter scorned him. Both quests involve acquiring Jesus' "wine cup" from Joseph and Basil. Hence there are opposing Grail quests on both the literal and figural planes in *The Silver Chalice*, one level epitomized by Basil and another one by his (or Christ's) enemies.

Like Simon, with whom she is partnered, the film's Helena is quite ambitious, and she is obviously planning to make herself great should Simon become great. Indeed, Helena's personal

Grail is the acquisition of freedom, wealth, and power. To these ends, she will assist whichever man, Simon or Basil, can best help her to achieve her quest. Nevertheless, the love between her and Basil is long-standing, and at least partly reciprocal. In Rome, she chastises Basil for not greeting her or kissing her as lovers should, and in Nero's palace she calls him both "a gifted artist" and "my lover." She claims, in fact, to love Basil as she has "never loved any other man." Saville's version of *The Silver Chalice* thus emphasizes the inevitable Hollywood love interest by milking Basil's love for both Helena and Deborra; much is made of his conflicting emotions. Indeed, the blurb on the back of the current DVD of *The Silver Chalice* announces that Basil is "torn between his adoring wife ... and a wily temptress." Nor is this comment merely a modern marketing gimmick; when the film was first released, top billing went to Mayo, followed by Angeli, as is still the case on the current DVD cover, which reproduces one of the early movie posters. Newman comes fourth, after Palance. Partly this love triangle generates suspense, partly it plays to audience or studio taste, but it also has the effect of rendering Basil into a sort of questing hero who must remedy a past mistake in order to achieve greatness or the love of a lady (or both).

Basil's temptation by Helena and the complications it causes in his relationship with Deborra thus have links with, or even inspiration from, similar scenes in medieval romance. Despite the associations of the Grail with Christ and with a certain religious asceticism, love tribulations do play a role of sorts in the medieval Grail Quest as well. Thus, in the French (or Vulgate) *Queste del saint Graal*, the model Grail knight is the virginal Galahad whose success is pre-determined by his physical and spiritual purity: he has neither experience of, nor desire for, carnal relations. Perceval and Bors likewise achieve the Grail, but it is made clear that Bors, as worthy as he is, is nevertheless not quite as pure or worthy as Galahad and Perceval, notably because he has had carnal relations once in the past (see, e.g., *Queste* 156). Malory retains this emphasis on sexual purity, as well as this hierarchy of Grail knights, in his *Le Morte Darthur*.[18]

What Basil's temptations by Helena most recall from medieval Grail narratives is Perceval's temptation by a fiend disguised as a woman. This story, too, appears in both the French *Queste* and Malory's "Sankgreall," and in both versions Perceval is on the verge of succumbing to sexual temptation when the pommel of his sword reminds him of the nature of his quest and causes him to make the sign of the cross, whereupon the beautiful woman disappears (*Queste* 105–11; *Works* 915.31–920.12). In the version of this trope in *The Silver Chalice*, Helena is not a fiend, and she does not disappear; but Basil does spend considerable time in the novel fighting the effects of a love potion that she concocts. For the cinematic adaptation, Saville and Samuels emphasize Basil's love for Helena for much of the film's 135 minutes. Consequently, one of the things Basil realizes in the course of his quest for knowledge of Christ and the Disciples, a quest necessary to finish sculpting their faces on the Chalice-Grail, is just how much he loves Deborra, not Helena. This realization, too, is part of the self-discovery and self-knowledge achieved during his Quest, but the realization effectively makes true love another figural Grail in the film. This self-knowledge also allows Basil to return to Deborra, not unlike the repentant sinners Bors and Perceval in medieval Grail narratives, where Bors and Perceval's contrition of their few past sins and avoidance of future ones enables their Grail success. Equally importantly for the movie, the pagan Basil is able to meet Peter and is eventually granted a vision of Christ, thereby enabling him to complete the Chalice-Grail and thus complete his own Grail Quest. In a significant confluence of themes, Basil's growing love of Deborra parallels, and indeed seems to be a precondition for, his growing love of Christ (and vice versa). In this way, too, the swelling of the Christian fold is arguably another figural Grail in both versions of *The Silver Chalice*.[19]

The Silver Chalice opens some years after the Crucifixion, with no initial mention of any Grail, and clearly Basil's Silver Chalice, created during the film, is not itself immediately presented as *the* Grail—but as noted, it is meant to *become* what we might term "the Grail," and, even before this designation, it does instigate several quests by Basil and others. Wood may go too far in claiming that "the enduring struggle for control of a talisman" is a universal element of Grail narratives (*Eternal Chalice* 178), but such a struggle does occur in *The Silver Chalice*. While Joseph and his allies, including Basil, struggle to keep Christ's Cup and the Chalice secret and safe, Christianity's enemies are equally keen to locate the Cup or Chalice or both. These enemy quests run parallel to, but also opposite of, Basil's quest. Basil's enemies wish to find the Cup-Grail in order to destroy it and thus discredit Jesus and his teachings: as noted, Mijamin and the Brotherhood hire Simon to debunk Christianity, thereby enabling Jewish males to become true men again—"men willing to fight and kill instead of pray"—and thus men to overthrow the Romans; Simon, meanwhile, wants the Cup-Grail to avenge himself against Peter, to destroy faith in Christ, and to elevate himself to position of new Messiah. In each case, we have various questors searching for the same precious object. Although Simon begins to believe himself truly a god, his quest to supplant Christ comes to an abrupt and highly unsuccessful end when Simon's final proof of his divinity, his ability to fly without magical or technological assistance, fails quite spectacularly. The Chalice-Grail is lost at the story's end, thereby allowing Newman his final (qualified) action scene as he rushes into the mob; in the novel, the Chalice is at last claimed by Mijamin (Costain 524–29), but in the film it is stolen first by Mijamin, and then—as Basil discovers when he manages to find Mijamin's dead body in the streets of Rome—looted by the mob who clearly murdered the thief before liberating his treasure. Simon's death, the course of biblical history, and Peter's oracle of the Grail's return assure viewers that, notwithstanding this loss, the missing Grail will resurface when needed.

Finke and Shichtman's claim that, "[i]n the Middle Ages, ... the Grail, whether pagan or Christian, is an object of mourning" (247) is arguably only partially true of medieval Grails and Grail narratives. In Saville's *The Silver Chalice*, on the other hand, nothing could be farther from the truth. Here, the Grail in both its forms, the Cup of Christ and Basil's Chalice, regularly brings joy to all who behold either or both manifestations of the Grail. Even those who never saw Christ, such as Basil or Deborra or even Luke, are uplifted by the Grail and encounter joy by being brought closer to Jesus through the Grail. Even the eventual theft and loss of the completed Chalice-with-Cup at the end of the film is, in Tolkienian terms, a qualified "eucatastrophe"[20]: there is temporary mourning for the loss of the Chalice, yes, but the sadness is immediately superseded by Basil and Deborra's realization of their mutual true love (another figural Grail), and by the consolation of Peter's prophecy that the Grail "will be restored" to future generations after "hundreds of years" and set right those who are lost and in need of spiritual guidance in a "world of evil."[21]

The quest in general, whether for a Grail, for the Golden Fleece, or for some other talisman, often brings with it self-knowledge or self-development for the hero, and in this sense, also, any sorrow over the loss of the Chalice at the story's end is superseded by Basil's realization that he genuinely loves Deborra—and also Christ. Helena's temptations are a thing of the past. And, for that matter, the fact that Basil is unable to retrieve the Grail at the film's close, thereby leaving his final Grail Quest unsuccessful, echoes the medieval tradition, where most knights actually fail to achieve the Grail. What Basil's failure to reclaim the Chalice most echoes is the failure of the first (extant) Grail hero, Chrétien's Perceval, whose quest is quite literally finished by those who come later: Chrétien's narrative is incomplete, and in the portion written by him Perceval sees a Grail and the Fisher King but fails to ask about the Grail. He later sets forth to redeem this mistake, and would presumably have succeeded had Chrétien completed the story. But it remained for the four post–Chrétien Continuations eventually to bring Perceval's quest to completion, and for Robert de Boron to take the Grail back to Christ. All of these back- and fore-stories are reflected in *The Silver Chalice* in Peter's prophecy that future questors in a later beleaguered age will locate Basil's Silver Chalice.

Scholars regularly note the importance of Robert de Boron to the development and Christianization of the Grail Legend. As noted above, it is Robert who provides a Christian back-story to Chrétien's unspecified "I graal." As Raymond H. Thompson observes, whether modern Grail narratives are pagan or Christian, their authors rely upon the Grail in whatever guise possessing "a rich history that precedes its manifestation to the Round Table" (545). An important part of that pre-history was provided by Robert in the late eleventh or early twelfth century. It is part of Costain's and then Saville's contribution to the Grail tradition that they, like Robert, provide a prequel to the Grail story. For this reason, if no other, *The Silver Chalice* is worthwhile as a Grail film. But Costain and Saville modify the traditional history of the Grail to focus not on Arthur's knights questing for the Grail, but rather on how Christ's Cup, lovingly preserved by Joseph, is merely the beginning of the Grail and its story. In this sense, *The Silver Chalice* offers an etiological account of the origins of the Christian Grail and the accompanying Grail Quest. Although the Chalice-Grail is lost at the conclusion of the film, Peter explicitly prophesies its future return, thereby locating this version of the Grail story at the forefront of a more prominent narrative tradition: for the eventual return of Basil's Grail links it to what will be future knights or questing heroes and heroines, including, from Basil's perspective, Perceval and Galahad and the medieval Grail seekers, but also including "new races" who will live in "great cities" and "fight long and bitter wars with frightening new forces of destruction" (Costain 533). In this mingling of medieval and modern Grail seekers, it is Costain's and Saville's Grail, rather than Arthur, that is once and future.

Notes

1. McCarten is one of the first reviewers to suggest the resemblance. Newman eventually tired of the comparisons to Brando and began to retort to reporters that the resemblance ran in the other direction: Brando resembled Newman.

2. For excerpts from reviews in *Variety*, *The New Yorker*, *New York Herald Tribune* and *New York Times*, see Quirk, *Films of Paul Newman* 42; also O'Brien 25.

3. This story is mentioned by both biographers, each of whom adds his own details, and each of whom misquotes Vidal: Quirk, *Paul Newman* 53–54; O'Brien 60–61. The precise extent of Vidal's rewrites of and contribution to *Ben-Hur* are contentious, but, since he had been blackballed in 1957 for refusing to work on the script, and since he was subsequently released by MGM after *Ben-Hur*, his own claims to have used the rewrite as a way out of his studio contract (Vidal 301–307) appear genuine.

4. As Loomis 274 observed, medieval Grail authors thus "seem to delight in contradicting each other on the most important [and even most basic] points." Naomi Mitchison's humorous solution to this plurality of Grails in her 1955 recounting of the story is to make them all valid, and to have each of the principal questing knights achieve one of the principal Grails.

5. For a sustained analysis of the Grail in *Indiana Jones*, see the essay by Joseph Sullivan, later in this volume.

6. I am indebted to Kevin J. Harty for suggesting that I explore this connection, as well as for inviting me to write this essay and for sharing his film expertise with me. At the time of going to press, three images of the Antioch Chalice, together with a short description, are available at the museum website: http://www.metmuseum.org/toah/works-of-art/50.4.

7. For the possibly negative aspects of the term, see the *Oxford Companion to the Bible*, s.v. "Christian."

8. Forty-six detailed photographs and twelve etchings of the chalice and all of its various figures can be studied in Eisen's *Great Chalice*, Vol. II.

9. If we adopt Mahoney's classifications of the dominant traditional Grail narratives, *The Silver Chalice* is thus primarily a Joseph version of the Grail story, with elements from the Perceval and *Queste* types mixed in for good measure (Mahoney 2–5).

10. This and the next several quoted descriptions come from Eisen, "Preliminary Report" 427–429. For a much more detailed account of all aspects of the Chalice, see the entirety of Eisen, *Great Chalice*, Vol. I. Pugh and Weisl link the composite nature of the Antioch Chalice to "the layering of history and fiction inherent in medievalism" (113). One could, along these lines, further link the composite nature of the Antioch Chalice to the composite Grails of *The Silver Chalice*.

11. "Incorrect" because, in *Great Chalice*, I: 10 and I: 133–36, Eisen clearly associates the inner Cup with the Last Supper.

12. Barber 91–96 offers a convenient overview of the scholarly positions on this issue.

13. According to Lacy 169, Robert's importance as an author of medieval French romance is arguably second only to Chrétien himself. Robert's story of Joseph and the Grail, alternately titled by modern scholars *Joseph* or *Roman de l'Estoire dou Graal*, is likewise "one of the most important documents in the history of the legend of the Holy Grail" (Roach 313).

14. Thus Pauphilet (esp. 21–26) argues that the Grail in the *Queste* is an immaterial object symbolizing humanity's search for God, while Gilson sees the *Queste's* Grail as a manifestation of Cistercian views on divine grace (321–327).

15. Malory 793.28 and 1030.19–20 (Caxton's Book XI, ch. 2 and Book XVII, ch. 20).

16. The wooden Grail of *Indiana Jones* may owe something to one of the other early twentieth-century Grail candidates, the Nanteos Cup. The Nanteos Cup is actually a late-medieval wooden bowl or mazer (see further Barber 299–300). On fertility myth and Boorman's *Excalibur* see Shichtman, as well as the essay by Raeleen Chai-Elsholz and Jean-Marc Elsholz later in this volume. I owe the *Mad Max* and gasoline-as-Grail suggestion to Kevin J. Harty; see also the essay by Paul B. Sturtevant on *Mad Max* below.

17. For cinematic accounts of various Grails, see Harty's "Grail on Film"; Finke and Shichtman 245–287. On *Monty Python and the Grail*, see the essay by Christine Neufeld, later in this volume.

18. While scholars accept Malory's indebtedness to the plot of the French *Queste*, there is considerable critical controversy about whether or not Malory adopts the same religious themes as his source. For an overview of, and proposed solution to, the issue, see my "Malory's Secular Arthuriad."

19. The idea that the Chalice's artist is "a Greek convert to Christianity" comes straight from Eisen, *Great Chalice*, I: 8.

20. "Eucatastrophe" is a term coined and defined by Tolkien in his magisterial essay "On Fairy-Stories" to note the chief function of faërie, the ultimate means of securing recovery and consolation: "the sudden joyous 'turn'" that "denies ... final defeat" to secure instead a "fleeting glimpse of Joy" (Tolkien 75).

21. In the novel, the prophecy, with slightly different wording but the same sentiment, is made by Luke, not Peter (see Costain 533).

Works Cited

Barber, Richard. *The Holy Grail: Imagination and Belief.* Cambridge: Harvard University Press, 2004.

Chrétien de Troyes. *Le Roman de Perceval ou Le Conte du Graal: Édition critique d'après tous les manuscrits.* Ed. Keith Busby. Tübingen: Niemeyer Verlag, 1993.

"Christian." *The Oxford Companion to the Bible.* Ed. Bruce M. Metzger and Michael D. Coogan. Oxford: Oxford University Press, 1993.

Costain, Thomas B. *The Silver Chalice.* New York: Doubleday, 1952.

Eisen, Gustavus A. "The Date of the Great Chalice of Antioch." *American Journal of Archaeology* 21.2 (April-June 1917): 169–186.

_____. *The Great Chalice of Antioch, on Which Are Depicted in Sculpture the Earliest Known Portraits of Christ, Apostles and Evangelists.* 2 vols. New York: Kouchakji Frères, 1923.

_____. "Preliminary Report on the Great Chalice of Antioch Containing the Earliest Portraits of Christ and the Apostles." *American Journal of Archaeology* Second Series 20.4 (October-December 1916): 426–437.

Evans, Helen C., with Melanie Holcomb, and Robert Hallman. "The Arts of Byzantium." *The Metropolitan Museum of Art Bulletin* 58.4 (Spring 2001): 1–68.

Field, P. J. C. "Malory and the Grail: The Importance of Detail." *The Grail, the Quest and the World of Arthur.* Ed. Norris J. Lacy. Arthurian Studies 72. Cambridge, England: D. S. Brewer, 2008.

Finke, Laurie A., and Martin B. Shichtman. *Cinematic Illuminations: The Middle Ages on Film.* Baltimore: Johns Hopkins University Press, 2010.

Gilson, Étienne. "La Mystique de la grace dans *La Queste del Saint Graal.*" *Romania* 51 (1925): 321–347.

Goetinck, Glenys Witchard. "The Quest for Origins." *The Grail: A Casebook.* Ed. Dhira B. Mahoney. Arthurian Characters and Themes 5. New York: Garland, 2000.

Harty, Kevin J. "Appendix: The Grail on Film." *The Grail, the Quest and the World of Arthur.* Ed. Norris J. Lacy. Arthurian Studies 72. Cambridge, England: D. S. Brewer, 2008.

Hatto, A. T., trans. *Parzifal.* By Wolfram von Eschenbach. Harmondsworth: Penguin, 1980.

Kondoleon, Christine. "The City of Antioch: An Introduction." *Antioch: The Lost Ancient City.* Ed. Kondoleon. Princeton and Worcester: Princeton University Press and Worcester Art Museum, 2000.

Lacy, Norris J. "The Evolution and Legacy of French Prose Romance." *The Cambridge Companion to Medieval Romance.* Ed. Roberta L. Kreuger. Cambridge: Cambridge University Press, 2000.

Loomis, Roger Sherman. "The Origin of the Grail Legends." *Arthurian Literature in the Middle Ages: A Collaborative History.* Ed. Loomis. Oxford: Clarendon, 1959.

Mahoney, Dhira B. "Introduction." *The Grail: A Casebook.* Ed. Dhira B. Mahoney. Arthurian Characters and Themes 5. New York: Garland, 2000.

Malory, Sir Thomas. *The Works of Sir Thomas Malory.* Ed. Eugène Vinaver. 3rd ed. Rev. P. J. C. Field. Oxford: Clarendon, 1990.

Marino, John B. *The Grail Legend in Modern Literature.* Arthurian Studies 59. Cambridge, England: D. S. Brewer, 2004.

McCarten, John. "The Current Cinema: In Old Jerusalem." *The New Yorker* 30 (January 15 1955): 66.

Meuwese, Martine. "The Shape of the Grail in Medieval Art." *The Grail, the Quest and the World of Arthur.* Ed. Norris J. Lacy. Arthurian Studies 72. Cambridge, England: D. S. Brewer, 2008.

Mitchison, Naomi. *To the Chapel Perilous.* London: Allen and Unwin, 1955.

Nutt, Alfred. *The Legends of the Holy Grail.* Popular Studies in Mythology, Romance and Folklore 14. London: Nutt, 1902.

O'Brien, Daniel. *Paul Newman.* London: Faber and Faber, 2004.

Pauphilet, Albert. *Études sur La Queste del Saint Graal, attribuée à Gautier Map.* Paris: Champion, 1921.

Pugh, Tison, and Angela Jane Weisl. *Medievalisms: Making the Past in the Present.* London: Routledge, 2013.

The Quest for the Holy Grail. Trans. E. Jane Burns. *Lancelot-Grail: The Old French Arthurian Vulgate and Post-Vulgate in Translation.* Ed. Norris J. Lacy. Vol. 4. New York: Routledge, 2010.

La Queste del saint Graal: Roman de XIII siècle. Ed. Albert Pauphilet. Paris: Champion, 1921.

Quirk, Lawrence J. *The Films of Paul Newman.* New York: Citadel Press, 1971.

_____. *Paul Newman.* Dallas: Taylor Publishing, 1996.

Roach, William. "The Modena Text of the Prose *Joseph de Arimathie.*" *Romance Philology* 9 (1955–56): 313–342.

Robert de Boron. *Le Roman de l'Estoire dou Graal.* Ed. William A. Nitze. Paris: Champion, 1927.

Saville, Victor. *The Silver Chalice*. Warner Brothers, 1954.

"Silver Chalice (1954) Music by Franz Waxman." *Film Score Monthly*. screenarchives.com. Web. 19 December 2012.

Sklar, Elizabeth S., and Donald L. Hoffman, ed. *King Arthur in Popular Culture*. Jefferson, NC: McFarland, 2002.

Shichtman, Martin B. "Hollywood's New Weston: The Grail Myth in Francis Ford Coppola's *Apocalypse Now* and John Boorman's *Excalibur*." *The Grail: A Casebook*. Ed. Dhira B. Mahoney. Arthurian Characters and Themes 5. New York: Garland, 2000.

Thompson, Raymond H. "The Grail in Modern Fiction: Sacred Symbol in a Secular Age." *The Grail: A Casebook*. Ed. Dhira B. Mahoney. Arthurian Characters and Themes 5. New York: Garland, 2000.

Tolkien, J. R. R. *Tolkien on Fairy-stories: Expanded Edition, with Commentary and Notes*. Ed. Verlyn Flieger and Douglas A. Anderson. Oxford 1947. London: HarperCollins, 2008.

Vidal, Gore. *Palimpsest: A Memoir*. New York, Random House, 1995.

Whetter, K. S. "Malory's Secular Arthuriad." *Malory and Christianity: Essays on Sir Thomas Malory's Morte Darthur*. Ed. D. Thomas Hanks, Jr. and Janet Jesmok. Kalamazoo: Medieval Institute Press, 2013.

Wood, Juliette. *Eternal Chalice: The Enduring Legend of the Holy Grail*. London: I. B. Tauris, 2008.

_____. "The Great Chalice of Antioch: On a Quest for the Holy Grail from Antioch to America and Back Again." juliettewood.com/papers/thegreatchaliceofantioch.pdf. Accessed 20 December 2012.

Lancelot du lac: Robert Bresson's Arthurian Realism

Joan Tasker Grimbert

It is no secret that modern French filmmakers revel in demystifying what they see as the most endearing "myths" of Western European culture. The subversive impulse can be seen particularly in films of the 1970s. It is hard to forget the acute discomfort at seeing an aging Klaus Kinski incarnate Roland in Frank Cassenti's *Chanson de Roland* (1978). Equally unsettling is Yvan Lagrange's *Tristan et Iseult* (1972), with its striking images of violence and explicit eroticism which, though clearly designed to reinforce the universal "mythic" dimension of the legend, effectively undermined our romantic vision of these famous lovers. King Arthur and his knights are also subjected to a certain—captivating—"deflation" in Eric Rohmer's *Perceval le Gallois* (1979). And then there is Robert Bresson's *Lancelot du lac* (1974), which takes aim at the romance between King Arthur's wife and his "first knight" and the unsuccessful quest for the Grail, a film from which that sacred object is curiously absent.[1]

Of this group of ardent demystifiers, Bresson remains in many ways the hardest to decipher, his intentions the most difficult to fathom.[2] He and Rohmer are both known as "Catholic" filmmakers, who treat subjects that have an obvious religious dimension, even though the subject matter of both *Lancelot* and *Perceval* can ultimately be traced back to Chrétien de Troyes, whose romances mostly celebrate a secular chivalry and are among the most delightfully ambiguous in medieval literature. Rohmer clearly recognized the humor and irony in Chrétien's *Conte du Graal* (*Story of the Grail*) and managed to convey it most effectively through most of the film. Yet he appended to the unfinished work a stunning ending that disambiguated the original romance by underscoring memorably the Christian allusions that were present, but left intriguingly undeveloped, by the author.[3]

Bresson, for his part, was not working from Chrétien's *Chevalier de la Charrette* (*Knight of the Cart*), which says nothing of the Grail, but does introduce into medieval literature the romance between Lancelot and Guenevere. The affair was to be developed at length a few decades later in the Vulgate *Lancelot-Grail* cycle. This huge, enormously popular and influential, thirteenth-century prose cycle features the *Lancelot* as its extensive centerpiece, framed, on the one hand, by *L'Estoire del Saint Graal* (*The History of the Holy Grail*) and *L'Estoire de Merlin* (*The Story of Merlin*) as a kind of "prequel," and, on the other hand, by

La Quête del Saint Graal (*The Quest for the Holy Grail*) and the *La Mort le roi Artu* (*The Death of King Arthur*), which cover the largely unsuccessful quest and its aftermath: the dis-integration of the Round Table and the death of all of its members.[4] The *Mort Artu* recounts the downside of the Arthurian legend, and it is this depressing view of the Arthurian world that informs *Lancelot du lac*.[5]

Bresson was aware that the legend had circulated in Europe much earlier than the thir-teenth century and that it had first taken root in Britain and France. When asked about future projects in an interview conducted by Michel Delahaye and Jean-Luc Godard after he had completed *Au hasard Balthasar* (*Balthazar*) [1966], Bresson confirmed that he was still interested in filming *Lancelot*, in both French and English, if possible, saying that what interested him was "to take up again an old legend known in all Europe" (663). Actually, as Godard knew, Bresson had intended to shoot *Lancelot* immediately after finishing his 1951 film *Le Journal d'un curé de campagne* (*The Diary of a Country Priest*), but lacked the requisite funds. In 1964, he wrote to George Cukor (who had admired his *Journal*), proposing to shoot *Lancelot* in English with Natalie Wood and Burt Lancaster, whom he considered the perfect actor to incarnate Lancelot, but the project fell through because Lancaster was com-mitted to another film.[6] It is almost inconceivable that a filmmaker who famously hated the idea of using professional actors actually contemplated making a film—in Hollywood, no less!—with American film stars at the top of their game, and it is hard to imagine what a bizarre production this version would have been.

As it is, the film that Bresson ended up making in 1974, though shot in French with French non-professionals—whom he calls *modèles* (models), as he habitually does—is highly unusual. His idiosyncratic interpretation of Lancelot is a function both of his particular mode of filmmaking, which sets him apart from his contemporaries, and of his desire to demystify the Arthurian legend, which he shares with them. Bresson based many of his films on literary works (by Diderot, Bernanos, Dostoevsky, and Tolstoy) and followed the actual trial transcripts for *Le Procès de Jeanne d'Arc* (*The Trial of Joan of Arc*) [1962]. For the *Lance-lot*, although he initially follows the basic outline of the *Mort Artu*, he changes the ending considerably, presenting a much bleaker vision not just of the fall of the Round Table, but also of Arthur's fellowship generally. One has the sense that he is working less with a par-ticular "source" than with the concept that he believes haunts the Western imagination—what he calls the Arthurian "myth," as if it were monolithic, rather than the multivalent legend that it is.[7]

In speaking to Delahaye and Godard of the Arthurian film he wanted to make, Bresson claimed that he would "not take up the purely fairy-tale element of the legend; I mean the fairies, Merlin, and so on," but rather "try to transfer this fairy-tale into the realm of feelings, that is to say, to show how feelings change even the air that one breathes" (663). By stripping away the fantastic element, Bresson arrives at what Julien Gracq calls his "Arthurian realism," a concept that Gracq considers almost an oxymoron in that the result is the implacable mate-rialization of a story that—in his view—has never known any climate other than that of myth, never lived anywhere but on the wings of the imagination (7). This poetic conception of the legend's origins and development is rather ingenuous, as no serious Arthurian scholar would see any part of the Arthurian legend as a fairy tale. But the marvelous does abound, and, although it is present even in the unusually sober *Mort Artu*, the plot of the *Lancelot du lac* is virtually devoid of that element. As one critic puts it, "Grimly, Bresson rips away nearly every vestige of romance, pomp, and magic from the material" (Dempsey 7).

Although in the Delehaye/Godard interview Bresson does not mention the Grail, he must have considered it to be another marvelous element that warranted, if not elimination, at least redefinition. When asked by the French press what he had found tempting about the subject matter of the *Lancelot*, he responded: "De le tirer de ce qui est notre mythologie. Et une situation, celle des chevaliers qui rentrent au château d'Artus sans Le Graal. Le Graal, c'est-a-dire l'absolu, Dieu (To draw it out of what is our mythology. And a situation, that of the knights who return to Arthur's castle without the Grail. The Grail, that is, the absolute, God)."[8] Although the concept of the Grail was clearly important to Bresson, he sought to treat it in a decidedly understated way, which must be why he ultimately rejected the idea he had once had of calling the film "The Grail." As he confided to Yvonne Baby, "Le titre que je désirais pour le film était 'le Graal' à cause justement de l'intensité de l'absence de ce Graal, au fur et à mesure que le film se déroule (The title that I wanted for the film was 'the Grail', precisely because of the intensity of the absence of this Grail as the film unfolds")
[15]. If Bresson had used his original title, viewers would probably not have understood this paradoxical—almost perverse—decision.

Many critics who appreciated what Paul Schrader in *Transcendental Style in Film* called the "transcendental" dimension of Bresson's earlier films, and what Susan Sontag (1966) termed his "spiritual style" (in an essay originally published in 1964), were puzzled by the turn his *œuvre* took after *Balthazar*.[9] In 1976, as he had completed *Lancelot* and was preparing to shoot *Le Diable probablement* (*The Devil Probably*) [1977], Schrader told him that he believed he had been "working off a given theology" from *Journal* up to *Balthazar*, whereas in the more recent films he was "foraging new terrain." But Bresson protested. He felt that his first films had been "a bit naïve, too simple" and explained the change seen in his later films by saying:

> The more life is what it is—ordinary, simple—without pronouncing the word "God," the more I see the presence of God in that…. I don't want to shoot something in which God would be too transparent…. The further I go on in my work, the more I see difficulty in my work, the more careful I am to do something without too much ideology…. I want to make people who see the film feel the presence of God in ordinary life [Schrader "Robert Bresson, Possibly"; rpt. Quandt 695].

To illustrate his point, Bresson refers to how the protagonists in *La Femme douce* (*A Gentle Creature*) [1969] and *Mouchette* (1967) set about to kill themselves, adding that at the end of those films: "There is a presence of something that I call God, but I don't want to show it too much. I prefer to make people feel it" (Schrader 1977; rpt. Quandt 695). Bresson seems surprised when Schrader's response reveals that he does not really feel the presence of God in *Lancelot*.

Do *we*? How does Bresson present the Grail, which he equates with the absolute, with God? If he believes that God's presence, or at least a moment of transcendence, can be felt in *Lancelot*, why does Bresson make it so difficult for us to sense it?

Tony Pipolo rightly calls *Lancelot du lac* "surely the darkest film anyone has made of

the Arthurian romances," noting that Bresson focuses on "the nadir of the Arthurian chronicle, the moment of the disintegration of the Round Table, the erosion of the chivalric
ideal, the decline of faith in what sustained it and the values it represented" (280). The film
opens on a particularly depressing note, with the return of those of Arthur's knights who
have survived the unsuccessful quest for the Grail. Although the Grail Quest precedes the
events in the film, "it haunts the narrative as yet another reminder of a crisis of faith and
loss of innocence, two of Bresson's abiding themes" (Pipolo 280). Lancelot tells Arthur that
he has returned without the Grail, adding, "The Grail has eluded me." As he tells Guenevere
in their first meeting, he did glimpse the Grail and was given to understand that his sinful
relationship with her lay at the root of his inability to approach the sacred object. This revelation prompted him to make a solemn vow to God to end their affair. But as Guenevere
suggests when he tries to break his earlier and equally solemn vow to her, carnal sin and the
love they share are surely less to blame than the barbarity to which Arthur's knights have
stooped. Refuting the notion that the court's moral decline was the result of their affair, she
says, "You were all implacable. You killed, pillaged, burned. Then you turned blindly on
each other like maniacs. Now you blame our love for this disaster."

    That Bresson shares Guenevere's verdict is clearly confirmed by the opening scenes of
the film, a series of five acts of graphic violence broken only by shots of knights careening
through the forest. We witness a decapitation and a disembowelment; we see a burning building with charred corpses and two armored corpses hanging from a tree—a stunning *memento
mori*!—and, perhaps most shockingly, a knight desecrating a church. Since the image of a
chalice appears after these scenes,[10] and we are told in the expository crawl that the thirty
knights remaining from the hundred who had set out on the quest were returning home,
the implication is that these knights are those same men, continuing the senseless behavior
that kept them from seeing the Grail. But to depict the action, Bresson uses metonymy and
parataxis, largely dispensing with the kind of causal connections that would help us contex-
tualize and understand it. Laurie Finke and Martin Shichtman rightly point out that this
lack of cinematographic suture produces uncertainty and anxiety in the viewer (249).[11]
Because these images are not "anchored," we have the sense that Bresson is presenting us,
both here and at the close of the film (which records the final battle, fought in that same
dark forest) with a picture of "war as anonymous and indifferent slaughter, with faceless
phantoms in the darkness battling and perishing beneath heavy armor that instantly turns
into scrap metal" (Rosenbaum 205). This vision of war is particularly striking in the final
scene, where Arthur's mortally wounded "first knight," whose horse has been felled, stumbles
over to collapse into the heap of his anonymous companions who have perished in the battle
that marks the ultimate demise of the Round Table. We recognize him by his distinctive
helmet, his horse, and his exclamation: "Guenevere!" In this context, his *cri de cœur* has a
very different function from Tristan's calling out "Iseult" three times as he expires in Thomas
of Britain's version of that legend.[12] Lancelot's utterance seems to be his final recognition
that Guenevere was right, that it was the knights' barbarous behavior and not the lovers' forbidden passion that brought down Arthur's realm. Although we think of the Grail quest
as a spiritual one, Arthur's knights have pursued it as if the quest were just another chivalric adventure. It is again Guenevere who tries to set Lancelot straight when she tells him:

"It is not the Grail, it is God you want, but God is not an object you can bring back with you."[13]

James Quandt points out that, whereas many critics have underscored the "transcendental" in Bresson's early films, others cite him as "a clear and supreme example of a materialist filmmaker, one whose images are solid and ineluctable as facts, whose use of sound places us in a dense, *material* world, and whose editing is based on principles of the relations between things" (10). Quandt notes that some critics offer inventories of images, gestures, and motifs that seem to support the latter view, even going so far as to suggest affinities with the *choisisme* of the *nouveau roman*, which describes objects obsessively. "But," he goes on, "how often in Bresson's films are objects and gestures—perceptible, factual, seemingly unambiguous—suddenly, mysteriously transformed into something ineffable: signifiers of an absent force or being?" (11). How difficult it is, in short, to categorize Bresson as *either* "transcendental" *or* "materialist," especially since both are rather vague, polysemic terms.

The ideas expressed in Bresson's *Notes on Cinematography* support both approaches, in that, for this filmmaker, meaning can only emerge from the physical juxtaposition of images. His montage, which he calls "*écriture*" ("writing"), is spare and precise: he favors images that are flat and inexpressive, or rather expressive only in relation to other images, whether closely juxtaposed or echoing each other at a distance (5).[14] Bresson considers aural motifs to be particularly evocative,[15] and, in the *Lancelot*, as countless critics have noted, the sound

The final apocalypse in Robert Bresson's 1974 film *Lancelot du lac*.

of armor clanging and of horses galloping and neighing, whether accompanied by visuals or not, is very striking. Consequently, we find ourselves in a world even more densely material than in Bresson's previous films, with the result that it is particularly difficult to perceive the transcendental element. We can easily identify with Lancelot when he tells the peasant woman whom he meets in the maze-like forest[16] on his return from the Quest, "I have lost my way." But unlike the many hermits that the knights encounter at the intersection of various paths in *La Quête del Saint Graal*, this woman cannot really enlighten him; she gives him only the most factual of information, telling him that he is in Escalot and offering to show him the way.[17]

Nowhere is Bresson's inimitable montage and its materialist thrust more striking than in the tournament. It is the longest and most elaborate sequence in the film and is placed at its very center. As Tony Pipolo notes, "Bresson turns the spectacle inherent in the [tournament] genre into a filmic one, a dazzling display of how the arsenal of cinema—framing, editing, sound, color, off screen space, synecdoche, and ellipsis—can depict and suggest action" (297).[18] This event is proposed by the knights of Escalot, and Arthur's demoralized knights prepare for it and participate in it with great enthusiasm, as if to demonstrate that their way of life still has validity, especially since the bravura performance of Lancelot, fighting incognito, clearly reveals his identity. But, here again, the failure of the chivalric experience, and indeed its materialistic dimension, is underscored: since the object of each joust is to unseat one's opponent, the image that Bresson shows repeatedly (eight times!—they are all Lancelot's victories) is that of a defeated knight falling off his charger; throughout, the camera is focused mostly on the ground.[19]

Since tournaments were originally held in times of peace primarily to provide knights with the opportunity to continue honing their fighting skills, they were *simulacra* of combat, and, indeed, increasingly ritualized and sterile forms of it. It is hardly surprising, then, that the tournament does not restore to Arthur's men the sense of fellowship that they had presumably had before setting out on the Grail quest. If anything, the tournament shows how hollow and fruitless their lives have become. Arthur, devastated by the loss of so many of his companions in the Quest, demonstrates his realization that his vaunted fellowship has ended when, believing that God has forsaken them, he moves to close the room that houses the Round Table. Bresson shows this iconic object only in fragmented form, evoking thereby the fracturing of the Round Table and the ideals it represents.[20] Gauvain, the only knight who appears to believe that all is not lost, protests the closing off of the Round Table, crying, "Give us a purpose!"—to which Arthur's only response is "Pray."

In our search for the transcendental in *Lancelot*, we might well ask if prayer still has any efficacy in the increasingly doomed Arthurian world. Early in the film Lancelot visits the chapel, apparently seeking God's help in reinforcing his vow to end his affair with Guenevere. But from the moment he enters, the cross that he approaches appears out of focus, reflecting a response that is nebulous at best, and more likely absent. This less-than-promising visit is cut short as we hear, and then see, the arrival of the messengers from Escalot, come to propose the tournament to Arthur. It is Lancelot's decision to participate in that event (from which he will emerge victorious, but wounded in the groin) that will keep him from meeting Guenevere according to the promise that he had made to her. Thus, if Lancelot does not return to his lover for the planned tryst, it is hardly to his credit. Throughout most of the film, he is left betwixt and between, having failed to renew his vow to God or to Guenevere—until after he has rescued her from prison. When the Queen insists that he must return her to Arthur in order to prevent further bloodshed, he somewhat petulantly refuses to capitulate, although eventually Guenevere manages to convince Lancelot that he must give her up.

Since the protagonists of Bresson's earlier films have, by the end, achieved redemption, we might have hoped that Lancelot and Guenevere, who struggled so with the conflict of two imperative loyalties, would be granted that grace. But this is not to be, or if it is, we see no sign of it, so overwhelmed are we by the materialist dimension, which Bresson underscores by the way in which he shoots all the combat scenes, featuring virtually anonymous knights both at the beginning and end of the film and in the central tournament scene.[21] The proliferation of objects, particularly in the final scene, is so striking that the transcendental element that we have come to expect at the end of Bresson's films—that moment of grace, the presence of God—is nowhere in evidence, unless the bird that we see taking flight at the moment of Lancelot's death represents his soul. But that seems unlikely. Although Bresson might maintain that the bird "evokes the presence of God," states Dempsey, it is the pile-up of armored corpses that we remember: "it is not grace but death which abounds—death with no life beyond it," he concludes (10). The significance of the bird's appearance is certainly open to various interpretations: Pipolo underscores the materialist theme of the film when he speculates that the bird is "presumably scanning the ground for prey" (307).

There is another potential element of transcendence that Bresson downplays considerably—the force of passionate love that has always been an integral part of Lancelot's character and that we have come to expect in his portrayal from the Middle Ages to the present. As Pipolo points out, the tournament sequence ("the most viscerally exciting") "in its breathtaking appeal to the aural, visual and tactile senses, approaches the orgasmic," whereas the dialogue that engages Lancelot and Guenevere, bearing as it does on their guilt, their tortured doubts, and God, "is wholly cerebral" (301).

Of course, it may be unfair to compare scenes governed by action with ones dominated by discourse, especially since the phrases that make up the characters' speeches are uttered by non-actors who, famously, are denied any expressivity by their director. Nevertheless, this "flattening" of the love scenes is in many ways quite as disorienting as the graphic violence portrayed nearly everywhere else in the film. Who can forget the jarring exchange in which Guenevere tells Lancelot, "Take this heart, this soul; they belong to you," only to hear him say, "It's your body I want?" Again, Lancelot's materialism drains what could be a touching moment of all potential transcendence. Is Bresson's willful deflation of this cherished romantic myth part of his impulse to inject "realism" into the Arthurian world, of his attempt to strip Camelot of all its "fairy tale" features? It is interesting to note that, although Bresson speaks of his intention to transfer the fairy tale element into the "realm of feelings" and does give the lovers three scenes in which to explore their emotions at length, nowhere in the trailer for the film is there any allusion to them or any sight of Guenevere. We see only a repetition of those relentless scenes of ignoble combat from the opening sequence and a couple of tournament scenes. The lack of allusion to the love theme is all the more surprising in that one of the few revelations Bresson gives in the film's pressbook concerns this passion: "Predestined love, passionate love battling against insurmountable obstacles. It's this love and its fluctuations which give their movement to the film. There you go, I've told you everything" (*Lancelot du lac* Pressbook).

In Bresson's film, the final massacre—which spares neither Arthur nor his best knights, Gauvain and Lancelot—brings the action of the film full circle in that it reflects the senseless violence of the opening scenes and the aching conviction that God has forsaken them. As John Pruitt observes,

> The action can be seen perhaps as not an unfolding narrative so much as a static analysis of a single moment in which a society loses its ways, and instantly dissipates and dies. The circularity of the film (as in *Pickpocket*) is a kind of denial of temporal progression and puts the action into a ritualised, symbolic realm, the end of which is sealed right at the beginning [8].

The film's oppressing circularity is reinforced by the fulfillment of the prophecy uttered by the old peasant woman at the beginning that "He whose footfalls precede him will not outlive the year." She answers in the affirmative when the little peasant girl inquires, "Even if the footfalls are those of his horse?" A bit later, when Lancelot arrives in Arthur's camp, Gauvain greets him, saying, "The first is last." Indeed, Lancelot, Arthur's "first knight" is not only the last to arrive at camp, he will also be the last to die in the final scene, and his horse's demise immediately precedes his.

Off screen, though, not everyone is dead, nor is everything resolved: we know that Mordred defeats the king's men, using archers perched in trees to pick them off as they ride through the forest.[22] We know that Arthur and Lancelot are both among the armored corpses we see at the end of the film, but we do not learn the fate of either Mordred or Guenevere. That these questions remain unanswered makes the film's conclusion even more despairing. The end of the *Mort Artu* is considerably less so. Arthur takes back Guenevere on the order of the Pope, but banishes Lancelot. Then, urged on by Gauvain, who cannot forgive Lancelot for—accidentally—killing his brother Gareth, Arthur leaves to make war on Lancelot, entrusting his realm and his wife to the care of Mordred, who immediately proceeds to betray his lord by seizing the kingdom and trying to gain possession of the Queen. The final battle will be, as in the film, between Arthur and Mordred, but Guenevere will already have fled to a convent where she will die shortly thereafter, and Lancelot, upon learning of her death and Arthur's disappearance, will retire to a monastery where, for four years, he will live an ascetic life of fasting and vigils and constant prayer. When he dies, one of his religious brothers has a vision of angels taking his soul up to heaven and is convinced of the efficacy of penitence.

These scenes in the literature do not ring totally true, or rather they work in the context of the thirteenth century but not in that of the twentieth, and it is not surprising that Bresson offers no redemption of this kind to either Lancelot or Guenevere. Nevertheless, Pipolo (281) suggests that one character—Gauvain—does find a kind of redemption similar to that achieved by other Bressonian protagonists, some of whom he resembles. Gauvain is the noblest of Arthur's knights (at least in the film), has the most faith in the possibility of rebuilding the Round Table and reviving the old ideals, confronts Mordred the most courageously, and stands up for Lancelot until the end. If he attacks his friend for killing Agravain and is, in turn, attacked by him, he assures Arthur that Lancelot's mortal riposte was legitimate and adds touchingly that, except for Lancelot's killing of his brother, "mon cœur est avec lui (my heart is with him)." Although he is not a Christ figure, notes Pipolo, "he fights the good fight and manifests the virtues of charity, humility, and mercy" (282). Indeed, a comparison with Lancelot is instructive. At one point Gauvain tells Guenevere that Lancelot is a saint and that he himself is not: "I go to mass. I take Communion at Easter. God does not ask any more of me. I am just as God wanted me." Lancelot, on the other hand, is clearly not just as God wanted him. He remains totally conflicted about his priorities and, in the end, decides that his vow to Guenevere takes precedence. For him, there is no redemption, just as there was no Grail, and God remains obstinately silent and unapproachable until the end.

In eliminating the magical dimension of the legend, Bresson naturally eschews the elements of Arthur's mystical death that offer some hope for his return. It would have run counter to his purpose to allow the king to be carried off to Avalon and Lancelot and Guenevere to die in religious institutions after repenting for their sins. Kristin Thompson echoes many critics when she states that *Lancelot* shares the "increasingly bleak outlook of Bresson's later films; rather than finding a religious or moral grace, as in the earlier ones, the characters now lose the grace they have in the face of a corrupt society's pressures" (441). In *Lancelot*, Bresson has taken a set of events that are part of our "mythical" past and tried to render them more real and concrete to today's viewers so that they can understand the ideological implications. With his next film, *Diable*, he returns to the modern world to trace the despairing path toward suicide of a student, Charles, who cannot abide the monstrous social, political and ecological decadence that surrounds him.[23] The director makes his point starkly— and most uncharacteristically—by inserting into this film stock footage of scenes of relentless destruction.[24] Bresson would go on to make only two more films, the last being *L'Argent* (*Money*) [1983], in which the filmmaker records his disgust with the current preoccupation with the false idol that is money,[25] and certainly the horrors that he highlights in *Diable* are all the result of callous people thoughtlessly intent on making money and nothing more. Given the thrust of these later films, which seem to reflect the darkening of Bresson's view of society, it is hardly surprising that in his *Lancelot* he presented a totally bleak, materialistic picture of the Round Table. It is tantalizing to imagine how this film might have turned out had it had been made back in the 1950s when Bresson's palette was lighter.

In beginning their analysis of three Grail films—Bresson's, Rohmer's, and Hans-Jürgen Syberberg's *Parsifal* (1982)—Finke and Shichtman state: "These are not lovable films—at least not at first viewing. They are difficult and require patience to watch. They are the product of cultures perhaps more used to grappling with intellectual issues and less afraid of challenging viewers than the culture that produces Hollywood films" (248). Nothing could be truer of Bresson's *Lancelot*, a film that may seem maddeningly opaque at first but which rewards the viewer who takes the time to explore it sequence by sequence, as the film's current availability on DVD invites us to do. Yet how many filmgoers apart from specialists in Arthurian film and dedicated Bressonians have the will and wherewithal to do so? But more to the point: it would seem that Bresson's demystification impulse is directed primarily to an audience that knows only the main outlines of what he is pleased to call the "myth." How can they appreciate the intricacy of the dark vision that his "Arthurian realism" presents if it is so elliptical and Bresson supplies so few cues? Moreover, as Julie Codell astutely observes, "Rather than a cinema of signs, Bresson's film is a cinema of signifiers without signifieds, a cinema of incompleted signs." Extending this comment to Bresson's use of the body of Arthurian legends, she goes on, "Bresson's characters are signifiers who remain separate from the signifieds of the legend—heroism, worthy death, Christian sacrifice, chivalry, love, honor, and the clear distinctions between the roles of good and evil, Christian and heathen, men and women" (277).

Medieval knights and their ladies were not as heroic as they are presented in Arthurian literature; or, more accurately, they are not as heroic as many dimly recall from reading such literary works. Even knowing this fact, we still want to believe to some extent in the ideals they incarnate. With Rohmer's *Perceval*, we can laugh at how the director follows Chrétien in poking fun at Arthur and his knights and the inflated ideals they represent, but somehow our vision of these figures survives intact. On the other hand, the stark impression left by Bresson's *Lancelot*, for all its artistry—or perhaps because of it—may be a little too unforgiving. But that is precisely the point.[26]

Notes

1. If *Monty Python and the Holy Grail* (1975), by Terry Gilliam and Terry Jones, had been made by a French director, I would have included it in this list of films made in the 1970s that seek to demystify our most cherished legends. See Brian Levy and Lesley Coote's essay on "the subversion of medievalism" in *Lancelot du lac* and *Monty Python*.

2. It is not surprising that, as Levy and Coote note (100), *Lancelot* has been far less frequently studied than other major Arthurian films (such as *Perceval le Gallois* and *Excalibur*) and that it has not received the enthusiastic reception accorded other Bresson films. This lack of attention to the *Lancelot*, as opposed to Bresson's other films, is reflected in the essays in Quandt, ed.

3. See my analysis of this film.

4. Thanks to Norris J. Lacy and his team of translators, the entire *Lancelot-Grail Cycle* is now available in English in ten paperback volumes from Routledge. Although this publication is essentially a reprint, some changes have been made. See my review of the paperback edition.

5. Jean-Marcel Paquette (193–194) states that, although Bresson nowhere identifies his source, he was clearly following the *Mort Artu*, no doubt Jean Frappier's 1936 translation, which would have been the most accessible to a non-specialist.

6. The details of this correspondence were published in the 1996 issue of *Positif*, cited by Keith Reader 116–117.

7. Jeff Rider, et al., claim that the Arthurian legend is viewed differently in France than in North America: "The past to which modern French treatments of the legend refer is not shadowy and mythological but datable and literary" (150). I think the distinction to be made in both cases, however, is that between scholars and non-scholars. I doubt very much that the average French person—or the average movie goer anywhere—is conversant with Chrétien's romances or the *Lancelot-Grail* cycle. In shooting *Perceval le Gallois*, Rohmer's enterprise is partly pedagogical: he wants his compatriots to be aware of Chrétien's *Conte du Graal*. In the case of the *Lancelot*, however, although Bresson knew the literary tradition, it is the "shadowy and mythological" view of the legend off of which he is playing.

8. www.mastersofcinema.org/bresson/Words/LancelotDuLac_pressbook.html (accessed May 22, 2012). This site is no longer available; although the English translation exists, it is somewhat faulty, as in the case of this particular quotation.

9. On this trajectory, see Quandt, "'All Things Conceal a Mystery.'"

10. As Finke and Shichtman (246 note), the Grail image at the beginning is somehow deformed.

It is true that something sticks out of the chalice on a diagonal to the right. It looks at first like a quill, but, since it is metal, it may be the top of a hand (covered in a gauntlet) reaching for the cup. The lighting, which comes from the upper left and leaves the lower right-hand part of the shot in darkness, reveals only the reflection on the top of the gauntlet.

11. See their excellent analysis of these scenes and the effect of Bresson's editing on the viewer, as well as their instructive comparison with Jerry Zucker's *First Knight* (249–252).

12. In this work, Tristan's appeal reflects his mistaken belief that his beloved has not heeded his call to come to Brittany to heal his wounds.

13. It is Guenevere's insight in part that makes me think the object projecting from the chalice is the top of a hand attempting, misguidedly, to take possession of the sacred cup—see n. 10 above.

14. Sandrine Siméon notes that Bresson's use of "spatial form" in the *Lancelot* recalls the same esthetic analyzed by Norris Lacy (1977) in the *Mort Artu*. In the film, the various segments relate to each other "according to visual or aural motifs and structural symmetry" (433).

15. "The ear goes more towards the within, the eye towards the outer" (*Notes* 28).

16. In the legend, the forest, where Merlin dwells, is a magical place. The film, which Bresson shot in the Breton forest, stresses its disorienting dimension. As Levy and Coote note, Escalot is the only place name that Bresson uses, "and the spirit of this place takes over the entire film, in the form of its doom-laden Breton forest" (106). When the knights return from their unsuccessful search for Lancelot following the tournament, they report, "No sign of Lancelot, but the forest was the devil." Indeed it is, notes Michael Wood, the site of "all sorts of hacking of human bodies and other knightly violence, headless trunks or trunkless heads spouting fountains of blood" (23).

17. If anything, she resembles Perceval's mother, who knew all too well the perils of chivalry and wanted to dissuade her son from becoming a knight. The parallel is even more striking when we recall that, at the beginning of the *Conte du graal* (both in Chrétien's romance and in Rohmer's film), Perceval is dazzled by the sights and sounds represented by the knights who suddenly appear before him.

18. Calling it "an exhilarating tour de force and one of the most spectacular passages of editing in film history," Pipolo likens it to the Gare de Lyon sequence in *Pickpocket*. See his excellent analysis on pp. 297–301. He cites Kristin Thompson's statistics: the sequence contains ninety-three shots, i.e., more than one-sixth of the 644 shots in the film. See her breakdown of the tournament in Quandt, ed. 454–455.

19. As Rider, et al., say about Bresson's earthbound focus in the film, generally: "This concentration on the earth thematizes the film's vertical dimension and knighthood's descent through it" (153).

20. As Pipolo notes, the rhetorical device of having a part stand for the whole (synecdoche), so characteristic of Bresson's style, in this film "seems to encode the overall moral and psychological crisis at the heart of the narrative, namely, the disintegrating social world it depicts and the personal breakdowns it generates" (284). Besides the Grail, the Round Table is, according to Finke and Shichtman, "the other great stranded object in the film" (253).

21. By the end of the film, the attentive viewer realizes that, when the knights are in full armor, some of the more prominent ones, such as Arthur and Lancelot, can be identified by the decoration on their helmets.

22. This detail may show the introduction of a new technology that will make cavalry seem inefficient and outmoded, just as the English longbows at the Battle of Crécy demonstrated the folly of the French who insisted on waging war in the traditional manner, while mounted on horseback. See Jean Sémolué 225, cited by Keith Reader, who adds, "History, lurking in ambush, has destroyed the time of myth, making this the most cosmically pessimistic of Bresson's endings" (120).

23. Of course, Charles's decision to kill himself rather than to go on living in a corrupt world is in some ways a courageous moral choice that seems less desperate than the knights' determination to preserve their lifestyle at all costs. We recall how Gauvain tells Guenevere that he would love God more if he didn't see so many baleful figures around him, but he perseveres.

24. They include horrific images, catalogued by Dempsey (10) as those "of fume-spewing factories and jets, poisoned animals and trees, mounds of garbage and trashed car hulks, a grounded tanker polluting the ocean, nuclear explosions, the baby seal hunt in Newfoundland, brain-damaged children of the Minamata mercury pollution."

25. In an interview with Michael Ciment, Bresson says: "Money is an abominable idol. It is everywhere. The only things that matter are invisible. Why are we here? What are life and death? Where are we going?" (716).

26. In any case, as Bresson states (63): "The public does not know what it wants. Impose on it your

decisions, your delights." As the translator points out, the original formulation ("tes volontés, tes voluptés")
is much stronger. I would translate it as "your will [or desires], your sensuous delights."

Works Cited

Arnaud, Philippe, Bernard Bénoliel, and Stéphane Dabrowski. *Robert Bresson: Éloge.* Milan: Mazzotta,
    1997.
Baby, Yvonne. "Du fer qui fait du bruit." *Le Monde* 29 September 1974: 15. English translation: "Metal
    Makes Sounds: An Interview with Robert Bresson." Trans. N. Jacobson. *Field of Vision* 13 (1985): 4–
    5.
Ciment, Michel. "I Seek Not Description But Vision: Robert Bresson on *L'Argent*." In Quandt, ed., 707–
    719.
Codell, Julie F. "Decapitation and Deconstruction: The Body of the Hero in Robert Bresson's *Lancelot du
    Lac*." In *The Arthurian Revival: Essays on Form, Tradition, and Transformation.* Ed. Debra N. Mancoff.
    New York: Garland, 1992.
Bresson, Robert. *Notes on Cinematography.* Trans. Jonathan Griffin. New York: Urizen, 1975. [Originally
    published in 1975 as *Notes sur le cinématographe*.]
Dempsey, Michael. "Despair Abounding: The Recent Films of Robert Bresson." *Film Quarterly* 34.1
    (Autumn 1980): 2–15.
Finke, Laurie A., and Martin B. Shichtman. *Cinematic Illuminations. The Middle Ages on Film.* Baltimore:
    Johns Hopkins University Press, 2010.
Frappier, Jean. *La Mort le roi Artu. Roman du XIIIe siècle.* Geneva: Droz, 1936.
Godard, Jean-Luc, and Michel Delahaye. "The Question, Interview with Robert Bresson." In Quandt, ed.,
    634–665.
Gracq, Julien. "Un compagnonnage d'exception," *Les Nouvelles littéraires* 23 September 1974: 7. Rpt. in
    Arnaud, et al., 55–56.
Grimbert, Joan Tasker. "Distancing Techniques in Chrétien de Troyes's *Li Contes del Graal* and Eric
    Rohmer's *Perceval le Gallois*." *Arthuriana* 10 (2000) [Special issue on Arthurian film guest-edited by
    Kevin J. Harty and Alan Lupack]: 35–45.
_____. Review of Norris J. Lacy, ed. *Lancelot-Grail, The Old French Arthurian Vulgate and Post-Vulgate
    in Translation* [paperback edition]. in *Encomia* 32–33 (2010–2011): 58–62.
Lacy, Norris J. "Spatial Form and the *Mort Artu*." *Symposium* 31.4 (1997): 337–345.
_____, ed. *Lancelot-Grail. The Old French Arthurian Vulgate and Post-Vulgate in Translation* [paperback
    edition]. New York, 1993–1996. Cambridge, Eng.: D. S. Brewer, 2010.
Lancelot du lac Pressbook. http://www.mastersofcinema.org/bresson/Words/LancelotDuLac_pressbook.
    html (accessed May 22, 2012). English version: http://www.ucalgary.ca/~tstronds/robertbresson.com/
    Words/LancelotDuLac_pressbook.html.
Levy, Brian, and Lesley Coote. "The Subversion of Medievalism in *Lancelot du lac* and *Monty Python and
    the Holy Grail*." In *Postmodern Medievalism.* Ed. Richard Utz and Jesse G. Swan. Studies in Medievalism
    XIII 2004. Cambridge, Eng.: D. S. Brewer, 2005.
Paquette, Jean-Marcel. "Lancelot's Last Metamorphosis," *Lancelot and Guinevere: A Casebook.* Ed. Lori J.
    Walters. New York: Garland, 1996. [First published as "La Dernière métamorphose de Lancelot."
    Cahiers de la Cinémathèque 42/43 (Summer 1985): 113–118. Trans. Marco D. Roman.]
Pipolo, Tony. *Robert Bresson: A Passion for Film.* New York: Oxford University Press, 2010.
Pruitt, John. "Robert Bresson's *Lancelot du lac*." *Field of Vision* 13 (1985): 8.
Quandt, James. "'All Things Conceal a Mystery': The Hidden God in Robert Bresson's *Au hasard Balthazar*
    and *Le Diable probablement*." In Quandt, ed., 493–507.
_____. "Introduction." In Quandt, ed., 1–23.
_____, ed. *Robert Bresson.* Rev. ed. Toronto: TIFF, 2011.
Reader, Keith. *Robert Bresson.* Manchester: Manchester University Press, 2000.
Rider, Jeff, et al. "The Arthurian Legend in French Cinema: Robert Bresson's *Lancelot du Lac* and Eric
    Rohmer's *Perceval le Gallois*." In *Cinema Arthuriana: Twenty Essays.* Rev. ed. Ed. Kevin J. Harty. Jef-
    ferson, NC: McFarland, 2002.
Rosenbaum, Jonathan. "The Rattle of Armour, the Softness of Flesh: Bresson's *Lancelot du lac*." In *Movies

as Politics. Berkeley: University of California Press, 1997. [First published in *Sight and Sound* 43 (Summer 1974): 128–30.]

Schrader, Paul. "Robert Bresson, Possibly," *Film Comment* 13.5 (1977): 26–30. Rpt. in Quandt, ed. 692–705.

_____. *Transcendental Style in Film: Ozu, Bresson, Dreyer*. Berkeley: University of California Press, 1972.

Sémolué, Jean. *Bresson, ou l'acte pur des métamorphoses*. Paris: Flammarion, 1993.

Siméon, Sandrine. "L'Esthétique 'spatiale' du *Lancelot* de Bresson." *Contemporary French and Francophone Studies* 15.4 (September 2011): 433–441.

Sontag, Susan. "Spiritual Style in the Films of Robert Bresson." *Against Interpretation and Other Essays*. New York: Doubleday, 1966. [First published in 1964.]

Thompson, Kristin. "The Sheen of Armour, the Whinnies of Horses: Sparse Parametric Style in *Lancelot du lac*." In Quandt, ed., 433–465. [Originally published in her *Breaking the Glass Armor: Neoformalist Film Analysis*. Princeton: Princeton University Press, 1988.]

Wood, Michael. "At the Movies: The Devil and Robert Bresson." *London Review of Books* 30.11 (5 June 2008): 23.

Perceval of the Avant-Garde: Rohmer, Blank and von Trier

Alan Baragona

Artists retell the stories surrounding King Arthur for reasons too numerous to list, but it is no surprise that makers of commercial and art films alike have been attracted to the heroic rise and fall of Arthur himself, or to the love tragedy of Lancelot and Guinevere. Meanwhile, the Holy Grail has become such a cultural touchstone that it is evoked daily for any ultimate goal, grand (a Super Bowl ring) or trivial (again, a Super Bowl ring, depending on your point of view). We cannot avoid the Grail. A Google search for "Holy Grail" as of the writing of this essay will return nineteen million hits; "Grail" by itself, roughly twenty-five and a half million. "Lancelot or Launcelot" returns fewer than two million. The Grail is all around us, so it is not surprising that it should show up in our films. Explaining the prominence of Perceval is a bit trickier. Chrétien's character is the archetype of the innocent going through an education by rite of passage, of course, and the *Bildungsroman* has become a staple of literature and pop culture since at least the eighteenth century. However, within fifty years of his creation, the first Grail knight was eclipsed by Galahad. Galahad's name has taken on a life of its own, almost inexplicably for a virgin Christ figure as a paragon of courtesy towards women—viz. Elvis as Kid Galahad. Meanwhile, the name "Perceval" evokes nothing special in our culture. Relegated to secondary status in the Grail story, despite the best efforts of Wolfram, he did not really regain the spotlight in the popular imagination until, in the nineteenth century, Wagner put him onstage, but so transformed as an ascetic and nationalist ideal that his earlier appeal as a naïve and somewhat comic young hero could be lost in the gravitas of his new, Wagnerian status. Outside of professional medievalists and their students, those who do know of him mostly know Parsifal, an icon of *Gesamtkunstwerk* and High Art.

If he has lost some of his cachet as a popular figure, though, Perceval has become a darling of the avant-garde in filmmaking, and the reasons for this cultural phenomenon are worth exploring. The range of his adaptability can be illustrated by examining three films of the 70s, 80s, and 90s: a well-known high concept art film (Eric Rohmer's 1978 *Perceval le Gallois*), a less well known, prototypically "indie" German television film (Richard Blank's 1980 *Parzival*), and a Grail surprise (Lars von Trier's 1996 *Breaking the Waves*), with a brief sidelong glance at a rare pop–Perceval (Robert Zemeckis's 1994 *Forrest Gump*). All of these films show, at the very least, that the character created by Chrétien de Troyes, elaborated by Wolfram von Eschenbach, and apotheosized by Richard Wagner still has the capacity to be transformed in the modern imagination.

Eric Rohmer's Perceval le Gallois

Rohmer's *Perceval le Gallois* is ground that has been well trodden by critics and scholars since it first premiered. Recurrent themes in books, articles, reviews, and interviews are Rohmer's conservative Catholicism and interest in morality, the literal presentation of Chrétien's text and the highly literary nature of the film itself, the filmic equivalents Rohmer found for Chrétien's narrative techniques, Rohmer's one major deviation from the poem at the end, the film's unique look, and especially two aspects of Rohmer's approach to the medieval poem, "distancing" and a sense of its "otherness," both of which are more problematical than they appear at first glance.

The film is well known enough that only a brief description should be required here. The look of the film is modeled on medieval manuscript illuminations. Costumes are authentic (Nickel 248); gestures and blocking, stylized. Sets are designed to imitate the proportions of figures in illuminations, with a castle, for example, that looks like a particularly fancy child's playhouse. The various forests that Perceval rides through are all represented by a small copse of silver trees, not much taller than the actors, each with four enormous leaves shaped into a spherical crown (looking somewhat more like they belong on *The Forbidden Planet* than in a twelfth-century fantasy landscape).

Rohmer began with a literal translation of Chrétien's text into octosyllabic couplets, even preserving occasional phrases from Old French that are understandable in modern French (Lacy 75). He also developed a correlative to Chrétien's narrative style and use of indirect discourse by having Perceval and other characters alternate between normal dialogue and third-person narration of what they are doing at any given moment.

The script follows the poem's plot closely. Rohmer deals with the challenge of filming an unfinished work by cutting the portions of the story that depict Gauvain's adventures after Perceval is last mentioned. The only significant addition is the performance of a passion play at the hermitage in which Perceval himself portrays Christ. The film closes with an open-ended depiction of Perceval riding off to continue his life's journey.

Discussions of the film attribute its stylized look and general aesthetic, major factors in putting distance between the audience and any emotional connection to what is happening on the screen, to a wildly varied range of influences: not only manuscript illumination, where the debt is obvious, but also Brecht, Rohmer's contemporary New Wave directors, medieval drama, and, of course, Chrétien himself.[1] And we should not forget that Rohmer and Claude Chabrol wrote a book about the master of casting a cold eye on life, and death, Alfred Hitchcock. At the same time, however, and sometimes in the same studies, writers will focus on Rohmer's appeal to human emotion or spiritual feeling in the staging of the passion play at the end[2] or his desire to have his audience identify with the innocence and naïveté of Perceval or his discovery of the power of love,[3] which would seem at odds with the contention that he wants his viewers to keep their distance from his characters.

Similarly, some critics assert that Rohmer wants modern audiences to see the medieval setting as alien,[4] and others that he wants them to recognize universal themes in the old story, especially moral principles that Rohmer addresses in all his films.[5] No one, however, mentions both possibilities in the same essay, so they do not seem to see these potentially contradictory positions as a matter of debate.

That "distancing" is a major part of the film's aesthetic is undeniable. It is consistent with Rohmer's other work and with the ideology of the French New Wave, which put a premium on "narrative telling" over "dramatic showing" (Williams 74). However, Rohmer's purpose seems to me to be different in *Perceval*. Like Pissarro and the Impressionists, Rohmer was older than the other New Wave *auteurs* such as Truffaut and Godard and "often seemed a throwback to many of the values the New Wave once opposed ... [a] moralist ... a literary sensibility ... a Catholic ... an unmistakably original, but decidedly conservative, talent" (Williams 71). There is strong evidence that in this case the distancing is meant to be only an initial effect, but the point is to take his modern audience beyond it.

The casting of Fabrice Luchini as Perceval at first seems to fit the mold of a character meant to distance the audience from emotional identification. Some reviewers, mostly Anglo-American, disliked him, because he was not beefy enough to be a convincingly realistic medieval warrior (one wrote, "'He looks as if he would be afraid to kill a mouse with a trap, much less joust with a man in armor'" [Rider, et al., 151]). However, he fits the medieval look of the film because he looks like knights as depicted in manuscript illuminations, slender and slightly curved in posture like a modern dancer, even in chainmail. "Although not quite the bloodless icon of medieval painting, Perceval does take on some of the ethereal, sinuous qualities of such figures" (Williams 78). Furthermore, his delivery of dialogue, coupled with his third person narration, appears, to American eyes and ears, at least, to have the flat affect associated with films that are aimed more at intellect than feeling. In fact, neither his resemblance to manuscript knights nor acting style were why Rohmer cast him. He says he chose Luchini for his "wide-eyed innocence and boyish figure" in order to capture Perceval's naiveté (Rider, et al., 151), traits that are true to Chrétien's character and that Rohmer wanted his audience to find appealing and probably identify with, since everybody is young once.

Luchini's portrayal of Perceval performing Christ confirms that Rohmer is taking his audience on a journey from seeing with the brain to seeing with the heart, and even the spirit. More than one critic has remarked that, at this point, Luchini acts with genuine feeling and that Rohmer's purpose, for the first time in the film, seems obviously to be to engage the emotions of the viewer (Harty 24; Wise 51; Grimbert, "Distancing Techniques," 39–40).

Not only Luchini's expressions, but also Rohmer's editing, seem intended to involve the audience. The staginess of the amateur theatrical is counterbalanced by the close-up of Perceval's foot being nailed to the Cross and spurting blood. Certainly, Rohmer, consistent with the Passion tradition, gives blood a mystical function (Gorgievski 175). It could be that, at this moment, Rohmer is reflexively slipping into a cinematic vocabulary inconsistent with what is being depicted. On the other hand, it could be a suggestion that the boundaries between the artificial and the real are being blurred, just as the line between the liturgical and the historical breaks down when the Eucharistic re-enactment of the Last Supper supposedly produces the same miracle of transubstantiation. Compare how the Vulgate *Lancelot-Grail Cycle* and Malory transform Galahad not just into Christ, but into the Eucharistic host itself in the Mass at the Grail Chapel.

Linda Williams notes in passing that Perceval suddenly "acquires a beard" (77), but this acquisition is significant. The abruptness of the shift to the "play within the screenplay," the unexplained facial hair, which is gone again in the final shot of Perceval, as himself again, riding off through the "forest," and the alternation of stylized staging with realistic blood all give the scene a dreamlike quality which signals that Perceval is not just joining a performance staged in the hermitage but has seamlessly entered a world of allegory even purer than the fantasy we have witnessed so far. The artificiality of the allegorical mode allows us to conclude that the staging of the Passion at the end by Rohmer is not only a liturgical performance of Christ by Perceval but a transformation of him into Christ, the ultimate fulfillment of Bernard of Clairvaux's idea of spiritual knighthood, which Rohmer has been aiming for all along.

This very medieval technique brings us back to the question of "alterity" in the film. Once again, the evidence at first supports the idea that Rohmer wants to present the Middle Ages as "other" than modern (Grimbert, "Distancing Techniques" 33). Jeff Rider, Richard Hull, and Christopher Smith connect the idea to the general French interest in the era and to Rohmer's literary approach to the film. They contend that French audiences found the Arthurian Middle Ages attractive for its strangeness, "historically, materially, and culturally" (150). They note that very few films with Arthurian settings had been made in France at the time. Thus, the "cultural and cinematic strangeness was seductive" to a director like Rohmer, who was "self-consciously independent and artistic" (150). Most importantly, the Anglo-American attraction to Arthurian legend is mythic; it is an heroic pseudo-history. But for Rohmer and the French, Arthurian legend was largely a matter of the "artistic greatness" of French literary heritage (150).

The literary nature of Rohmer's interest in the period informs his presentation of the story. He is not interested in depicting an historical Middle Ages, or even a medieval fantasy in quasi-historical mode. Instead, Rohmer sought "'to rediscover the vision of the medieval period as it saw itself. This it seems to me one can attempt to accomplish, while we will never know the Middle Ages as they really were'" (Tesich-Savage 50). This belief is consistent with what Rohmer also said about his depiction of the nineteen century through the style of its own artists in *La Marquise d'O* (Grimbert, "Distancing Techniques" 34). It is also consistent with the notion that art is not about reality but about the fact of how reality is perceived.

In "How to Tell a True War Story," Tim O'Brien says that the truth a war story must capture is how war felt to the soldiers, not how it really was. So when a listening patrol hears sounds of a cocktail party in the jungle, the true war story must not discover what they really heard but convey what it felt like to hear those sounds. When a soldier steps from shadow to light and is instantly obliterated by a rigged mortar shell, the storyteller must convey that the last thing the soldier felt was being blown apart by sunlight, his final reality. In the same way, Rohmer is depicting the way the Middle Ages seemed to the manuscript illuminators of the time. When we want to know how medieval authors and readers visualized, for instance, Palamon and Arcite, we look not only at the text, where visual descriptions may be sparse, but at the manuscript illustrations.

Trying to understand what medieval readers imagined while reading and trying to reproduce it, however, may be two different things. Donald L. Hoffman calls into question whether any such endeavor can succeed. Even an exact replication of the style of medieval illumination, he contends, will feel quaint, which is clearly not what the illuminators intended (45). One is reminded of Borges's joke about Pierre Menard, who "rewrites" *Don Quixote* for the twentieth century simply by copying Cervantes word for word, because a passage written by a sixteenth-century author means one thing, but the verbally identical passage written by a twentieth-century man, with all the possible associations that have accrued to it over 300 years, is entirely different. In the same way, *Perceval's* medieval style becomes a commentary on medieval "otherness" whether Rohmer intends it or not.

Nevertheless, if Rohmer, on the one hand, believed that the literal past was irrecoverable and alien, he was also using the literary past to highlight, instead, the similarities between the past and the present. This appropriation of past artistic styles is consistent with the Modernist methods of Picasso's forays into primitivism, because he found the aesthetic of African tribes compatible with his own modern ideas about art. Lucy Fischer and Linda Williams have said much the same thing about Rohmer's attraction to medieval art. Fischer says "in filming a medieval romance, Rohmer is clearly regarding the genre as a narrative 'ancestor' of the cinema. His aim, as a self-proclaimed conservative, is to pay it homage. His goal, as a modernist, is to tap it for new artistic forms" (21). Williams refers to medieval literature's "fragmented, digressive narratives, one dimensional characters and total disregard of reality that seems very similar to the scrambled narratives and anti-realism of our own recent literature" (72).

It seems likely that, while at first keeping the audience at an emotional distance that appears also to be a cultural distance, he is finally inviting the audience to see Chrétien as a modern sensibility. What at first seems alien will come to feel familiar. Grimbert confirms this possibility when she talks about Rohmer's translation of Chrétien's Old French into a modern idiom, taken from his "Notes sur la traduction et la mise en scène de *Perceval*": "He sought to prove that these dictates—*littéralité* and *compréhensibilité*—were not incompatible" (34). Rohmer takes the connection beyond recognizing modern style in the medieval. As a conservative Catholic, Rohmer is turning to the Middle Ages also to explore the roots of his own moral system. Critics frequently point out that the religiosity of *Perceval* is consistent with the moral questions he examined in his earlier works, especially the *Six Contes moraux* (Grimbert, "Distancing Techniques" 33; Rider, et al., 155), one of which Truffaut called "the most moral cinema event there can be, ... one of the first devoted to the importance of marriage...." (Grimbert, "Truffaut's *La Femme d'à Côté*" 195). Lucy Fischer even says, "Rohmer's films are descendants of the medieval romance" because his "pensive Catholic heroes" are like romance knights, and "Chrétien's *Perceval and the Grail* contains the ideological roots of Rohmer's world-view" (21). Kevin J. Harty avers that "Rohmer finds the soul of the medieval period and in it a lesson for the present" (24).

Everything old is new again.

Richard Blank's Parzival

Richard Blank's *Parzival* is less well known than Rohmer's *Perceval*. Although it was not Blank's first film, it does not even show up on IMDB, the earliest film in the list being one made the following year. It was shown several times on European television but was never marketed on video. Consequently, scholars have had little access to it, and almost nothing has been published about it outside of half of an essay by Ulrich Müller in *Cinema Arthuriana*. It is not as stylish or visually ambitious as *Perceval* with its low budget and found settings, but, in some ways, it is even more typical of the avant-garde for those reasons and others.

Like Rohmer, Blank comes at his craft from a literary angle. "[F]ilm is a medium to bring a story to life; a means, not an end. What is really worthwhile, according to Blank, is the attempt to make a statement as storyteller and artist through film" (Sunnen 4). In fact, he wanted to be a writer before he became a filmmaker. Blank began his artistic career studying writing at the Literarisches Colloquium Berlin (LCB) in the mid–60s with classmates like Tom Stoppard. At the LCB, he took a drama course in which he wrote short scenes, but he never studied screenwriting (Sunnen 1). The scenes were written collaboratively, and he has carried over that preference for collaboration in his filming. "We discovered that everyone had completely different ideas. In this way we learned not only how to write, but how to tolerate criticism and to understand that there is never one solution—there is no 'reality'" (Sunnen 2).

Also like Rohmer, Blank's Catholic upbringing has influenced his avant-garde sensibility and given him a sense that the past is not "other" but intertwined with the present. In one of his several treatises on filmmaking, *Drehbuch*, about storytelling, Blank writes,

> "Perhaps my rather odd concept of time is the reason for my aversion to the 'classical' story. I developed concurrent notions of time from an early age along with the normal course of chronological time. From childhood I have believed in the real presence of Christ in the liturgy of the Roman Catholic mass. This religious alternative to 'historical' time was complemented in a profound way at the beginning of my studies: I read André Malraux and took on his theory of the *musée imaginaire*, the idea of historical periods as present in our consciousness" [quoted in Sunnen 6].

Like the very Catholic Rohmer, "Blank sees the historical and ahistorical as inextricably joined in the mind. He refer[s] to the ahistorical as '*Heilszeit*,' or 'sacred time'" (Sunnen 6).

The most immediately striking difference between Rohmer's and Blank's films, of course, is the visual style. In addition to what I have already discussed, Rohmer went to great technical lengths to reproduce the flatness of medieval art in a medium that gives the illusion of three dimensions. He built a soundstage in a semicircle, so that, when the camera would pivot in a pan shot following actors moving along the arc, it would appear as if they were moving in a straight line but disorient the viewer's eye in a way that flattened the perspective (Williams 80). By contrast, the look of Blank's film is more conventional; however, such a look is arguably more suitable for his source. As it happens, the difference in some ways correspond to the distinction Annemarie Mahler makes between the ways Chrétien and Wolfram themselves convey a visual reality. Mahler begins by comparing the way Chrétien first describes Blancheflor, and Wolfram first describes Condwiramurs in a corresponding scene. Chrétien's description is as flat as an illumination, "front-face" and static (538). Wolfram's is full of movement and shifts perspective to different observers from different distances. Chrétien's "portrait is detailed, two-dimensional, precise, symmetrical, frontal—Wolfram's is vague, in motion, three-dimensional" (538–539).

Blank's path to the Middle Ages, moreover, was very unlike Rohmer's. Rohmer prepared himself to undertake Chrétien for years. As a high school teacher in 1964, he had made a television film that consisted of stills of manuscript illuminations with a voiceover telling the story (Rider, et al., 149). In preparation for filming *Perceval*, he made a close study of manuscripts and rehearsed his actors for a year in how to imitate the gestures and postures in the illuminations (Williams 78). Because of the nature of his project, Blank did not have this kind of preparation. The film was one of a series of dramatizations of works of literature for German television. Blank had already done episodes on *Peter Schlemiel* and *Dracula*, but he had never read *Parzival* and had to give himself a crash course in the poem and the criticism (Sunnen 4). These conditions, however, suited Blank, who was schooled in improvisation and felt comfortable creating a work that feels improvised instead of meticulously polished.

In fact, the film opens with an improvised scene. The actor and musician Wolfram Kunkel is on a street in Cologne singing Old High German lines from Wolfram von Eschenbach, accompanying himself on a hurdy-gurdy and dressed like either a modern hippy or a medieval peasant. He answers questions from onlookers about what he is singing. Blank pulls a Hitchcock and guides the line of conversation by speaking with Kunkel as if he were a man in the crowd (Sunnen 6). In later unscripted scenes, Kunkel chooses to perform twentieth-century poems by Walter Mehring and ad-libs much of his exchanges with people who gather to hear.

After the opening, the titles roll over a grainy photo of a ruined, perhaps bombed out, building. Kunkel walks out of the darkness and says, "I am Kunkel. I am to be Parzival." Thus the reenactment begins. Kunkel finds himself in what appears to be an attic or perhaps a ruined theater prop room amid the dust and debris of years. Alternating between voiceover and actual speech, he ruminates on how we remember the Middle Ages. He passes what appear to be banners of Hieronymus Bosch's scenes of the Black Death, of Hitler as a knight in shining armor ("Der Bannertrager" or "The Standard-Bearer"), and of David's "Napoleon Crossing the Alps." There are mannequins, mostly figures of women, and a live actress, Eva Schukardt, who is posed like one. Jump cut to Kunkel sitting amid the detritus and reading a book. It is *Parzival*. He is at once a student and an actor studying Wolfram's poem to prepare himself to play his main character.

This interpretive choice solves a problem that Rohmer faced but did not really resolve. In a publicity release for *Perceval* (Fischer 33n), Rohmer described his actors as narrators who "'become absorbed by the text and actually end up acting the part they were simply asked to speak'" (Fischer 22). This back story that his actors are really narrators who get caught up in the text and begin acting out their tale means that Rohmer conceives that he is showing the audience what is inside the narrators' heads. Instead of distancing the audience, Rohmer is drawing them into the actors' imaginations. The trouble with this idea, of course, is that Rohmer does not do anything to convey it to the viewers, because the whole concept is within his own imagination and not on the screen. There is an old saying in the theater, "If you can't play it, you can't say it." But Blank found a way to play it. Blank's audience sees Kunkel reading a text before he starts to act it out. They hear him working through the character and themes in both words and action. Far from being distanced from Parzival, the viewer can inhabit him along with the storyteller, who is both Kunkel and Blank.

Not yet in character as Parzival, Kunkel begins to narrate the back story of Herzeloyde, sometimes reading Wolfram's verse from the dusty book in modern German, sometimes reciting or paraphrasing, walking through the attic and picking props out of the dirt: a shield, a battle-axe, clothing. We see two boys in medieval dress sorting through costumes. Parzival's first encounter with knights is recounted rather than depicted, but a realistic stuffed horse stands in to represent the knights, much like a chess knight. When Kunkel dons the motley clothes of a fool that Herzeloyde gave him, his impersonation proper of the character begins, though he will alternate between Parzival and a fictive version of himself throughout the film.

When Parzival determines to leave and become a knight, Blank cuts to an outdoor scene, a naked, dead Herzeloyde half buried in a plowed field as a woman's voice takes over the narration momentarily. As the camera zooms out, we see a modern cityscape or perhaps a factory in the distance. The position of Herzeloyde's body is paralleled by the position of Schukardt as the sleeping lady in the tent back in the attic surrounded by medieval looking props.

The horse turns out to be on wheels operated by the two boys with a winch so that the Red Knight can actually ride it when he comes on the scene to be killed by Parzival, and Parzival has a mobile steed as he undertakes to become a knight. As Parzival contemplates what it means to have killed someone and to undertake a quest alone for the first time in his life, Blank cuts to modern Cologne again and a conversation between Kunkel and the crowd about loneliness. Blank will follow this pattern throughout the film, alternating between enacting Wolfram's story mostly in the allegorical attic, sometimes elsewhere, and modern street scenes that comment on the themes just depicted.

In this way, Blank covers the entire story, though he does so in a kind of shorthand. For an hour and a half, Blank encapsulates the story in a slow, "epic pace" (Müller 179). Blank solidifies the connection between medieval and modern in various ways. The same actor plays Gurnemanz as a rather smug, conservative old man as and an officious but somewhat sympathetic clerk that Kunkel, playing himself, must deal with for performing in the street without a license. In the medieval scenes, a mixture of live actors and mannequins will represent the characters, and some of the actors are in modern dress. Throughout, Schukardt is seen painting a mannequin in black and white stripes to represent Feirefiz. Kunkel, dressed as Parzival but smoking a cigarette as if on a break backstage between scenes in a play, continues to contemplate and comment on what Parzival is (or is not) learning. There seems to be some tension between Kunkel and Schukardt in their own persons, perhaps a reflection of the relationship between Parzival and Kondwiramurs. All but one of the major female characters is played by Schukardt, and that is Obilot, the young girl who has a crush on Gawan, also played by Kunkel, but with a beard. The resolution comes with a feast with all the characters, including Feirefiz now come to life. Kunkel/Parzival muses on the greater lessons from the poem:

> Wolfram knew how to treat the Grail; in the book he hardly mentions it. Instead he speaks of the complex relationships among people. Variety, family. All the people of the Grail are related. We are all family. The human family ... knights in combat, killing, murder. Killing in combat is fratricide. I, Parzival, become the Grail knight at the end of the tale. Wolfram spends 12 pages on this. The other 403 pages, in standard German, newly bound and sold in any train station's book shop, deal with how we human beings live with one another on Earth. Lady Earth. One hardly dares say "Mother Earth" anymore. Now, towards the end, when we expect to focus on the Grail, Wolfram is ... high-spirited. There is celebration! People have come together.... So many have come together who did not know each other. Were I to name their homes and lands, no one could remember them all.... A fairy-tale ending. So many women, now free. And a Grail King who has learned to ask questions and speak to other people.... Where striped people are accepted by the family, all ends well [trans. Sunnen].

This last statement is accompanied by an image of, first, Kondwiramurs and then Parzival putting their cheeks against Feirefiz's and coming away with wet black and white stripes on their faces. Ending on an image of racial harmony may betray a particularly modern preoccupation, but that theme and all the others in Blank's summation are there in Wolfram.

The attic "carries associations of a mythical picture of European philosophy and theology: the large 'cavern of memory' as presented and defined by Augustine in his *Confessions*. The plot emerges from this 'mythical cave,' whose tradition stretches back from Jung to Plato, that is, from the collective memory of both the main actors and from their analysis and exposition of Wolfram's text" (Müller 179). Like Rohmer, Ulrich Müller argues, Blank is emphasizing themes that are universal and fundamental, regardless of historical change, including "ecological and environmental issues," the connectedness of the human family, love, and especially the importance of women's suffering in the past and the belief that equality of women represents hope for the future (179). Despite the upbeat tone of the ending, notes provided by WDR, the television network that first broadcast the film, make clear Blank's view that Wolfram's hopes are a work in progress: "'Struggle and controversy still rule; women are still the main sufferers; human society has still not been realized'" (Müller 179).

Possibly influenced by a Freudian reading of the importance of Herzeloyde to Parzival's psyche, Blank puts the role of love and women in the forefront of his story. He feels that Wolfram is critiquing masculine competition whether in economics or in knightly combat. In an interview with Anke Wagemann, Blank said he believes Wolfram's Gawan does not learn how to love until he is taught by the innocent young Obilot, "the most important female character"; he even says that he sees Gawan as "part man and part woman" (Sunnen 4–5). In the film, Parzival concludes men should "trust women more than God," a sentiment probably more extreme than Wolfram would approve. The phrase, in fact, is a loose, but powerful, translation of Wolfram's lines "Friend, when thy time has come for strife / Then may some lady pledge her life," which Parzival speaks after being insulted by Kundrie. It expresses Blank's interpretation that Wolfram believed "the 'old soldier' mentality of the knights of the Round Table cannot continue in this feminine world" (Sunnen 5, quoting Wagemann).

Though presenting these themes as universal, Blank's treatment of the story is deeply rooted in contemporary Germany. There can be no question that the film can be seen as a commentary on Germany in the early 1980s. Just as Gurnemanz gives Parzival advice about how to survive the medieval world of chivalry, the modern clerk, played by the same actor, gives the street performer Kunkel advice about overcoming poverty. He reminisces about what it was like as a boy to stand in the wreckage of Germany after World War II, and we know that the actor is old enough to have experienced what his character describes. The voiceover narrative links the beginnings of German cities to Wolfram's era. In an interview in 2012, Blank said that what interested him about the period was how the Crusades led to foreign influences in Europe, the rise of capitalism, and the shift from an agrarian to an urban culture (Sunnen 4). As such, the rise of a modern Germany out of the Middle Ages is reiterated in the resurrection of post-war Germany referenced throughout the film, just as the juxtaposition of the modern city with the wreckage of the attic/prop room is clearly meant to evoke the destruction in post-war Germany and its rebuilding.

Three years later, Hans-Jürgen Syberberg's film of Wagner's *Parsifal* seems to follow in Blank's footsteps. "Syberberg's film begins aurally with the stops and starts of a rehearsal, the sounds of an orchestra and singers tuning up. What is shown, however, is a landscape littered with photographs of ruin, suggesting, primarily, the destruction of a post–World War II landscape dotted with the fragments of Western civilization" (Hoffman 48).

Some thirty-five years after the war but with the Berlin Wall still firmly in place, the memories of destruction and disruption were still fresh in German minds. How appropriate to examine the wreckage of a divided Germany by depicting a lost soul, literally divided between character and the actor who portrays him, trying to come to terms with his own predicament.

Lars von Trier's Breaking the Waves

Perhaps the most radically avant-garde transformation of Perceval on film features another divided central character, but it looks least avant-garde in style and is the most difficult to recognize as a Perceval story at all. Lars von Trier's *Breaking the Waves*, despite its provocative story line, looks like conventional, even gritty, realism, especially compared to Rohmer's and Blank's films. Nor, with its modern Scottish setting and female heroine, would anyone realize at first that it is a Grail story, even someone familiar with the tradition. Only at the end of the film does von Trier drop the pretense of *verismo*, and does the Arthurian nature of the characters and themes become apparent.

Other films have coded the Perceval story in a modern setting. *The Water Boy*, which did it for comedy, is treated elsewhere in this volume. *Forrest Gump* is virtually a bullet-pointed list of conventions from the Perceval tradition.[6] Zemeckis uses conventional tropes in creative but ultimately comfortable ways. Not so von Trier.

The plot of *Breaking the Waves* ("an act of nature that is also a kind of endlessly repeating climax" [Nelson 228]) raised controversy from the start for its lurid premise. In broad outline, Bess, a young, mentally challenged Scot from a fundamentalist Christian sect in a coastal community, marries Jan, a worldly Scandinavian from a North Sea oil rig. She blooms in the relationship but becomes completely dependent on him. When he goes back to the rig, she prays to God to bring him home quickly. Jan comes home soon but paralyzed from a freak accident, and Bess blames herself and her selfish prayer. After falling into despair, Jan asks Bess to take a lover and describe her trysts to him, so he can still experience sex with her vicariously. At first she balks but eventually carries out his wishes. Remarkably, he improves physically, so Bess goes to greater extremes for sexual liaisons in hopes of curing him fully.

As she pursues her plan, she goes into a downward spiral in the community and is scorned as a slut, a sacrifice she is willing to make. At one point, trying to push a broken down motorcycle up a hill, she is sneered at and pelted with stones by a group of young boys, and the audience starts to become aware of echoes of the Via Dolorosa in her experience ("'Breaking the Waves'"; Nelson 237). Eventually, she goes aboard a ship in the harbor, where she is brutalized and dies from her injuries. Now it is Jan's turn to feel overcome with grief and guilt that he expresses at her funeral, in which, Ophelia-like, she is buried with an abbreviated ceremony because of the circumstances of her death. Yet he has improved physically so much that he only wears a neck brace and can walk again with a cane. He goes back out on the oil rig, where the miraculous nature of his cure is confirmed. Though nothing physical is showing up on the sonar, the rig is surrounded by the sound of ringing bells from the sky. Jan and the other workers look up to see gigantic, Notre Dame–like bells ringing in the clouds. The final shot looks down from the bells through the clouds at the oil rig below.

Critics were divided over whether the film was flawed and, if so, what those flaws were. Some condemned it for the perversity of its sexual premise. Some philosophers and sociologists took it so seriously that they held a panel on the film's examination of sin, love, faith, and evil ("'Breaking the Waves'"). Much of the "grassroots" reaction was carping that the latter third of the film was simply ludicrous (Nelson 228). Cinéastes were divided. Some criticized von Trier for violating the aesthetic principles of his own group, Dogma95, which was committed to avoiding illusionist techniques (Nelson 228; Nochimson 48). Jan Simons argued that the film is consistent with the Dogma95 manifesto despite the miraculous ending ("Von Trier's Cinematic Games" passim), while Victoria Nelson argued that von Trier's work should be seen not so much in light of the Dogma95 manifesto as through the lens of a neo–Expressionism ("The New Expressionism: Why the Bells Ring in *Breaking the Waves*" passim).

Nelson calls the miracle at the end "a poison pill" to modernist sensibilities (230), but insists that it is part of the Expressionist method to take things like "the pastel sentimentalism of a turn-of-the-century postcard or Italian roadside shrines, an unholy alliance of 1940s Hollywood movie kitsch with organized religion" (230) and to retool the clichés in the higher purpose of allegory (233). The only problem with Nelson's case is that she doesn't carry it back far enough. Once the miracle occurs, it becomes evident in retrospect, but only in retrospect, that von Trier, deliberately or not, has reached back to a much older set of conventions, not only the all too familiar tradition of the Christ figure but the related, less well known tropes of the Perceval story, with Jan as Fisher King and Bess as a female Perceval. Von Trier says he can't remember how he first came up with the story, based on a dimly remembered, unidentified book from his childhood, but he was looking for an innocent main character and found "several references within myself, and others from external influences, possibly from experience of other art forms" (Björkman 78). It is perfectly possible that Perceval, the prototype for the naïf, was waiting in his subconscious to be chosen. Walking back through the film with the miraculous healing in mind puts the correspondences in high relief.

The film begins *in medias res.* It opens with a close-up of Bess's face, looking at once sheepish and impish. She has already met Jan, a Scandinavian who works on "the rig," a North Sea oil rig, and is facing a tribunal of stern male Scottish elders, asking for permission to marry. They question whether she is fit to marry. The question and her childlike demeanor and the tone of her response ("I know I am") are the first suggestions that Bess is mildly retarded but willful. They also refer to Jan as "an outsider," the first indication that Bess belongs to a reclusive religious community. The next scene reinforces the impression that Bess is a woman-child. She is in a wedding dress outside waiting for a helicopter to bring Jan in for the wedding, and she is angry, because he is late. When he does land, she hits him playfully, but the petulance is real. Like Perceval, Bess is a naïf, though she is more than just a case of arrested development. Also, like Perceval, but for very different reasons, Bess is isolated from the outside world, first by virtue of being on the northernmost coast of Scotland, and second as part of a cultish religious sect. Their suspicion of the modern world corresponds to Perceval's mother's fear of the culture of chivalry. It is probably coincidence that Perceval first encounters knights by the sound of their rattling armor and, when the elders

Stellen Skarsgård as Jan and Emily Watson as Bess in Lars von Trier's film *Breaking the Waves* (1996).

ask Bess what good outsiders have ever brought them, she answers, "Their music." In a case where parallels seem so obvious in hindsight, one has to fight the impulse to find them everywhere.

On the wedding night, it is clear that Bess is a virgin. Jan asks her how she was able to stave off all the boys, and she says, "I was waiting for you." When he laughs, she chides him for not taking her seriously. The next day, Bess kneels in the bare chapel and says a prayer of thanks to God for love and for Jan, but then, Gollum-like, she speaks to herself in God's voice, a scolding tone telling her to "be a good girl." She seems genuinely upset and says "I didn't mean it like that," illustrating her conflicts about sex. She promises like a child to "be really, really good," but what follows is a scene of explicit sex (possibly a cut back to the wedding night—von Trier shares Blank's and Malraux's notion of concurrent time and refuses to be pinned down by chronology). Bess thanks Jan mid-coitus, presumably for awakening her sexuality. However, later scenes repeat this pattern of Bess praying to God and then schizophrenically criticizing herself as if God is speaking through her. Again, like Chrétien's Perceval, Bess is at once an innocent and highly sexual. Bess, however, is not ignorant of religion, as Perceval is, but trapped and torn by it.

Bess's joy in sex is juxtaposed with scenes of more innocent marital joys. Jan and Bess go to a cinema and watch an old Lassie movie. Bess's reaction is entirely girlish, but Jan exhibits real affection as he watches her watch the film with wide-eyed wonderment. Culture clash soon undermines wedded bliss. At a funeral in Bess's parish, Jan is appalled to hear the deceased condemned to Hell by the preacher and a bit surprised that Bess accepts that judgment unquestioningly, but he takes her unthinking faith as another aspect of her childlike charm. Nevertheless, the conflict between a severe Christian fundamentalism and a personal kind of secular humanism foreshadows the moral questions to come, and the funeral foreshadows Bess's own burial in disgrace.

The next "chapter," "Life Alone," shows Bess's trouble adjusting to Jan's absence when he is back on the rig, laying the groundwork for her willingness to do anything for him when the accident occurs. Worse, when she prays to God to bring him home quickly, and he is brought off the rig because of an accident, she believes that it is the fault of her prayer, which makes her feel guilty but also is a sign to her that she has special powers with the deity. Like Perceval, Bess, at least in her own mind, makes mistakes with dire consequences and needs to find a way to make them right.

When she is told by doctors that Jan might be better off dead than completely paralyzed, she places life (and life with him) above everything. Subsequent scenes show Bess, Jan, and her best friend Dodo, a nurse, trying to adjust, but while Jan shows signs of good cheer, depression sets in. In a tortured scene, Jan, left alone by Bess, tries to grasp a bottle of sleeping pills pincer-like between his almost useless arms and raise it to his mouth to commit suicide—failing, of course. Afterwards, he tells the nurse that he feels as bad for Bess, saddled with a crippled husband, as for himself. When they married, "she blossomed," but now hopes of a normal marriage are dashed. The scene establishes the psychological plausibility that Jan can ask Bess to have sex with other men and tell him about it as much for her own sexual fulfillment as for his, and she will do it in order to give him the will to live, which she cherishes above all. When Jan tells Bess that only love can keep him alive, he means sexual love; when she agrees to his plan, she does so for a love that is sentimental and self-sacrificial.

We cannot dismiss the possibility that von Trier is challenging Christianity here with a modern secular view that sexual love and emotional love are ultimately the same. His and Bess's Grail, after all, is life, but Jan says one cannot have life without love, and neither can one have life without sex. However, it is equally possible that von Trier is presenting us with the same type of secular-spiritual split that Rohmer sees in Chrétien, only this time in terms of love instead of chivalry. Of course, this dichotomy is also a medieval trope, the conventional division between *amor* and *amicitia*, always with the possibility that *amor* will slip into *luxuria*. It may be significant that the first man Bess tries to seduce for Jan's sake is one of his doctors, a man of modern science at the opposite extreme from her family on the secular-sacred continuum, and yet he acts humanely and morally. In her eyes, though, he is making it harder for her to keep Jan alive emotionally, even as he is helping to keep Jan physically so. She begins lying to Jan about sexual encounters, and Jan appears to improve, so she comes to believe that she can really save him by having actual sex. In another schizoid conversation with God, she compares herself to Mary Magdalene.

Eventually Bess has real sexual encounters. She decides to offer herself to the ugliest, most dangerous men she can find. This tactic will keep her from taking actual, sinful pleasure in adultery and is an extreme measure that she hopes will lead to an even greater improvement in Jan. Ironically, this chapter is called "Faith." We have already seen that her decision leads to a depiction of Bess as a suffering, slutty Christ figure. It is worth asking why a modern equivalent of Christ, with buffeting, scourging, and eventual sacrificial death, when feminine, must therefore be sexual. It was not always so. Contrast Perceval's sister in *The Vulgate Cycle* or Malory, a female Christ figure precisely because she is chaste. Of course, she sacrifices herself without enduring a Passion, like Bess, perhaps because she is as much a figure of Mary as of Jesus. In *Breaking the Waves*, the Passion of the Female Christ is connected to sexual passion in a gray area between love and lust, and we must ask, is this von Trier's sexism, or is it satire?

When Dodo, the nurse, another figure of reason and modern science, scolds her for shaming herself for nothing but a twisted, irrational illusion, Bess turns on her and sounds as stern as the elders. Dodo is also an outsider. "You're not from around here, are you?" asks Bess with a certain amount of scorn. Von Trier is turning fundamentalist Christianity on its head. What should an obedient wife do if her husband requires her to sin? What should a father do if his God requires him to sacrifice his son? It is worth noting that, when von Trier takes the doctrine of obedience to an unacceptable but logical conclusion, he is following the path of medieval heretics, like the Cathars, who were accused of taking the orthodox doctrine that we are purest at the moment of baptism and following it to its heretical but logical conclusion that babies should be killed when baptized to be assured of heaven. What Bess does is logically the same. Scotland, the Promised Land of Error?

Bess's conservative doctrine becomes twisted and entangled with Jan's psychosexual fantasy. God has told her to honor her husband, so she must do as he wants. God has also shown her that she has power to channel His will, so she has a moral obligation to save her husband as God's work, as Perceval has the moral obligation to heal his uncle. So once Bess's

Grail, the miraculous healing of Jan, has been achieved, what does the miracle of the bells signify? Is it an announcement that Bess, despite her shameful burial, is in fact saved? Is it a celestial celebration of the ascent into heaven of a Grail Queen/female Christ? Film experts looking for an allusion at the end generally point to the spiritual bells at the end of *Ordet*, by Carl Theodor Dreyer ("'Breaking the Waves'"), another Danish director, like von Trier, who also happens to have been brought up in a strict Lutheran family, perhaps like Bess, and whose 1955 film is about a character who is thought to be the Second Coming of Jesus. Or could von Trier's bells be a sly reference to the Christmas bell that rings when the angel Clarence gets his wings in *It's a Wonderful Life*? If we are left wondering to what degree von Trier is making fun of the serious religious, social, and sexual issues the film addresses, we should remember that scholars are still asking the same question about Chrétien de Troyes.

It would not be true to say that the character of Perceval appeals to avant-garde film-makers because he is a *tabula rasa* onto which every artist can sketch his or her own image. That would be a better description of King Arthur, who seems to be all things to all people. As different as Rohmer's French Perceval, Blank's German Parzival, and von Trier's Scottish Bess are from each other, they have enough in common that suggests a continuing, fundamental appeal of the original Grail knight. He is an innocent but seriously flawed, deeply human hero, divided and fluid in identity (including gender). He must quest not only into unknown territory but also in search of an unknown goal, unsure what questions to ask or whether to ask questions at all. He must improvise, backtrack when things go wrong, and start entirely new, unpredictable and unforeseen searches. He is flying blind. Perceval/Parzival might be a pattern for avant-garde artists themselves. One can only imagine where he will be riding next.

Notes

1. For the influence on Rohmer's "distancing" of medieval illuminations and Chrétien's own technique, see Grimbert, "Distancing," and Williams, "Eric Rohmer and the Holy Grail"; for the influence of Brecht, see Hoffman, "Re-Framing Perceval," and Runte, "Review of *Lire le Moyen Age?*"; for the influence of the New Wave, see Williams, "Eric Rohmer and the Holy Grail"; and for the influence of medieval drama, see Wise, "Review of *Perceval* by Eric Rohmer."

2. See Williams, "Eric Rohmer and the Holy Grail" and Wise, "Review of *Perceval* by Eric Rohmer."

3. See Grimbert, "Distancing Techniques" and Hoffman, "Re-Framing Perceval."

4. Sources that assert "otherness" include Grimbert, "Distancing Techniques"; Rider, et al., "The Arthurian Legend in French Cinema"; and Zumthor, "Critical Paradoxes."

5. See Fischer, "Roots"; Grimbert, "Distancing Techniques"; Insdorf, "France and the New York Film Festival"; Little, "Review of *Le Moyen-Age Au Cinéma*"; Rider, et al., "The Arthurian Legend in French Cinema"; Williams, "Eric Rohmer and the Holy Grail"; and Wise, "Review of *Perceval* by Eric Rohmer."

6. Forrest is a childlike innocent. His first name suggests Perceval's isolation in nature. He is brought up in isolation by his mother because she is a single woman (rather than a widow) and because of his mental and physical handicaps. As in earlier versions, the distinctions among the characters of the Grail knight, a wounded knight, a Maimed King, the Fisher King, and Christ himself are blurred. Forrest starts out as a "maimed" character himself, and he is cured in an encounter with a king, in his case, Elvis. Jenny is a modern, flawed substitute for Blanchefleur. Rather than the half-black half-brother, Feirefiz of Wolfram and Wagner, Forrest has a black brother in arms, named, appropriately for a brother, "Bubba," and their personal affinity is emphasized by the fact that both are mentally challenged. Lt. Dan, of course, is a reluctant Fisher

King/Maimed King, who is cured by the miracles of modern science rather than a miraculous Grail, but his real cure is mental and is effected by the idealism of Forrest. In the same, very modern way, Forrest's quest is a psychological one, not for a Grail but for personal identity, which is also true of Chrétien's Perceval, who does not know who he is.

Works Cited

Björkman, Stig. "Trier on von Trier." *New England Review (1990–)* 26.1 (2005): 69–92.

"Breaking the Waves." *International Dictionary of Films and Filmmakers.* 2001. Encyclopedia.com. 15 July 2013. http://www.encyclopedia.com.

Fischer, Lucy. "Roots: The Medieval Tale as Modernist Cinema." *Field of Vision* 9–10 (Winter-Spring 1980): 21–33.

Gorgievski, Sandra. "From Stage to Screen: The Dramatic Compulsion in French Cinema and Denis Llorca's *Les Chevaliers de la table ronde* (1990)." In *Cinema Arthuriana: Twenty Essays, rev. ed.* Ed. Kevin J. Harty: 163–176.

Grimbert, Joan Tasker. "Distancing Techniques in Chrétien de Troyes's *Li Contes del Graal* and Eric Rohmer's *Perceval le Gallois.*" *Arthuriana* [Screening Camelot: Further Studies of Arthurian Cinema] 10 (Winter 2000): 33–44.

_____. "Truffaut's *La Femme d'à Côté* (1981): Attenuating a Romantic Archetype—Tristan and Iseult?" In *King Arthur on Film: New Essays on Arthurian Cinema.* Ed. Kevin J. Harty. Jefferson, NC: McFarland, 1999.

Harty, Kevin J. "Lights! Camelot! Action!—King Arthur on Film." In *King Arthur on Film: New Essays on Arthurian Cinema.* Ed. Kevin J. Harty: 5–37.

Harty, Kevin J., ed. *Cinema Arthuriana: Twenty Essays.* 2002; rpt. Jefferson, NC: McFarland, 2010.

_____, ed. *King Arthur on Film: New Essays on Arthurian Cinema, rev. ed.* Jefferson, NC: McFarland, 1999.

Hoffman Donald L. "Re-Framing Perceval." *Arthuriana* [Screening Camelot: Further Studies of Arthurian Cinema] 10 (Winter 2000): 45–56.

Insdorf, Annette. "France and the New York Film Festival." *The French Review* 52 (May 1979): 955–956.

Lacy, Norris J. "Arthurian Film and the Tyranny of Tradition." *Arthurian Interpretations* 4 (Fall 1989): 75–85.

Little, Marie-Noëlle. "Review of *Le Moyen-Age Au Cinéma.*" *The French Review* 61 (March 1988): 646–647.

Mahler, Annemarie E. "The Representation of Visual Reality in *Perceval* and *Parzival.*" *PMLA* 89 (May 1974): 537–550.

Müller, Ulrich. "Blank, Syberberg, and the German Arthurian Tradition." In *Cinema Arthuriana: Twenty Essays, rev. ed.* Ed. Kevin J. Harty: 177–184.

Nelson, Victoria. "The New Expressionism: Why the Bells Ring in *Breaking the Waves.*" *Salmagundi* 116/117 (Fall/Winter 1997): 228–237.

Nickel, Helmut. "Arms and Armor in Arthurian Films." In *Cinema Arthuriana: Twenty Essays, rev. ed.* Ed. Kevin J. Harty: 235–251.

Nochimson, Martha. "Review of *The King Is Alive.*" *Film Quarterly* 55 (Winter 2001): 48–54.

Rider, Jeff, Richard Hull, and Christopher Smith. "The Arthurian Legend in French Cinema: *Lancelot du Lac* and *Perceval le Gallois,*" in *Cinema Arthuriana Twenty Essays.* Ed. Kevin J. Harty: 149–162.

Rohmer, Eric. "Notes sur la traduction et la mise en scène de *Perceval.*" *L'Avant Scène du Cinéma (Perceval le Gallois)* 221 (1 February 1979): 6–7.

"Rohmer's Perceval." Interview with Gilbert Adair. *Sight and Sound* 47 (1978): 231.

Runte, Hans R. "Review of *Lire le Moyen Age?* by Alain Corbellari; Christopher Lucken." *The French Review* 71 (May 1998): 1055–1057.

Simons, Jan. "Von Trier's Cinematic Games." *Journal of Film and Video* 60 (Spring 2008): 3–13.

Sunnen, Don. "An Interview with Richard Blank: Eloquence in Word and Image." Paper delivered at the International Congress on Medieval Studies, Kalamazoo, MI, May 2013.

Tesich-Savage, Nadja. "Rehearsing the Middle Ages." *Film Comment* 14 (September-October 1978): 50–56.

Williams, Linda. "Eric Rohmer and the Holy Grail," *Literature Film Quarterly* 11 (1983): 71–82; rpt. in
    The Grail: A Casebook. Ed. Dhira B. Mahoney. New York: Garland, 2000.
Wise, Naomi. "Review of *Perceval* by Eric Rohmer." *Film Quarterly* 33 (Winter 1979–1980): 48–53.
Zumthor, Paul. "Critical Paradoxes." *Modern Language Notes* [French Issue] 102 (September 1987): 799–
    810.

Hans-Jürgen Syberberg's *Parsifal*: Remystifying Kundry

Jon Sherman

Perceval and the Holy Grail have captivated audiences since the twelfth century, so it is not surprising that the oldest surviving film based on the legends of King Arthur focused on this aspect of the Arthurian tradition (Harty 6). More surprising perhaps is the fact that this adaptation—made in the era of silent films—was based on Richard Wagner's *Parsifal*. The success in New York of the premiere of the opera in 1903 was enough to captivate audiences and encourage filmmakers to explore the possibilities of capturing Wagner's final work on film (Harty 6; Mertens 254). Over the years, a number of subsequent cinematic adaptations of *Parsifal* have been made, including another silent film in 1912 and a sound version in 1953 (Mertens 254). In addition to the films of the opera—Hans-Jürgen Syberberg and others make a clear distinction between *Opernverfilmungen* [opera films] and "Fernsehdokumentierung und –übertragung aus den Opernhäusern [televised documentations and broadcasts from opera houses]" (Syberberg 30)[1]—there have been numerous recordings of *Parsifal*, many still available on DVD. The Holy Grail is as inspirational in the late twentieth and early twenty-first centuries as it was in the Middle Ages, and Wagner's operatic interpretation of the Grail knight Parsifal continues to intrigue audiences, as perhaps even P. Craig Russell's *Opera Adaptations*—a graphic novel retelling of opera narratives, which includes Wagner's *Parsifal*—implies.

One hundred years after *Parsifal*'s premiere in 1882, Hans-Jürgen Syberberg decided to make another film of Wagner's opera. The funding for the project and the filming of Syberberg's adaptation were plagued with difficulties, including withdrawn financial support, actor and singer scheduling conflicts and editing issues (Syberberg 40–56; Olsen 143). The end result, however, is a film that remains essentially faithful to Wagner's *Parsifal*, but that adds captivating and at times overwhelming images and sets to Wagner's opera. Syberberg's adaptation of *Parsifal*—although essentially unknown to non-enthusiasts—has received scholarly attention similar to perhaps better known Arthurian films such as John Boorman's *Excalibur* (1981) or even *Monty Python and the Holy Grail* (1975), and includes numerous articles and a book-length study of the film by Solveig Olsen.

Parsifal has also received unusually high praise from Arthurian scholars. Volker Mertens calls it "die künstlerisch bedeutenste Adaptation [the most important artistic adaptation]"

(Mertens 254), and Ulrich Müller claims—twice—that it is "[o]ne of the most interesting and exciting opera films ever made" (Müller 256; Müller and Wunderlich 320). John Christopher Kleis comments on the difficulties of staging and producing *Parsifal* and Syberberg's success therein, claiming that "[i]t is the great distinction of Hans-Jürgen Syberberg's *Parsifal* (1982) that he struggles to remain true to the interpretation of that opera that he has chosen inasmuch as Wagner's tangled intentions allow" (109). Kleis later adds more direct praise, stating that *Parsifal* "uses cinematic resources to fully engage the piece better than any opera film I have seen" (120). Olsen points out the great complexity of *Parsifal* stating that "[i]n view of the surrealistic setting and surprising details of the film, any viewer would need to see his *Parsifal* repeatedly, preferably in short segments, to gradually comprehend the film" (Olsen 295). Although *Parsifal* may only appeal to a very specific audience, its target viewership was impressed with Syberberg's creation.

Syberberg's intentions with the film are in part revealed in his book *Parsifal: Ein Filmessay*, written in a stream-of-consciousness style during the filming and editing of the movie. Although Syberberg claims that he never planned on interpreting Wagner, this result is unavoidably the case. The driving idea behind the film, however, was to create a *Gesamtkunstwerk*—one which Wagner would approve of—with all the possibilities film provides, which are at best difficult, if not impossible, to realize in stage performances (Syberberg 33–34). Syberberg even suggests that "Richard Wagner selbst war es, dessen Ansprüchen die Bühne nie gerecht werden konnte [It was Richard Wagner himself, for whom the stage simply could not suffice]" (Syberberg 21), implying Wagner's operas anticipated—or at least required—some of the possibilities that modern technology and cinema effects offer.

While Syberberg's *Parsifal* remains essentially faithful to Wagner's opera, the director made a number of changes to his adaptation that slightly alter the focus of the film. These alterations, however, are limited to staging and static and projected images, since "Syberberg preserves every word and note of the work [Wagner's *Parsifal*]" (Olsen 295). Although many of the changes are quite minor, three deviations take on additional significance and are particularly salient. The first major change Syberberg made was to complement the overture—usually performed with the curtain down, and hence without visual accompaniment—with images drawn from the opera itself, from contemporary history, and from art. The second was to cast a woman to play Parsifal for significant portions of the second and third acts. And the third was to change one element of the ending of *Parsifal*, or better, not to change anything, but to add a final scene to Wagner's opera. All of these changes shift the focus of *Parsifal* towards the figure of Kundry[2] and perhaps the role of women in general, and seem to reintroduce an element to Wagner's opera that was present in its medieval source, but that the composer had removed or downplayed in *Parsifal*.

Wagner first read Wolfram von Eschenbach's *Parzival* in the summer of 1845 and allowed his idea for an opera to germinate for almost forty years (Sadie 137; Beckett 1). After being introduced to his protagonist and to the Holy Grail, Wagner turned to Wolfram's sources and read Chrétien de Troyes' unfinished *Perceval* and its medieval French continuations (Beckett 1). Although Wagner believed that Wolfram lacked an understanding "für die Gattungsprinzipien des Epos [for the principles of the epic]" (Dahlhaus 216) and that "all the substance [of Wolfram's romance] was in his own interpretation of a legend naively presented by the poor confused medieval poet," (Beckett 3) he took an in-depth look at the medieval sources, before making his—quite significant—changes. Syberberg also was interested in exploring the medieval roots of Wagner's work (Bolduc 205–207; Olsen 132, 153–155), but his engagement is focused on Wagner far more than on Wolfram. In fact, "Wolfram's name is usually suppressed. He appears mainly in visual references and, in the book to the film, in paraphrases" (Olsen 155), although Chrétien de Troyes, at least, is mentioned by name (Syberberg 109). Syberberg was aware of the medieval sources and drew on them at times for imagery, but he was not creating something entirely new, as Wagner had done, but took the opera—essentially unchanged—and exceeded the limits inherent in stage performances and created a film "mit allen Möglichkeiten der Darstellungen und Musik und was Film vermag [with all the possibilities of representation and music and whatever film is capable of]" (Syberberg 19). Syberberg's *Parsifal* engages primarily with Wagner and is quite literally "eine Reise durch Wagners Kopf [a journey through Wagner's head]" (Mertens 255) as the setting is in part the composer's death mask. "Wagner's presence" is—not surprisingly—"palpable throughout the film" (Olsen 295). It is therefore interesting to note that, for at least one character in the film, Syberberg has returned some of the mystery found in Wolfram's text, which Wagner had removed.

Anyone familiar with both Wolfram's *Parzival* and Wagner's *Parsifal* will have noticed the multitude of changes that Wagner made to his source material. One of the most significant alterations that the composer made was to the figure of the sorceress Cundrîe. As Wagner was writing his final opera, one of the last difficulties plaguing him involved the Grail messenger and her role in *Parsifal*. The final pieces for his opera fell into place when he realized that the "fabelhaft wilde Gralsbotin [fabulous wild Grail messenger]" and the seductress were one and the same, and this identification allowed him to conflate Wolfram's Cundrîe and Orgeluse into one character (Dahlhaus 219). Kundry is, for Wagner, the figure who connects the main characters: Amfortas, Parsifal and Klingsor (Beckett 8). Cundrîe's part in Wolfram's *Parzival* is relatively small, even if her role in Parzival's path to understanding is not unimportant. Wagner, however, takes this essentially insignificant figure and moves her to the center of his drama, and Syberberg's film adds further depth to this complicated character and reintroduces some of the mystery and ambiguities found in the medieval text which are absent in Wagner.

Wolfram von Eschenbach's Cundrîe

One of the more interesting figures in Wolfram von Eschenbach's *Parzival*—a narrative filled with complex and often contradictory characters—is the sorceress Cundrîe. Although one must view her as a minor figure in a romance that is over 20,000 verses long, Cundrîe sets both Parzival and Gawan on their respective paths, making her the driving force behind the narrative's two main threads. Winder McConnell even refers to her as one of "the four most significant women in Parzival's life" (208), even if her presence in the narrative's action is minimal. She is also an oddly ambiguous figure, as she fulfills a number of surprising and boundary-crossing roles in Wolfram's romance. Cundrîe is an "intermediary between the grail castle, the Arthurian court and Schastel Marveile" (McConnell 215) and also a link to the heathen realms—although she seems to belong to none of them. Her role as Grail messenger is confusing as the Grail is an obvious Christian symbol, yet she is clearly a heathen. She is a sorceress—or at least that is what she is called—although she never uses magic in Wolfram's narrative. She is perhaps the most knowledgeable person in *Parzival*, but she is horribly misshapen and is, therefore, not received at King Arthur's court as her education and position in the Grail world would seem to demand. In short, Wolfram has given a minor character a major role not only in the hero's journey, but also in other narrative threads in *Parzival*, and then shrouded her in dichotomies that lend her an air of mystery.

Cundrîe is introduced into *Parzival*—as so many of Wolfram's characters are—in a protracted, yet obscuring, manner. First, the narrator informs the listeners that "hie kom von der ich sprechen wil [here comes someone I want to speak about]" (312, 2). The audience is further informed that Cundrîe is "ein magt gein triwen wol gelobt [a maiden well praised for loyalty]" (312, 3), but a shadow is then cast upon this compliment with the addition that "wan daz ir zuht was vertobt [except when her courtliness was filled with rage]" (312, 4). The description of Cundrîe as being praised for *triuwe* [loyalty]—one of the core values of medieval German courtly society—except when her courtliness turns to rage, is a disconcerting introduction for a woman who has not yet even been named. The paradoxes surrounding her continue as her mount and its trappings are described. She is riding a mule, a base and inappropriate animal for a courtly lady, but the mule's bridle was "geworht mit arbeite, / tiwer unde rîche [made with great effort, rare and expensive]" (312, 12–13). Finally, her learning is praised—which will be discussed below—and her misshapen body is described so that, from the outset, Cundrîe is a dichotomy.

Additionally, although Cundrîe is the Grail messenger and a source of insight and information for King Arthur's court, the narrator stresses that she is the bringer of sorrow, pain, and ill tidings. Before she has even been named, the narrator states that "Artûs her si brâhte pîn [she brought misery to King Arthur's court]" (312, 18), a sentiment repeated later in the comment "vil hôher freude si nider sluoc [great joy she struck down]" (312, 30). The narrator seems to view Cundrîe in a light which attracted Wagner to this figure, even if the medieval narrative provides little motivation for his suspicion or condemnation—motivation which Wagner, of course, will provide. Further statements like "si zuct in schimpfes dâ genuoc [she caused them problems enough]" (313, 16) and "mir tuont ir mære niht ze wol [her news did not please me]" (314, 22) may have been the seeds that attracted the nineteenth-century composer to this ambiguous character, but also that encouraged him to add to her story, in order to explain the narrator's unease.

Even the geographic referents associated with Cundrîe in Wolfram's *Parzival* seem intended to portray her as a bridge between the worlds of the narrative and also a dichotomy. She is from the Far East, sent by Queen Secondille from India to King Arthur's court. She traverses all the geographic and narrative threads of the romance, teaching Queen Arnîve, bringing food to Sigune, informing King Arthur's court of Parzival's brother, visiting the Grail castle and Arthur's court, and even riding off towards the adventure at Schastel Marveile after chastising Parzival. When she enters King Arthur's court—her first appearance in the narrative—she is also wearing "the latest fashion from London" (McConnell 210), so that she is associated with the extremes of the known world from Britain to India, an impressive geographic spectrum in a medieval narrative.

Cundrîe is also unusually well-educated—especially for a female figure in medieval literature—and her knowledge is repeatedly stressed. The narrator praises her education, which would have been the apex of learning at the time, and finally names her:

> alle sprâche si wol sprach,
> latîn, heidensch, franzoys,
> si was der witze kurtoys,
> dîaletike und jêometrî:
> ir waren auch di liste bî
> von astronomîe.
> si hiez Cundrîe:
> surziere was ir zuoname [312, 20–27].

[She spoke all languages, Latin, Arabic, and French, and was gifted in the sciences, dialectic, and geometry. She was also knowledgeable in astronomy. Her name was Cundrîe and she was called "the sorceress."]

Later her knowledge of science and medicine is reinforced in a scene in which Cundrîe is not even present. Queen Arnîve explains to Gawan that she attained her healing knowledge as follows:

> Cundrîe la surziere
> ruochet mich sô dicke sehn:
> swaz von erznîe mac geschehn,
> des tout si mich gewaltec wol.
> sît Anfortas in jâmers dol
> kom, daz man im helfe warp,
> diu salbe im half, daz er niht starp [579, 24–30].

[Cundrîe the sorceress visits me often. She has taught me much about what can be accomplished through medicine. Ever since Anfortas began suffering, so that people attempted to cure him, this salve helped him, so that he didn't die.]

A final mention of her learning—especially in terms of language and astronomy—occurs in book fifteen, when the narrator states that "[s]iben sterne si dô nante/heidenisch [she named seven stars in Arabic]" (782, 1–2), and then proceeds to describe their attributes (782, 6–15). Albrecht Classen even views her as the embodiment of knowledge in *Parzival* and states that "knowledge is exemplified" in the figure of "the grail messenger Cundrie" (193). In a world where most people are illiterate and few women are provided the opportunity to study, Cundrîe embodies the pinnacle of medieval education.

In addition to her extensive learning, Cundrîe is almost preternaturally knowledgeable about the Grail, King Arthur's court and Parzival's family and exploits, perhaps explaining her epithet *la surziere*, the sorceress. Upon her arrival at King Arthur's court, she chastises Parzival for his unknightly behavior, indicating that she is aware of what transpired— although she was not present—at Munsalvæsche. She also comments on both Parzival's mother and father, demonstrating that her knowledge of his family reaches into the past, and later provides—indirectly—information about Parzival's brother. In addition to knowing more about Parzival's life than he does himself, it is also Cundrîe who brings King Arthur's court news of the adventure at Schastel Marveile, setting the Gawan story in motion. Not only is Cundrîe better educated than most men, she is also unusually well-informed about almost everything that transpires in the narrative.

Already an intriguing figure because of her unusual education and her mysterious knowledge of both Parzival and the Grail kingdom, a number of dualities and ambiguities make this complex figure one of the most interesting—if minor—characters in Wolfram's romance. Her dual nature as Grail messenger and heathen, as sorceress who does not use magic and as highly educated woman is further underscored by the duality surrounding her name, which she shares with Gawan's sister. Although there are a number of figures in Wolfram's narrative who share names, none but Cundrîe are significant characters.[3] After Cundrîe has chastised Parzival for his behavior, she introduces King Arthur and his court to the adventure at Schastel Marveile, a castle in which both the king's mother Arnîve and Gawan's sister, also named Cundrîe, are held prisoner—although Gawan's sister will not be named until later. When Gawan's sister finally appears in the narrative, the first mention of her name could be mistakenly taken to be that of the sorceress. As Clîas relates his mishap at Schastel Mar-veile, he reveals the names of the four queens who are being held captive there: "der heizet einiu Itonjê, / diu ander heizet Cundrîê, / diu dritte heizt Arnîve, / diu vierde Sangîve [the one is called Itonjê, the second Cundrîê, the third Arnîve, the fourth Sangîve]" (334, 19–22). It is not immediately clear that this Cundrîe is not the sorceress, but Gawan's sister, adding further uncertainty to both the character and the name.[4] Later, the second Cundrîe is revealed to be Gawan's sister, but her introduction into the narrative is ambiguous.

Perhaps more interesting is the fact that Cundrîe is a presence even when she is not actually present in the narrative. After she has departed from King Arthur's court, the narrator returns to the information she provided about the eponymous hero: "von Cundrîen man och innen wart / Parzivâls namn und sîner art [from Cundrîe we also learned Parzival's name and his ancestry]" (325, 17–18), forcing the audience to think of the sorceress even in her absence. During a discussion at King Arthur's court, a heathen woman provides information about Parzival's brother, telling Parzival that "Cundrîe nant uns einen man, / des ich iu wol ze bruoder gan [Cundrîe named a man who could well be your [Parzival's] brother]" (328, 3–4), and thereby reminding the listeners not only of the sorceress, but also of her extensive knowledge of Parzival's family. Later, when Parzival asks Sigune how she provides for herself, alone in the woods, she tells him that:

> dâ kumt mir vonme grâl
> mîn spîse dâ her al sunder twâl.
> Cundrîe la surziere
> mir dannen bringet schiere
> alle samztage naht
> mîn spîse (des hât si sich bedâcht),
> die ich ganze woche haben sol [438, 29–439, 5].

[My food is brought to me, without fail, from the Grail. Cundrîe the sorceress quickly brings me every Saturday night my food, she decided to do that herself, for the whole week.]

Here again the mention of Cundrîe reinforces her importance in the narrative and heightens the connection of this heathen woman to the Holy Grail. As mentioned above, her name is also invoked by Queen Arnîve when she praises Cundrîe's medical skills (579, 24–30). Even when Cundrîe is not a part of the narrative's action, the audience is constantly reminded of her, and she serves—much like the final image of Syberberg's film—as an eerie presence looming nebulously over Wolfram's narrative.

Richard Wagner's Kundry

Richard Wagner realized the potential found in the character of Cundrîe and was clearly captivated by Wolfram's sorceress. He obviously takes his inspiration from Wolfram, but, like the revised spelling of her name, "the character and history of Wagner's Kundry are largely new" (Müller 250). The Kundry found in *Parsifal* is arguably entirely Wagner's creation. This new character maintains a number of elements found in the medieval source, including some of her ambiguities and dualities, but these have been shifted away from their mysterious and contradictory nature, as Wagner has explained away—and in one case cleared up—some of the uncertainty surrounding her. Kundry's complexity, however, remains undiminished, and Dahlhaus even finds her to be the "komplizierteste und widerspruchvollste Gestalt in Wagners Dramen [most complicated and contradictory figure in Wagner's dramas]," so not just in *Parsifal*, but the most complicated figure in all of Wagner's work (219). By making Kundry the Grail messenger and the seductress responsible for Amfortas injury and the loss of the spear, Wagner does not add mystery, but a dual role which is the result of—and therefore explainable by—Klingsor's magic.

Similar to his medieval source, Wagner's Kundry emerges in the narrative with some degree of ambiguity. When she first appears, she is called "die wilde Reiterin [the wild rider]" (Wagner 19). Her appearance causes one squire to ask, "Flog sie durch die Luft? [Did she fly through the air?]" (Wagner 19) and another to comment, "Jetzt kriecht sie am Boden hin [Now she is creeping along on the ground]" (Wagner 21). A further similarity she maintains with Wolfram's Cundrîe is the vast geographic area she traverses serving the Grail and its king. When Gurnemanz asks, "Woher brachtest du dies? [From where did you get this?]," she replies, "Von weiter her, als du denken kannst [From farther away than you can conceive]," which turns out to be "Arabia" (Wagner 21). Like Wolfram's Cundrîe, Wagner's Kundry traverses—and therefore also connects—the worlds encompassed in his narrative, making her "the wandering, disturbing, tragic, erotic presence that haunts Wagner's Grail community" (Finke and Shichtman 487).

As Kundry takes on additional significance in Wagner's opera, she loses some of her otherworldly mystery. Undoubtedly, her role is clearly expanded from its medieval sources. She is introduced into Wagner's narrative even before his protagonist, Parsifal. She subsequently appears in proportionately more of the narrative and plays a more active role in the events—past and present—that shape the opera. In Wolfram, she sets Parzival's journey in motion, "[b]ut within the context of Wagner's plot, also Kundry contributes to Parsifal's development. She helps him acquire an identity by giving him a name and other information. She prods his memory activating self-scrutiny. Even when posing as danger she helps empower him" (Olsen 309). Her role in at least part of Parsifal's development is the same in Wagner as in Wolfram. In the opera, however, she is also responsible for Amfortas's wound and the loss of the spear, already a substantial addition to her function in the medieval romance. These events from the opera's narrative past are coupled with her temptation of Parsifal in the present, further expanding her role. Adding yet more complexity, "Wagner ties the concept of the evil seductress as the origin of sin in this grail story to that of the errant Jew, thereby coupling female sexuality with Judaism in the figure of Kundry" (Bolduc 204). Although the composer expands Kundry's importance in the narrative and makes her a far greater presence in his opera, he demonizes her contributions to the Grail kingdom by making her in part responsible for its downfall.

What Wagner removes from the medieval Cundrîe are her mystery and some of her ambiguity. By ending *Parsifal* with her baptism, the composer clears up one question confounding readers of Wolfram's *Parzival*. The Grail messenger, at least at the opera's conclusion, is no longer a heathen serving the Grail community, but a Christian. Additionally, one scene in Wolfram's romance seems unexplained and unmotivated, but makes perfect sense for Wagner's seductress. When Cundrîe meets Parzival the second time, she falls at his feet and begs his forgiveness: "si viel mit zuht, diu an ir was, / Parzivâle an sînen fuoz, / si warp al weinde umb sînen gruoz, / sô daz er zorn gein ir verlür [she fell with dignity, as was her nature, at Parzival's feet and begged, crying, for his greeting, to show that he forgave his anger towards her]" (779, 22–25). It is unclear, however, why she needs to be forgiven (Beckett 9). In Wagner's opera, Kundry is the reason Amfortas has been wounded and the spear lost, so her feelings of guilt and her need for forgiveness are clear. The element of the seductress makes Kundry's role in the opera more complex, but it explains away some of the ambiguity found in Wolfram's *Parzival*. It also explains the medieval narrator's comments about Cundrîe bringing King Arthur's court pain and suffering. There is nothing in Wolfram's romance which motivates these narrative asides, but, in Wagner, Kundry's role in the sorrows of the Grail kingdom is clear.

Hans-Jürgen Syberberg's Kundry

Like Wagner, Hans-Jürgen Syberberg was captivated by the figure of Kundry—and eventually by the actress Edith Clever who would portray her. Wagner transformed Wolfram's Cundrîe into a central figure in the Amfortas-Klingsor-Grail story, and Syberberg adds importance to Wagner's character, further highlights her role in the opera, and reintroduces some of the mystery Wagner removed from the medieval romance's Cundrîe. Where Wagner demystifies, Syberberg seems to take inspiration from the medieval poet, and relishes the mystery and ambiguity. Olsen comments that "[l]ike Wolfram, Syberberg only hints at less accessible dimensions in his work" (155), one link between the two that is not mediated by Wagner. Syberberg's interest in Kundry is not surprising, in that "[p]rogressive stage interpretations in recent years have attempted to rehabilitate Kundry and womankind generally, allowing them a more prominent role in the final act of redemption" (Sadie 146). But the director's focus moves beyond "rehabilitation," to the point that Kleis even claims that Syberberg "gives her (and the themes she embodies) undue prominence" (119) in the film. "Undue"

Edith Clever as Kundry in Hans-Jürgen Syberberg's 1982 film *Parsifal* (British Film Institute).

is perhaps unfair, but Syberberg's "focus on Kundry suggests a different reading" of Wagner's sorceress (Olsen 321), and indeed, Syberberg highlights Kundry's maternal aspects and her role as redeemer, balancing in many ways the negative side of Wagner's seductress.

The director accomplished this shift in the focus and depiction of Kundry in a number of ways, including choosing an exceptional actress with a distinguished career (Edith Clever) who "is a star artist in a class by herself" for the role of Kundry (Olsen 315). The disconnect created by having a separate voice (Yvonne Minton) and body (Edith Clever) for Kundry, also adds to the dichotomy and mystery of the character, and is one which Syberberg put considerable thought into:

> Kundry aber in Körper und Stimme zu teilen, muss zu tun gehabt haben mit meinem Versuch, diese von einem einzigen Menschen undarstellbare Komplexität so aufzuteilen, daß nicht wie bei der Figur des Parsifal Mann und Frau sich zur Idee des paradeisischen Menschen ergänzen, sondern die Erscheinung der Person in sich selbst zu trennen, und das nicht auf psychologische Weise. Was Richard Wagner zusammentat, die Zusammenstellung von Gut und Böse, von Verführung

und Erlöserin, von Verfluchter und Gralsdienerin, ergibt eine Verschmelzung jenes Risses in der Welt, den darzustellen von einer Person kaum möglich ist [Syberberg 54].

[Dividing Kundry into body and voice, must be related to my attempt, to divide the complexity, which one single person could not portray, and that differently from the way it was done with the figure of Parsifal-man and Parsifal-woman who complete themselves in the idea of the ideal human, but to separate the appearance of the person in him/herself, and not in a psychological way. What Wagner put together, the combination of good and evil, of temptation and salvation, of cursed-one and Grail servant, creates a combination of the rift in the world, which would be impossible for one actress to embody.]

And, of course, the opportunity provided by film of shooting close-ups, which force viewers to focus exactly where the director chooses, allowed Syberberg—with repeated close-ups of Kundry appearing throughout the film—to make the audience direct their gaze, frequently, at this captivating figure.

Among the significant changes that Syberberg made to Wagner's opera are the visuals accompanying the overture, the introduction of Kundry in the narrative and the final image of *Parsifal*, all of which will be discussed below. While these additions—and the inclusion of three actors to play Parsifal—appear most striking, Syberberg himself found his changes to the Grail ceremony to be the most pronounced, along with, of course, his change to the opera's final image of Kundry:

In diesem Film gibt es keine Gralszeremonie der oben beschriebenen Art, und das ist wohl die augenfälligste Abweichung vom üblichen Theaterritual, wenn man einmal davon absieht, daß Kundry diejenige ist, die überlebt [Syberberg 104].[5]

[In this film there is no Grail ceremony as described above, and that is the most obvious deviation from the usual theater ritual, if one ignores the fact that Kundry is the person who survives.]

Although the Grail ceremony is re-imagined in the film, it is the fact that Kundry is the final image of *Parsifal*, and perhaps that she is alive at all, which appears to be the greatest deviation Syberberg makes from Wagner's opera, as the libretto makes it clear that the sorceress dies.

Another striking addition Syberberg's *Parsifal* makes to Wagner's opera is the "extraordinarily complex opening sequence" of the film (Finke and Shichtman 485). Wagner's *Parsifal* begins, like most operas, with an overture that is "designed to signal the audience to take their seats" and "is conventionally performed with the theatre curtain down so there is nothing for the audience to look at while they listen to the music" (Finke and Shichtman 486). Syberberg's film, however, not only offers the audience something to look at, it provides an almost overwhelming visual collage of images that include photographs of a world in ruins, art, a book with an illustration of the Round Table, dramatic action (with actors) recreating scenes from the opera, and a reenactment of Kundry's betrayal of Amfortas with puppets. Although Volker Mertens was not referring specifically to the overture, but to the entire film, his comment that "Syberberg's Bilderwelt, und das ist der einzige Einwand, überwältigt nicht nur den Zuschauer, sondern auch die Musik [Syberberg's imagery, and that is the only complaint, overwhelms not only the audience, but also the music]" (258) is particularly applicable to *Parsifal*'s overture. This opening sequence adds a new dimension to Wagner's opera, especially for the figure of Kundry.

Among the numerous images and scenes, which Syberberg has accompany the overture is one in which Kundry assists Klingsor in stealing the spear and wounding Amfortas. The scene is striking in part because it has a young Parzival (actor) watching the puppet-theater scene of Kundry, Klingsor and Amfortas, so that the film audience ends up watching the watcher, giving them and the episode itself a disorienting sense of viewer and viewed. More importantly, however, the scene—reproduced with puppets—is only recognizable or understandable to an audience already familiar with the opera, so Syberberg is not removing suspense or drama from the story by showing what is to come. By making the episode where Kundry and Klingsor steal the spear one which is repeated—once during the overture with puppets and then as part of the narrative later in the opera—Syberberg highlights this event and reminds audiences very early in *Parsifal* of Kundry's role in the spear's theft, long before the opera narrative addresses it.

Additionally, the overture also adds an entirely new dimension to the opera's sorceress Kundry, by reintroducing some of the duality found in Wolfram von Eschenbach's Cundrîe to Wagner's figure. During the many scenes accompanying the musical introduction, Syberberg has cast Edith Clever, the actress who plays Kundry, in the role of Parsifal's mother Herzeleide. While Kundry has yet to appear in the opera and the audience cannot, therefore, yet know that the woman playing Parsifal's mother will also play the role of Kundry, this addition further expands the ideas that will later be associated with Kundry. One of these scenes has the young Parsifal receiving his bow from his mother—played by Clever—and another has Herzeleide sleeping with an open book (Bolduc 206).

The recognizable image of the Round Table, clearly visible in the book, is perhaps another reference to the medieval sources of Wagner's opera, connecting Wolfram's Cundrîe and Herzeloyde with Wagner's and Syberberg's through the actress Edith Clever. In Wagner's opera, Kundry is already savior and seductress, bringing much needed aid to the suffering Amfortas, but also the cause of that suffering. Using the same actress for the role of Herzeleide and Kundry makes a visual connection that also adds a parental element to this already complex character, so that "the two maternal manifestations, Herzeleide as queen in heaven and Kundry as queen in exile, share Clever's face" (Olsen 305). The overture's puppet theater and the scenes that depict Parsifal's mother serve to focus the audience's attention on the figure of Kundry, but also reintroduce some of the duality found in the character's medieval antecedent.

Kundry's first appearance in the film is, therefore, ambiguous. The character is introduced before the stage action of the opera officially begins, in the puppet theater during the overture. The actress who plays Kundry also first appears at this time, playing the role of Parsifal's mother, but the sorceress Kundry, also played by the actress Edith Clever, is not introduced until the first act—as Wagner's libretto dictates. In Wagner's opera, Kundry is introduced flying through the air and then crawling along the ground, and Syberberg's adaptation only adds to this. In yet another visually striking scene—and one in which the squires sing their comments about air and earth, as in Wagner—Kundry appears in the film emerging out of the water like a goddess or nature spirit. As mentioned above, Kundry's first appearance in Wagner is noteworthy, but Syberberg has returned some mystery to this figure who in the film appears out of air, earth, and water.

Subsequent scenes with Kundry are filled with close-ups of her face and shots which focus only on the sorceress, adding to her centrality in Syberberg's adaptation. Kleis notes that she "has her own playing space," even when engaged in conversation with other characters, and is usually removed or turned away from them, making her visually ostracized (111–112). She is alone in groups, and the camera is drawn repeatedly to her. Even when she is no longer part of the action or the dialogue, Kundry is still the focus. After Gurnemanz has explained how he knows Klingsor, for example, Parsifal arrives and kills the swan. In the film, Gurnemanz's story ends, swan singing begins, and the camera once again returns to Kundry, who is lying in a pile of leaves, at which point she jumps up and runs away. Much like Wolfram's sorceress, who is a presence even when she is not present, Syberberg's Kundry is the camera's focus, even when she is not engaged in conversation with other characters, nor the topic of their discussion.

Syberberg's film also deviates significantly from Wagner's libretto in the final scenes, which further highlights his remystification of Kundry. After Parsifal sings the final verses of Wagner's opera ("Höchsten Heiles Wunder! / Erlösung dem Erlöser! [Highest of Holy miracles! Redemption for the redeemer!"]), the stage directions indicate that "Kundry sinkt, mit dem Blicke zu ihm auf, langsam vor Parsifal entseelt zu Boden [Kundry sinks, looking up at him, slowly in front of Parsifal to the ground, dead]" (Wagner 157). The opera ends with Kundry's death, and Parsifal's final lines indicate at least that her transgressions have been forgiven. Syberberg ends his film in a very different manner, one that does not so much remove Kundry from the narrative as Wagner does, but ends with her presiding over it. The film's final scenes see Kundry, now wearing a crown, slowly lie down in a bed next to Amfortas, in complete contradiction to Wagner's stage directions. Olsen comments that "[t]he libretto instructs her [Kundry] to collapse and die during the Grail ceremony, leaving the others alive. The film restores her to dignity first before letting her expire at Amfortas' side" (286), a sentiment she later repeats: "[b]y endowing her with a crown and resting place next to the Grail king, Syberberg restores her to the dignity of her original position" (311). From this scene of Grail king and queen, the camera shifts to a crack in Wagner's death mask, which slowly opens to reveal the male and female Parsifals. The two embrace so that, like Amfortas and Kundry, the two sides of Parsifal are now visually reconciled. The male and female Parsifal are blended out and replaced by the film's penultimate image: a "Totenkopf aus der Wiener Kapuzinergruft [skull from the Imperial Crypt in Vienna]" (Syberberg 229). This scene then fades to the film's final image, which is of Kundry leaning over a glass orb, with her hands and hair encircling and framing the sphere. Inside is a model of the Bayreuth Opera house (Syberberg 229). The camera first slowly zooms out, allowing a complete view of Kundry and the glass orb, and then zooms back in on just Kundry's face. As the final notes of the opera sound, Kundry slowly closes her eyes and the film ends with Kundry presiding over Wagner's opera house.

The visual additions to the overture, the scene with Kundry emerging from the water, and the final image of the film further highlight the significance which Syberberg accords the sorceress. This focus is also apparent in Syberberg's book about the making of *Parsifal*. The first indication of the heightened importance of Kundry is visible on the book's cover, which shares the film's final image of Kundry leaning over a crystal ball. The use of this image as the book's cover art, coupled with the dedication "für Edith Clever," demonstrates the importance the actress and the character had acquired for the director. Throughout the work, Syberberg comments repeatedly on the role of Kundry and the skill of both the actress Edith Clever and the singer Yvonne Minton in capturing this character, as seen in a number of comments mentioned previously. Perhaps more revealing, however, of the importance Syberberg placed on Wolfram and Wagner's sorceress are the stills and photographs that accompany the book. There are eighty photos of the set, actors, singers, orchestra and director included in *Parsifal: Ein Filmessay*. Many of these are of two or more people, but thirty-five are just of Edith Clever—either in her role as Kundry or as Herzeleide. Some of these pictures occur together in groups creating a photo montage exploring the actress's facial expressions and body language. One of these photos is a two-page spread of fifty-six video stills just of Clever (Syberberg 36–37). Pages 148 through 155 are also stills of Kundry from act two, in different guises of guilt and anger after her attempted seduction of Parsifal. Pages 174 through 181 again are solely photos of Kundry expressing her despair. Pages 256 through 259 include another four photos just of the sorceress in the third act. In addition to the thirty-five images of Edith Clever, there are another two dozen of her with one other character: Kundry and the young female Parsifal, Kundry and the young male Parsifal, Kundry and Amfortas, Kundry and Gurnemanz, and another two-page spread of Kundry at Klingsor's feet (Syberberg 118–119).

For Syberberg, the role of the sorceress assumed even greater importance than that already accorded her by Wagner and the overwhelming number of pictures of her in *Parsifal: Ein Filmessay* offers another visual indicator—already apparent in the film itself—of her heightened significance for the director.

Syberberg makes three striking changes to Wagner's opera. The first is the inclusion of powerful visuals during the overture, which begins the process of returning mystery and duality to the figure of Kundry. The second is the use of three actors to play Parsifal: one young boy, one young man and one young woman. While such triple casting does little to affect the audience's perception of Kundry per se, it does slightly shift the focus of *Parsifal* towards questions of gender roles, and perhaps alleviates some of the misogyny often associated with Wagner's work. This addition at least parallels his interest in Kundry—the dominant female character in *Parsifal*. And the final significant change that Syberberg makes in his cinematic adaptation of Wagner's opera is to remove Kundry's death scene and to conclude his film with the sorceress looking into her crystal ball. This change, perhaps more dramatically than all the other major and minor divergences, causes Kundry to become the ultimate visual associated with the film. Kleis even comments that "[t]he film's final image [...] revives a slight suggestion [...] that the whole affair has somehow taken place in Kundry's mind" (119). Whether the audience is supposed to ponder that possibility or not, Kundry is left unquestionably as the dominating figure in Syberberg's film. That this image is also used on the film posters, on the DVD cover, and for Syberberg's book *Parsifal: Ein Filmessay* further demonstrates the significance the director placed on her. Kundry's role of seductress has been toned down in the film, her maternal side heightened, and the image of the mysterious "wild woman" rising from the water—an odd addition, since she arrived on horseback—makes Syberberg's sorceress a complex continuation of Wagner's, but one with revived elements found in the opera's medieval antecedents.

Notes

1. Unless otherwise noted, all translations are my own.

2. I have maintained Wagner's spelling for the characters found in the opera and in Syberberg's film (Kundry and Herzeleide), but used the most common medieval spelling for figures such as Cundrîe and Herzeloide when referring to Wolfram von Eschenbach's narrative. In direct quotations, I have, of course, kept whatever spelling (with or without diacritical marks) that the author adopted.

3. I discuss the duality of Cundrîe's name in the chapter on Wolfram von Eschenbach's *Parzival* in my dissertation. The other minor figures who share names never occur in close proximity, so there is never any confusion as to which of the two characters Wolfram is describing.

4. Wolfram himself is not consistent in his spelling of names. He frequently varies the spelling of the sorceress's name, so the discrepancy here is not an indicator that this character is indeed another figure.

5. Syberberg describes Wagner's Grail ceremony and his original intention to remain true to his source (105–106), before he decided to depart from Wagner's stage direction.

Works Cited

Beckett, Lucy. *Richard Wagner: Parsifal.* Cambridge: Cambridge University Press, 1981.

Bolduc, Michelle. "Mourning and Sexual Difference in Hans-Jürgen Syberberg's *Parsifal.*" In *Queer Movie Medievalisms.* Ed. Kathleen Coyne Kelly and Tison Pugh. Burlington, VT: Ashgate, 2009.

Campbell, Mary Baine. "Finding the Grail: Fascist Aesthetics and Mysterious Objects." In *King Arthur's Modern Return.* Ed. Debra Mancoff. New York: Garland, 1998.

Classen, Albrecht. "Reading, Writing and Learning in Wolfram von Eschenbach's *Parzival.*" In *A Companion to Wolfram's "Parzival."* Ed. Will Hasty. Columbia, SC: Camden House, 1999.

Dahlhaus, Carl. *Richard Wagners Musikdramen.* Stuttgart: Philipp Reclam jun., 1994.

Finke, Laurie A., and Martin Shichtman. "Remediating Arthur." In *A Companion to Arthurian Literature.* Ed. Helen Fulton. Singapore: Wiley-Blackwell, 2009.

Harty, Kevin J. "Lights! Camelot! Action!—King Arthur on Film." In *King Arthur on Film: New Essays on Arthurian Cinema.* Ed. Kevin J. Harty. Jefferson, NC: McFarland, 1999.

Kleis, John Christopher. "The Arthurian Dilemma: Faith and Works in Syberberg's *Parsifal.*" In *King Arthur on Film.* Ed. Kevin J. Harty. Jefferson, NC: McFarland, 1999.

McConnell, Winder. "Otherworlds, Alchemy and Pythagoras, and Jung: Symbols of Transformation in *Parzival.*" In *A Companion to Wolfram's "Parzival."* Ed. Will Hasty. Columbia, SC: Camden House, 1999.

Mertens, Volker. "Gralkino: Syberberg, Rohmer, Boorman, Gilliam." In *Der Gral.* Stuttgart: Philipp Reclam jun., 2003.

Müller, Ulrich. "Wolfram, Wagner and the Germans." In *A Companion to Wolfram's "Parzival."* Ed. Will Hasty. Columbia, SC: Camden House, 1999.

_____, and Werner Wunderlich. "The Modern Reception of the Arthurian Legend." In *The Arthur of the Germans.* Ed. W.H. Jackson and S.A. Ranawake. Cardiff: University of Wales Press, 2000.

Olsen, Solveig. *Hans-Jürgen Syberberg and his Film of Wagner's "Parsifal."* Lanham, MD: University Press of America, 2006.

Russell, P. Craig. *Opera Adaptations.* Vol. 2. New York: Nautier, Beall and Minoustchine, 1990.

Sadie, Stanley. *Wagner and His Operas.* New York: Macmillan, 2000.

Sherman, Jon. *The Magician in Medieval German Literature.* Dissertation. University of Illinois, Urbana-Champaign, 2008.

Syberberg, Hans-Jürgen. *Parsifal: Ein Filmessay.* München: Wilhelm Heyne Verlag, 1982.

Wagner, Richard. *Parsifal: Textbuch, Einführung und Kommentar.* Ed. Kurt Pahlen. Mainz: Schott Musik GmbH, 2008.

Wolfram von Eschenbach. *Parzival.* Ed. Gottfried Weber. Darmstadt: Wissenschaftliche Buchgesellschaft, 1963.

"Lovely Filth": Monty Python and the Matter of the Holy Grail

Christine M. Neufeld

The Quest for the Holy Grail according to medieval sources is, as most medievalists will attest, not a search for the correct answer, but rather for the right question. Success in this endeavor depends on the questing knight's proper attention to a signifying landscape. Only when the hero knows, observes Norris J. Lacy, "that a sign is a sign of *something* ... will he understand what the question will be" (2). Little wonder then that Monty Python's "holy grailing" in a landscape littered with signs illegible or gleefully misread has frequently been interpreted as a cheeky tarnishing of the transcendent shimmer of Quest narratives both medieval and modern.[1] A film which Python Graham Chapman impishly referred to during its production as a "great anticlimax," *Monty Python and the Holy Grail* not only refuses its audiences a Grail, but also wreaks havoc with the codes upon which audiences of Grail quests rely.[2]

According to Richard H. Osberg and Michael E. Crow, in contrast to the Grail films like *Excalibur, Indiana Jones and the Last Crusade* and *The Fisher King*, where "words still seem to have power—signifier and thing signified have a hieratic, sacerdotal relationship, symbolized by the Grail as an incarnation of Truth," in *Monty Python and the Holy Grail* "language collapses into incomprehensibility in an endless deferral of meaning" (40). John Cleese actually stakes a claim to this postmodern idiom for Monty Python in a *New Yorker* interview with Dave Eggers:

> CLEESE: "Each thing we do also mocks the form it's in. The books, the records, the films—that's part of what we do. We recognize the form that we're in. That's postmodernism, isn't it? And I think we were there before postmodernism. We precede ... was it Deru—What's his name, the French guy?"
>
> EGGERS: "Derrida?"
>
> CLEESE: "Right. We precede him. In fact, I think he stole his stuff from 'The Holy Grail.'"

If Cleese's comment reminds us of a "French guy" he once played who also claims to have that which cannot be possessed (and "it's very nice"), it is perhaps because that comment draws attention to a discursive shift from principle to intellectual property, from the conceptual to the material. Postmodernity becomes a "special property" (the Latin definition of *idiom*) and as such becomes "stuff" that can be "stolen." In a similar vein, in the first episode

81

of the film's "The Quest for the Holy Grail" section, the claim by Cleese's French Taunter that Guy de Loimbard "has already got one" shocks Arthur partly because it treats the Grail as an actual object rather than as a symbol of spiritual enlightenment.[3] Indeed, the term "one" suggests the Grail is even potentially a replicable commodity. Arthur's "sacred task" from God thus falters at the outset upon the material reality of an actual thing he must now retrieve (by way of Trojan Rabbit or Badger) rather than attain in more spiritually symbolic endeavors that certify his worthiness. The correct heroic question in response to the Grail's presence is never so banal as Arthur's plaintive, "Well ... can we come up and have a look?" Nevertheless, this essay proposes to emulate King Arthur's forensic impulse by having a look precisely at the material objects in Monty Python's narrative and to show how the film's use of these objects participates in, rather than undermines, a broader Grail tradition.

A film that begins with a mist-shrouded medieval landscape pierced by a Catherine wheel and ends with contemporary police shoving knights into a prisoner transport van certainly invites a reading that vaunts the triumph of modernity over the fetishism of the medieval past. This iconoclastic impulse is most evident in the film's treatment of the most significant material objects of the medieval heroic quest: the mount, the sword, the fortress. Seen from a medieval perspective, the skepticism or disinterest shown in response to King Arthur's claims to sovereignty is legitimate since he does not possess the requisite objects to validate his authority. In Scene One, even if Patsy wasn't banging coconuts together, a horseless King Arthur would come across as a bit of a "loony." For to take the *cheval* out of *chivalry* undoes the very identity of the knight, by definition a mounted warrior, whose mastery over his equine companion signals his own self possession.[4] The ensuing debate between Arthur and the soldiers owes its absurdity to the rapid shift from the social valences of chivalry to bickering about mundane matter bereft of social value. In fact, the soldiers quickly overlook Arthur's insistence on the illusion and become preoccupied instead with the material puzzle posed by his anachronistic prop.

> SOLDIER: You're using coconuts.
> ARTHUR: ... What?
> SOLDIER: You're using two empty halves of coconuts and banging them together.
> ARTHUR: (*scornfully*) So? We have ridden since the snows of winter covered this land, through the Kingdom of Mercia.
> SOLDIER: Where did you get the coconuts?
> [...]
> SOLDIER: What? A *swallow* carrying a *coconut*?
> ARTHUR: It could grip it by the husk.
> SOLDIER: It's not a question of where he grips it; it's a simple matter of weight-ratios ... a five-ounce bird could not hold a one pound coconut.
> ARTHUR: Well, it doesn't matter. Go and tell your master that Arthur from the Court of Camelot is here.
> SOLDIER: Look! To maintain velocity a swallow needs to beat its wings four hundred and ninety-three times every second. Right?

Thus Arthur's first essay as King of the Britons fails not merely because of the accoutrements he lacks, but because of the anachronism of the objects he possesses.

The important role of the correct material object in the Arthurian narrative becomes even more apparent in Arthur's encounter with Dennis, the Constitutional Peasant. Arthur's invocation of Excalibur as the emblem of his Divine Right illustrates a familiar treatment of the material object. The editorial introduction to a *Yale French Studies* special issue on Material Culture in the Middle Ages neatly summarizes the common approach: "substance becomes the locus, as well as sign, of meaning; from the material we glean the intangible" (2). Arthur's proclamation relies on this logic: "The Lady of the Lake, her arm clad in purest shimmering samite, held Excalibur aloft from the bosom of the waters to signify that by Divine Providence.... I, Arthur, was to carry Excalibur ... that is why I am your King." While various scholars comment on the contrasting linguistic registers representing competing medieval and modern political ideologies at work in this scene, we should also attend to how the material realm functions here.

Obviously, Arthur's Malorian reference to "purest shimmering samite" in the presence of peasants in rags slinging mud into a sack registers a similar political critique as the famous observation in the preceding Plague Village scene that a king is identifiable primarily in that "he doesn't have shit all over him." Dennis's verbal assault on King Arthur, consequently, works to bring the King in contact with base, or in this case, common, matter.

> DENNIS: Look, strange women lying on their backs in ponds handing over swords ... that's no basis for a system of government. Supreme executive power derives from a mandate from the masses, not from some farcical aquatic ceremony.
>
> ARTHUR: Be quiet!
>
> DENNIS: You can't expect to wield supreme executive power just because some watery tart threw a sword at you.
>
> ARTHUR: Shut up!
>
> DENNIS: I mean, if I went round saying I was an emperor because some moistened bint had lobbed a scimitar at me, people would put me away.

Dennis's rant demystifying Arthur's privilege proceeds by way of material analogy. The Lady of the Lake goes from being a lady to a "strange woman," then a "tart," and finally a "bint," with an increasing sexism rendering her objectification more explicit. The symbolic resonance of the Lake is domesticated, not to mention physically diminished, as Dennis transforms it from a "pond" to the pejorative, physical aspects, "watery" and "moistened," of the Lady herself.[5] Likewise, Dennis reduces the highly individuated sword, Excalibur, from its function as status-enhancing prestige object to one tool among many: "some sword." In the end, he denies even the sword's practical value, as his dismissal of it as "scimitar" may evoke for an audience sensitive to the pattern of diminution less the weaponry of a medieval Saracen and more the props wielded in the ceremonies (aquatic or otherwise) of modern day Shriners. Such a dismissal of Arthur's most defining object is made even more trenchant by the fact that when faced with this challenge to his sovereignty Arthur does not, in fact, wield the sword strapped to his side. Dennis experiences the "violence inherent in the system" at an overwrought Arthur's hands, while the King's sword remains decoratively sheathed. Subsequently, even when Arthur later uses his sword, Excalibur as a unique object has vanished from the narrative altogether.

If Excalibur is merely a prop, then it should come as no surprise that Camelot is, as

Arthur (Graham Chapman) confronts Dennis the Peasant (Michael Palin) and his Mother (Terry Jones), as his trusty steed Patsy (Terry Gilliam) looks on in the 1975 film *Monty Python and the Holy Grail*.

Patsy mutters, "only a model." The dismissal of Camelot as "a silly place" effects Monty Python's removal of the third object from the network of objects that traditionally collaborate in creating the identity of the medieval chivalric hero. From *Beowulf* to *Sir Gawain and the Green Knight*, the fortress symbolizes a medieval ruler's success, a product of his unhampered access to material goods, and emblematic of his ability to provide materially for the community. In fact, if we consider the few interior castle scenes the film does afford us—the "flashback" to Camelot, Swamp Castle, and Castle Anthrax—we will note they portray castles as spaces dedicated to creature comforts in the form of extravagant feasts, and, in one case, exciting underwear. Granted, the castle can also be read as a feminine space, both in medieval romance and in the adventures of the two knights who do enter castles in *Monty Python and the Holy Grail*. Lancelot's confusion at not finding a damsel in distress in Swamp Castle and the "peril" Galahad (almost) faces in Castle Anthrax portray castles as spaces filled with confined women or feminized men, like Herbert and the festively accessorized guards of Swamp Castle, in contrast to the masculine world of adventure. In fact, Lancelot, clearly the most puissant of Arthur's knights, must escape being domesticated himself through the Swamp Castle King's marital machinations. Nevertheless, while the knight errant has always been a peripatetic figure Monty Python renders this a more unfortunate chronic condition in that King Arthur seems incapable of gaining access to *any* castle he encounters.[6]

    If Camelot as the material monument of his accomplishments is "only a model," Arthur's attempts to access the "real" thing only expose his impotence. Rebuffed at the first castle by the guards' empirical perspicacity, at the second by various livestock projectiles, and at Castle Aargh by buckets of excrement, Monty Python's Arthur is continually thwarted until in the end, he, too, is covered in shit. The resistance he faces is profoundly material in that his interlocutors refuse to look through the objects he invokes to the chivalric values they signify. Consequently, Arthur's discourse falters much like the Swamp King's does when, in response his proclamation to his son, "One day all *this* will be yours," Herbert inquires innocently, "What? The curtains?" Robbed of the signifying objects that constitute his heroic identity, Arthur is instead repeatedly confronted with resistant matter, objects that resist interpellation into his heroic idiom, about as useful to him as the Constitutional Peasants' harvest of dirt.

By severing the hero from his mount, his sword, and his fortress—incidentally the very objects that facilitate the emergence of the feudal system that produces the knight as an historical phenomenon and fictional character—*Monty Python* challenges its audience's sentimental medievalism wherein these objects function as material vestiges of a simpler, nobler time. This iconoclastic impulse is apparent in the film's mockery of the "silliness" of cinematic representations of the Middle Ages akin to the "brief shining moment" of the musical *Camelot*. The film contests the pastoral Greenwood of Robin Hood films and the elegance of mid-century epic representations of Camelot by confronting its audience with an exaggerated material reality of the Middle Ages with all the subtlety of a wooden board to the forehead. *Monty Python*'s Arthur encounters a medieval world not seen in Arthurian romance of any period. And, as the warty faces of Dennis's wife, the Old Woman and many others suggest, this world is physically ugly, with the human barely distinguishable from the livestock incessantly underfoot. From the buckled figures scrabbling in the mud around a cart full of corpses in the Plague Village, to the filthy faces and ragged clothing of the peasants, to the concept of communal dirt farming, Monty Python uses dirt as their primarily tool to dismantle cinematic medievalist fantasies, a strategy highlighted in both commentaries the Pythons contributed to the Collector's Edition DVD.[7] After recounting Michael Palin's challenges playing the "mud-eater" role in the Plague Village, director Terry Jones summarizes: "I think our look for the Holy Grail, we were sort of going for the Middles Ages that was dirty and everyone had to have their teeth blackened and everybody was wallowing in mud. In actual fact, I don't think the Middle Ages was actually like that. ... but when we showed it everyone thought it was very authentic."[8] Michael Palin makes a similar point in his commentary on the Constitutional Peasants scene: "Once again there is this sort of idea well, what are medieval peasants doing? They are either eating mud, collecting mud or putting it in piles."[9]

Drawing on what scholars would now identify as the stereotype of the abject Middle Ages, Monty Python's attempt to create what Michael Palin calls a "fully realized historical world" constructs the Middle Ages as a space of physical deprivation, disease, ignoble inquisitorial violence, a place above all filled with vulnerable, very material, bodies.[10] Even accepting the inevitable self-reflexivity of the Pythons (most evident in their gestures to the theatrical, somber medievalism of Bergman's *The Seventh Seal*) and the more nuanced understanding Jones and Gilliam convey in their commentary, Monty Python's vision nevertheless invokes material reality as a form of authenticity that resists the Arthurian fantasy. This impulse is most obvious in the medieval object they deploy as a set piece: the Catherine or "breaking" wheel, a torture device in which a person is lashed spread-eagle to a wagon wheel, bludgeoned until all limbs are broken, and then mounted, still bound to the wheel, to die slowly from exposure and assaults of carrion-eating birds.[11] The Catherine wheel appears not only as the first object we see in the *Monty Python and the Holy Grail*, but also at the beginning of Arthur's encounter with the Constitutional Peasants. Recognizable to all as an instrument of torture and execution, for those familiar with Terry Gilliam's visual registers it also evokes a landscape reminiscent of Brueghel the Elder's *Triumph of Death* as a counterpoint to the Pre-Raphaelite opulence audiences might expect of an Arthurian film. Thus, much in the manner of the enormous cumbersome baggage strapped to backs of servant/horses like Patsy and Concorde, Monty Python's portrayal of the Middle Ages is one which saddles medieval bodies with the weight of material reality.

Monty Python's evacuation of the objects significant to the heroic subject and literal besmirching of the filmic medieval world, as well as its heroes, with base matter is all the more provocative in a narrative quest that has as its aim the ultimate medieval object: the Grail. In its most familiar form as the chalice of the Last Supper brought to England by Joseph of Arimathea, the Grail is the emblem of the Arthurian world's most utopian endeavors, and thus poses the greatest threat to an iconoclastic agenda. Can there be a Grail quest in a muddy world that refuses to signify?

The film acknowledges the highly symbolic function of the Grail in the first of its two most explicitly metafictional scenes, where the characters interact directly with animation. *Monty Python and the Holy Grail* highlights the traditional unrepresentability of the transcendent in the conventional heroic narrative when God appears to Arthur and his knights:

> GOD: [...] What are you doing now?
> ARTHUR: I'm averting my eyes, Lord.
> GOD: Well, don't. It's like those miserable Psalms. They're so depressing. Now knock it off.

Arthur's averted gaze reminds audiences of the Judeo-Christian tradition informing Western literature which frequently conceives of the divine as that which cannot or should not be encountered empirically: from Moses and the Burning Bush to Christ's *noli me tangere*. Attendant to this ideology is the prohibition among the religions of the book—though practiced variously and frequently contended—against the depiction of the divine for fear that adherents could not distinguish between the material image and the divine force it represents. Monty Python's God may demand Arthur knock off his tiresome obeisance, but the God Arthur encounters is markedly mediated. An animated, rather than acted, God dramatizes this mediation, implicitly acknowledging the seductive mimetic qualities of the film medium, even in a film about "The Book of the Film." Furthermore, this cartoon God is distinct from the rest of Gilliam's animation in the film. Whereas his other cartoons appear hand-drawn even as they reference manuscript illumination, Gilliam's God appears more like a paper doll. Gilliam informs us in the commentary that this cartoon is a manipulation of a cut up photo of W. G. Grace, one of England's most famous cricketers. The addition of the crown and Grace's distinctively Edwardian beard create an image reminiscent of turn of the century magazine illustration, with the layers of remediation generating the sense that God and the cartoon Grail he shows the knights are always already modified copies of someone else's images, inevitable approximations of that which they signify.

Galahad's adventure at Castle Anthrax further invites the audience to read the Grail as another of the film's simulacral medieval objects, like Excalibur or Camelot, copies of originals exposed as fictions themselves. Fighting his way through hostile elements, Galahad perceives a promising sign: a Grail appears to him hovering over a castle looming in the distance. Inside, however, he encounters a rather unlikely set of presumable Grail keepers, who threaten the very chastity that qualifies him in medieval narratives as worthy of the Grail:

GALAHAD: I have seen the Grail! I have seen it—here in this castle!

DINGO: No! Oh, no! Bad ... *bad* Zoot!

GALAHAD: What is it?

DINGO: Bad, wicked, naughty, Zoot.... She has been setting fire to our beacon, which—I just remembered—is Grail-shaped ... this is not the first time we have had this problem.

GALAHAD: It's not the *real* Grail?

DINGO: Oh ... wicked, *wicked*, Zoot ... she is a bad person and must pay the penalty.

Castle Anthrax's appropriation of the Grail for the purposes of its frisky inhabitants domesticates the most sacred of medieval objects. The Grail-shaped beacon is not merely an empty signifier; it once again renders a unique medieval object as a common tool. Furthermore, Dingo's "I just remembered" suggests the beacon's shape is only incidentally Grail-shaped— the form does not signify. Even less substantial than a model of Camelot, the Grail here is a projection, a sham apparition, and nothing more. In a sense then, Galahad's confrontation with the rather more earthly priorities of Castle Anthrax's inhabitants at the moment he thinks he has reached the end of his spiritual quest parallels the audience's encounters with pedestrian matter which does not gesture beyond itself to a transcendent sublime; it is a film after all in which knights dedicated to the Grail also seek shrubberies.

This suspicion that the Grail itself may be pedestrian or utilitarian matter may appear familiar to the postmodern Grail quest audience that believes itself beyond the fetishism of the past. In "On the Cult of the Factish Gods," Bruno Latour outlines how "modernity" seeks to distinguish itself from what it perceives as the fetishism of the cultural (or, in our case, historical) Other who crafts divinities or demons out of "mere" matter and then is naïve enough to be convinced these objects have power. In fact, Monty Python clearly depicts such thinking in The Witch Village scene when Terry Jones' Bedevere is confronted with the tautological logic of peasants who dress up a woman to look like a witch in order to corroborate their belief that she is in fact a witch. The woman, whose powers cannot be confirmed since the man she turned into a newt apparently "got better," receives no better treatment at the hands of the "wise" Sir Bedevere. The knight's eccentric inductive reasoning ultimately brings Eric Idle's peasant to the conclusion:

VILLAGER: If ... she ... weighs the same as a duck ... she's made of wood.

BEDEVERE: and therefore...

VILLAGER: A Witch!

If this syllogism were indeed how medievals approached matter, then the Grail becomes the quintessential fetish. In fact, Latour's reference to the historical etymological associations of the term suggests the felicity of this terminology for such objects in the Arthurian literary context:

Even though all etymological dictionaries agree on the origins of the term, Charles de Brosses, who invented the word fetishism ... linked its origins with fatum, or destiny, the source of the French noun, fée, "fairy," and of the adjective form in the noun-phrase objet-fée, "fairy-object" ... [3].

Dennis the Peasant's anarcho-syndicalist rant conveys that fairy-objects have no place in the modern world.[12] Moreover, the film portrays the thinking that produces such objects as a channel for the violent impulses of the witch-hunting peasants or the clerical wielders of the Holy Hand Grenade of Antioch. These scenes extend the film's logic that to grant agency to mere matter facilitates the "violence inherent in the system" that mystifies power relations through a shell-game of signifying objects.

Given the ubiquitous Protestant slant of modern Anglo-American culture, it is tempting to read medieval relics as fetishes, the fairy-objects of the Middle Ages. However, just as Latour challenges modernity's construction of the "native's" understanding of the fetish, recent work by scholars of both the early and late Middle Ages demonstrates that medieval attitudes toward material culture were more complex and nuanced.[13] In particular the role of the material world and its relationship to the transcendent was a topic of medieval debate. "Holy matter," remarks Caroline Walker Bynum, "was both radical threat and radical opportunity in the later Middle Ages," a fact that has implications for our understanding of Grail in particular (20).

A brief consideration of the medieval English Grail tradition reveals diverse medieval attitudes towards materiality. For instance, several scholars have noted how limited the Grail tradition is in medieval English literature, a curious condition given the role Glastonbury plays in versions of the Grail legend involving Joseph of Arimathea.[14] Mary Flowers Braswell observes that, in contrast to the circulation and proliferation of Grail legends from the twelfth century onward on the Continent, the Grail quest makes relatively few appearances in English literature and art before Malory (470–471). Late medieval works that do treat the Grail, the alliterative *Joseph of Arimathea*, Henry Lovelich's *The History of the Holy Grail*, and, of course, Malory's "Tale of the Sankgreal" in the *Morte Darthur*, closely follow their French sources, though with a few notable interventions. Scholars have remarked that, whereas French romances often feature the Grail as an apparition, Malory treats the Grail as an object.[15] Consider for instance what Phillip C. Boardman refers to as the "almost shockingly pedestrian" initial appearance of the Grail in the castle of Pelles, where it seems indistinguishable from other magical devices in Arthurian romance: "It is a handy magical vessel in the back room, trotted out whenever guests must be fed, a wounded knight needs to be healed, or someone troubled with madness must be cured" (127). The uniqueness of this English Grail as a particular kind of object becomes more evident through Robyn Malo's innovative reading of Malory as discursively constructing the Grail as an actual relic, thereby raising practical concerns about the accessibility of holy objects in a fifteenth-century society profoundly engaged by devotional objects of all sorts.[16]

One reason proposed by various scholars for why the English Grail tradition makes of the Grail an historical blood relic, with the container as contact relic often rhetorically conflated with the effluvial relic it bears, is due to popular cults related to blood relics in medieval England, such as the one dedicated to "The Blood of Hailes." Hailes Abbey in Gloucestershire claimed to be in possession of a cruet of Jesus's blood from the Crucifixion, supposedly collected and preserved by a holy Jew. Neither medieval treatise writers, nor modern scholars, miss the opportunity to point out the similarity of this story to Grail legends featuring Joseph of Arimathea.[17] Considering the Grail as a particular kind of object, the relic, and foregrounding the relic as a medieval object, rather than as a celestial sign, draws attention to the very practical, occasionally downright skeptical, concerns such objects precipitated in some of their medieval audiences. If veneration of the Holy Blood of Hailes, as Richard Barber has argued, influenced Malory's Grail vision, ambivalence towards the very same object may have actually contained earlier English impulses to engage artistically with the Grail.

Braswell, for instance, builds a convincing case for the "conspicuous" absence of the Grail material in fourteenth century England, and in Edward III's reign in particular. The paucity of artistic objects, narratives or visual art, featuring the Grail in this period is especially intriguing considering Edward's identification with King Arthur and his preoccupation with the material artifact, as evidenced by his commission of the building of the Round Table at Winchester and his founding of The Order of the Garter in 1348. One theory Braswell proposes to account partially for this "lacuna" in the English Arthurian tradition is the controversy surrounding the Blood of Hailes: "Hoping it would rival the relics of the Passion housed at Sainte Chapelle—the Holy Lance, the crown of thorns, the relic of the True Cross, among others—the monks at Hales [*sic*] found that the object was instead embroiled in a theological controversy" (477). The Holy Blood as relic posed a challenge to theological interpretations of Christ's Resurrection, for to believe in the integrity of the resurrected Christ's body placed into question the presence of his blood as an earthly remainder. This tenet forced those who believed in Holy Blood relics to account for the legitimate anachronicity of the blood. In the case of Hailes, this potentially problematic anachronicity was magnified in the accusation that monks were, much like Chaucer's Pardoner, passing off the stuff of the barnyard as miraculous matter: "The acrimonious debates over the Blood of Hales [*sic*] raged throughout the reign of Edward the III and beyond, the substance being referred to as 'an unctuous gum' like 'birdlime,' or 'the blood of a duck, renewed from time to time by its custodians'" (Braswell 478–479).

Aside from proving that, contrary Monty Python's portrait of Sir Bedevere, medieval inductive reasoning could indeed pass the duck test—if it looks like a duck, swims like a duck, and quacks like a duck, then it's probably not a witch—the medieval ambivalence towards the Grail that Braswell reads as potentially symptomatic of the debate about Holy Blood relics in England is instructive. This theological dilemma distills an issue posed by other relics, such as the contact relic that popular culture imagines Joseph of Arimathea's chalice to be. While there are various scholarly treatments of the concept of the relic, for our purposes I propose that we consider what it means that the relic is by definition anachronistic: an object out of place and, often, out of time.[18] In fact, the contact relic is all the more appealing because it once was a mundane object—a drinking cup, a winding cloth, a nail—indistinguishable from other utilitarian matter. The relic is created, to follow Patricia Cox Miller's reasoning, through an aesthetic transformation that embeds mundane matter in rhetoric and art. Aesthetically diverted, the mundane object becomes elevated, but its social value or force depends on the perceiver's ability to recognize its anachronism, its mediated nature.[19] The possible manipulation implicit in the mediation of relics preoccupied medieval theologians as well as religious dissidents. It is this understanding of the Grail as a medieval object informed by complex medieval attitudes towards materiality and mediation that invites us to consider the possibility that *Monty Python and the Holy Grail*, with its preoccupation with anachronistic objects, does not in fact abort the Grail Quest. Instead, the film offers a significant narrative contribution to a continuing English Grail tradition that has always wrestled with the matter of the Grail.[20]

Distinguishing the Grail from the other signifying objects of the heroic quest through medieval thinking about relics invites a reconsideration how mundane objects actually function in *Monty Python and the Holy Grail*. As Arthur and his knights discover, pedestrian or utilitarian matter is not necessarily as innocuous as it seems. One perception of the material world is of matter as inert, waiting, like the Trojan Rabbit, to be filled with human significance in order to affect the world. Another, however, recognizes that even the most inconsequential seeming object can have a force of its own which, as Arthur learns with the Rabbit at Caerbannog, one scorns at one's own risk. Bill Brown's work on the category the "Thing" provides a lens with which to appraise the eccentric matter encountered on Monty Python's Grail quest. Working with Heidegger's distinction between the Object (already socially interpolated through its preconceived utility) and the Thing (an excess of both matter and meaning—most easily grasped when an object is broken or out of place), Brown invites us to reexamine the force inherent in the Thing:

> As they circulate through our lives, we look *through* objects (to see what they disclose about history, society, nature, or culture—above all, what they disclose about us) but we only catch glimpses of things.... The story of objects asserting themselves as things, then, is a story of a changed relation to a human-subject and thus the story of how the thing really names less an object than a particular subject-object relation [4].

Seen from the perspective of Thing Theory the anachronistic objects—coconuts, swallows, ducks, curtains, shrubberies—do not dislocate the narrative but rather draw our attention to the vitality of material things as a theme in the larger Grail cycle beginning in the Middle Ages.

Monty Python and the Holy Grail is not the only Grail quest to be littered with unusual things. *La Queste del Saint Graal*, Lisa Cooper points out, presents a "veritable catalog of furniture": "A stream of chairs, tables, and beds flows through the narrative until some of the most notable furniture floats off—quite literally on a boat—to the city of Sarras" (26). In her reading of these "fictional furnishings," Cooper argues that, even as attaining the Grail is presented as a move beyond the material world itself, the Quest presents an "insistent materiality" in that questers must account for the "curious artifacts" in the fictional landscape before they can proceed (27). Not merely plot devices or spiritual signifiers, artifacts like the bed of Solomon direct our attention to their own histories, becoming central to the quest, demanding the reader's sustained engagement, and ultimately contributing to the *Queste*'s climax. Accepting Cooper's premise that the non-human in the narrative landscape of a Grail quest is not merely an interruption of the hero's trajectory can reconstitute the "interruptions" in Monty Python's Quest, like the recurring swallow meme. After the first scene's extended discussion of swallow flight paths, the swallows continue to hover in the audience's consciousness because they appear in what seem to be parenthetical asides to the action. Prior to adjudicating the witch trial, Sir Bedevere is tying a coconut to a dove and releasing it. Furthermore, Scene 24 finds the narrator temporarily distracted by various avian concerns:

NARRATOR: Meanwhile, King Arthur and Sir Bedevere, not more than a swallow's flight away, had discovered something.... Oh, that's an unladen swallow's flight, obviously.... I mean, they were more than two laden swallows' flights away ... four, really, if they had a coconut on a line between them.... I mean, if the birds were walking and dragging the....

ARMY: Get on with it!

NARRATOR: Anyway, on to Scene 24, which is a smashing scene with some lovely acting, in which Arthur discovers a vital clue and in which there aren't any swallows, though I think you can hear a starling ... (sound of strangling).

The narrative insignificance of swallows gets turned on its head, however, in the film's penultimate scene, the Bridge of Death. Faced with the Bridgekeeper's materially-focused questions ("What is your favorite colour?"; "What is the capital of Assyria?"), King Arthur's attention to the inconsequential matter earns him his only unqualified triumph in the film:

BRIDGEKEEPER: What is your name?

ARTHUR: It is Arthur, King of the Britons.

BRIDGEKEEPER: What is your quest?

ARTHUR: To seek the Holy Grail.

BRIDGEKEEPER: What is the air speed velocity of an unladen swallow?

ARTHUR: What do you mean? An African or a European swallow?

BRIDGEKEEPER: Er ... I don't know that ... aaaaargh!

BEDEVERE: How do you know so much about swallows?

ARTHUR: Well, you have to know these things when you're a king, you know.

Arthur's response to Bedevere effects a neat metafictional twist for an audience that must now reconsider what matter really "matters" in this quest. In this manner, *Monty Python and the Holy Grail* follows in the tradition Cooper identifies in the *Queste*, where material objects exert force not only as narratological devices or spiritual signifiers, but also as reminders of the material world, a materiality Cooper ultimately identifies with the *Queste* text itself.

A reorientation from the traditionally significant Object to the Thing that resists signification becomes especially important for an understanding of the film's climactic moments, beginning at the Cave of Caerbannog, as a commentary on the Grail quest. The scene begins, of course, with a relic: the Holy Hand Grenade of Antioch. Even as the Holy Hand Grenade comically illustrates the anachronism of the relic, its fictional provenance in Antioch—aside from being one the three locations associated with the Grail's frequent companion object, the Holy Lance—still functions symbolically for an audience that associates medieval relics originating in the Orient with Crusading violence. Moreover, Brother Maynard's reverential reading from the Book of Armaments demonstrates that this signifying object explicitly orders the world, functioning much in the manner of the objects Monty Python jettisoned from the heroic narrative. Notably, even here this order is disrupted by an eruption of insignificant matter into the text with the extensive list of food stuffs featured in St. Attila's feast: "and the people did feast upon the lambs and sloths and carp and anchovies and orang-utangs [*sic*] and breakfast cereals and fruit bats and—." In this case, however, the matter is contained, at least for the moment.

The Holy Hand Grenade of Antioch is not Monty Python's final treatment of the relic, however. The knights' encounter with the dying words inscribed into the cave wall by Joseph of Arimathea offers a different approach to the relic. Contact relic or not, the cave inscription recalls other Grail narratives that feature inscribed stone objects as conduits for divine revelation. Furthermore, Lisa Robeson argues in her reading of the *Queste* that such inscribed monuments can function like saints' relics when explicated by a religious figure:

> Relics are created because the Holy Spirit is present in the saint's body, even after the body is dead; these bodies enable miracles to occur. In the *Queste*, on stone monuments and other hard surfaces, the Holy Spirit codifies written texts whose messages ultimately open a door to a revelation not permitted to any other than the select Grail knights. The inscriptions are a means of transcendence first of the normal parameters of human understanding and second of time itself [437].

Arthur and his knights' encounter with the inscribed cave wall certainly evokes episodes Robeson cites from the *Queste*, such as when Lancelot learns how Joseph of Arimathea's descendants bring the cup of the Last Supper to Logres from a hermit who explains an inscription on a stone cross he has discovered (434). Of course, in contrast to Lancelot, when Monty Python's questing knights come face to face with the ultimate signifying landscape the message is clear as, well, mud:

ARTHUR: What does it say?

MAYNARD: It reads, "Here may be found the last words of Joseph of Arimathea. He who is valiant and pure of spirit may find the Holy Grail in the Castle of aaarrggggggh."

ARTHUR: What?

MAYNARD: "...the Castle of aarrgggggh."

BEDEVERE: What is that?

MAYNARD: He must have died while carving it.

LANCELOT: Oh, come on!

MAYNARD: Well, that's what it says.

ARTHUR: Look, if he was dying, he wouldn't bother to carve "aarggggh." He'd just say it!

MAYNARD: Well, that's what's carved in the rock!

GALAHAD: Perhaps he was dictating.

ARTHUR: Oh, shut up. Well, does it say anything else?

MAYNARD: No. Just, "aarrgggggh."

The knights' extended semiotic confusion at this sign—Is it nonsense? An exclamation? A proper noun?—has, of course, been read as the quintessential postmodern moment where language collapses into incomprehensibility and meaning is endlessly deferred. Approaching the cave inscription as the last in a network of resistant, inscrutable things, however, offers another interpretive possibility.

I contend that medieval discourse around anachronistic things allows us to perceive the knights' experience in the Cave of Caerbannog as an encounter with a miraculous thing.

Shannon Gayk's reading of another "inassimilable thing," the enigmatic grain in Chaucer's *Prioress's Tale*, proves helpful here: "The miraculous thing's resistance to interpretation ... registers epistemological limits rather than possibilities, and in so doing, mirrors back the subject's desire to force things into semiotic submission" (141). What distinguishes the cave inscription as a miraculous Thing in contrast to the other resistant things that precede it depends on our understanding of the events that follow. We can, for instance, read the knights' escape from the Legendary Black Beast of Aaaargh as a playful version of the miracles Robeson describes, with contemporary metanarrative playing the role of medieval metaphysics: "As the horrendous black beast lunged forward, escape for Arthur and his knights seemed hopeless, when suddenly ... the animator suffered a fatal heart attack.... The cartoon peril was no more ... the quest for the Holy Grail could continue." The second of the two scenes featuring animation intervening directly in the otherwise mimetic film medium, this multiply metafictional episode ruptures normal narrative parameters, introducing another layer of time through its self-reflexivity. Even more noteworthy, this metanarrative generates questions remarkably similar to those Gayk attributes to the wondrous Things of medieval religious genres:

> [They] draw attention to the shifting relationships between animate and inanimate things, between living and dead matter, between objects and subjects. Such attention helps us to consider the continuities and sites of rupture between human beings and the material things they interpret and use.... Chaucer's representation of these things lies less in what they might signify than in how their resistance to signification both unsettles and reconstitutes their human observers [139].

Perhaps it is too neat to suggest that Arthur's success in the adventure that follows at the Bridge of Eternal Peril represents a reconstitution of sorts for the hero. In any case, since the audience is actually the witness to the "miracle," its impact on us is more pertinent. Our own discomfiture in the face of the narrative's inassimilable things invites us to reconsider the nature of the Grail we expect to see as the quest nears its climax. For if Grail is a Thing, rather than the ultimate signifying Object, then it offers not the Truth, or the unification of signifier and signified, but wonder.

This concept of the Grail as a wondrous Thing seems especially apt given the shape-shifting quality of the Grail as object in medieval literature. Listing the Grail's various incarnations generates a rather Rabelaisian recital of matter: Chrétien's *gradale* or platter, Wolfram von Eschenbach's acheiropoietic *lapsit exillis* or inscribed stone, Robert de Boron's chalice, *Peredur's* salver bearing a severed head. Even a single artifact like Monty Python's film can set off the Grail's transmogrification, as viewers of the DVD Extras section entitled "Sacred Relics" soon discover.[21] When asked to give a brief synopsis of *Monty Python and the Holy Grail* for BBC Night Line, Graham Chapman claims: "It's about a search for the Holy Grail, you see, which is a large sort of creature, a bit like a dodo, with a big beak, and people are trying to find this [pause] grail."[22] Meanwhile, the English translation of the Japanese version of the film features Arthur inviting the French taunters to join his search for the "Holy Sake Cup." Notably, the Grail's resistant nature seems to affect the Japanese translator for, when Arthur initially announces his quest to the French guards, the subtitles state only: "We are looking for something sacred."[23] The Grail as some "thing" echoes through medieval and more modern Grail narratives, from Wolfram von Eschenbach's "*daz was ein dinc, daz hiez der Grâl* (that was a thing that was called the Grail)," to Tennyson's reference to it as "This Holy Thing."[24] Thus, taking the Grail tradition as a whole, the Grail as Thing in contrast to an Object like Excalibur can be understood as substance without form, its force lying in what Bill Brown identifies as the Thing's "specific unspecificity" (3): "Temporalized as the before and the after of the object, thingness amounts to a latency (the not yet formed or not yet formable) and to an excess (what remains physically or metaphysically irreducible to objects)" [5].

Read in the light of these aspects of latency and excess, the film's (anti-)climactic conclusion can be interpreted as honoring the thingness of the Grail in that it shares its medieval predecessors' hesitation to represent the Grail physically. In her survey of the shape to the Grail in medieval art, Martine Meuwese muses: "Was it the many forms and functions of the Grail that confused artists or made them reluctant to represent it" (27)? Monty Python's own refusal takes the form of a collision of quest paths in the final scene. Arthur, still in the romance hero's idiom in which the signifying landscape and various objects are hermeneutically ordered around the heroic subject, intersects with a familiar contemporary trope: the forensic quest of the police detectives following a trail of physical evidence. As the film progresses, we see the detectives standing with evidence bags among the Knights of Ni's shrubberies, as well as picking their way over the bones outside of the Cave of Caerbannog. These material objects become the nodes that bring the two timelines together, much like the relic is a node between two temporally and spatially distinct narratives: one in which the relic initially appears as mundane matter, the other where its diversion has made it wondrous. Monty Python's representation of the contemporary narrative's empirical approach still makes the human subject the ordering force in an otherwise inert material landscape. The empirical mode offers us no better alternative for understanding the matter of the Grail; in this idiom, it would simply be bagged as evidence. Thus, ultimately Monty Python seems to reject its own disenchantment of the medieval world by way of historical accuracy. The Historian's demise at the hands of the deadly material realities of the Middle Ages—pointedly highlighted by the murdering knight's use of the film's only actual horse—results in the end to the contemporary indictment of the knightly questers based on a trail of material objects without context and with no clear proof of their guilt. The collision stalls both quests. The medieval hermeneutic effort is interrupted through its containment by the modern one; the modern empirical one, through a potentially mistaken sense of its completion. This leaves only one final quest remaining: our own.

In the final moment of the film, when the policeman's hand blocks the camera, Monty Python places the audience very much into the scene. Reconstituted by our own encounters with the inassimilable things in film's narrative landscape, haunted by the one magical moment the film does allow when the remarkable self-propelling boat brings Arthur and Bedevere to Castle Aaargh, we may perceive in the film's own resistance to interpretation, its abrupt ending, not a refusal of signification but an invitation to reconsider the film itself as an artifact. The film's metafictional moments, especially Gilliam's animations that take such delight in medieval manuscripts illuminations, offer a vision of a world that acknowledges the vitality and significance of Things. Much like the anachronistic objects that seem to interrupt Arthur's quest, Gilliam's non sequitur animations, inassimilable to the quest narrative itself, are the sites of wonder that reconstitute the audience's desire, its sense of what "matters" about this Grail film. In fact, Gilliam's playful sketch of a scribe unable to work because the weather is being too noisy is a fitting exemplum of shifting subject-object relations that wondrous Things can generate. His inspiration, Gilliam claims, comes from how he perceives the medieval imagination:

> There is something about the whole medieval world where reality and fantasy were so blended. I don't know if the line was very clear where they separated. People did believe in devils and demons and ghouls and angels. And they were there. And so if you believe in them and they are around in the imagery around you then they were acting in the world, they affected things and that's a different mentality than what we seem to have today. It's always intrigued me and so in some sense it's in the film.... I think in a strange way the freedom with which we approached things in the film, jumping from ideas to different forms of reality is not an unmedieval way of thinking.[25]

Given the film's consistent mockery of the metaphysical certainties of the heroic landscape, I choose to read Gilliam's identification of the "medieval way of thinking" not as a tendency towards belief, but as a capacity for wonder. Consequently, by disabusing us of our projections onto the Grail as Object, Monty Python frees the Grail from the iconic system to which it has become beholden as a way of opening up its unforeseeable potential. A wondrous Thing itself, *Monty Python and the Holy Grail* leaves us with new questions rather than the answers we have come to expect so that the Quest may continue.

Notes

1. See, for instance, Brian Levy and Lesley Coote, "Subversion of Medievalism." See also George Reisch's essay in *Monty Python and Philosophy: Nudge Nudge, Think Think!* in the Popular Culture and Philosophy series.
2. All citations of Python commentaries and interviews, unless otherwise indicated, are my personal transcriptions of materials presented in the Special DVD Features of the *Monty Python and Holy Grail* Collector's Edition (2004). The BBC Film Night interview, "On location with the Pythons" (broadcast 19 December 1974), can be found under the category "Sacred Relics" on Disc Two.
3. All citations from *Monty Python and the Holy Grail* are my own transcription of movie dialogue. The Collector's Edition does include the original 1974 screenplay (Methuen 2003). However, not all dialogue and scenes in the final movie appear in the original screenplay.
4. See Jeffrey J. Cohen's discussion of the role of the horse in medieval knightly identity in the chapter "Chevalrie" in *Medieval Identity Machines*.
5. The diminishing logic becomes even more apparent if one is familiar with the song "Soggy Old Blondes" composed by Eric Idle. Elaborating on Dennis' original speech, the lyrics effect a more gradual diminishment: from "lake" to "pond" to "pool" to "shower." The only record of the song I can find is on YouTube: http://www.youtube.com/watch?v=-UhW6rO5TpQ (accessed 3 June 2013).
6. Brian Levy and Lesley Coote also note this in "Subversion of Medievalism."
7. Disc One of the Collector's Edition offers two commentaries on the film: one features directors Terry Jones and Terry Gilliam; the other features the remaining Python cast, Eric Idle, Michael Palin and John Cleese. All citations from these commentaries are from my transcription and will be identified as Commentary One (Directors) and Commentary Two (Pythons), by speaker and with scene select titles to help locate the comment.
8. Commentary One, Terry Jones, "Plague Village."
9. Commentary Two, Michael Palin, "Constitutional Peasants."
10. Commentary Two, Michael Palin, The Historian bit at the end of "The Trojan Rabbit."
11. This torture device is frequently referred to as the Catherine wheel because St. Catherine of Alexandria was said to have been condemned to such an execution.

12. Though the jargon-laden discourse deployed by Dennis neatly illustrates Bruno Latour's point in "The Cult of the Factish Gods" that modernity demands the destruction of the native fetish only to replace it with theories of social forces (what Dennis calls "the System") that still rob the individual of agency as an actor (10–11).

13. For instance, see work by Patricia Cox Miller (Early Church), Cynthia Hahn (Early and High Middle Ages), Caroline Walker Bynum (Late medieval Europe), and Robyn Malo (Late medieval England).

14. See essays by Mary Flowers Braswell and Phillip C. Boardman.

15. See Robyn Malo in *Relics and Writing* (101) and Dorsey Armstrong in *Gender in Malory* (150). I am especially grateful to Robyn Malo, who generously offered to share her monograph with me prior to its official publication.

16. According to Lisa Robeson, Jean Frappier and Pauline Matarasso have also contended that the Holy Grail operates as a saint's relic in the *Queste del Saint Graal* (431). However, as Lisa Cooper explains: "most readings of the *Queste* have remained rather insistently directed to the adjective 'saint' that became attached to the noun 'graal' in the thirteenth century" (27).

17. Malo lists medieval references (101). For modern discussions, see Braswell and Barber.

18. See Malo for an incisive overview of scholarly approaches to relics (13–14).

19. Andrew Cowell builds an argument similarly informed by Arjun Appadurai's "aesthetics of diversion" in "Swords, Clubs, and Relics" (16–17).

20. For another essay arguing for *Monty Python and the Holy Grail* as a continuation of the Grail tradition, see Wlad Godzich.

21. Disc Two. Monty Python offers its own amusing play on the concept of the "relic" with the list of items under the category "Sacred Relics": Coconuts; Japanese Version; BBC Film Night; Old Rubbish; Artefacts; Photos; Trailers; The Cast.

22. Disc Two, Sacred Relics: BBC Film Night interview.

23. Disc Two, Sacred Relics: English Subtitles in Japanese version.

24. Bk. 5, st. 235, line 20 in Wolfram von Eschenbach's *Parzival*. Line 124 in Tennyson's "Holy Grail" in *Idylls of the King*.

25. Commentary One, Terry Gilliam, "A Herring."

Works Cited

Appadurai, Arjun. "Introduction: Commodities and the Politics of Value." In *The Social Life of Things: Commodities in Cultural Perspective*. Ed. Arjun Appadurai. Cambridge, Eng.: Cambridge University Press, 1986.

Armstrong, Dorsey. *Gender and the Chivalric Community in Malory's* Morte d'Arthur. Gainesville: University of Florida Press, 2003.

Barber, Richard. *The Holy Grail: Imagination and Belief*. Cambridge: Harvard University Press, 2004.

Boardman, Phillip C. "Grail and Quest in the Medieval English World of Arthur." In *The Grail, the Quest and the World of Arthur*. Ed. Norris J. Lacy. Rochester: Boydell & Brewer, 2008.

Braswell, Mary Flowers. "The Search for the Holy Grail: Arthurian Lacunae in the England of Edward III." *Studies in Philology* 108.4 (Fall 2011): 469–487.

Brown, Bill. "Thing Theory." *Critical Inquiry* 28.1 (Autumn 2001): 1–22.

Burland, Margaret, David Laguardia and Andrea Tarnowski. "Editors' Preface: Meaning and Its Objects." *Yale French Studies* 110 (2006): 1–4.

Bynum, Caroline Walker. *Christian Materiality: An Essay on Religion in Late Medieval Europe*. New York: Zone Books, 2011.

Cohen, Jeffrey J. *Medieval Identity Machines*. Minneapolis: University of Minnesota Press, 2003.

Cooper, Lisa. "Bed, Boat, and Beyond: Fictional Furnishings in *La Queste del Saint Graal*." *Arthuriana* 15.3 (Fall 2005): 26–50.

Cowell, Andrew. "Swords, Clubs, and the Relic: Performance, Identity, and the Sacred." *Yale French Studies* 110 (2006): 7–18.

Eggers, Dave. "Sixteen Tons of Fun." *The New Yorker* 20 December 2004: 166. *Academic OneFile*. 16 March 2013.

Gayk, Shannon. "'To wonder upon this thing': Chaucer and the *Prioress's Tale*." *Exemplaria* 22.2 (Summer 2010): 138–156.

Godzich, Wlad. "The Holy Grail: The End of the Quest." *North Dakota Quarterly* 15.1 (Winter 1983): 74–81.

Lacy, Norris J. "Introduction: Arthur and/or the Grail." In *The Grail, the Quest and the World of Arthur.* Ed. Norris J. Lacy. Rochester: Boydell & Brewer, 2008.

Latour, Bruno. "On the Cult of the Factish Gods." *On the Modern Cult of the Factish Gods.* Durham: Duke University Press, 2010.

Levy, Brian, and Lesley Coote. "Subversion of Medievalism in *Lancelot du Lac* and *Monty Python and the Holy Grail.*" In *Postmodern Medievalisms.* Ed. Richard Utz and Jesse Swans. Rochester: Boydell & Brewer, 2005.

Malo, Robyn. *Relics and Writing in Late Medieval England.* Toronto: University of Toronto Press, 2013.

Meuwese, Martine. "The Shape of the Grail in Medieval Art." In *The Grail, the Quest and the World of Arthur.* Ed. Norris J. Lacy. Rochester: Boydell & Brewer, 2008.

Miller, Patricia Cox. "The Little Blue Flower Is Red." *Journal of Early Christian Studies* 8.2 (2000): 213–246.

Monty Python and the Holy Grail: Collector's Edition. Dir. Terry Jones and Terry Gilliam. Burbank: Columbia TriStar Home Entertainment, 2003.

Osberg, Richard H., and Michael E. Crow. "Language Then and Now in Arthurian Film." In *King Arthur on Film: New Essays on Arthurian Cinema.* Ed. Kevin J. Harty. Jefferson, NC: McFarland, 1999.

Robeson, Lisa. "Writing as Relic: The Use of Oral Discourse to Interpret Written Texts in the Old French *La Queste del Saint Graal.*" *Oral Tradition* 14.2 (1999): 430–446.

Tennyson, Alfred, Lord. *Idylls of the King.* Ed. J.M. Gray. New York: Penguin Classics, 1983.

Wolfram von Eschenbach. *Parzival.* Ed. Karl Lachmann. Berlin: De Gruyter, 2003.

John Boorman's *Excalibur* and the Irrigating Light of the Grail

Raeleen Chai-Elsholz with Jean-Marc Elsholz

> My life has been spent dancing with the mystery of light.
> *Excalibur* was an attempt to make the world more luminous.—*John Boorman*[1]

Entyrde a sonnebeame, more clerer by seven tymys than ever they saw day, and all they were alighted of the grace of the Holy Goste. Than began every knight to beholde other, and eyther saw other, by their semyng, fayrer than ever they were before.... Than entird into the halle the Holy Grayle covered with whyght samyte.... Seyde sir Gawayne, "But one thing begyled us, that we might nat se the Holy Grayle: hit was so preciously coverde" [Malory 521–522].

In these words, Thomas Malory translated from the Old French *Queste del Saint Graal* (c. 1225) the first appearance of the Grail at King Arthur's court. Intense light, like Malory's "sunbeam seven times brighter than daylight," had been a feature of medieval Grail narratives since as far back as Chrétien de Troyes's *Perceval ou la Quête du Graal* (c. 1183). While some romances placed the Grail in a luminous setting, others described the radiance proceeding from the Grail itself. Medieval texts were less consistent in their descriptions of the Grail artifact and of the possibility of gazing upon it; meanwhile, representations of the Grail in art likewise varied widely and were sometimes at variance with the texts they illustrated (Meuwese 13). Was the Grail a cup? A shallow bowl or deep dish? A stone as in Wolfram von Eschenbach's *Parzival* (c. 1200)?[2] A "preciously covered" unseen vessel as in Malory's *Morte Darthur* (1485)? A mutable gleaming chalice as in John Boorman's *Excalibur*?

Discussing the relationship of John Boorman's 1981 film classic, *Excalibur*, to its purported source, Malory's *Morte Darthur*, Norris J. Lacy enumerates some of the salient differences between this late medieval retelling and the late twentieth-century screenplay by Rospo Pallenberg and John Boorman. Lacy concludes that Boorman "follows Malory sporadically if at all" ("Mythopoeia" 123), for

> even the briefest comparison of the film and the medieval text reveals that Boorman modifies the story in substantial and significant ways, innovating in fact and detail alike, in an evident if not entirely successful attempt *to enhance the cinematic impact* of his presentation ["Mythopoeia" 122; italics added].

These remarks are revealing, but not solely because they confirm what any medievalist suspected: that Boorman's film is inscribed within a mythopoeic continuity instead of being a faithful cinematic copy of Malory. Rather more importantly for the present study, Lacy's findings demonstrate that Boorman's crafting of "cinematic impact" was of greater importance to the director than the plot's fidelity to Malory's text. The significance of the cinematic impact of *Excalibur* as it relates to Arthurian mythopoeia offers a way of thinking about the Grail episodes in Boorman's film. Lacy views them as one of Pallenberg and Boorman's most original and significant "innovations" ("Mythopoeia" 125–126).

In *Excalibur*, Boorman's montage of the Grail—transmuting from a chalice, to Arthur, to searing light—reveals the hidden properties of the physical object, the chalice that Perceval brings back to Camelot. Before Perceval's eyes, the Grail morphs from a cup to the form of Arthur, presented as a "Grail bride" in what appears to be a combination of nuptial veil and full armor. This scene is in keeping with Boorman's mostly de–Christianized approach where, for instance, the "priest" in druid-reminiscent trappings waives a sprig of mistletoe at the sword in the stone and officiates in vague rituals where the Crucifix-object appears more akin to a stylized sword.[3] In *Excalibur*, the human figure most closely linked to the Grail through Perceval's vision is King Arthur. By contrast, many medieval texts depict the Grail as a mystical vessel linked to the person of Christ, not Arthur, at least ever since Robert de Boron's *Roman de l'Estoire dou Graal* (c. 1200) [Lachet 28]. Boorman's Grail thus seems to sit uneasily in the company of medieval texts, like Malory's *Morte Darthur*, that depict the Grail object in (quasi–)Eucharistic settings. Nevertheless, it is less a question of the shape of the physical object or what it is made of—both of which vary greatly from one medieval text to the next. It has long been recognized that

> Grail myths are founded upon the existence of a magical object—sometimes a precious stone, sometimes a cup—whose increasingly complex symbolism caused its material original to be forgotten, to the extent that one of Chrétien de Troyes's continuators came to believe—and rightly so—that as a 'medium' of supraterrestrial visions, the Grail could be almost anything [Nelli 18].[4]

In underscoring the Grail's connection with visions, René Nelli identifies the object with visionary perception rather than with a material form. It is within this continuity that Boorman's *Excalibur* is inscribed.

The Grail is one of the distinctive constituent elements of Arthurian legend that Boorman attaches to his film to assert its place in the continuity of the tradition. Yet instead of passively illustrating any specific episode from one of the many medieval renderings of the Matter of Britain, the filmmaker exploits medieval currents of thought about the nature of vision and the physical world, and extends and renews them through the art of cinema. Boorman's choice of depicting the Grail in the form of a shining chalice offers a point of view emerging from his thinking about preexisting figures of the Grail. More especially, however, the depiction of the Grail in *Excalibur* offers an opportunity to explore ways of "figuring" or representing the ineffable, a question that looms large in works of art and literature from the Gothic era.

The art of cinema makes us believe we are watching a story, yet everything in a film is nothing more than projections of light. What film audiences actually are looking at is not an army of extras in warrior costumes, nor a car chase, flying bullets, people undressing, amber waves of grain, or anything like that. They are looking at a flat, matte, big white screen. They are watching light projected through a strip of film. Almost the same is true of television or DVD: audiences are looking at a light-bearing display and watching pixels. Whatever the media involved so far, in reality there is no movement, no flesh, no rivet-popping deep-sea pressure, no wind, no metal—no Grail.

All of the images conveyed by a movie depend less on sight than on the audience's capacity for vision and envisioning. This process entails more than letting data in through the eyes; it is the active, neuro-sensorial conjoining of visual data to create a "world" from flashes of light on the screen. The eye of the beholder creates settings and motion to make the picture and bring the players to life. Upstream of the spectator's creative participation is the filmmaker's ability to use lighting effects to create images and atmospheres in interaction with the light used to project them. The viewer's translation of physical perceptions into mental pictures in response to the film director's marshaling of light is fundamental not only to the art of cinema in general, but also, more particularly, to grasping Boorman's Grail imagery.

The concept of light as the basis of cinematic worlds would have struck a chord with medieval philosophers as well as with the medieval audiences of Arthurian romance. Grail legends took the shape of romance in the Middle Ages during the age of Gothic art and architecture, at a time when thinking about the nature of light and matter was in full efflorescence. Medieval philosophers were theorizing about the human capacity for vision and envisioning in terms of light, from their perspective of what matter or substance was.

The neoplatonic philosophy that underpinned their thinking was not transmitted in a single thread directly from Plotinus to the Renaissance; rather the influence could be fragmentary or subject to specific ways of reading and rhetorical models (Pranger 217–218). The vein of neoplatonism that stemmed from Pseudo-Dionysius the Areopagite infused twelfth- and thirteenth-century theologies of light, which assimilated light with substance. Analogous to the role light plays in the creation of cinematic worlds, light was the very essence of things and the source of all beauty to medieval philosophers; it was more than just a metaphor (Elsholz 206–207 and 210–212). Robert Grosseteste (1175–1253), for instance, states that "light is more exalted and of a nobler and more excellent essence than all corporeal things." He goes on to explain that all bodies proceed from light; differences in form are due to different levels of density or complexity (Grosseteste 10 and 15).

In *Excalibur*, the Grail that appears to Perceval is a gleaming chalice, then a gleaming Arthur, and lastly a penetrating gleam with no physical shape. On this level, Boorman's film shows us a Grail that conforms to medieval traditions. Special vocabulary denoting radiance like that of Boorman's shining Grail is employed in many Arthurian romances from Chrétien de Troyes down through the Middle Ages. Paul-Georges Sansonetti has collected descriptions of luminous brilliance in Arthurian romances to demonstrate that the term *vermeil* ("*rede and as bryght os ony fyre*," Malory 603) variously and simultaneously denotes the shimmer of fine cloth, the shine of gilt, the burnish of gold, the sparkle of metal, the luster of skin and hair, the radiance of the sun, and the blaze of fire (Sansonetti 26–28). Boorman translates the brightness, fire, luminosity, shine, color, and sparkle that inhabit medieval Arthurian romances onto the big screen in the abundance of bright metallic reflections, "vernal glows," and mysterious glimmers that punctuate the scenery of *Excalibur* (Elsholz 220; Kennedy). Thus material manifestations like water, lightning, the Grail castle, armor, and cloth all share the property of luminosity in the film *Excalibur*, as in the special terminology of Grail narratives.

Boorman achieves visually, in the aesthetic storyline of *Excalibur*, what medieval romance established lexically in *vermeil* as a basis of unity of physical matter. A kind of shared beauty results from the fluidity of identity between material things, since the fundamental substance of each thing—however imperfect and dim, or perfect and luminous—is light. Indeed, Boorman's use of cinematic effects translates medieval thinking about visual perception, specifically in relation to the possibility of portraying inexpressible mysteries. As will be developed further on, to perceive the Grail in *Excalibur* is to perceive the aesthetic unity of matter and light in Boorman's film, and to allow for the fluidity of the boundaries that demarcate material objects or bodies (sword, Grail, king, armor, flesh) and elements (fire/lightning, water, stone/earth, metal).

The strand of medieval philosophical thinking about matter and light that found its way into literary creations furthermore involved a certain fluidity between material and spiritual realms: there was no ironclad division between physical form and spiritual effect. The physical experience of beauty that is seen with the eyes translates into metaphysical meaning that is "seen" with the mind's eye. A selection of a few verses by Abbot Suger (c. 1081–1151) from the gilded bronze doors at the Basilica of Saint Denis famously expresses this idea:

> Bright is the noble work;
> but, being nobly bright, the work should
> brighten minds, so that they may travel through true lights,
> to the true light....
> The dull mind rises to truth through that which is material
> and, in seeing this light, is resurrected from its former submersion
> [Suger 47 and 49].[5]

Thus the brilliance of the various and sundry "lights" of the material world, for example here the gilded bronze doors of the Basilica, can illuminate the mind, which can then experience the wholeness of intelligible light. As John Scotus Eriugena (c. 815–877) observed based on Pseudo-Dionysius,

> Our spirit can rise to what is not material through the conduit of what is.... This is possible only because all visible things are "material lights" which reflect "intelligible lights." This rock or this piece of wood is a light for me.... As soon as I see such things and others like them in this stone, they become lights for me; that is to say, they illuminate me.[6]

In *Excalibur*, during Arthur's brief "training period" with Merlin in the forest, the two discuss the nature of the dragon. Boorman's *mise-en-scène* calls upon the eyes (of Arthur, of the owl, of Merlin) to observe the properties of the dragon that shine forth in the things of the material world. "Its scales glisten in the bark of trees," Merlin explains to Arthur, "and its forked tongue strikes ... yes, like lightening!" At that point, a forked lightning bolt strikes and illuminates a similarly forked tree, where glistening serpents flickered their forked tongues. Boorman hereby exploits the possibilities of formal identity (that is, identity of shape or form) at the same time as at the cinematic level the film establishes through light a certain identity of substance with and between the things of the material world it projects. The world of *Excalibur* is created by projecting light through film; this "extradiegetic" light-projecting process informs and inhabits the created diegesis. In *Excalibur*, the oneness of the material world is expressed in the figure of the dragon and the gleams and glimmers of its metallic reflections that are an integral part of everything and vice-versa.

When the dragon is presented within both the narrative and the visual storylines as burning fire—"a beast of such power that if you were to see it whole in a single glance it would burn you to cinders!" Merlin tells Arthur—the spectator is invited to explore the allusion in all of the figures that Boorman's cinematography puts into play, for Merlin pointedly tells the Boy King, "it is everywhere; it is everything." The lightning bolt of the dragon's forked tongue transmutes into the forked waterfall under which Arthur and Lancelot joust. Whether in the shape of a waterfall or as a pool, the dragon's gleam is everywhere. Water, for instance, can be the shimmering metallic surface in which the shiny scales of the Lady of the Lake's "chain mail" dress dissolve, or the opaque depth where Merlin captures a quicksilver fish—likewise part of the dragon. The dragon is a visual rebus that Boorman takes care to confine to the formal register (in the "shape" of metallic light in all of its forms), representing it directly only in metallic figures, like the statues at the entrance to Camelot and on its rooftops, or the shimmering dragon emblazoned on the Pendragon banner matching Arthur's shield. A dragon head pours forth a stream of water that Guenevere uses when tending the young king's wounds. Dragon statues shine dimly in the halls of Tintagel, and metallic dragon figurines decorate Arthur's throne. All of these recall the general principle of the dragon's radiance, everywhere and in everything.

After extracting the gleaming metal sword from the glowing stone, the young Arthur exclaims to Merlin in the forest, "Excalibur! It's part of the dragon, too!" Later on, when the King thrusts Excalibur into the earth between his wife and his most loyal knight, asleep in the forest, the sword stabs Merlin in his shimmering lair within the coils of the dragon. The magus cries, "Excalibur! Into the spine of the dragon!" When Excalibur is driven into the earth, it is driven by the same action into Merlin and the dragon, thus illustrating the principle of oneness (rather than actual identity) that Merlin had failed to teach Arthur completely—or that Arthur had forgotten by now.

Finding the sword planted between them when they awaken, the lovers lament the "loss" of Excalibur. Lancelot exclaims, "The King without a sword—the land without a King!" This line makes no apparent sense here: the King is still alive, the land is still there; the only thing missing is the sword, and it is right there in front of them waiting to be returned. Lancelot's outcry is coherent only if the King is somehow equivalent to the land, and the sword to the King; it follows, here again, that the principle of oneness links King, land, and sword. Brightness deserts the kingdom, leaving its King tarnished and depleted, the people impoverished, and the land dark and sterile when Arthur witnesses his betrayal by Lancelot and Guenevere.

In terms of cinematic impact and aesthetic logic, the King's sword is not confined to its narrative role as a "symbol and instrument of his authority" (Lacy, "Mythopoeia" 124); rather it functions as a variable emblem. It would be a mistake to reduce Boorman's art to a series of images each of which "stands for" or "symbolizes" something else. Instead the fluidity of boundaries between material bodies parallels a similar fluidity of significations. The dragon's metallic gleam can be perceived throughout the projected world of *Excalibur*. Nevertheless, there is no rigid code or formula for assigning meanings. Rather the glimmer of the underlying dragon is a matrix for interpretation. At once light-bearing and truce-building, Excalibur is in Merlin's words "what cannot be broken," yet Arthur breaks it; what is intended to heal also hacks; what is part of the dragon can be driven into its own spine; what is united with the Grail is separate from it.

In Boorman's depiction, the Grail's esthetic emblem or "figure" is the cup or chalice. This material form enters the film subtly, almost unnoticeably. At the Duke of Cornwall's festivities in Tintagel, it appears on the table in front of which Igrayne dances under the covetous gaze of all in attendance, most especially that of her husband and Uther. With a chalice depicted on his shield and banner, Lancelot makes his appearance at the waterfall bridge as Arthur's most skillful opponent and most devoted ally. Arthur and Guenevere drink from a chalice at their wedding, witnessed by all of the attendees. Thus, in the narrative storyline, the cup as a possible incarnation of the Grail appears to symbolize both divisive lust and its opposite, unifying love—a reminder of what Morgana asks Merlin to show her. "Here ... all things meet their opposites," Merlin tells her as they view scenes of desire occurring simultaneously within the dragon.

The cup emblem is asserted gradually. It becomes more than an accessory and takes center stage when, at a banquet in Camelot, Gawain accuses the Queen's desire of destroying the unity of the Round Table. She proposes that he drink from a cup to partake of Lancelot's goodness. The cup passes around the table the long way, from hand to hand and gaze to gaze. All eyes are upon the cup in Gawain's hand when he rejects the shining premise of unity and overturns it. Later on, the elevation of the chalice in the chapel of Camelot and the lightning that strikes Arthur as the priest speaks of Mordred is a reminder of the King's incest with his sister. This repetition of the theme of desire would appear to indicate that Boorman's cup figure invokes a symbolism of lust and error. Indeed, Morgana solicits such a reading toward the end of the quest in the eerie lair of Mordred's throne when she tells Perceval there is no Grail and offers him a "replacement" cup. To tempt the knight to doubt that the Grail exists, she brings the Grail down to the level of any other cup and raises pleasure-oriented cups to the level of the Grail, arguing that "there is no Grail.... There are many pleasures in the world, many cups to drink from."

The break in the plot is sudden when Perceval rejects Morgana's offer, and, in fact, the action of the Grail that Perceval will find is the exact opposite of that of the cups which betoken destructive desire. Unlike the cup of Lancelot's goodness that Gawain refuses to accept from the Queen, thereby imperiling the cohesion of the Round Table, the Grail will bring the knights together and reanimate Arthur. As Perceval will perceive, the physical drinking vessel is not the Grail. The part the cup-objects play in the narrative plot is not representative of the role the Grail performs in the aesthetic storyline that Boorman deploys in his film. The Grail's subtle action permeates and informs the visual universe of *Excalibur*. Emblematized as a cup, but operating on an entirely different plane than the series of drinking cups, the aesthetic of the Grail intersects with the narrative at several points, the most telling of which operates through Perceval, and will enable him to complete the Grail quest.

Although Grail-like objects recur in the film's iconography almost from the beginning, the first verbal reference to the Grail occurs—quite abruptly—after Mordred's birth. The "unholy child" is born at Tintagel during an intense lightning storm, signaling that the event causes a disturbance in the dragon. Meanwhile, in Camelot an apparently stray bolt strikes Arthur's breastplate. Reading the scene in terms of plot and narrative representation, Lacy notes that "while the lightning strike may appear to be an unnecessary physical elaboration of the King's decline and Camelot's decadence, it is consistent with Boorman's method, which provides parallel sequences on the physical and moral levels" ("Mythopoeia" 125). When one shifts the focus away from plot to look at Boorman's motion picture, furthermore, it becomes apparent that the lightning strike is consistent with the filmmaker's method most especially on the visual and aesthetic levels. The flash of lightning is not "unnecessary" because here it emblematizes the unity of matter in *Excalibur*. In what might be termed Boorman's "dramaturgy of light," the bright stroke of lightning floors the lackluster King as it forcefully illustrates the absence that is causing realm's demise and simultaneously points to the remedy. The blaze from the bolt striking Arthur's body within its metal skin initiates the Grail quest. Here again, it is a question of light, the essential substance. Arthur takes the clue and reacts by telling his knights, united (albeit imperfectly without Lancelot) at the Round Table one last time: "We must find what was lost: the Grail. Only the Grail can restore leaf and flower. Search the land, the labyrinths of the forest to the edge of within. Only the Grail can redeem us."

When asked how to find this Grail, Arthur gasps feebly, "Portents. Signs. Follow...." The scantiness of the information that he gives the knights bespeaks the difficulty of their quest. Furthermore, it is unclear how finding the Grail solves the problem of the missing sword; unclear, that is, unless the principle of oneness is operating between the Grail and the sword. If the Grail is somehow equivalent to the sword, and it with the land and the King, then oneness binds all four of these seemingly separate entities, each consisting of an ostensibly distinct substance: the metal of the sword, the stone of the land, the flesh of the King. What of the Grail? Is it metallic like the sword? Or flesh, or stone, like the other two entities? The bright flash that launches the quest defines the nature of what is being sought.

Boorman's film permits signs to be multivalent within the interpretive matrix of the dragon's metallic gleam, like the "tokens" that the quest knights are supposed to read in various ways in Malory's *Sankgreal* (Tiller 91). The portents and signs that Arthur had advised his knights to heed could be misinterpreted. They must seek the Grail without any standard interpretive system to guide them all in their "quest for its 'preciously covered' meaning," and this results in "incomplete seeing" (Tiller 84). How will they recognize a portent, and what signs can be trusted? The danger of believing one's eyes and applying a schematic method of interpretation is illustrated in several scenes, as Perceval finds upon greeting a kneeling knight who is not the hoped-for companion, but a dead body propped up in its rusted armor. Boorman plays with this idea of seeing incompletely in his depiction of Mordred. The boy's smooth, lustrous gold armor would have denoted its wearer's perfection elsewhere in the film, as Lancelot's glistening silver armor did. It makes Perceval believe Mordred is good. And the boy's strange, maniacal laughter is perceived by the weary Perceval as innocent joy. It has been remarked that "the instability of interpretation underscores the complexity of 'seeing' in Malory's Grail quest" (Tiller 91)—likewise in Boorman's film.

To be able to see truly means to contemplate in terms of the dragon: after all, Arthur had told the quest knights to seek "to the edge of within." The Grail, therefore, is not elsewhere; it is within. Merlin had tried to teach Arthur that the dragon is within everything. This is the object of the quest, the hidden knowledge that the knights should be seeking. The aim is not to take possession of an object, however precious it may be, but to uncover its secrets, to access the knowledge (Lachet 27). The two characters in *Excalibur* who have a command of such knowledge are able not only to change shapes, but also to see through them: Merlin can transform Uther into the semblance of the Duke of Cornwall; Igrayne sees her husband, but the child Morgana can see through him. When Morgana transforms herself into Guenevere, she knows Arthur will be unable to perceive his sister because he has forgotten the secret. Sight cannot be trusted; insight or "looking within" is the way to full vision.

This is how Boorman's semi-conscious Perceval, his life literally hanging by a thread in the tree where Mordred's thugs have strung him up, is able to perceive the Grail for the first time. His closed, dying eyes are pierced by a searing light that proves to be a threshold into the Grail castle, depicted as a luminous Camelot. There he perceives a shining chalice. Filled by sparkling drops, it pours bright red blood (reminiscent of the "blood of Christ" proffered in a chalice by the celebrant at Arthur and Guenevere's wedding).[7] Unable to answer the questions asked of him and fearfully struggling to extricate himself from the castle, Perceval falls from the castle's drawbridge in the vision, and physically from the tree where his body has been hanging. He regains consciousness, his eyes open, and realizes the Grail has eluded his grasp.

The desolation of his surroundings challenges Perceval's perseverance. Even water is dark and ominous, recalling the episode of Uther's death and the images of the Wasteland at the beginning of the quest. This is the landscape as it appears when the unity of the realm is broken. When, at the beginning of the film, Uther momentarily heeds Merlin's lesson, that Excalibur "is to heal not to hack," the truce with Cornwall is sealed between opposing camps on either side of the forest's bubbling brook, and so the realm is "healed" from war. The special properties of luminous waterfalls, pools, and fountains to heal and restore appear throughout *Excalibur*. Uryens dubs Arthur knight and King in the water of Camelyarde's moat, and afterwards Guenevere tends Arthur's wounds beside a calm pool, water flowing from a dragon-head fountain next to them. Later on, Arthur's enraged desire to overcome Lancelot breaks both Excalibur and the mysterious bright knight at the foot of a waterfall.

In the adjacent shimmering pool appears the Lady of the Lake, presenting Arthur with a brand new Excalibur, whole again. In the world of *Excalibur*, liquid can repair metal. It can mend flesh, too, for Lancelot, whose prone body in shining armor blends with the bright streams and pools of the cataract, recovers simultaneously. Nevertheless, when it is deprived of its luminosity, water is heavy and muddy, as it was when Uther waded painfully and laboriously from the site of his ambush to deprive his assailants of Excalibur by driving it into the stone. It is an oppressive and murderous element when rain darkens the land, starves and sickens the people, and freezes and drowns the quest knights. Now Perceval witnesses the

The enraged Arthur (Nigel Terry) breaks the sword Excalibur in John Boorman's 1981 film *Excalibur* (Chai-Elsholz and Elsholz collection).

gruesome murder of Uryens at the side of a pool. With his last gasp, Uryens urges Perceval to continue the quest. Perceval himself nearly drowns later when, harried and beaten by a lynch mob egged on by Lancelot, he tumbles into a river. As he drowns, his soiled armor falls away, and Perceval emerges fresh, clean, and bright straight into another vision. There is a blinding light. He walks toward it, his shining skin illuminated by it.

Perceval's second vision of the Grail shows it to be a brilliant chalice morphing into a veiled, armored Arthur. The veil that covers the chalice-cum-Arthur-cum-"bride" is a permutation of the elements in Arthur and Guenevere's wedding ceremony, during which Guenevere holds her glistening veil over the chalice to drink, and then over Arthur for the nuptial kiss. When the Grail first appears in the *Morte Darthur* it is likewise "preciously coverede" (Malory 522). Combined with armor, the veil is a reminder of the feminine/masculine cup-and-sword motif that appears from time to time in the film (in stylized form on the stained glass window through which lightning strikes Arthur, for instance, or the cup-and-sword shaped "cross" at the foot of which Arthur later finds Guenevere praying in her convent). At any rate, both the wedding and the Grail secret are *loci* of unification.

The voice in the Grail castle vision asks Perceval again: "What is the secret of the Grail? Who does it serve?" This time the knight correctly answers: "You, my lord," and then specifies, "You are Arthur." Perceval thus acknowledges the disembodied voice as that of Arthur. Perceval knows who the Grail serves—but was not asked what the Grail is. Arthur's voice again addresses him. "Have you found the secret that I have lost?" Here it will be recalled that the demise of the realm began when the King "lost" Excalibur, and that, curiously, the remedy was to find the "lost" Grail. The recovery of these lost things takes the form of literal and figurative enlightenment, of a soul that is healed, of a secret remembered.

And so the Grail is, in fact, a secret that was lost. Perceval pronounces it: "You and the land are one." The enigma of the Grail (the unity of King and kingdom) is a shortcut back to the enigmatic dragon ("it is everywhere; it is everything"). These two mysteries sharpen the viewer's awareness of visual clues and point to the figurative bases on which the film is elaborated.

Thus Boorman's Perceval perceives the gleaming Grail object in a waking dream and "sees" its oneness with the substance of the King and the realm as a whole. The scene harkens back to Merlin's very first lesson to the Boy King in the forest on the day Arthur withdrew the sword from the stone: "You will be the land, and the land will be you. If you fail the land will perish. As you thrive the land will blossom." Later on, during the victory celebration on the hilltop the night Arthur announces the fellowship of the Round Table, Merlin cautioned the assembly of knights, "It is the doom of men that they forget."

Now in possession of the secret that has been forgotten, Perceval brings back from his quest the chalice whose contents will heal the King. "Drink from the chalice, and you will be reborn and the land with you," Perceval tells the weak and ailing Arthur. The King is revitalized. "I didn't know how empty was my soul until it was filled," says Arthur, underscoring the liquid's effect on his soul. Indeed, the chalice and its contents are both a vision and a material object. Perceval brings a liquid-bearing chalice back to the physical world from his visionary encounter with the larger-than-life, light-radiating Grail.[8] Whatever it is that the chalice contains replenishes Arthur spiritually, and physically as well, thus underscoring the connection between material and spiritual "lights" that was current in medieval philosophy. When Arthur partakes of the chalice's contents, the whole realm blossoms with new life.

The light Perceval finds in the Grail castle, and from which the Grail proceeds, is more than the light that the objects in the film reflect. It is the very light with which the filmmaker constructs the world of *Excalibur*. In other words, the metadiegetic process (light brings to life everything within the film) becomes significant on the diegetic level (the King and his realm are brought back to life). When Perceval brings the Grail back to Camelot, he is bringing the very light through which that world is constructed.

Boorman's pointed use of various elements in *Excalibur* has attracted critical attention and frustrated critics. According to one such critic, "whether the motifs of fire, water, and rock are sufficient to provide unity, only the viewer can judge" (Whitaker 142). Yet above and beyond viewer response, the aesthetics of the Arthurian romance tradition offer a powerful assessment that goes beyond personal judgment. When metal and flesh are added alongside the already noted motifs of fire, water, and rock, it is entirely possible to read the aesthetic unity of the film as a continuation of medieval theories of light. Boorman's vision is not only in keeping with the vocabulary of Grail romances, but also harmonizes various incarnations of the Grail as represented in medieval narrative: it is shimmering brightness, a luminosity so bright that it replaces seeing with envisioning. The Grail is not so much a variable chalice-shaped object as something that is consistently *vermeil*: luminous, shining, blazing a-bright, dispensing its light to irrigate the realm. At the time when "in Frensshe dyvers and many noble volumes" (Caxton's preface; Malory xiii) were being composed about Arthur and his knights, subsequently inspiring Malory, influential schools of medieval thought abolished the discrete nature of objects and elements: fire, water, air, earth, metal, and flesh were believed to share light as their essence.

In this way, light could be liquid, too, flowing forth not *like* liquid, but *as* liquid. Medieval poets and theologians relied on the formal correspondences between light and stream, between luminosity and liquid, to carry their message. The springs, brooks, and rivers that a theologian referred to at once as water and light were part of a more general poetic vision, where they might be expressed as a river of light or a sea of light. The identity of light and stream occurs in mystical writings as well (Curtius 361).[9] In much the same way as the art of cinema depends on light to create a world of images and things, the basic substance of the medieval material world was light, whether in dark, complex, imperfect matter, or in luminous, simpler, more perfect bodies.

When the King is "perfected," filled by the light that he drinks from the Grail, his dingy clothing and appearance are replaced in the following scene with gleaming new armor and youthful vigor. He and his bright knights ride purposefully through the land where leaf and flower have been restored, under a gentle shower of petals. A stream of shining armor wends its way over hill and dale under the unfurled dragon banner (Pendragon, or "pan" dragon, the all-encompassing). Thus animal, vegetable, and mineral entities all benefit from the irrigation, but also participate in it with their own light in their own fluid form. Expressed in the translated words of one influential medieval philosopher, "light possesses of its very nature the function of multiplying itself and diffusing itself instantaneously in all directions. Whatever performs this operation is either light or some other agent that acts in virtue of its participation in light" (Grosseteste 10). In Boorman's film, when Excalibur was lost, the land and its people withered, becoming rusty, dark, and infertile; now everything is revived by the Grail's irrigating light. The "enlightenment" that occurs when the Grail-secret is recovered is the unifying principle irrigating the realm; in the shape of liquid (petal raindrops, stream of armor, liquid to drink), it revives the constituent parts of the land, binds them together, and repairs what was broken.

The world of *Excalibur* may be termed "mythical," to borrow from Boorman's own words when he stated he was not striving for "historical truth" (Yakir 49)—even assuming there could be such a thing in Grail legends. The mythical world of *Excalibur* is not the natural world, nor is it specific to a single literary work. Instead, as Merlin tells Morgana during her initiation within the coils of the dragon, "Here all things are possible." The passage of time in *Excalibur* is not subject to that of the natural world either. The film's aesthetic storyline, which accompanies and diverges from the narrative plot, offers "tokens" for seeing, so that the viewer can find his or her way through the mythical world. Cyclical time, the properties of daylight and darkness, and material distinctions are all as many "portents" and "signs" that can lend themselves to interpretation, but also complicate it.

Boorman explains that the "filmmaker functions as a Merlin in the sense that he tries to organize the world" (Yakir 50). Seasons come and go in Excalibur; the "winter" of the wasteland apparently lasts the whole of Mordred's life, but nevertheless includes a series of changes in season. The "spring" following the accomplishment of the Grail quest is extremely fleeting, and branches bloom immediately as the knights ride by.[10] There is a succession of night falls in the episode of Arthur's initiation, which appears to last only a day. Yet even the night in the forest is full of glimmers and reflections of light, and everything is perfectly visible as if by the light of day. Night can be bright when the gleaming knights are joined together by Merlin's torch on a hilltop where Arthur declared the founding of the Round Table. Day can be dark during the final battle between Mordred's and Arthur's armies, when the dragon's breath obscures the light that had revived the land. Yet even then light is never far away. Several times it looks like day is about to break, but then the sun sets in a bright red halo behind Arthur's head. The narrative reiterates this motif of cyclical time-warps in terms of cycles whose duration, beginnings, and ends are incommensurable. Arthur tells Guenevere that the fellowship of the Round Table was "a fair time that cannot be forgotten. And because it will not be forgotten, that fair time may come again." The question of "when?" cannot be addressed in terms of months or years in the mythical world. There cyclical time functions like a promise. The King and his knights ride out, Arthur says, "to defend what was and the dream of what could be."

The aesthetic narrative of Boorman's film, which depicts the Grail quest as a search for the light that irrigates the world of *Excalibur*, offers a new way of illuminating the quest. The metallic gleam of the all-encompassing dragon, which informs the King's sword and the Grail as well, has its parallel in the artistic creation surrounding the Arthurian tradition in the Middle Ages. Metal was widely used in art, under the influence of the theology of light during the long Gothic age that extended from the twelfth to the fifteenth century, a period corresponding to the flowering of the Matter of Britain. The abundant use of gold backgrounds in illuminated medieval manuscripts, including those that contain Arthurian texts, reminds us that metalworking is an art that enhances and surpasses narrative descriptions of arms and armor, brilliance and radiance. The metaphysical paradigm of light that the term *vermeil* conveys in Grail literature has its analogue in pictorial metal in the form of the gold backgrounds and highlights in Gothic works of art.

To transpose these effects from the illuminated page to the big screen is a technical challenge. Cinematographic images cannot refract light as gold leaf or other metals can, and, in fact, analysis of Boorman's film reveals through freeze frames and screenshots that the films images are actually dull. The matte screen has minimal reflective capacity, and so images that are projected onto it cannot shine or reflect light. The title image of the film presents the word EXCALIBUR as glistening metal. Boorman achieves this effect with kinetic light, in other words, light that is portrayed by the movement of the film through the projector. By making the Grail in *Excalibur* "shine" through his use of kinetic light, Boorman's creative genius offers new possibilities in the quest for the irrigating light of the Grail. The filmmaker's innovative application of kinetic light to depict the Grail stands within the tradition of medieval authors and artists who invented ways of expressing and performing luminosity as a representation of the indescribable mystery of the Grail.

When war is waged, a truce broken, or a King betrayed, light withdraws from the world of *Excalibur*, leaving only faint glows and glimmers. Yet the desolation can be repaired when what has been lost (sword, Grail, secret) is found, and life-giving light flows into the realm once more. Light flows through *Excalibur* repairing, restoring, and healing. Boorman's film cycles through scenes of brightness to scenes of darkness punctuated by reflections of light, and then back to brightness again, and so forth—likewise, in the finale, when Arthur sends Perceval to look for a calm pool into which he is supposed to throw Excalibur. To convince him to do so, Arthur promises to Perceval that "one day a king will come and the sword will rise again." When the knight finally casts Excalibur into the water, the Lady of the Lake takes the sword, and in the next shot three ladies take the King. He is borne away with them across the water on a barge ... to be healed? If a parallel is drawn with the Lady of the Lake episode at the foot of the waterfall, the sword will be returned and the wounded warrior healed. The return of the sword to the watery realm sets the scene for Arthur's eventual return. The barge carrying Arthur sails away on a path of light (moonlight after a sunrise?) reflected on the water's surface. The powerful image of the glowing red sunset acknowledges the cyclical nature of the romance; Arthur may yet return (Harty, "Roll the Final Credits" 245–246). The scene includes the very medium by which rebirth and renewal is effected in *Excalibur*: liquid light. The brightness restored to the realm by the Grail's irrigating light, obscured temporarily during the final battle, now bears the promise of its own return in the shimmering path of Arthur's departure.

Notes

1. John Boorman, personal correspondence with Jean-Marc Elsholz, April 2012.
2. Background and editions are provided in Lachet 275–277 for the *Queste* (ed. Pauphilet); 43–47 for *Perceval* (Chrétien de Troyes); 325–327 for *Parzival* (Wolfram von Eschenbach). One reference edition each is included in the list of works cited below.
3. As Kevin J. Harty notes, "Arthur is the Grail King, but the Grail is stripped of any Christian associations. In a film where the king and the land are one, the Grail is the central symbol of a murkily defined pagan fertility ritual" ("Arthurian Legends" 20). Indeed, the "church" where Arthur and Guenevere are married is a clearing in the forest conducive to the discussion between Merlin and Morgana about their (other)worldly knowledge of the (super)natural.
4. Les mythes du Graal reposent sur l'existence d'un objet magique—tantôt pierre précieuse, tantôt coupe—dont le symbolisme de plus en plus complexe a fini par faire oublier l'origine matérielle, au point que l'un des continuateurs de Chrétien de Troyes a osé penser—avec raison—qu'en tant que 'support' d'une vision supraterrestre, il pouvait être n'importe quoi (Nelli 18).
5. Nobile claret opus, sed opus quod nobile claret,
   Clarificet mentes ut eant per lumina vera
   ad verum lumen....
   Mens hebes ad verum per materialia surgit,
   Et demersa prius hac visa luce resurgit [Suger 46 and 48].
6. John Scotus Eriugena, *De Caelesti Hierarchia*, cited in Erwin Panofsky. *Architecture gothique et pensée scolastique* (Paris: Minuit, 1967), 39–40; English translation emended from Elsholz 219.
7. Lachet (29) notes that *Le Haut Livre du Graal: Perlesvaus* (1200–1210 or 1230–1240) contains the first reference to the Grail as the recipient of blood dripping from the Holy Spear, a possible reference for the image of drops falling into the Grail in Perceval's first vision in Boorman's film. See also note 8.
8. In the conflation of Arthur with the Fisher King, Lacy notes a reminiscence of *Perlesvaus* in Boorman's film ("Introduction" 9–10 and 10 n26). Another interesting connection to *Perlesvaus* is the fact that "the Grail is transmuted from a chalice into a luminous vision of Arthur in armor, and then back into the chalice, but this time it is not an image but the object itself: the vessel that can be grasped by Perceval and brought back to Arthur," as Lacy had observed previously ("Mythopoeia" 127), but without exploring the parallel with the episode of Cahus who, upon waking from a dream, hands Arthur a gold candlestick that he stole while in a dream. Cahus then dies of a wound that he received during the dream (Bryant 4–5).
9. The authors Curtius cites are Alain de Lille, Dante Alighieri, and Mechtild of Magdeburg.
10. The "O Fortuna" movement of Carl Orff's *Carmina Burana* is particularly relevant to the theme of cyclicality, as it sets to music a thirteenth-century Latin poem on the waxing and waning of fortune by analogy with the moon.

Works Cited

Bryant, Nigel, trans. *The High Book of the Grail. A Translation of the Thirteenth-century Romance Perlesvaus.* 1978; rev. ed. Cambridge, Eng.: D. S. Brewer, 2007.

Chrétien de Troyes. *Perceval, ou le Conte du Graal.* Genève: Droz, 1959.

Curtius, Ernst Robert. *European Literature and the Latin Middle Ages.* Trans. and intro. Colin Burrow. 1953; rpt. Princeton: Princeton University Press, 2013.

Elsholz, Jean-Marc. "Elucidations: Bringing to Light the Aesthetic Underwriting of the *Matière de Bretagne* in John Boorman's *Excalibur.*" In *Palimpsests and the Literary Imagination of Medieval England: Collected Essays.* Ed. Leo Carruthers, Raeleen Chai-Elsholz, and Tatjana Silec. New York: Palgrave Macmillan, 2011.

Grosseteste. *Robert Grosseteste on Light (De Luce).* Trans. and intro. Clare C. Riedl. Milwaukee: Marquette University Press, 1942.

Harty, Kevin J. "The Arthurian Legends on Film: An Overview." In *Cinema Arthuriana.* Ed. Kevin J. Harty, 3–28.

_____. "Roll the Final Credits: Some Notes on Cinematic Depictions of the Death of Arthur." In *The Arthurian Way of Death: The English Tradition.* Ed. Karen Cherewatuk and K.S. Whetter. Cambridge, Eng.: Brewer, 2009.

Harty, Kevin J., ed. *Cinema Arthuriana: Essays on Arthurian Film.* New York: Garland, 1991. See also Harty, ed. *Cinema Arthuriana, Twenty Essays.* 2002; rpt. Jefferson, NC: McFarland, 2010.

Kennedy, Harlan. "*Excalibur*: John Boorman—In Interview." *American Film* (March 1981). http://americancinemapapers.homestead.com/files/Excalibur.htm.

Lachet, Claude, ed., trans., and pres. *Les Métamorphoses du Graal (Anthologie).* Paris: Flammarion, 2012.

Lacy, Norris J. "Introduction: Arthur and/or the Grail." In *The Grail.* Ed. Norris J. Lacy. 1–12.

_____. "Mythopoeia in *Excalibur.*" In. *Cinema Arthuriana.* Ed. Kevin J. Harty. 121–134.

Lacy, Norris J., ed. *The Grail, the Quest and the World of Arthur.* Cambridge, Eng.: D. S. Brewer, 2008.

Malory, Thomas. *Works.* Ed. Eugène Vinaver. 2nd ed. Oxford: Oxford University Press, 1971.

Meuwese, Martine. "The Shape of the Grail in Medieval Art." In *The Grail.* Ed. Norris J. Lacy. 13–27.

Nelli, René. "Le Graal dans l'ethnographie." In *Lumière du Graal.* Ed. René Nelli. Paris: Cahiers du Sud, 1951.

Nitze, William A., and Thomas A. Jenkins, eds. *Le Haut Livre du Graal: Perlesvaus.* 2 vols. Chicago: University of Chicago Press, 1932–1937.

Pauphilet, Alain, ed. *La Queste del Saint Graal.* Paris: Champion, 1923.

Pranger, M. B. *Bernard of Clairvaux and the Shape of Monastic Thought: Broken Dreams.* Leiden: Brill, 1994.

Robert de Boron. *Le Roman de l'Estoire dou Graal.* Ed. William A. Nitze. Paris: Champion, 1995.

Sansonetti, Paul-Georges. *Chevalerie du Graal et lumière de gloire.* Menton: Exèdre, 2002.

Suger. *Abbot Suger on the Abbey Church of St. Denis and its Art Treasures.* Ed. and trans. with notes Erwin Panofsky. Princeton: Princeton University Press, 1946.

Tiller, Kenneth J. "'So precyously coverde': Malory's Hermeneutic Quest of the *Sankgreal.*" *Arthuriana* 13 [*Rhetorical Approaches to Malory's* Le Morte Darthur] (Fall 2003): 83–97.

Whitaker, Muriel. "Fire, Water, Rock: Elements of Setting in Excalibur." In *Cinema Arthuriana.* Ed. Kevin J. Harty, 135–143.

Wolfram von Eschenbach. *Lieder, Parzival und Titurel.* Ed. Karl Lachmann. Berlin: De Gruyter, 1926.

Yakir, Dan. "The Sorcerer." *Film Comment* 17 (May-June 1981): 49–53.

The Da Vinci Code
and the Myth of History
Susan Aronstein

One of the many acts in the media circus leading up to the release of Ron Howard's film version of *The Da Vinci Code* took place in the British High Court. Two of the authors of *Holy Blood, Holy Grail*, Michael Baigent and Richard Leigh, filed a case that threatened to delay the hotly-anticipated release of the film; they sued Random House, the publisher of Dan Brown's novel, arguing that Brown's bestseller relied on "a sequence of connections that no one had made before (them)" and thus had copied their "central theme" (Suthersanen). Baigent and Leigh lost their case in April 2006, and *The Da Vinci Code* premiered as planned while the two erstwhile historians prepared their appeal, which they lost the following year. While it may seem that *Baigent and Leigh v. Random House* is but a side-show in the larger public reception of Dan Brown's novel, more interesting to legal debates than to film studies, the questions addressed in this case are central to the cultural debates occasioned by *The Da Vinci Code*—its embrace by conspiracy theorists and New Age seekers, its demonization by the Catholic Church and other Christian groups, its dismissal by academics, and its acceptance by a significant portion of the reading and viewing public.

The court's decision rested on the assumption that "facts" could be separated from fiction, from "their selection, arrangement, and compilation," and that facts, in themselves, are not "protected." Indeed, the court argued, "there is no copyrights on ideas expressed in a work which claims to be a book of history" (*Baigent and Leigh v. Random House*). Therefore, the Claimants had no "exclusive property rights" as they could not "monopolize historical research or knowledge" (*Baigent and Leigh v. Random House*). Essentially, the court argued, genre matters; as it did so, it bought into what Laurie Finke and Martin Shichtman, building on the work of Levi Strauss, Hayden White and Frederic Jameson, identify as "the myth of history," the assertion that history and literature can be "conceived of as entirely separate entities belonging to disciplines with largely incompatible goals" (3). This myth relies, as did the court, on the premise that there are things "out there"—facts, events, dates—that exist independently of their "selection, arrangement, and compilation," of their narration. The court's argument that "facts" cannot be copyrighted stems from what Finke and Shichtman call this "common sense" version of history: "fictions are made, while facts are discovered and therefore indisputable" (15).

Facts, however, as Finke and Shichtman, applying Latour and Woolgar's analysis of scientific discourse to history, remind us, are also "made," not discovered; "an utterance becomes a fact when it has been cut off from the circumstances of its production, its making. A fact is an utterance whose history has been erased. The past controversies, struggles, conflicts, debates, alliances, negotiations, and trials of making have all been rendered invisible" (15). "A fact speaks for itself because no one needs to speak for it; attribution of authorship would undermine its status as fact" (15). Indeed, the history of *The Da Vinci Code* (both novel and film), the texts that inspired it, the texts it inspired, and the debates surrounding it, are the history of the making and unmaking of fact, of the blurring of the lines between fiction and history, of the question of a "usable past." This essay explores *The Da Vinci Code*'s opening of the black box of historical fact by examining the textual transmission of its secret history—from the 1970s and Henry Lincoln's series of television documentaries for BBC's *Chronicle*, to 1982 and Lincoln, Baigent and Leigh's history book, *Holy Blood, Holy Grail*, thence to 2003 and Dan Brown's page-turning conspiracy thriller, *The Da Vinci Code*, and, finally, to Ron Howard's 2006 film of Brown's novel. In this exploration, I will focus on genre and history, remediation and authority, experts and the public, on networks and alliances—on the making of (Grail) history.

The Grail Facts

> "The simple association of the Grail and the cup is a relatively late development. Malory perpetuated this facile association."—*Holy Blood, Holy Grail*, 286
>
> "Robert! Has he been telling you the Holy Grail is a cup?"
> —*Ian McKellan as Leigh Teabing in the film version of* The Da Vinci Code

The first fact that is made and unmade in this chronicle of *The Da Vinci Code* and its reception is the "fact" of the Grail. Until the publication of Brown's novel in April 2003, if people thought about the Holy Grail as anything other than a code word for the ultimate find ("the Holy Grail for dieters," "the Holy Grail of influenza research," "the Holy Grail of car makers"[1]), they accepted "the facile association"—perpetuated not so much by Malory as by Monty Python in the contemporary world—between the Grail and the cup. Brown's version of the Grail, however, may be the most widely-disseminated of the twentieth century. Eighty million copies of *The Da Vinci Code* have been sold; the critically-derided 2006 film based on the novel has made over $750 million on the big screen and an additional $100 million in DVD sales. The video game has brought in another $2 million. Add rentals, library-loans, and book/DVD sharing to this number.[2] Now consider the industry that has capitalized on its success: television specials, spin-off books, commercial tours. After *The Da Vinci Code,* the association between the Grail and the cup will never be "facile" again.

But this version is not, as Baigent and Leigh argued in their case, Brown's version of the Grail (and indeed, Brown has never claimed that it is); the redefinition of the Grail as not cup but metaphor is the culminating movement of *Holy Blood, Holy Grail*'s historical argument, the piece of evidence that made the final connection among the Templars, the Priory of Sion, the royal bloodline and the medieval Grail romances: "The Holy Grail, then," the authors argue, "would have symbolized both Jesus's bloodline and the Magdalene, from whose womb that bloodline issued, but it may have been something else as well ... official records pertaining to Israel's royal line ... Jesus's marriage license and/or the birth certificates of his children. Any or all of these items might have been referred to as the Holy Grail" (402). This redefinition of the Grail, according to Baigent, Leigh and Lincoln, proved that the "facts" of history should be read quite differently; it exposed what Brown would later call the "dark con of man" (131), opening Latour and Woolgar's "black box," calling into question Western culture's official history, as it exposed the networks and alliances that went into both the making of this history and the repression of the true, secret, Grail history.

That a redefinition of the Grail should be at the center of a paradigm shift, of a change in the way we see and interpret history, is in keeping with the Grail tradition. From the twelfth-century on, the coming of the Grail has heralded a change in dispensation, a new way of seeing, a move from the secular to the spiritual. Grail romances posit the Grail as what Derrida calls a "fixed origin" to "orient, balance, and organize the structure" (278). To seek the Grail—to see it more openly, to understand its essence and purpose—is to seek this unique center, "a full presence that is beyond play," one that "represents coherence itself" (Derrida 278). But there are many Grails—the cup of Christ, the cauldron of plenty, the lost truth that the king and the land are one, the sacred feminine; it, like Lévi-Strauss' *mana*, functions as a floating signifier, "a symbol in the pure state, and therefore capable of becoming charged with any sort of symbolic content" (Derrida 290). Thus, the history of the Grail tradition both promises a fixed center and demonstrates Derrida's assertion that "central presence ... has never been itself, has always-already been exiled into its own substitute ... (it) has no natural site ... (is) not a fixed locus, but a function" (280).

And, beginning with Robert de Boron and the thirteenth-century *Queste del San Graal*, the Grail has functioned to provide the proper perspective for an understanding of history; in this tradition, the romance narrative will pause to insert (much as does *The Da Vinci Code*) large chunks of discursive prose that place the Grail in both earthly and sacred history, locating the Grail in typological history, the last of a long line of artifacts that provide the key to the interpretation of historical events, assuring a master narrative of history, a narrative moving inexorably from *arche* (the tree of the knowledge of good and evil) to *telos* (Christ triumphant). In the eighteenth and nineteenth century, this "historical" Grail was adopted by the occultist tradition, where it became the centerpiece of several accounts of a hidden, conspiratorial history underlying mere surface appearance. These secret histories took the form of a benign conspiracy undertaken and preserved through the generations by a group of initiates (i.e., the Priory of Sion) in possession of profound knowledge—a *gnosis* illuminative of the true nature of sacred, ultimate reality (the Grail and the Bloodline). This knowledge, the occultist tradition argued, poses a threat to existing religious and political authority, authority that seeks to suppress and/or destroy the truth. Thus, history takes the form of a struggle between the forces of an unenlightened and repressive orthodoxy and the defensively hidden possessors of a carefully maintained and transmitted truth; "[Occultists'] understanding of historical process," as Leon Surette observes, "tends to derive from the paradigmatic case of an archaic wisdom or practice suppressed—and often opposed—by authorities committed to a degenerative or corrupt version of the true, archaic faith" (50).

Thus, *Holy Blood, Holy Grail's* (and, through it, *The Da Vinci Code's*) exposure of the massive cover-up of an explosive truth, of a suppressed history, is nothing new; in fact, many of its methods and some of its conclusions closely mirror these early occultist texts, most notably occultist A. E. Waite's *Hidden Church of the Holy Grail* (1909).[3] What made these books radical was not so much their arguments as it was their movement, through *The Da Vinci Code,* from esoteric texts and into the mainstream where their version of history resonated with multiple groups: feminists, arm-chair conspiracy buffs, religious skeptics, new-age seekers. As it did so, this version of the "truth" garnered converts, formed networks and alliances, restoring, or at least claiming to restore, the "facts" of history to "the history of (their) production" (Finke and Shichtman 15). The familiar (Christian) story—Jesus the celibate prophet, Mary Magdalene the prostitute who washed his feet, the Crucifixion and Resurrection, Peter as the rock upon which Christ had built his church, Christ's divinity, the Church as the guardian and transmitter of religious truth—was questioned, thrown back into the arena for debate. Another story emerged: Jesus, the married man, his pregnant widow to whom he entrusted his church, the secret—the Grail—of the *sang real*, Jesus as mortal man, the worship of the feminine ruthlessly suppressed by the Church, the secret survival of the Merovingian kings, the mystery of Templars and their lost treasure, and the information discovered in the secret dossiers about the Priory of Sion, with its ludicrous list of Grand Masters stretching from Leonardo Da Vinci to Jean Cocteau, who sought to guard and protect the secret.

From Paperback to Television: Henry Lincoln *and* Le Tresor Maudit

> The international bestseller *The Da Vinci Code* owes its existence to a chance purchase made at a spinning stall outside a small provincial bookshop in central France.... There would be no books, no films ... no tourist trail if Henry Lincoln hadn't made a discovery that eventually took him beyond the confines of that little red paperback.—*The Original Da Vinci Code*

When Henry Lincoln stumbled across the secret message in the *Le Tresor Maudit's* reproduction of the "cryptic documents" purportedly found by Saunière at Rennes-le-Chateau and became obsessed with the connection between this discovery and Sauniere's sudden and unexplained wealth, he was an aspiring television writer, with 17 episodes of *Dr. Who* and a B-horror movie *The Curse of the Crimson Altar* (based on an H.P. Lovecraft story and starring Boris Karloff and Christopher Lee), to his credit (*Original*). And his original fascination with the story was clearly inspired by its television-potential; Lincoln pitched it to the executive producer of BBC's *Chronicle* series and spent the next three years being fed codes and clues by Gerard de Sede, the book's author; at the end of this process, Lincoln had become a convert; convinced that he had stumbled onto a vast conspiracy, a secret history, he eventually teamed up with fiction-writer Richard Leigh and photojournalist turned filmmaker, Michael Baigent to continue his research into the mystery of Rennes-le-Chateau. These discoveries formed the basis of three *Chronicle* installments: *The Lost Treasure of Jerusalem* (1972), *The Priest, the Painter and the Devil* (1974), and *The Shadow of the Templars* (1979).

Each of these "documentaries" repackaged eighteenth- and nineteenth-century occultist inventions as it revealed hidden connections—between Rennes-le-Chateau and the Templars, between the Templars and Isaac Newton, between the Holy Grail and the Temple of Solomon, ultimately connecting the dots among all of the above to disclose a hidden history.

As part of the BBC's respected *Chronicle* series, Lincoln's exposé was presented as "history," speculative history, perhaps, but history nonetheless. The final program in the series, *The Shadow of the Templars*, demonstrates the ways in which Lincoln uses the television medium to make his history "real," to establish the evidence, the networks, and the alliances, that speak for his facts. The documentary begins with a montage of images—stone effigies, codes, a chalice intersected by a lance, pentacles—and resolves to an establishing shot of Lincoln standing by the effigies of Templar Knights in London's Temple Church (a scene that will be repeated in Ron Howard's film). Speaking directly to the audience, he promises to "shed a new and startling light on these long dead knights of Christ," to penetrate the "smokescreens" constructed "to conceal one astonishing and simple truth." The camera cuts to Lincoln entering the church at Rennes-le-Chateau, the location of the mystery that started him on his quest, and follows him into the crypt, where Lincoln stops in front of a tapestry/bulletin board featuring a stylized representation of mounted Templar knights. Here, Lincoln promises to take us with him on his quest to "show us the trail, how the pieces, which seem to have no connection, fit together." "Never," he assures us, "has a new element been contradicted." As he speaks, Lincoln covers the board with a collage of images—landscapes, portraits, documents, geographical representations. Picking up a piece of the puzzle, he tells us we will "begin with a part of the underlying structure." The camera pans closely on the photo and then dissolves into Lincoln climbing the hill to the ruins of Bezu, ruins that, Lincoln tells us, "resonate with gold and greed and mystery and lies."

This initial sequence encapsulates the documentary's technique, the ways in which it constructs Lincoln's "trail" as a faithful reading that leads to "truth" or "fact": his admission that his pieces seem random, the construction of the puzzle, the use of the camera to turn image into video, and, as we see later, history into film, story into presence. Again and again, Lincoln acknowledges that his theories are improbable, ludicrous even; "some of these names," he declares after reading through The Priory of Sion's Grand Masters, "are so illustrious that the list seems just the sort of grandiose pedigree that would be created for itself by a lunatic fringe body of eccentrics playing at secret societies." But before the audience really has a chance to agree, Lincoln continues, "It's too easy to make assumptions and not keep an open mind." Viewed from the right context—a "medieval" context that Lincoln and the crew's camera provide, we can see connecting threads: the rose, the cross, the pentacle. As Lincoln takes his pieces from the board, he declares, "so many intangible maybes, yet underneath it all, a hard core of fact." "The real treasure," Lincoln concludes, "is a secret ... the hidden body of knowledge reserved only for the initiate," and Mary Magdalene is the medium of that revelation.

These television "documentaries" tell the tale of Lincoln's romp through the "obscure byways of history" ("Shadow"). In them, Lincoln presents alternate facts; his networks and alliances consist of voices from the past, preserved in manuscripts and stone, in architecture and geometry. In these shows, the medium of television functions as part of Lincoln's network; it makes his facts "visible," and the use of editing—cross-cuts and camera pans, montage and superimposed images—argues for the connections that Lincoln proposes, connections that, Lincoln suggests, unmake history as we know it, pointing to an esoteric society stretching back to the Templars and still very much alive in the present, guarding "the real treasure," "not gold and jewels," but a secret ("Shadow").

From Small Screen to Large Book: Holy Blood, Holy Grail

> To our bemused bewilderment we found ourselves attracting as much celebrity (or more accurately, notoriety) as if we had staged a coup d'etat in the Vatican.... We also attained certifiable shock-horror status as a news story—Holy Blood, Holy Grail, 10

The *Chronicle* documentaries fared relatively well with audiences, but, in the days before DVRs and On Demand, they were ephemeral, an hour's evening amusement. As such, they attracted little outside attention; the experts, on the whole, ignored them. But *Holy Blood, Holy Grail*'s remediation of the authors' "ten years of research into the obscure byways of history" from new to old media constituted an authorizing gesture ("Shadow"); 496 pages of densely argued prose, shelved in the history section of the bookstore, replaced the television romp. Furthermore, in the series, Lincoln alone had spoken for his facts; *Holy Blood, Holy Grail* brought other players into the network, popular reviewers and blurb-writers. These players validated the book as "meticulously researched" and "enough to seriously challenge traditional Christian beliefs, if not alter them." Baigent, Leigh and Lincoln's challenge to traditional history and belief—and traditional academics—catapulted its authors to infamy. They were "ambushed" (their words) by the Bishop of Birmingham on BBC's *Omnibus*, accused of errors of fact and rampant speculation, and castigated by the academic establishment, with Marina Warner leading the charge (*Holy Blood,* Introduction).[4]

Like the television documentaries, *Holy Blood, Holy Grail* begins with a "mystery" (i.e., Rennes-le-Chateau and Saunière), moves to a series of seemingly unrelated "facts," speculates as to their meaning, and then draws conclusions. But the book replaces the use of cameras and editing with an authoritative academic tone, bolstered by a rhetorical sleight of hand. First it posits a link, then the prose slides from the subjunctive ("if," "perhaps") to the indicative, a slide that allows the authors repeatedly to insist that the fragments are not random, their connections not coincidence, their pattern coherent:

> Why should the Grail finally surface precisely when it did—at the very peak of the Crusades? Was it coincidence that this enigmatic object, ostensibly nonexistent for ten centuries, should assume the status that it did at the very time it did—when the Frankish kingdom of Jerusalem was in its full glory, the Templars were at the apex of their power, when the Cathar heresy was gaining a momentum that actually threatened to displace Rome? Was this convergence of circumstances truly coincidental? Or was there some link between them? ... Only by examining these "fantasies" (the Grail Romances) closely could we hope to determine whether or not their recurrence in our inquiry was indeed coincidental or the manifestation of a pattern—a pattern that in some way might prove significant [284].

In this passage, the authors float the premise of "fantasies" as coded history; and, as they "closely" examine the medieval Grail texts, they "find" what they are looking for. "It is also possible that something is being implied by these ostentatious connections of the Templars with the Grail. For if the Templars are indeed guardians of the Grail, there is one flagrant implication—that the Grail existed not only in Arthurian times, but also during the Crusades" (295). They take the implication and run with it, moving from *Perlesvaus* to *Parzival* to posit a secret order protecting both the Grail and the Grail family—now to move again from romance to history. "At the same time, however (the romances) told us nothing that was historically useful. If we hoped to find an actual historical prototype for the Grail family, we would have to look elsewhere. The clues were meager enough" (301). "*Parzival* ... is said to be of Angevin blood" (302); Angevins are associated with Templars and the Holy Land; the Priory documents connect the Angevins with the Merovingians. Geography comes to their aid: Wolfram's poem is set in France. Parzival's homeland, Waleis, is not Wales at all, but Valais in Switzerland, whose capital is Sidonensis, modern name, Sion. Final conclusion? "Wolfram is hiding something—*Parzival* and his other works are not merely romances, but also initiation documents, depositories of secrets" (303). From here, to Cabalism, more Merovingians, the bloodline's exile to Britain and the Grail's connection with the blood of Christ.

"At this point," the authors write, "we paused to review the evidence at our disposal. It was leading us in a startling yet unmistakable direction. But why, we wondered, had this evidence never been subpoenaed by scholars before" (309). Rather than blaming a massive cover-up by an academic community controlled by the Church, the authors indict the Enlightenment's valorization of analysis over synthesis and the academy's emphasis on specialization. In other words, experts in Grail romances are not historians, historians don't read Grail romances, and no one takes them as factual. No one else has been willing to see the "kernel of historical truth" (310). "But," *Holy Blood, Holy Grail* argues, "reality, history and knowledge cannot be segmented and compartmentalized according to an arbitrary filing system of the human intellect.... One must be able to link data and make connections between people, events, and phenomena widely divorced from each other.... In short, one must synthesize—for only by such synthesis can one discern the underlying continuity, the unified and coherent fabric, which lies at the core of any historical problem.... Finally, it is not sufficient to confine oneself exclusively to the facts. One must also discern the ramifications of the facts, as those repercussions and ramifications radiate through the centuries, often in the form of myth and legend" (312). Thus, from Grail romances to the royal bloodline: a "plausible hypothesis that makes coherent sense" connects the fragments, redefines the Grail, and reveals "a living and plausible Jesus—a Jesus whose life is both meaningful and comprehensible to modern man" (399).

In this passage, the authors expose the limitations of traditional networks and the facts as we think we know them. In fact, using the tools of the master, as it were, they write a book that is received as history to upend the endeavor of history itself, arguing for a view of history that is distinctly postmodern, that the facts cannot be understood outside of the networks and alliances that went into their making, that we have no unmediated access to history. All that we can hope for is a "plausible hypothesis that makes coherent sense" (399). Furthermore, that hypothesis did more than romp through the byways of history; to suggest that the Templars found the Grail and that Isaac Newton and Jean Cocteau belonged to a secret society is one thing; to posit that Jesus was mortal man and the Church knew it, to redefine the "Holy Grail," is another. One is an ingenuous puzzle; the other threatens the center. No wonder church and academia colluded in an attempt to reseal the black box of historical fact.

History to Novel: The Da Vinci Code

> "*The Da Vinci Code* is nothing short of a modern day apocryphal gospel."—*Beal*
>
> "The book is everywhere. You can't be a modern youth without having read it."
> —*Cardinal Bertone, quoted in Mexal* (1085)

Holy Blood, Holy Grail introduced the secret history of Mary Magdalene, the bloodline, and the Priory of Sion to the general reading public, caused a stir, and then quietly retreated to conspiracy theory websites and the remaindered shelves. Then Dan Brown's novel incorporated Baigent, Leigh and Lincoln's "historical" syntheses into a page-turning airplane read that—in spite of its clunky prose—shot to the top of *New York Times* bestseller list, and remained on the list for 166 weeks. The market-forces and *Zeitgeist* that propelled *The Da Vinci Code* to this remarkable success are beyond the scope of this essay.[5] Here, I will focus on Brown's repackaging and authorization of Baigent, Leigh and Lincoln's theories for a popular audience. The novel wraps *Holy Blood, Holy Grail*'s historical speculation in a familiar generic package, a fictional wrapping that lends their theories a factual authority, as the "facts" about the Priory of Sion and its secret require the novel's readers to re-evaluate their generic expectations.

At the beginning of the novel, it seems as though we are dealing with a straight-forward detective story. Saunière's murder, the bizarre disposition of the body, and the calling in of Langdon as an expert witness all point to a police procedural that will focus on the identity of Sauniere's killer; but then Brown introduces Opus Dei and the "secret," and the detective novel slides into a conspiracy thriller. Add Gothic trappings—crazed albino monk, flagellation, night-shadowed Louvre, gargoyle-festooned crypts and churches, secret rituals, suppressed histories, codes and riddles—and we are in the familiar territory of what Victoria Nelson identifies as the "faux Catholic." Yet, from the moment that Robert Langdon relates the history of the Templars, their secret treasure, and the Priory, all of these genres serve to frame the novel's central Grail Quest. This generic sleight of hand authorizes *Holy Blood, Holy Grail*'s history, picking up where Baigent, Leigh and Lincoln left off. If medieval Grail romances encode secret history, Brown's modern Grail romance affirms and concludes that history; of course, the irony here is that this "confirmation" takes place within a fictional text. However, it is precisely this fictional status that allows Brown to elevate *Holy Blood, Holy Grail*'s theories to "fact." If the fiction lies within the pages of his novel, the facts must lie outside of those pages, as Brown confirms on *The Da Vinci Code*'s opening page:

Fact:
The Priory of Sion—a European secret society founded in 1099—is a real organization. In 1975 Paris's Bibliothèque Nationale discovered Documents known as Les Dossiers Secrets, identifying numerous members of the Priory of Sion, including Sir Isaac Newton, Boticelli, Victor Hugo and Leonardo Da Vinci [1].

The Da Vinci Code further authorizes Baigent, Leigh, and Lincoln's theories by taking the Marina Warners of the world out of the equation; instead of a debate between traditional, analytical academics and a television script-writer, novelist and filmmaker, the novel chronicles a contest between respected academics and a repressive orthodoxy. Brown goes out of his way to establish Langdon and Teabing's academic credentials; in the words of Langdon's publisher as he responds to the Harvard symbologist's book on the Sacred Feminine (clearly a version of *Holy Blood, Holy Grail's* more provocative arguments), "You are a Harvard historian for God's sake, not a pop schlockmeister." Langdon calms him down by presenting a bibliography of books written by established academics—his network—including Sir Leigh Teabing, a "British royal historian" (177). As *The Da Vinci Code* continues, the narrative bolsters both men's academic authority with their command of historical facts and trivia, a constant stream of information imparted in both dialogue and inner-monologues, to support their assertions.

These facts are not their only allies; as Stephen Mexal argues, the novel's studied realism, its pedantic use of details (many of them inaccurate) about real places and objects, validates Langdon and Teabing's history lectures, even as those lectures (in much the same way as does *Holy Blood, Holy Grail*) slide from "historical to imaginative to conjectural" (1093). "Their very specificity bespeaks accuracy, and so the reader, having already verified the essential realism of the fiction ... perhaps literally verified it by finding the Pavillion Dauphine on a map, or buying an issue of *Boston* magazine, further confirms ... the sense of being in history" (1093). Brown's use of specific, verifiable "realistic" details, in short, functions much as Lincoln's use of landscapes, manuscripts, and diagrams. The very materiality of these things lends weight and evidence to the speculation at the heart of their Grail theses.

The novel's narrative provides final confirmation for the "facts" presented in *Holy Blood, Holy Grail* as these facts provide Langdon with the knowledge he needs to unravel the multiple riddles that stand between him and the Grail: Saunière's coded messages, the symbols and engravings on the key, the clues embedded in the cryptex, the true history of the Priory, the significance of the missing apple on Newton's tomb, the rose as a symbol of both the Magdalene and secret knowledge, the Louvre's pyramid as a joining the ancient symbols for male and female.

Langdon derives his prowess as symbologist and Grail historian from Baigent, Leigh and Lincoln's history; this prowess allows him to follow the signs the Priory left behind, to prove worthy, to find all the Grails: the bloodline, the archive, the bones of Mary Magdalene; his successful quest provides final fictional "proof" of *Holy Blood, Holy Grail's* historical "facts."

As Langdon finds the Grail, the truth of the secret history that exposes the "dark con of man," *The Da Vinci Code* reveals that the *arche*, the center, of Western Christianity is not presence but supplement, unraveling the structure and its myths. As Victoria Nelson observes, "the novel's function is simply the unmaking of the godhead, not the putting of the goddess or any deity in its place. The supernatural is not present as an active agency. The Catholic Church," she concludes, "is right to be upset ... the function it serves in secularizing Jesus is not to promote a dialogue about Christianity ... but rather to help deliver a deathblow to the Christian trinity" (ch. 2).

From Realistic Novel to Gothic Film: Ron Howard's The Da Vinci Code

"I am requesting that a disclaimer appear on the screen prior to the start of the movie indicating that the film is purely a work of fiction."—*William Donahue, President of the Catholic League in a March 18, 2005, letter to Ron Howard*

What's odd is that the church, on the whole, ignored the novel until Hollywood threatened to bring it to the big screen. When Archbishop Amato and the Catholic League weighed-in in the days leading up to the release of Ron Howard's film adaptation, Stanley Kauffmann observed, "The film medium has just been given a tremendous salute, negative, but tremendous. Only when the film version of *The Da Vinci Code* loomed did Christian protests swell around the world. Hail then, wry though the hailing be, to the immediacy and ubiquity of film" (28). And swell they did; alarmed by the tremendous reach of a summer blockbuster able to pull in audiences reluctant to commit to reading even Brown's page-turning, sound-bite prose, the faithful organized protests, picket-lines, and boycotts.

The faithful may have been even more alarmed had their spokesmen been reading film theory. The summer blockbuster, in the words of Peter Biskind, is never "just a movie" (i). It performs ideological work, and as Robert Burgoyne observes, the work of historical film is inextricably caught up with the creation of public memory (a fact that Tammy Kennedy explores in her article on *The Da Vinci Code*'s influence on the popular perception of Mary Magdalene). "Film," Burgoyne argues, "engages the viewer at the somatic level, immersing the spectator in experiences and impressions, that like memories, seem to be [what Nietzsche calls] 'burned into'" (quoted in Kennedy). Because "film uses images that read like 'real memory,' viewers forget that what they are watching is fictional" (Kennedy). Thus, Ron Howard's *The Da Vinci Code*'s remediation of the written word (here, not only Brown's novel but also, through it, Lincoln's original *Chronicle* documentaries and the "historical" investigations in *Holy Blood, Holy Grail*) promised a dangerous (to believers around the world) immediacy, one that would "burn" the "heretical" arguments of the earlier texts into its viewers' memories.

And yet, in the end, even devout Catholics concluded that the film was no threat, merely a bad movie presenting "a tamed and twisted version of divine femininity" (Cunneen). However, I would argue that the domestication of *The Da Vinci Code* in Ron Howard's film stems from more than the fact that it is an unsuccessful movie (although I am not prepared to go so far as to argue that it is a good movie). Columbia Pictures may have declined to begin the film with a disclaimer, but the entire film is that disclaimer. If Dan Brown's novel validated Baigent, Leigh and Lincoln's "history" by placing it within a realistic fiction, closing the black box and presenting their hypothesis as "fact," Ron Howard's film calls attention to its status as cinema, reopening that box and reinscribing the debates surrounding its production. It reveals the "shocking" truth of Brown's novel, but works oddly against its own revelation using both cinematography and narrative to question *The Da Vinci Code*'s version of historical truth.[6]

While Brown goes out of his way to code Baigent, Leigh and Lincoln's historical-faction as "fact," incorporating a paraphrased version of *Holy Blood, Holy Grail* into his novel, Howard, as Nickolas Haydock observes, codes them as fiction (194–206). As he does so, he remediates the television documentaries that started it all, transforming their use of cinematic technique to provide immediacy by enveloping the viewer in images that read not like memory but like film; color filters, flash editing, and superimposed shots all aggressively call attention to the technologies of film. The "history" sequences in the first half of Howard's movie—Langdon's lecture on the Templars and the Priory of Sion and Teabing's Grail narration—draw their shape, materials and visual images straight from the television documentaries; each begins with the expert authority—the voice of the narrator recounting historical fact supported by a cinematic reenactment of the tale he relates; the images on the screen confirm the authority of the tale, providing immediacy, and access to the historical past. In the television documentaries, these images both match the narration and displace it; the voice in the background seems secondary to the event unfolding before our eyes; the historical film runs without interruption, only returning to the image of the expert, who draws conclusions and maps out the next step in his history, once the tale is over. For all their B-movie qualities, these histories strive for cinematic realism, lit naturally, filmed without filters, and cut to continuity. Not so in *The Da Vinci Code*, where Howard's use of colored-filters and the grainy quality of the sequence calls attention to it as film, as artifice, as a version of the tale. In addition, the fact that the film cuts between the cinematic reenactment and the narrator, often using superimposition and split-screens to have both narrator and flashback in the same frame, constantly reminds us that we have not been granted unmediated access to the past—that we are, in fact, watching *a version* of the past, not *the* past.

Teabing's reading of Da Vinci's *The Last Supper* also remediates the television documentaries to call attention to their status as *made* not *discovered*; Teabing plays Henry Lincoln, in his study, surrounded by Grail artifacts, with a camera and technology to help him make his point. The camera allows him to manipulate Leonardo's work, highlighting the figure he claims is Mary Magdalene (hidden in plain sight) and then the "chalice" between her and Jesus, reversing the positions of the figures, to reveal the Magdalene leaning on her "husband." The fresco fades from the computer screen, and Teabing is provided with a space upon which to manipulate the phrase San Greal as he propounds the thesis of the *sang real*. Langdon, whom the camera shows watching Teabing with a pained and incredulous expression, dismisses the whole performance as "balloon animals," a party trick, an illusion of likeness.

The portrayal of Langdon in this sequence is key to the film's reopening of Brown's black box. In the novel, the story at the heart of *Holy Blood, Holy Grail* unfolds as a tag-team effort with Teabing and Langdon expanding upon and supporting each other's assertions. While Teabing is the acknowledged expert, Langdon, through his own research into the imagery of the sacred feminine, has also clearly drunk the Kool-Aid; "the historical evidence supporting this," he assures Sophie, "is substantial" (254). Furthermore, the novel's version of this exposition presents the origin of the "dark con of man" as an unambiguous political ploy. In announcing Christ's divinity, according to Teabing and Langdon, the Council of Nicea did not resolve a theological debate; it created a theological truth in the service of political expediency. "It was all about power.... Christ as Messiah was critical to the functioning of Church and state: Many scholars claim that the early Church literally *stole* Jesus from his original followers, hijacking His human message and using it to expand their own power" (233).

The film both strips Teabing of his authority—he is a Grail enthusiast in the film, not a respected Royal historian—and substantially rewrites this sequence, casting Langdon (still a Harvard professor) as the barely-tolerant skeptic, the voice of reason, reigning in Teabing's flights of fancy. The facts about the Priory and the Grail are not presented as cut off from the circumstances of their making; we see here the competitions, debates and alliances. Langdon scoffs at Teabing's assertions of a "secret war" fought by a globe-spanning Priory—that was "exposed as a hoax in 1967." "And *that*," Teabing fires back, "is what they want you to believe." This initial exchange sets the tone for what follows—Langdon's skeptical insistence on facts and evidence, Teabing's fanatical, if charming, proclamations.

As the film moves towards its conclusion, the explosive truth that, in the novel promises to shake the very foundations of history, further undermines that truth, cinematically recoding Langdon's discoveries as beatific visions, affirmations of faith, rather than as denials of it, granting the symbologist access to a world beyond the material one. Langdon's ability to see truly is first evidenced as he tells Sophie the story of Newton's funeral. Technically, this sequence presents another historical flashback, another moment in which Howard must insert large chunks of discursive prose into his film. As such, we might expect the same techniques here as have been previously used by Howard in the film: color filters, crosscutting, superimposition, and split screens. This history lesson, however, employs an entirely different technique, using the technologies of cinema to bring the past into the present. As Langdon lectures Sophie, the dignitaries attending Newton's

Audrey Tautou as cryptologist Sophie Neveu and Tom Hanks as symbologist Robert Langdon outside the Louvre in Ron Howard's film of Dan Brown's *The Da Vinci Code*.

funeral materialize on the streets of modern London, framing the shot of Westminster Abbey; a long shot of Newton's funeral procession entering the Abbey follows, but the landscape remains in the twenty-first century, with scaffolding on the Abbey and the London Eye in the distance; the camera pans up, the Eye disappears, and a crane-shot pans over the funeral inside the Abbey; the camera pans down in a shot that mingles past and present, funeral attendees and modern tourists; Langdon and Sophie move to the front of the frame, the historical figures fading out as they reach Newton's tomb.

This sequence employs several film-technologies, but, unlike the earlier historical sequences, it does so in the service of immediacy; film brings the two periods together, allowing the viewers a glimpse of the past. Of course, this past is completely unproblematic; Newton's funeral is a matter of historical record, and the glimpse we are shown need not have anything to do with the Priory of Sion and its secret history. But this sequence also signals the film's movement towards the enchantment of the material, the affirmation of transcendence, a movement that is completed when Langdon successfully solves the next part of the riddle. While up to this point in the film Langdon's decoding of codes and riddles has been depicted as a rational process, this sequence presents the answer to him in a beatific vision that displaces his earlier attempt to read the tomb rationally. As Langdon moves towards the center of an empty chapel, ringed with glowing stained glass windows, the music picks up, beginning to swell; a medium shot from behind shows Langdon gazing into empty space, Newton's tomb begins to materialize before him; the camera pans 180 degrees, the tomb solidifies, the light comes up on Langdon; the camera continues to pan and glowing objects materialize in front of the tomb; the camera cuts to Langdon's rapt face; the music swells and the sparking objects morph into planets and a glowing orb; and the camera circles into a close shot of the miraculous vision, and then up to a crane shot of the tomb and planets, before slowly panning down the tomb to a tight close of the statue's empty hand. The music soars ridiculously, and the camera switches to Langdon's face surrounded by what Steven Spielberg calls "god light"—bright and golden, seemingly lit from within (Baxter, 20). The vision has been received, the riddle solved, the Grail all but achieved.

And in the end, the Grail, "the greatest cover-up in human history," turns out to be utterly irrelevant. At Rosslyn, Langdon and Sophie find the archives, but, as Sophie observes, "Saunier took the location of Mary's sarcophagus with him, so there's no way to prove empirically that I am related to her. What would you do Robert?" Langdon responds by dismissing the whole secret history as so much "noise":

> Sophie, the only thing that matters is what you believe. History shows us that Jesus was an extraordinary man, a human inspiration. That's it. That's all the evidence has ever proved. But when I was a boy, when I was down in that well.... I thought I was going to die; Sophie, what I did I prayed; I prayed to Jesus to keep me alive so I could see my parents again, so I could go to school again, so I could play with my dog. Sometimes I wonder if I wasn't alone down there. Why does it have to be human or divine? Maybe human is divine. Why couldn't Jesus have been a father and still be capable of all those miracles, like turning water into wine? Who knows? His blood is your blood. Maybe that junkie in the park will never touch a drug again; maybe you healed my phobia with your hands. And maybe you're a knight on a Grail quest. Well here's the question: A living descendent of Jesus Christ, would she destroy faith or would she renew it? So again I say, what matters is what you believe.

This speech slides from secret history to official history, from evidence to faith. Truth lies in personal experience—the praying boy who wasn't alone in that well, the water turned into wine, Sophie's healing hands. Langdon's defense of faith redirects the film's final sequence (based on the novel's Epilogue). Both texts end with the "symbologist" kneeling at the entrance to the Louvre, where "the Holy Grail 'neath ancient Roslin waits." In the novel, Langdon's pious act acknowledges the lost power of the sacred feminine; in the film, it functions—in spite of the camera's reverent pan down to reveal a medieval effigy of a woman—as a beatific vision, a moment of transcendent faith, the final revelation of "truth." Music swells, the camera swirls, depth of time and space collapses as Langdon kneels beneath starry skies, in a moment straight out of the end of *Il Paradiso*, where the truth of the feminine—of the rose—leads to the knowledge of God; Mary Magdalene merges with Mother Mary.

In the end, Ron Howard's film sought to have it both ways—to exploit the massive popularity of *The Da Vinci Code* and its explosive truth and to defend centuries of historical beliefs; the Grail may prove to be a code for secular "facts" about Mary Magdalene and the *sang real*, and it may refer both to the sacred feminine and to the bones of the Magdalene, but its true function affirms the faith it purports to destroy—it bestows sacred vision on the pious deserving. In this film, history—secret or otherwise—is irrelevant; what matters is what you believe.

The Da Vinci Code *and Public Memory: Networks and Alliances*

The black box of Christian history remains, however, open. Brown's novel threw the facts of this history back into the public domain, where competing networks and alliances continue to produce books, television and DVD specials, tours and classes, and websites. On the one side, there are the traditional historians and theologians who attempt to reassert the established narrative even as they capitalize on *The Da Vinci Code*'s success; on the other, there is a network of new-age, conspiracy theorist believers and popular readers for whom, as Mexal's discussion of user-comments and blogs demonstrates, the novel's version of history remains in play, in spite of the fact that the *Secret Dossier* has been exposed as a hoax and no matter how many times the History and Discovery Channels, established academics, and outraged Catholic theologians try to convince them otherwise.

Just ask the guides at Rosslyn Chapel, which saw its annual visitor count climb from 30,000 to 150,000 the year the film was released as those who wished to "see" Brown's history for themselves journeyed to Scotland.[7] But what they saw in the film was only a model—a built-to-order reproduction of the exterior and a "genuine" interior, give or take the Masonic symbol that the production crew affixed (without the Trust's knowledge) on the archway leading to the crypt—an addition that defaced the fourteenth-century stone with a white mark that the guides call the Hollywood circle. Here, the believers come, seeking the "truth" of history: a woman who claimed to be the direct descendent of Christ, a man who chained himself to the "apprentice pillar," and another who came with an axe, seeking to hew through the stone of Rosslyn, in quest of the Holy Grail.

Notes

    1. These phrases were the result of a Google search performed on 8 June 2013.

    2. Box office figures are from IMDB.com. See http://www.imdb.com/title/tt0382625/business?ref_=tt_ql_dt_4, accessed 4 June 2013; DVD sales figures are from The Numbers, http://www.the-numbers.com/movies/2006/DVINC.php, accessed 4 June 4 2013; books sales and video game sales figures are from CBC News, http://www.cbc.ca/news/arts/story/2013/05/13/f-dan-brown-inferno.html, accessed 4 June 2013.

    3. Versions of the Templar History can be found in dozens of sources, some more respectable than others. For a scholarly discussion of "the secret tradition," see Richard Barber, *The Holy Grail: Imagination and Belief* (Cambridge: Harvard University Press, 2004) and Malcolm Barber, *The New Knighthood: A History of the Order of the Temple* (Cambridge: Cambridge University Press, 1995).

    4. Marina Warner reviewed the book for *The Times of London* 18 January 1982.

    5. For a more detailed discussion of these issues, see Kent Drummond 60–72.

    6. Robert Torry and I discussed the film's domestication of the novel in more detail elsewhere in our essay "Chivalric Conspiracies: Hollywood's Templar Legacy." In this essay, I will focus on the film's presentation of "history."

    7. These stories were collected on a June 26, 2013, visit to Rosslyn Chapel.

Works Cited

Aronstein, Susan, and Robert Torry. "Chivalric Conspiracies: Hollywood's Templar Legacy." In *Hollywood in the Holy Land*. Ed. Nickolas Haydock. Jefferson, NC: McFarland, 2009.

Baigent, Michael, Richard Leigh and Henry Lincoln. *Holy Blood, Holy Grail*. New York: Dell Publishing, 1983.

Baigent and Leigh v. Random House. A3 2006/0971. British Court of Appeal. 2007. *Cesnur: Center for Studies on New Religions*. 28 May 2007. Accessed 15 June 2013. http://www.cesnur.org/2007/mi_davinci_en.htm

Baxter, John. *Steven Spielberg: The Unauthorized Biography*. New York: Harper Collins, 1998.

Beal, Timothy. "Romancing the 'Code.'" *Chronicle of Higher Education* 52.40 (9 June 2006). Web. 22 May 2013.

Biskind, Peter. *Seeing Is Believing: How Hollywood Taught Us to Stop Worrying and Love the Fifties*. New York: Holt Paperbacks, 2000.

Brown, Dan. *The Da Vinci Code*. New York: Random House, 2003.

Cunneen, Joseph. "Deciphering the 'Da Vinci Code.'" *National Catholic Reporter* 2 June 2006. Web. 29 May 2013.

The Da Vinci Code. Dir. Ron Howard. Columbia Pictures, 2006.

Derrida, Jacques. "Sign, Structure, and Play in the Discourse of the Human Sciences." In *Writing and Difference*. Trans. Alan Bass. London: Routledge, 1978.

Drummond, Kent. "Culture Club: Marketing and Consuming *The Da Vinci Code*." In *Consuming Books: The Marketing and Consumption of Literature*. Ed. Stephen Brown. London: Routledge, 2006.

Finke, Laurie A., and Martin B. Shichtman. *King Arthur and the Myth of History*. Gainesville: University of Florida Press, 2004.

Haydock, Nickolas. *Movie Medievalism: The Imaginary Middle Ages*. Jefferson, NC: McFarland, 2008.

Kauffmann, Stanley. "Films Divining Divinity." *The New Republic* 6 September 2006: 18. Web. 22 May 2013.

Kennedy, Tammy M. "Mary Magdalene and the Politics of Public Memory: Interrogating *The Da Vinci Code*." *Feminist Formations* 24.2 (2012). Web. 29 May 2013.

Mexal, Stephen, J. "Realism, Narrative History, and the Production of the Bestseller: *The Da Vinci Code* and the Virtual Public Sphere." *The Journal of Popular Culture* 44.5 (2011): 1085–1101.

Nelson, Victoria. *Gothicka: Vampire Heroes, Human Gods and the New Supernatural*. Cambridge: Harvard University Press, 2012. Kindle edition.

The Original Da Vinci Code. Michael Bott. The Disinformation Company, 2005. [DVD]

"The Shadow of the Templars." *Chronicle*. BBC. 27 November 1979.

Surette, Leon. *The Birth of Modernism: Ezra Pound, T.S. Eliot, W.B. Yeats and the Occult.* Montreal: McGill Queens University Press, 1994.

Suthersanen, Uma. "Copyright in the Courts: *The Da Vinci Code.*" *WIPO (World Intellectual Property Organization) Magazine.* Web. June 2006. Accessed 15 June 2013. http://www.wipo.int/wipo_magazine/en/2006/03/article_0004.html.

Waite, Arthur Edward. *The Hidden Church of the Holy Grail, Its Legends and Symbolism Considered in Their Affinity with Certain Mysteries of Initiation and Other Traces of a Secret History in Christian Times.* London: Rebman Limited, 1909.

Percival in Cooperstown:
Arthurian Legend, Baseball Mythology and the Mediated Quest in Barry Levinson's *The Natural*

James Jesson

Barry Levinson's 1984 film of Bernard Malamud's novel, *The Natural*, is a Quest story for a mass-media age. Its hero, slugger Roy Hobbs (Robert Redford) of the New York Knights baseball team, is a Percival-like innocent who travels from the country to the city to pursue his Quest to be "the best there ever was" in the game. Yet his adventures ultimately reveal the city to be a Wasteland and his initial object of "fame and achievement" to be a false Grail, which must be replaced by the pursuit of "honor and love" (Olton 214). The film, therefore, uses the traditional shape of the Arthurian Quest narrative, in which the Grail is associated with higher spiritual values, in contrast to corrupt worldly ambitions. Levinson updates this story not only by staging the Quest within a baseball season (as his source text, Bernard Malamud's 1952 novel, had done), but also by focusing on the simultaneous mediation of Roy's Quest by the sports-journalism industry. As Roy's magical 1939 season unfolds, reporters cover him relentlessly, and the film depicts his season being documented in newsreels, radio broadcasts, newspaper and magazine covers, and even baseball cards. The film makes this sports-media industry stand in for the more general worldly corruptions—the Wasteland of the modern city and the modern, commercialized sports world—that Roy must both resist and cure. By criticizing the sports media, *The Natural* ultimately becomes a paean to a long-lost, innocent, and uncorrupted game of baseball and its place in a simpler, rural American past. As such, the film fuses Arthurian myth with the American legend of Cooperstown, the pastoral site of baseball's mythical invention in 1839.

By placing his hero's Quest in conflict with the impersonal forces of mass media, Levinson demonstrates the potential for Arthurian myth to be translated to contemporary contexts. The mass media in the film not only report on Roy's actions; they also can lead him astray, influencing him to chase false Grails rather than the true one that he ultimately achieves. Yet, as I will argue ultimately, Levinson's film neglects to follow the full implications of his thesis and to acknowledge that the past he romanticizes is largely an invention of the same media that *The Natural* vilifies. Thus, his film also reveals a potential pitfall for modern

Arthurian adaptations: that the template of Arthurian legend, if deployed too broadly, can misleadingly idealize a past that never was.

The Arthurian "Template"

Levinson's *The Natural* retains the rough outline of Malamud's plot, but also makes some significant changes that are often criticized for betraying the spirit of Malamud's work and its incorporation of Grail legend. In the film, gifted teenaged pitcher Roy leaves his family farm and sweetheart, Iris, for a tryout with the Cubs. Before his big chance, however, he is shot by a femme fatale in a Chicago hotel, leaving his potential unfulfilled. Fifteen years later, in 1939, Roy mysteriously reappears in the game and makes his Major-League debut with the Knights.[1] Now an outfielder and phenomenal power hitter—thanks in part to his Excalibur-like bat, Wonderboy—Roy pledges his services to the team's manager and co-owner (and Fisher King figure), Pop Fisher (Wilford Brimley), who oversees a losing team that plays in a Wasteland of a stadium. Roy's outstanding hitting turns the losing Knights into winners, despite a conspiracy on the part of gambler Gus Sands (Darren McGavin) and Pop's partner, "the Judge" (Robert Prosky), to maintain the Knights' losing ways—Gus wins by betting against the Knights, and the Judge hopes to force Pop to retire. Along with this plot to derail the team, Roy faces threats of a more personal nature from two other antagonists: Pop's beautiful niece, Memo Paris (Kim Basinger), whom Gus uses to tempt and distract Roy (and even to poison Roy before the season's final games), and sports columnist Max Mercy (Robert Duval), who is determined to deflate the magic of Roy's season by uncovering secrets from Roy's mysterious past.

The film's most notable departure from Malamud's story is its conclusion. While the novel's Roy loses a playoff game by striking out in his last at bat, Levinson's Roy hits a dramatic ninth-inning home run, winning the pennant for the Knights. Roy's differing fates reflect his varying depictions in novel and film. Physical appetites mislead Malamud's imperfect Roy, who misses the season's final series after overeating prodigiously (rather than being poisoned by Memo, as he is in the film), and who also accepts a payoff from the Judge and Gus to throw the playoff game (a payment that Levinson's Roy rejects). As Peter Turchi notes, compared to Malamud's anti-hero, Levinson's is stronger and less driven by worldly desires; this Roy's enemies generally come from without rather than within, leaving Roy's character largely untainted (154).

Another significant change is in the character of Iris. In the novel, Iris is a stranger who shows up mysteriously at one of Roy's games and stands during one of his at bats, inspiring him to hit a home run and break a terrible slump that had begun during his affair with Memo. Malamud's Roy largely fails to recognize Iris as his spiritual guide, as he is alternately attracted to and repelled by her fertility (at 33, she is already a grandmother, in contrast to the sterile Memo). Levinson makes Iris Roy's childhood sweetheart, and her son, Ted, is the product of their lovemaking just before young Roy's departure for Chicago. When she is reunited with Roy in 1939, Levinson's Iris helps to show him the way of the true hero, and the film's final scene depicts Roy, Iris, and Ted joined as a happy family in the farmland of Roy and Iris's youth.

By giving Roy greater integrity, the film tends to present a simple story of "good over evil" (Griffith 158), and it is often dismissed, therefore, as Hollywood schmaltz. Vincent Canby's *New York Times* review comments that the film turns Malamud's "brooding moral fable" into "a fairy tale," and a later appraisal by Rob Silberman complains that "the whole tenor of the book is changed, simplified, and cheapened" (Canby 15; Silberman 5). Most critiques of the film draw a relationship between infidelity to the source and the film's "hokey" and "simplified" character (Silberman 5). Many critics conclude, along with James Griffith, that Levinson's Boy-Scoutish depiction of Roy means that any "challenging plot and characterization must go the way of the mythic allusions: onto the cutting room floor with everything else thought to be 'too much' for a 'mass audience'" (163). While I would suggest that the film's depiction of a mediated Quest makes it more complicated than generally has been acknowledged, it is undoubtedly true that Levinson's adaptation simplifies the moral landscape of Malamud's original.

Levinson also executes what Barbara Tepa Lupack has called a "Retreat from Camelot"— from the rich tapestry of Arthurian allusion in Malamud's novel (80). Critics have thoroughly explored Arthurian allusions in the novel, from Roy's resemblance to Percival (Westbrook 185) to the generally Grail-like nature of his Quest, which focuses less on attaining an object than on achieving the "transcendence" that results from "a transformation that slays the 'lower' self" (Richman 31).[2] Critics examining the film have also identified a number of correspondences, with Bert Olton noting that Roy is "like the Fisher King, Amfortas, Parsifal, Perceval, King Arthur, and Galahad all rolled into one" (214).[3] As this comment suggests, the Arthurian correspondences are fairly loose in the film, and the novel draws such comparisons more precisely. As Lupack writes, Malamud much more specifically links Pop Fisher to the Fisher King and Roy to Percival, and his work is more attentive than Levinson's is to such Arthurian themes as "the new hero who displaces the aging one" (with the teenaged Roy striking out an aging star, only to be similarly felled himself, years later, by a rookie pitcher) and the association of the Grail with fertility—through both the Wasteland imagery associated with Knights Field and the contrasting love interests, Memo and Iris (81, 83–84). Therefore, the function of Arthurian stories in the film is most accurately described as a rough "template" for the film, which is "Arthurian" mainly in the sense that "it is modeled on the redemptive Quest" (Umland and Umland 163).

The Cooperstown Myth

The film melds this Arthurian template with the distinctly American mythology of baseball and, particularly, the myth of the game's American origins. While the modern game of baseball actually developed primarily in urban centers (the New York Knickerbockers, founded in the 1840s, were most influential in codifying the game's rules), baseball legend holds that a military cadet named Abner Doubleday invented the game in the upstate New York village of Cooperstown in 1839 (Voigt 1: 5, 7–9). This myth, created in the late nineteenth century by business interests in the professional game, served two related ideological purposes: first, the myth patriotically asserted baseball's essentially American character, and, second, it depicted baseball as a reflection of American frontier and agrarian values, and disassociated it from the perceived corruption of modern cities (Voigt 1: 5–6; Seymour 1: 8–12). Steven A. Riess has argued that the baseball "ideology" that developed in the progressive era—the same period in which *The Natural* opens—was closely associated with the "agrarian" and "arcadian" myths inherited from the nineteenth century. The former held that "the countryside ... bred character and patriotism while the city fostered opposed vices," while the latter held that communing with nature provided spiritual benefits for urbanites (227–228). Baseball ideology connected the game with these values not only through the symbolism of green ballparks as urban oases but also through the legend of the game's invention "in a rustic setting in upstate New York" (Riess 228).

The myth of baseball's American invention was created in 1889 and promoted by sporting-goods magnate and baseball executive Albert G. Spalding, whose handpicked committee of experts certified the Doubleday story, with scant evidence, in a 1907 report (Seymour 1: 9). While evidence has clearly shown that baseball, in fact, evolved from English games like rounders and cricket, the Major Leagues nonetheless celebrated the centennial of its American "invention" in 1939. The United States Postal Service also lent authority to the centennial when it issued a commemorative stamp featuring "a sandlot scene ... as the central motif, with a house, barn, church, and school in the background, thus associating baseball with these time-honored American symbols" (Seymour 1: 11).

The Natural never mentions Doubleday or Cooperstown directly, but there are several signs that the filmmakers are consciously drawing on the myth. One of these is setting Roy's magical season in the centennial year of 1939—while Malamud's novel does not specify a year. Players in the film wear the patches that Major Leaguers wore in 1939 to commemorate the centennial, thus drawing attention to the Doubleday myth. The centennial celebrations in 1939 also included the founding of the Baseball Hall of Fame in Cooperstown, where the game's best players are "enshrined," like heroes from legends of old. The film alludes to this element of the centennial as well, at one point depicting a former player's plaque that recalls the inductees' memorials at Cooperstown.[4] These allusions allow the film to draw on the spiritual resonances that Cooperstown continued to have for baseball fans, even forty-five years after 1939. As baseball historian Harold Seymour comments, "[w]ords such as 'shrine,' 'pantheon,' 'sanctuary,' 'relics,' and 'pilgrimage' are constantly used in newspaper descriptions of Cooperstown" (1: 4). The mythic quality of the film, therefore, is enhanced by its subtle yet unmistakable references to the game's mythical founding and the perpetuation of its legends in Cooperstown.

The film also celebrates the agrarian and Arcadian values that Riess associates with the "baseball ideology," and that are closely associated with the game's supposed pastoral birth. Roy's agrarian roots are idealized, beginning with the film's opening shot: bathed in a golden, pre-dusk glow, an adolescent Roy chases a fly ball through an overgrown wheat field and falls into the stalks as he catches it. The film soon suggests that the family farm where Roy grows up is not simply a beautiful setting but also the source of strong values. In the next scene, Roy's father, Ed, teaches him to pitch next to a weathered barn. As he catches Roy's pitches, Ed also instructs his son on the character required of a true hero: "You got to develop yourself. The secret is confidence and concentration. You got them, you don't need much else."

The film associates such advice with farm and nature landscapes, as this early scene is echoed by another flashback, later in the film, to Roy's childhood. This time, Ed imparts similar wisdom ("A clear mind and the ability to see from the heart. That's the real strength"), while teaching Roy to fish in an idyllic river setting. Roy brings these heartland values with him on his Quest in the urban Wasteland of New York. He also carries a symbol of the land and its values in the form of his bat, Wonderboy, which the young Roy carved from a tree under which his father had suffered a fatal heart attack. Kevin Thomas Curtin writes that Wonderboy, "a phallic fertility token from the heartland of America," helps Roy "bring new life to an urban wasteland being sucked dry by evil forces" (230). When he gets his first game-winning hit at Knights' Field, for example, a rainstorm suddenly begins, restoring a previously parched field in a nod to the Grail knight's restoration of the Wasteland. The spiritual values of the pastoral/agrarian roots of baseball, it seems, can cure the corruptions of the urban game.

Baseball in the Wasteland

What is the source of this corruption in the Wasteland? The film suggests that it is the game's commercialization and the saturation of media coverage, which interfere with a pure, innocent enjoyment of the game. These are the film's ultimate villains, and each is associated with the urban game. Roy encounters both when, as a teenager in 1924, he leaves the farm for his tryout with the Cubs, accompanied by the scout, Sam Simpson (John Finnegan), who has discovered him. And, like Percival, who fails to heal the Fisher King and his land in his first visit, Roy also fails initially, prompting the long hiatus from baseball until his second chance in 1939. Along the way to Chicago, Roy encounters the commercialized game personified by fellow train passenger "The Whammer" Whambold (Joe Don Baker), a slugging Major League star modeled on Babe Ruth. Also on board is a mysterious and beautiful woman dressed in black named Harriet Bird (Barbara Hershey). Harriet, as we will soon discover, is the perpetrator of a string of unsolved murders of great athletes, and she appears to be targeting the Whammer as her next victim.

The Whammer is immediately associated with wealth and media-generated celebrity: he appears first in a dining car of the train with the columnist Max Mercy, and, while the pair play a game of hearts, the Whammer deliberately flashes a large, diamond-studded ring at Harriet, who is sitting nearby. When the train stops for thirty minutes at a carnival site, Roy and the Whammer show off their respective skills—Roy pitches balls at a stack of bottles while the Whammer hits in a batting cage, attended by a carnival barker. The scene of these heroes playing carnival games implies that they are trivializing their talents in a baldly commercial venue. Meanwhile, we see the Whammer's implication in the commercialized game through his essentially economic relationship with baseball fans. As he hits, adoring young boys cheer for him and stand next to the net separating them from the star. And when his fans cheer for him to hit another round of balls (prompted by newspaperman Max, who seems more a promoter of the star than an objective observer), the Whammer declines and instead hawks tickets to his upcoming game in Chicago.

Despite its reflection of the game's commercialized elements, the carnival scene ends with a brief return to the values of Cooperstown and the uncorrupted game, when Roy and the Whammer face off in an impromptu tournament. After Max mocks Roy's pitching skill, Sam bets that his prospect can strike out the Whammer on three pitches. Encouraged by Harriet, who enthuses, "Oh, I love a contest of skill," the players retreat to an open field to settle the bet. Several critics justifiably consider this face-off to be one of the film's strongest moments.[5] The diffuse light of the pre-dusk "magic hour" gives a romantic glow to the scene, which occurs across the train tracks from the carnival. Away from the carnival's commercial setting, the fans now have closer access to the players. Previously separated from the Whammer by netting, the bystanders now observe the players without any separation; the proximity of fans and players in this scene recalls the overflow crowds at turn-of-the-century professional games, who often would sit on the grass, either in front of the outfield fence or along the foul lines (Riess 60). While Max stands behind the plate to call balls and strikes (and thus, as a sportswriter, still passes symbolic judgment on the contest), Roy's fastballs drive Max farther back in fear, suggesting a momentary retreat of the media's influence.

For the moment, at least, Max's worldly cynicism is replaced by wonder, as a slow-motion shot captures the wind-up and delivery of Roy's third strike, and a halo even forms when Roy's head passes before the sun. Levinson similarly uses slow motion in subsequent magical moments, emphasizing the timeless quality of truly mythic events, which displaces mundane, worldly concerns. Such moments include Roy's first hit for the Knights, when he literally knocks the cover off the ball; his final, pennant-winning home run; and an earlier home run in which the ball shatters a scoreboard clock. These moments, when Roy fully realizes his heroic potential, emphasize that, like "Sir Percival and the other heroes of medieval romance ... Roy Hobbs is a figure very much out of time" (Lupack and Lupack 215).

Yet, despite the temporary retreat of the media's influence at the carnival, which allows for a brief moment of wonder, the media's authority over the game clearly persists. Having earlier proclaimed the Whammer the "best there is now and best there ever will be," Max now prepares to crown a new king, and we see him sketching a cartoon of Roy defeating the Whammer. The early showdown between Roy and the Whammer, therefore, opposes the direct—occasionally magical and timeless—communing of players and fans to the cynical, commercial world of the Majors, in which heroes are made and unmade by the verdict of the press as much as by their heroic deeds.

Speaking to a *Sports Illustrated* reporter to promote the film, Robert Redford offered a comment that seems to express *The Natural*'s attitude toward modern baseball. According to Redford, "With contemporary baseball, there's just too much television. I feel as if I'm pummeled by analysts and instant replays.... It's an incredible invasion of the imagination.... I don't respond to the current assault on my senses. I prefer to know less and imagine more" (Fimrite). Curtin cites this statement as evidence that the film sought to restore a mythic character to the game, which had been diminished by "the relative flatness and bias-through-abbreviation" that characterizes much sports journalism (228). Curtin further writes that, in the film, "[l]iving myth becomes the antidote to cynicism"—particularly the cynicism that developed after 1939, "the last year of America's relative innocence and confidence before assuming her place in the on-going wars of the planet" (226–227, 234). The 1939 season, moreover, was the year in which radio broadcasting definitively entered the game, eventually paving the way for the pervasive television coverage that Redford laments.[6] With its mythic, slow-motion moments, *The Natural* suggests not simply a more innocent time, but specifically a time before mass media completely consumed baseball.

Despite his momentary defeat of the cynical forces that have come to control the game, Roy fails in his initial heroic Quest because he is tempted by the commercialized sport's promises of earthly glory and fame. Roy reveals his ambition for these rewards after his defeat of the Whammer. When Harriet—now taken with the young upstart rather than the older star—asks Roy what he "hope[s] to accomplish" with his talent, Roy answers, "When I walk down the street, people will look at me and say, 'There goes Roy Hobbs, the best there ever was.'"[7] Roy's comment suggests that he has been influenced by the media and commercial forces represented by Max Mercy. After all, Roy's statement echoes Max's description of the Whammer as "Best there ever was. Best there is now and best there ever will be." Harriet clearly recognizes the emptiness of this goal of worldly fame, and when Roy tells her about his ambition, she responds simply, "Is that all?" When Roy checks into his Chicago hotel, awaiting his tryout with the Cubs, Harriet invites him to her room in the same hotel and prompts Roy to repeat his boast, asking, "Will you be the best there ever was in the game?" When he answers, "That's right," she immediately shoots him in the stomach. As Sidney Richman writes of this scene in Malamud's novel, Harriet thus fits the role in the Grail tradition of the antagonist "sent to test the hero's worthiness, and exact punishment when he fails" (32).

When Roy returns to the game in 1939, Max remains a major antagonist—both to Roy's success and, symbolically, to the direct, innocent appreciation of the sport. After fifteen years, Max finds Roy only vaguely familiar. As Roy's magical season develops, Max frequently attempts to remove its shine, acting as an overly rational force against the romantic spirit that the filmmakers clearly value. When Roy, incredibly, knocks the cover off the baseball in his first at bat—an event immediately followed by shots of Roy and Pop besieged by photographers as they walk toward the dugout—Max theorizes that Roy's bat does not meet the league's specifications. Trying to uncover the hero's secret in another scene, Max searches the newspaper's morgue for references to Roy, a scene that further associates Max with the media's deadening effect on the sport's vibrancy. Max is clearly portrayed as a leech on the game—Kael notes that Duval "sneers and grovels and acts parasitic" ("Candidate" 172)— and this point is expressed most directly when Roy asks, near the end of the film, if Max has ever played baseball. "No, I never have," Max responds, "But I make it a little more fun to watch, you see. And after today, whether you're a goat or a hero, you're gonna make me a great story." Max cares only for the story and will, for its sake, deflate the game's magic through the over-analysis and "invasion of the imagination" that Redford complained of in his *Sports Illustrated* interview.

Through Max's portrayal, the film not only blames the sports media for this assault on the imagination but also implicates it in the game's commercial corruption. Max clearly has ties to Gus Sands (a character who evokes one of the darkest moments of baseball legend, the 1919 Black Sox gambling scandal), and Max introduces Roy to the gambler at a nightclub—Richman compares this scene in the novel to the Grail-Quester's trip to the "netherworld" (33). Max, therefore, introduces Roy to the temptation to make easy money by throwing games and thus wasting his talent. There is also the hint of a partnership between Max and the Judge, the Knights' co-owner. When Max finally remembers his earlier encounter with Roy in 1924, he digs up police photographs of Roy and Harriet. The Judge eventually uses these same photographs to try to blackmail Roy into missing the final playoff game, suggesting that he received the photographs from Max. Such associations between the sports media and the game's moneyed interests are historically accurate. Media historian Robert W. McChesney has demonstrated the "symbiotic relationship" between sports and mass media over the last century and a half, and Riess writes that baseball's growth in the first two decades of the twentieth century depended on "a vigorous public rela-

Robert Redford as Roy Hobbs in Barry Levinson's 1984 film *The Natural.*

tions campaign waged by baseball magnates and sportswriters willing to cooperate in any way to promote the game" (McChesney 49; Riess 13).

The collaboration of financial and media interests is illustrated most strikingly in the film by a newsreel depicting the funeral of a former player, Bump Bailey. Bump, a hard-hitting but lazy right fielder, initially holds the starting role that Roy eventually wins. When he senses the threat that Roy poses to him, Bump starts playing harder, but his efforts have a fatal consequence when, chasing a fly ball, he collides with the outfield fence. The film cuts directly from this collision and a shot of teammates calling for help to the newsreel that documents his funeral at Knights Field. The newsreel's voiceover refers to the funeral as a "stirring ceremony," but it looks more like a media spectacle. The film presents the service as suspect by depicting it through the mediation of the newsreel only.

The ceremony's centerpiece, the scattering of Bump's ashes over the stadium from a biplane, seems both overblown and deliberately cinematic. By cutting between a panning shot of the passing plane and shots of the players' confused reactions, the filmmakers suggest that this event is a tribute less to the players and more to the owners' magnanimity. Moreover, the ceremony honors a player who was not only lazy and selfish but also, we later learn, being paid by Gus to throw games. The newsreel foreshadows this revelation by capturing Gus in a front-row seat. The newsreel ends with a shot of a freshly minted plaque honoring Bump, an allusion to the similar plaques at the Baseball Hall of Fame. Here, therefore, is the essence of the game's corruption as portrayed in *The Natural*: an alliance of commercial and media interests that lionizes what is worst about the game.

Significantly, this scene echoes, but drastically changes, one in Malamud's novel, in which Roy, at a later point in the season, is honored with a "Roy Hobbs Day" at Knights Field (108). Typically for his character in the novel, Roy reveals his flaws at this event; rather than humbly thanking the fans who have organized the tribute, Roy egotistically promises to "do my best—the best I am able—to be the greatest there ever was in the game" (108). By transforming this ceremony into Bump's funeral (never mentioned in the novel), Levinson shifts the focus from Roy's inner failings to the external dangers that he must negotiate and the side of the game that he must resist: the media-driven manufacturing of heroes, which can tempt one with worldly fame but lead only to spiritual or (in Bump's case) physical death.

The Knight and the Lady in White

Malamud's highly flawed hero makes the wrong choices repeatedly and ultimately realizes, "I have to suffer again" (230). Levinson's Roy, in contrast, takes better advantage of his second chance, and he eventually learns to abandon his Quest for fame. As Turchi notes, Levinson's heroic Roy is destined to succeed because the filmmakers have given him a self-awareness and understanding of his heroic role that Malamud's anti-hero lacks (154). Yet the film's middle two acts preserve some of the sense from the novel that Roy is moving toward "a destiny he ... only half understands" during much of his Quest (Richman 30).[8] The success of Roy's Quest for understanding comes to hinge on the contrast between two potential love interests: Iris, his long-lost sweetheart, and Memo, Pop's niece and Bump's ex-girlfriend. Roy's relationship with each becomes entangled in the relentless media coverage that accompanies Roy's every move. While Memo—reminiscent of Harriet in many ways—represents the temptations of sex and worldly rewards like wealth and fame, Iris will eventually help Roy to the correct understanding of his heroic role. But her assistance is delayed as she first becomes obscured from Roy by the media frenzy accompanying his accomplishments.

Iris, having heard of Roy's heroics with the Knights, comes to see Roy play in Chicago, where she has settled after leaving the family farm. When she stands during his final at bat in the game, Roy looks at her spot in the stands but seems only unconsciously to recognize her; still, the sight inspires him to hit a home run that breaks a prolonged slump. After the game, he rushes toward her section of the stands, but a group of cameramen crowds around him and blinds him with flashbulbs, delaying the reunion with Iris. The close-up of a flashbulb, which puts viewers in Roy's disoriented position, becomes a prominent motif in the film's second and third acts.

Roy's confusion at this point in the season is exemplified by the newspaper story that appears in New York that evening. Above separate pictures of Iris in the stands and Roy looking up toward her, the headline reads, "The Knight and the Lady in White." Still engaged in an affair with Memo, Roy should realize the truth of the newspaper's headline—that Iris is the key to his successful spiritual Quest and Memo a distraction from it. Yet Roy fails to see what would be evident to anyone who reads this headline. The problem for Roy is that the story is published in New York, while he is still in Chicago. We see the headline only because Memo has a copy of the newspaper in New York, and she, naturally, has no interest in discussing this Madonna-like Lady in White. Rather, fulfilling her role as the temptress, she tries disingenuously to claim Iris's attractions as her own. When she calls Roy, she claims to be wearing nothing but a white slip—a clear, but obviously muddled, attempt to project Iris's innocence—but we see that she actually wears a black evening dress. And when Roy asks if she has heard about the Knights' victory, Memo responds that she heard the game on the radio, while the camera focuses on the newspaper story and the photographs of Roy and Iris, revealing another lie. Here Memo's identity as the misleading temptress is tied up with the media that document Roy's Quest and that can equally lead him astray. Indeed, as Roy is distracted by his affair with Memo, he starts to be covered in the society pages as much as the sports pages, with photographs of Roy and Memo at nightclubs appearing in one section, while his batting slump is reported in another.

In contrast, Iris represents Roy's path to the true Grail of a return to home and its agrarian values. Her name associates Iris with "redeeming fecundity" (Lupack and Lupack 216), and, although she lives in Chicago now, she has kept her family farm (when he learns this detail, Roy says, "Good. It's home"). With Iris's help, Roy finally finds redemption and completes his Quest in two stages, as he attains true wisdom and defeats the forces of the mass media. The first of these stages comes when Iris visits Roy in the hospital as he is recovering from being poisoned by Memo, apparently at Gus's direction, before the Knights' final regular-season series. During the visit, Roy echoes his conversation with Harriet of years earlier. Now, however, instead of proclaiming faith in his immanent fame, Roy laments potential glories lost: "For sixteen years I've lived with the idea that I could be—could have been the best in the game.... I could have broke every record in the book." As Harriet had, Iris finds this goal insufficient, and she asks, "And then?" In response, Roy again echoes the earlier conversation with Harriet, saying that, had he not lost his prime years, people who saw him walking down the street would have called him the best who ever played the game.

While Roy's response suggests that he still longs for worldly fame, Iris redirect's Roy's attention from material to spiritual attainments. In a speech taken from Malamud's novel, but moved to a later point in the film for greater emphasis, Iris tells Roy, "I believe we have two lives.... The life we learn with and the life we live with after that. With or without the records, they'll remember you. Think of all those young boys you've influenced. There are so many of them." This speech makes Roy think of his father, the earlier imparter of country wisdom, and, overcome by emotion, he exclaims, "God, I love baseball." Spiritually, Roy has shifted his sights from worldly fame to the fortifying values of his father, the farm, and the pure connection between players and fans that the film idealizes.

The next stage of Roy's redemption comes in the playoff game, which, significantly, is the first night game depicted in the film. In one establishing shot, two film cameramen are shown on the stadium's roof, next to one of the light standards. By picturing cameras alongside the lights, the shot suggests the economic incentives that made night baseball increasingly popular among team owners after the first Major League night game in 1935 (Katz 5–6). Originally a way to sell more tickets (and, former Indians pitcher Bob Feller has suggested, more alcohol), night baseball became a necessity as television contracts became more lucrative for teams (Katz 6–7).

In the game, Roy, still weak from the poisoning, strikes out in his early at bats. Meanwhile, Iris is in the stands with her son Ted, though she has not revealed to Roy that he is Ted's father. Seeing Roy's struggles, Iris sends him a note that informs Roy of his paternity. After reading the note, Roy in his last at bat hits a home run into the light standards, bursting one bulb and causing sparks to cascade onto the field. The close-up shot of the ball destroying the bulb recalls the many earlier close-ups of flashbulbs popping in Roy's face. Roy's home run, therefore, symbolically strikes back at the media and commercial forces that had earlier derailed his Quest. With Iris's help, he is ready to return to the farm, where the film's final shot portrays Roy playing catch with Ted. The Grail of the pastoral game, far from the corruptions of the urban, commercial sport, is achieved.

Conclusion

The Natural's focus on the mediated hero relates it to other contemporary Arthurian films that retell the Grail story. Like George A. Romero's *Knightriders* (1981) and Terry Gilliam's *The Fisher King* (1991), *The Natural* represents mass media as a threat to social bonds. The motorcycle-riding knights of *Knightriders*, who perform in a touring Renaissance fair, momentarily disband when a faction breaks off from the troupe to join up with a promoter who promises wealth and fame—values directly opposed to the knightly code promoted by their leader, Billy (Ed Harris). And *The Fisher King*'s protagonist, Jack (Jeff Bridges), undertakes a Grail Quest that redeems his anti-social past as a radio shock jock. As Rebecca A. and Samuel J. Umland note, despite these three films' divergent settings and stories, they share qualities as postmodern renderings of Arthurian legend (153–154). As in *Knightriders* and *The Fisher King*, redemption in *The Natural* comes when the hero rejects the lure of media-generated fame for social bonds—when Roy gives up his Quest to be "the best there ever was" and submerges his ego within the family unit.

The Natural's examination of mass media also places it firmly within Levinson's canon, as his films often explore the false promises that mass media will improve our lives and our connections with others. This is the case in films like *Bugsy* (1991), centered on a gangster (Warren Beatty) who quixotically dreams of a film career in 1940s Hollywood; in *Good Morning Vietnam* (1987), about an Armed Forces radio DJ in Vietnam (Robin Williams), whose sense of humor makes him popular with listeners but who truly connects with his fellow soldiers and the Vietnamese only when he leaves the booth; and, most notably, in *Avalon* (1990), the story of an extended immigrant family driven apart by the post-war forces of suburbia and television. In *Avalon*, when the young Krichinsky brothers immigrate from Russia to Baltimore before World War I, they share a flat in a building named Avalon. The familial cohesion that helps this first generation establish itself in America dissolves as the next generation becomes wealthier (thanks to a discount appliance business specializing in televisions), moves to the suburbs, and replaces large family gatherings with isolating time before the television. Despite its title, *Avalon* adheres to Arthurian legend even less than *The Natural* does; it is Arthurian only to the extent that its title suggests, in Levinson's words, "this mythical place, an earthly paradise" that the Krichinsky family has lost (Levinson and Thompson 106). Yet the two films are connected by such nostalgia for an idyllic past. And this feature is also each film's greatest flaw.

Avalon's opening sequence, which bears a striking resemblance to the dramatic, pennant-winning home run in *The Natural*, illustrates this similarity. In the sequence, we see Sam Krichinsky (Armin Mueller-Stahl), the moral heart of *Avalon*, arriving in Baltimore on July 4, 1914, while an older Sam describes the moment in a voice-over. Baltimore, he says, was "the most beautiful place you have ever seen in your life." The scene's visuals support Sam's reminiscence, at least ostensibly: a low-angle shot shows the young Sam, with a dazzled look on his face, walking through the Electric Park amusement grounds, surrounded by brilliant electric lights on the ground and bursting fireworks in the air. The shots are so formally composed and so dazzlingly beautiful—recalling the quintessentially cinematic scene of cascading sparks as Roy rounds the bases at the end of *The Natural*—that an audience must suspect Sam of hyperbole. Indeed, as Pauline Kael writes in her *New Yorker* review, "Early on, there's a comic tinge to Sam's feeling that the time of his arrival in Baltimore ... was the high point of his life and of the nation's history"; yet, as the film pursues its thesis about television and the decline of families, "we seem expected to believe that [1914] really was a high point of innocent expectations" ("Hits" 107). Rather than recognizing Avalon as a mythical place existing in memory alone, the film suggests that its "earthly paradise" actually once existed.

The Natural makes similar missteps in idealizing 1939 as a better time for baseball and for American life. Silberman rightly complains that the film treats the past as an attractive, but uncomplicated backdrop. The film "never acknowledges the Depression" or baseball's pre–Jackie-Robinson racial segregation, and it generally presents the late 1930s as "a simpler, better, more colorful time" (Silberman 6). *The Natural*, of course, also reveals the corruptions already present in the game (and also, implicitly, in the country) in 1939. Yet its impulse, like *Avalon*'s, is to contrast these ills with the ideal of a better, even-more-distant past. And this past—the mythical pastoral roots of baseball—also fails to bear historical scrutiny.

The Natural ends with a return to the farm and the agrarian and Arcadian ideals, linked to the Cooperstown myth, that opened the film. The film's final image of Roy playing catch with his son Ted, as his father Ed had once done with him, suggests a retreat to the past, away from the modern game, which will only become more commercialized and media saturated with the rise of television and night games. The image of a less commercial, more rural past in baseball's history, however, goes against the historical truth. The Cooperstown legend, as mentioned above, obscures the game's historically urban origins; the legend also distracts from the sport's very early association with moneyed interests. While the game evolved from English pastimes, baseball as we know it was developed not by simple country folk but by upper-class urbanites. The first baseball club, the "aristocratic New York Knicker-bockers," not only codified some of the game's early rules in 1845 but also fiercely protected the belief "that organized baseball ought to be a gentleman's game" (Voigt 1: 8–9). Moreover, baseball truly developed, as Riess's research makes clear, through collaborations among team owners, urban machine politicians, and prominent gamblers, with many of the early baseball magnates falling into several of these categories (61–72, 76).

At the same time, the myth of the game's pastoral roots was developed deliberately by the figures who controlled this urban, commercial business enterprise. The myth was trans-mitted through methods as diverse as the naming of playing venues—Riess notes that, when Yankee Stadium opened in 1923, it was the first Major League team's home not to have a rural-sounding name like "park," "field," or "grounds" (108)—and the notion, frequently perpetuated in news stories, that players came primarily from rural backgrounds (Riess 168). As sportswriters collaborated with owners in "trying to enhance baseball's image and par-ticularly its rural connections" in the early twentieth century, stories of the off-season employ-ment of "ballplayers who were farmers ... were much more likely to be presented than tales about ballplayers working as bartenders or miners" (Riess 168). Again, the association of the game with rural values was seen to be more attractive than linking the game to typically urban or industrial experiences. Yet Riess's research suggests that, while contemporary writers claimed that up to sixty percent of Major League ballplayers in the 1910s were from rural backgrounds, the actual numbers were more likely between fifteen and twenty percent (168–171, 180–181). Such conflicts between mass-media narratives and reality show the role of sports journalism in creating the pastoral myths of baseball.

Ironically, therefore, for all its suspicion of sports journalism, *The Natural* follows that profession's lead in romanticizing and mythologizing the game, despite the film's occasionally perceptive examination of the ownership-media nexus. Malamud's novel had arguably used its flawed baseball hero to suggest "the inadequacy of America's popular heroes [such as Babe Ruth, one model of Roy's character] as either paradigms of conduct or as spirits of regeneration" (Candelaria 72). In contrast to this scrutiny of hero-making by the sport's owners and journalists, Levinson's film lionizes its hero. The film thus acts much like the early sportswriters who "tended to glorify sports heroes and present them as larger-than-life figures" and to dutifully ignore those heroes' moral lapses (McChesney 57; Riess 23; Katz 107). Roy is a mythical hero of the sort who never was, and a throwback to a game that never existed.

Yet, perhaps the film should not be faulted too much for its historical inaccuracies. As Redford's comments to *Sports Illustrated* suggest, the film celebrates imagination as a cure to the onslaught of information in contemporary culture. The magic moments, presented in slow motion, argue for the time- and history-destroying force of the heroic act. In moments like Roy's defeat of the Whammer in a "contest of skill" and his light-shattering final home run, the film's power increases as the story retreats from historical fact. Where

The Natural might fail as history, it often succeeds as myth, specifically as a modern day expression of the continuing appeal of the Quest for the mythic Holy Grail.

Notes

1. In Malamud's novel, Roy makes his Major League debut in an unspecified year, sixteen years after the shooting in Chicago.

2. Westbrook writes that "Percival ... the precursor of Roy Hobbs, is characterized by his ignorance, his alien origins and outsider status, his natural aptitude for knighthood, and his potential role of redeemer of or successor to the Fisher King and thus of restorer of fertility" (185).

3. Roy is wounded like Amfortas and the Fisher King, and he is also the knight who must heal the wounded king (Pop Fisher). Like Parsifal, he must wander for years before returning to the Grail Castle. And he resembles Percival, the country bumpkin who becomes a great knight; Arthur, who brandishes a magical weapon; and Galahad, whose spiritual purity allows him ultimately to achieve his Quest (Olton 214–217).

4. For an account of the founding of the Hall of Fame and the opening ceremonies in 1939, see Katz 13–38.

5. See, for example, Griffith 158–159 and Silberman 6. Deford comments in a 1984 review that the scene "may be as fine an interlude as we've ever witnessed in any film about sport." Kael lists Joe Don Baker's turn as the Whammer as one of several performances in the film that "stand apart from the sludge of moral uplift" characterizing *The Natural* ("Candidate" 101).

6. Long-time baseball announcer Red Barber identifies 1939 as the watershed year in baseball broadcasting. As he recalls, baseball-team owners feared that broadcasting, by allowing fans to enjoy games for free, would diminish attendance, and the three New York teams agreed to ban broadcasting of their home games for five years during the late 1930s. In 1939, however, Brooklyn's new general manager, Larry MacPhail, brought Barber to the Dodgers and instituted regular radio broadcasting. As Barber says, "from that time on there's been no Question. Radio, television, more fans, more money" (Ward 237).

7. Roy's response echoes what Ted Williams, the star Red Sox outfielder from 1939 to 1960, reportedly once told a friend: "All I want out of life is that when I walk down the street folks will say, 'There goes the greatest hitter that ever lived'" (Ward 271).

8. Deeanne Westbrook also explores Roy's inability, in the novel, to understand his situation. Westbrook argues that a key feature of Malamud's book is the dramatic irony of readers recognizing the mythic and symbolic roles that are hidden from Roy: Roy "will fail, not because ... he knows too much but because he knows too little. Readers know that he inhabits the Freudian wastes, but he does not know this" (188).

Works Cited

Canby, Vincent. Review of *The Natural. New York Times* 11 May 1984: 15.

Candelaria, Cordelia. *Seeking the Perfect Game: Baseball in American Literature.* New York: Greenwood Press, 1989.

Curtin, Kevin Thomas. "*The Natural*: Our Iliad and Odyssey." *Antioch Review* 43.2 (1985): 225–241.

Deford, Frank. "'The Natural': Hit or Myth?" *Sports Illustrated* 21 May 1984. Web. 16 May 2013.

Fimrite, Ron. "A Star with Real Clout." *Sports Illustrated* 7 May 1984. Web. 16 May 2013.

Griffith, James. "Say It Ain't So: *The Natural*." *Literature/Film Quarterly* 19.3 (1991): 157–163.

Kael, Pauline. "The Candidate." *The New Yorker* 28 May 1984: 100–101.

_____. "Hits." *The New Yorker* 22 October 1990: 104–108.

Katz, Lawrence S. *Baseball in 1939: The Watershed Season of the National Pastime.* Jefferson, NC: McFarland, 1995.

Levinson, Barry, and David Thompson. *Levinson on Levinson.* London: Faber and Faber, 1992.

Lupack, Alan, and Barbara Tepa Lupack. *King Arthur in America.* Cambridge, Eng.: D.S. Brewer, 1999.

Lupack, Barbara Tepa. "The Retreat from Camelot: Adapting Bernard Malamud's *The Natural* to Film." In *Cinema Arthuriana: Twenty Essays.* Rev. ed. Ed. Kevin J. Harty. Jefferson, NC: McFarland, 2002.

Malamud, Bernard. *The Natural*. New York: Farrar, Straus and Giroux, 2003.

McChesney, Robert W. "Media Made Sport: A History of Sports Coverage in the United States." *Media, Sports, & Society*. Ed. Lawrence A. Wenner. Newbury Park, CA: Sage, 1989.

Olton, Bert. *Arthurian Legends on Film and Television*. Jefferson, NC: McFarland, 2000.

Richman, Sidney. *Bernard Malamud*. Boston: Twayne, 1966.

Riess, Steven A. *Touching Base: Professional Baseball and American Culture in the Progressive Era*. Westport, CT: Greenwood Press, 1980.

Seymour, Harold. *Baseball*. 3 vols. New York: Oxford University Press, 1989.

Silberman, Rob. "Mr. Smith Goes to the Ballpark." *Jump Cut: A Review of Contemporary Media* 31 (1986): 5–6. Print.

Turchi, Peter. "Roy Hobbs's Corrected Stance: An Adaptation of *The Natural*." *Literature/Film Quarterly* 19.3 (1991): 150–156.

Umland, Rebecca A., and Samuel J. Umland. *The Use of Arthurian Legend in Hollywood Film: From Connecticut Yankees to Fisher Kings*. Westport, CT: Greenwood Press, 1996.

Voigt, David Quentin. *American Baseball*. 3 vols. University Park: Pennsylvania State University Press, 1983.

Ward, Geoffrey C. *Baseball: An Illustrated History*. New York: Knopf, 1994.

Westbrook, Deeanne. *Ground Rules: Baseball and Myth*. Urbana: University Illinois Press, 1996.

Terry Gilliam's *The Fisher King*

Cory James Rushton

During the publicity rounds for *The Fisher King* (1991), actress Mercedes Ruehl recalled her degree in English Literature at the College of New Rochelle, where her senior thesis was on T. S. Eliot's *The Waste Land*. She claims that her experience of the Eliot poem was the deciding factor in her decision to be in the film: "And of course, Eliot based the poem on the quest for the Grail. When I auditioned for *The Fisher King*, it was like an old talisman coming back" (Rickey). It turned out to be a good decision, as she won a supporting actress Oscar for the role of Anne Napolitano, the long-suffering girlfriend of Jeff Bridges' damaged protagonist Jack Lucas. This sense of destiny at work is also found in subsequent interviews with the cast and crew: script-writer Richard LaGravenese (whose subsequent screenwriting credits include *The Bridges of Madison County*, *The Horse Whisperer*, *Beloved*, and the recent Liberace bio-pic *Behind the Candelabra*) said this: "At times it appeared that for some people working on the movie, individual journeys were being made towards their own particular Grails. This was certainly true for me. I hear it is common; that a movie you're working on can begin to reflect the life you're having around it. For that experience, and for the gift of working with such extraordinary people, I am deeply grateful to those who made it all possible" (Stubbs). This comment might be simple Hollywood-speak, LaGravenese's acknowledgment that crews often experience a deep connection between their own lives and the film they're working on. But this particular film seems to invite reflection on ideas of community, masculinity, happenstance, and destiny. Most of all, it invites contemplation of trauma as metaphor, or madness as sanctity, even as it seems to resist contemplating questions about violence. What is perhaps surprising is how little attention the film's madness *as* madness has received, as critics and scholars alike have tended to accept both the film's own (very traditional) ideas about trauma and the New Age edifice which the film builds on that trauma.

The Fisher King represented two firsts for Monty Python alumni Terry Gilliam: it was the first of his films not to involve any other member of the Python troupe, and he worked from someone else's script rather than his own. Gilliam considers the film to be part of his "American trilogy," with *12 Monkeys* (1995) and *Fear and Loathing in Las Vegas* (1998), which are generally (but not entirely) less overtly surreal than his earlier solo films, the Trilogy of Imagination—*Time Bandits* (1981), *Brazil* (1985), and *The Adventures of Baron Munchausen* (1988)—or his earliest non–Python film, *Jabberwocky* (1977) [Pirie]. While the film was considered important enough to earn a Criterion DVD release, it is difficult to determine its importance in cinema history. Certainly, there was a period when Arthurian scholars noticed it: Kevin J. Harty's 1999 collection on Arthurian film contains one essay devoted to the film (Blanch), and two that make significant reference to it (Osberg/Crow and Miller). Yet other disciplines that might have found something interesting in the film, notably in its depiction of insanity/madness, have not discussed it: Lisa D. Butler and Oxana Palesh's discussion of dissociation includes a list of thirty-seven films, but *Fisher King* is not one of them; oddly, it does include Ang Lee's superhero film *Hulk* and *The Matrix* (Butler and Palesh 64). A further element in the odd and underwhelming critical response to the film is the reception of Gilliam himself: given Gilliam's persistent interest in medieval and Arthurian topics, it is odd that a book like Darl Larsen's 2003 examination of Monty Python's use of history and Renaissance drama has only a handful of references to Gilliam, while Terry Jones and Michael Palin are imagined as the driving forces in Python's tendency to historical parody and medieval legend.

Early Gilliam films share three themes: an interest in the visuals of the Middle Ages or of a pseudo-medieval aesthetic; the relationship between madness, eccentricity, and whimsy; and a concern with commerce. Before turning to the medieval and the eccentric, it is worthwhile to briefly explore how commerce (and innovation) fit into the Gilliam canon, given that the baleful effect of commerce is one of the themes most observers have noticed in *The Fisher King* (as if it was unique to that film). *Jabberwocky* is deeply concerned with the conflict between tradition and economic innovation: the film's protagonist, Dennis Cooper, is despised by his own father for trying to create a more efficient business model. When he goes to the walled city, he is not planning an adventure in which he'll kill a bloody monster: he hopes to make it financially, and thus win the hand of his beloved, only to find himself in an outright fairy tale—even marrying a princess against his will, a traditional happy ending that is unhappy for Dennis. Gilliam's genre play is a persistent feature of his work: in *Jabberwocky*, a character who wants to be Horatio Alger accidentally becomes Guy of Warwick, just as *The Fisher King* will play with the nature of protagonists and the meaning of success.

The same generic conflict between modern-style commerce and traditional adventure comes in the prologue to *Monty Python's The Meaning of Life* (1983), a segment directed by Gilliam independently from the rest of the movie: the Crimson Permanent Assurance sequence. An old British family firm has fallen into the hands of a big American company (called, helpfully, the Very Big Corporation of America), thanks to the monetarist policies of their own government. The British look as if they have not changed since the turn of the twentieth century; the American overseers look like the yuppies of *Fisher King*, all blue-grey suits and slick hair. (The point is made, perhaps too explicitly, in a brief dream sequence translating the office into a Roman slave galley.) When one of the accountants is sacked, the remaining accountants overthrow the Americans, killing at least some of them, and the building is transformed into a pirate ship, its sails once scaffolding intended to preserve its crumbling façade. The accountants then engineer hostile take-overs of American corporations, their office equipment doubling as pirate weapons, rendering the metaphor of modern predatory financial practice ludicrously real. A key scene in *Jabberwocky* involves the lords of the city conspiring to keep the monster alive because it drives people into their city, where they are in turn forced to buy everything from the lords; the viewer sees them conspire while literally riding other human beings, conflating the stifling hierarchical tradition of Dennis's medieval village with a more modern but equally exploitative mercantilism. *The Fisher King* shares a deep concern with the corporate world, and with money itself, with these earlier films.

The Fisher King's New York setting engages with this interest in commerce, and with the social consequences of wealth and disparity. The engagement with the pseudo-medieval comes in the visions and the subject matter, but it is paradoxically the New York cityscape which will tie all three together and bring the film's aesthetics in line with Gilliam's other work. The look of the film has been read too much in isolation: Osberg perceptively notes the predominance of the newspapers blowing around the streets, collecting in doorways and "marking liminal and transitional narrative junctures" (Osberg 194). In fact, Gilliam's films (whether with Monty Python, or early solo work like *Jabberwocky* and *Time Bandits*) are often visually cluttered with a ragged aesthetic that hints at the run-down and neglected. One of the elements of *Holy Grail* most praised by critics and scholars is that it is "one of the most authentic-looking films ever made about the Arthurian legend" (Hertzberg 69), which Larsen roots in the "filth" of the sets (Larsen 68); this sense of filth and dirt is extended into the commercial urban setting of *Jabberwocky* and its most obvious successor, the run-down New York of *Fisher King*.

The 90s were a transitional decade for New York, the city slowly recovering from the malaise and crime of the 70s through a resurgence of the financial markets—exactly the source of social tension in the *Fisher King* between the haves and have-nots (Blanch 129–130). It is a newspaper clipping, a picture of Carmichael's sitting room, which leads Parry to believe that Carmichael has the Grail. Those bits of paper, whether newsprint or old books in Parry's basement refuge, are, as Osberg notes, best seen as "the torn and detached pages of apparently once coherent narratives" (Osberg 195). But they are also messages, capable of being pieced together (but perhaps not back together, for the new narrative will by necessity be different than the old one). In that, Gilliam's New York has rather more access to its past than the city in *Jabberwocky* does, and is about on par with the monks in *Holy Grail*, capable of reading Aramaic and the manual for the Holy Hand Grenade of Antioch. The difference here is that this New York is on the verge of being reclaimed, something the film commemorates by linking Parry's trauma and healing with a new vision of the city itself.

The film's most prominent "new narrative" is that of the Grail itself. *The Fisher King*'s version of the Grail legend, as Robert J. Blanch notes, may seem idiosyncratic to Arthurian scholars, as it not based on Arthurian legend but on a New Age masculine self-help book, Robert A. Johnson's *He: Understanding Masculine Psychology* (1989), in which the Grail and the knight who seeks it are metaphors for the perceived plight of modern masculinity. In one obvious sense, either the film's version of the Grail is tailor-made for it, or the film is tailor-made for this version. This is Parry's re-telling of the Grail narrative:

> It begins with the king as a boy, having to spend the night alone in the forest to prove his courage so he can become king. Now while he is spending the night alone he's visited by a sacred vision.

Out of the fire appears the Holy Grail, symbol of God's divine grace. And a voice said to the boy, "You shall be keeper of the grail so that it may heal the hearts of men." But the boy was blinded by greater visions of a life filled with power and glory and beauty. And in this state of radical amazement he felt for a brief moment not like a boy, but invincible, like God, so he reached into the fire to take the grail, and the grail vanished, leaving him with his hand in the fire to be terribly wounded. Now as this boy grew older, his wound grew deeper. Until one day, life for him lost its reason. He had no faith in any man, not even himself. He couldn't love or feel loved. He was sick with experience. He began to die. One day a fool wandered into the castle and found the king alone. And being a fool, he was simple minded, he didn't see a king. He only saw a man alone and in pain. And he asked the king, "What ails you friend?" The king replied, "I'm thirsty. I need some water to cool my throat." So the fool took a cup from beside his bed, filled it with water and handed it to the king. As the king began to drink, he realized his wound was healed. He looked in his hands and there was the Holy Grail, that which he sought all of his life. And he turned to the fool and said with amazement, "How can you find that which my brightest and bravest could not?" And the fool replied, "I don't know. I only knew that you were thirsty."

This version equates thirstiness with masculine discontent, the modern western male's perceived inability to love or be loved, and threatens to collapse the Grail's potential for historical specificity (cup of the Last Supper, cauldron of plenty) into a heal-all, even a placebo. Osberg and Crow acknowledge that the "permutations of the Grail myth and the ideological agendas connected with it are as multifarious as are the treatments of the Arthurian matter," but argue that *Fisher King* is one of three films in which the Grail is "a stable signifier, the sign under which individuals (and concomitantly their societies) are healed and restored"; the other two are John Boorman's *Excalibur* and the third Indiana Jones film, *The Last Crusade* (Osberg and Crow 58). The film would appear to insist on that stability at the level of the dialogue when Parry suggests that the king in his story is "sick with experience," but the film remains confused about precisely what is being healed: is to be "sick with experience" simply to have suffered a trauma? The connection between the king's actual wound—a hand burned by the very vision that promises to heal the burn at the same time—and an ability to feel emotionally connected is not at all clear, especially given that a burned hand here replaces the more traditional emasculating wound to the groin. In *Excalibur*, the Grail explicitly connects the health of the king with the health of the kingdom, while in *The Last Crusade* the Grail clearly tests virtue. The Grail in the *Fisher King* is never so clearly explicated.

Even in its ambiguities, the film's narrative fits the events of Jack's recent past: a man with delusions of grandeur is burned by his own ambition, and a fool wanders in to help heal him. But then the film reverses this sequence so that the wounded man helps the fool, who it turns out is also wounded: but Parry's story does not account for the fool's presence. Indeed, Parry only seems to remember the actual traumatic event at the end of the film, so his allegorical counterpart is all action without specific motivation (as his answer to the king's question makes clear). But there are other disconnected elements: the fool succeeds where the best and brightest have failed, but we never hear that they tried in the first place; the manner in which the vision of the Grail prompts the delusion of divine grandeur at least implies a failure of the divine will whose intention was to help rather than harm; the "But" in the following sentence confirms that the boy's reaction was not God moving in mysterious ways, but the boy acting in defiance; the role of the fool seems to eclipse that of the divine and the royal, leaving the king a bystander in his own story. The fool succeeds in a test that the king did not realize was even happening. The shell of the narrative suggests a test which never really occurs: the vision of the Grail is a divine accident, the coming of the fool a coincidence. Osberg and Crow rightly note that Jack's being "the one" "registers a range of significations" which include his responsibility for the death of Parry's wife, his role in acquiring the Grail, and his being "the one whose expiation of guilt will heal Parry's madness" (Osberg and Crow 45). This range looks particularly over-determined given the artificial nature of the quest, and the very real question of whether Parry is in fact healed of his "madness" (rather than his madness simply becoming something else, which seems equally plausible for reasons discussed below).

Anne initially remembers the Grail as "Jesus's juice glass" before positing a Manichaean vision of the universe divided between women/God and men/devils, who need to be brought together through sexual attraction:

> I don't believe that God made man in his image. 'Cause most of the shit that happens comes from man. No, I think man was made in the Devil's image. And women were created out of God. 'Cause after all, women can have babies, which is kind of like creating. And which also accounts for the fact that women are so attracted to men ... 'cause let's face it ... the Devil is a hell of a lot more interesting! Believe me, I've slept with some saints in my day, I know what I'm talking about. So the whole point in life is for men and women to get married ... so that God and the Devil can get together and work it out. Not that we have to get married. God forbid.

The thematic significance of love, then, is obvious in the film: Parry has lost love in one of the most traumatic ways possible, and seeks to connect with a new love; the sign that Jack is "healed" of his own wounds is his return to the loving Ann, and his acknowledgment that he needs her (he had earlier refused that emotional connection, claiming that men will say anything to have sex). When directly prompted by her own admission of love, and her broad hint that, while he does not need to respond in kind it wouldn't hurt anything, he chooses to say nothing. Like the film's Grail, love's meaning is fluid and sometimes either paradoxical or twisted: love is both the root cause and the solution of the crisis of masculinity disguised as a crisis of sanity. It is not just Jack and Parry (and perhaps the equally-wounded but passive Lydia) whose stories are deeply invested in the idea of "love." But so is the story of the killer, Edwin.

What sends Edwin off to kill is not just that Jack says yuppies are the enemy; it's that Jack responds to Edwin's claims to have met a woman at the yuppie bar with a reminder of a previous call, in which Jack humiliated Edwin by getting him to ask a cashier out (unsuccessfully), and arguing that this time will be exactly the same. In other words, Edwin—whether he is deluded or not—sees the possibility of love across these class lines, and Jack brutally shuts that possibility down. While the film then reimagines Edwin's crime as the Red Knight who haunts Parry, Edwin himself is never mentioned again. He existed solely to reveal something flawed in Jack, which breaks something in Parry, which in turn breaks something in Jack. But Edwin is the first broken individual in the film's chain of pain, never healed by the power of the Grail (whatever that is) because he has killed himself and thus cut himself off from the potential for change. The film's cases of madness are prompted by an originary marginalized disaffection that is never healed because it belongs irrevocably to the past, curiously distanced from the rest of the movie and not matched by anything in

Parry's allegorical story. We hear Edwin's voice, and we see his picture on the news, while the act he commits appears metaphorically in the visually arresting, but voiceless, Red Knight.

Whether intentionally or not, Edwin ends up looking much like Balin, the hapless knight who wounds the Fisher King in Malory's *Morte Darthur* (and his source, the *Suite du Merlin*), a figure whose end is lamented by virtually no one despite—or because of—his role in the providential history of the divine's interaction with humanity. Balin is a tragic figure: the best knight in the world who will nonetheless do a terrible thing, condemning a kingdom to barrenness by wounding its king. In Malory's version, the links between event and consequence are obscure and confusing; by allowing a woman he does not know to kill herself, Balin condemns himself to wounding an unrelated man in an unrelated adventure (Malory 45), eventually dying himself in combat with his own brother. As Elizabeth Edwards has argued, there is an "extraordinary intensity of mood [in Balin's story], the sense of fatefulness that contradicts the apparent randomness of events" (27). The way in which mood takes the place of (and to some extent acts as) causality in Malory's story of Balin may be a greater influence for Gilliam than any specific event in that story.

The Fisher King shares this mood, the events of the film united through the figure of Edwin, as those in Malory are united by Balin. Just as Balin plays no role in the healing of the Fisher King and the achievement of the Grail, serving only to set the relevant chain of events into motion, so Edwin has no place in Parry's allegory of suffering, redemption, and male pair-bonding—yet the Red Knight, the traumatic memory of that act, does have a place, absorbing into itself the darker side of the city. Edwin's madness is important as a sign that his society is also sick, and that Jack Lucas is at best a bad solution to that sickness, his mockery manifesting itself not as cure but exacerbation. New York feels like a place of alternating beauty and violence, a place where two young men can spend their evenings killing the homeless with no consequence. The Red Knight appears between these two thugs to drive that point home.

There are, of course, medieval theories and representations concerning madness available to a director with Gilliam's astute sense of history, even leaving aside (for a moment) the film's engagement with the connection between the illness of the ruler and the corresponding illness of the society ruled. Whether Gilliam is aware of the medieval tradition of the Holy Wild Man, as he might well be, or by contrast he is simply an unconscious heir to it, the idea of the man who "may well be mad by normal standards in that his love for God prevents him from acting 'reasonably' like other men, valuing life, comfort, and kindred," who seems to "forsake worldly pleasures for almost intolerable hardship" (Doob 138), would seem to operate within the hobo-hero of *The Fisher King*. Doob argues that "throughout history one man's saint is another man's idiot" (138). According to Doob, the Holy Wild Man "chooses to be a fool so that he may be wise" as opposed to the Unholy Wild Man, who is "driven mad by God's grace so that he may suffer and eventually be saved" (139), which does not seem to describe Parry; but her first example of the Holy Wild Man is Sir Orfeo, eponymous hero of a fourteenth-century romance (158–207), who does choose ten years of exile in the wilderness, renouncing his throne, but only after the Fairy King violently abducts his wife. It is worth noting that *Sir Orfeo* was translated by no less a figure than J. R. R. Tolkien in 1979, making it just possible that LaGravenese (if not Gilliam) was aware of this medieval poem in which the hero lived like a homeless man following the loss of his wife to a powerful and otherworldly knight. But whether Orfeo is a conscious source is not a deal-breaker: it is enough to note how closely Parry's situation mirrors Orfeo's, suggesting that the film responds to something authentically medieval.

Mental illness has been directly associated with the Fisher King in the past, during the reign of Henry VI (1422–1461, 1470–1471). Henry, who came to the English throne (and, technically, the French throne as well) at a very young age, never really grew into the king his people were hoping for. Usually passive where kings were expected to be active and aggressive in pursuit of their rights and those of their kingdom, Henry "seemed more like a child than the father of his country" (Lerer 15). The passivity of Henry's reign is coterminous with a rise in English interest in the Grail, notably in Malory and the chronicler Hardyng. Prior to the fifteenth century, English Arthurian narratives had not been much interested in the French quest for the Grail: even the extant Middle English version of Perceval's story replaces the Grail material with some aggressive giants and a stereotypical, almost clichéd, battle (Rushton 166–167). The fifteenth century saw an increased interest in the French Grail materials (both the originals and in English adaptation/translation), and Jonathan Hughes argues that contemporaries saw the Fisher King's wasteland in a nation wracked by the Wars of the Roses, a conflict largely prompted by Henry's weakness (Hughes 67). Henry's illness manifested itself in at least one, and possibly two, long periods of catatonia, during which others ruled in his name. The absence of the foundational principle of England's monarchy—a virile, active king capable of making decisions—caused widespread anxiety. The Fisher King, in all medieval versions, is the nightmare of ineffective royal rule made real: a king who cannot perform as king, in any sense of the word. As Anna Klosowska writes, "the Fisher King's inability to hunt and mount, mentioned in both Chrétien and Wolfram, may be intended to define not so much the extent of his handicap, but rather the sexual and gender characteristics of the castrated King" (50). Indeed, he is called the Fisher King because the only comfortable activity remaining to him in the earliest versions is to fish, a decidedly un-aristocratic pursuit.

In this sense, Jack is closer to the figure of the Fisher King than Parry is, for Jack's lethargy following the Edwin massacre is an abrogation of his masculine identity: he gives up media power, signified by his signature song "I've Got the Power," for a life of mooching in Anne's home and business. The link between masculinity and virility is complicated by a scene in which a reluctant Jack, hurting after his initial adventure with Parry, is carefully and patiently seduced by Anne. While the film does not allow Jack to be impotent, his strength is rooted in the love of a good woman. Anne's patience, and her role in the full redemption of the misanthropist Jack, is an aspect of the film that feels almost irredeemably old-fashioned. This sense is not just typical Hollywood—although it is that—but a direct consequence of the film's other field of reference, the men's movement of the early 90s. "Hollywood's interest in the plight of masculinity is nothing new," writes Angela Stukator, "masculinity in jeopardy and male redemption trajectories mark every period of American cinema, continually revised and renewed within the parameters of shifting generic paradigms" (Stukator 214). In fact, the perpetual crisis of masculinity seems to have become important the moment men were invented: the medieval romance, home of the original

Fisher King, is obsessed with what it means to be male, and to be in love, and with changing paradigms for normative relationships between men and women. Stukator argues that *The Fisher King* represents "a decisive shift in the cultural construction of masculinity" best marked by the publication of Robert Bly's *Iron John* (1990), a seminal book for the genre which includes LaGravenese's source, Johnson's *He.*

In Bly, Iron John (protagonist of a Grimm fairy tale) is "the Wild Man, a man who bypasses both macho and supersensitive man" symbolized by the "soft male" (men who eschew control and authority) and "flying boys," men "who soar in a balloon of self-importance, narcissism, and arrogance": Jack Lucas is a flying boy, while Parry's boisterous behavior and tendency to strip down and yell at the moon, situates him closer to the archetype of the Wild Man (Stukator 215–216). Parry is also capable of finding what appears to be a balance between a vigorous male sexuality and a respect for women, exemplified by his teasing conversation with Anne over dinner: "I'm surprised some man just doesn't come in here and snatch you up all for themselves" he says, "You have a great set of ... dishes." Anne has dismissed the idea of "saint as lover," opening up a space for Parry's cheeky flirtation, neither saintly nor misogynist. Parry's trauma, outside of his debilitating visions of the Red Knight,

Robin Williams as Parry (left) and Jeff Bridges as Jack, the two latter-day Grail Knights in Terry Gilliam's 1991 film *The Fisher King.*

manifests itself as the Iron John vision of masculinity, but without any kind of social, day-to-day border (such as a job, a mortgage or other markers of adult identity).

Parry's madness is arrestingly close to what Foucault identified as "the true secret of madness" for the "proto-psychiatric practice" of the late eighteenth and nineteenth century: "Whether you believe yourself to be a king or believe that you are wretched, wanting to impose this certainty as a kind of tyranny on all those around you basically amounts to 'believing one is a king'; it is this that makes all madness a kind of belief rooted in the fact that one is king of the world" (27–28). Parry does not believe that he's a king, but his belief that Jack is "the one" forces the latter into a harrowing re-examination of his past shock jock life and his current situation, and in turn that new sense of self forces Jack to play Parry's Grail game. Parry forces his narrative, cobbled together from myth and legend, into and onto Jack's story. In fact, he essentially transforms Jack's angry depression into something closer to a benevolent version of Parry's own illness (best categorized under the sizable label of the dissociative): Jack's recovery "is dependent on his ability to discover and embrace the mythic" (Stukator 217). Osberg and Crow may have overstated the case when they argued that *Fisher King*'s Grail was "a stable signifier" (54). Parry's response to the Grail, indeed his belief that it is the Grail, is entirely individual until he has basically over-written Jack's own belief structure and personality. When Jack thinks he sees the Red Knight during his break-in at the Carmichael house, his perception of reality has been hijacked by Parry's.

In a similar vein, the film's most overtly magical or whimsical sequence—the Grand Central Station waltz in which commuters engage in spontaneous dance as Parry pursues the unknowing Lydia—is coded as romantic. This sequence is the only one Gilliam claims is entirely his own, and not in the script at all:

> "The waltz is the only thing that I would claim total credit for because it wasn't in the script," Gilliam says. "A scene takes place at Grand Central Station, so I was there watching the rush hour develop, watching the swarm begin. It started slowly, then the tempo increased and I thought, 'My god, wouldn't it be wonderful if all these thousands of people suddenly just paired up and began to waltz?' And the producers foolishly enough said, 'What a good idea!' Bingo, it's in the film" [Stubbs].

The ballroom pattern of the dance reclaims something grand for the architecture of Grand Central Station, restoring light and color to a place that has perversely become workaday. The sequence apparently takes place only in Parry's head, although the real world effects of the other entity in his head, the Red Knight, might give the viewer pause. For a moment, Parry has transformed the world, and as viewers, we are forced to follow along. Lydia, however, is not; Parry's gaze remains focused on her as she makes her way through the dance, in a sense reducing the dance itself to a metaphor for the business of life. While her walking becomes less clumsy during the dance, and she does move for the dancers, her gaze never wavers. That Parry can enforce a certain view of the world onto Jack—his male friend—and not Lydia—his love interest—testifies to the film's persistent focus on the importance of men as friends and women as inspiration (Lydia) or test (Anne). The waltz is illusion: but the film is more subtle than that here, for the scene is immediately preceded by Jack's conversation with the film's third significant homeless figure, a homeless veteran begging for change (Tom Waits). When Jack objects that a man who gives the veteran change did not even look at him, the veteran shrugs:

> "He's payin' so he don't have to look. See ... guy goes to work every day, eight hours a day, seven days a week. Gets his nuts so tight in a vice that he starts questioning the very fabric of his existence.... See, I'm what you call kind of a 'moral traffic light' really. I'm like sayin', "Red! Go no further! Boooo-ee boooo-ee boooo-ee....'"

The *Fisher King* insists that illusion is everywhere, and that, however distasteful, it may even be necessary, a constant dance between beauty and horror in which every individual finds a way to distance themselves from what they are experiencing. Parry's is simply more extreme than most.

In clinical terms, "dissociation" would cover both Parry's illness and whatever Parry "is" at the end of the film:

> An assumption shared by both classical and modern dissociation literature is that dissociative experiences lie on a continuum ... ranging from everyday nonpathological experiences such as the phenomena of daydreaming, highway hypnosis, and transient depersonalized experiences, to psychopathological conditions involving persistent and pervasive disruptions of memory and identity [Butler and Palesh 63].

Parry is on the extreme end of the continuum, not only believing himself to be a kind of knight and abandoning his earlier identity (even his original name), but suffering visions of the Red Knight which can leave him utterly helpless, almost catatonic—so much so that, when attacked near the end of the film, he makes no move to defend himself against his physical opponents. Oddly, Parry no longer seems to have access to the band of homeless friends who help him rescue Jack from the same fate: Parry's friendship with Jack moves him closer to the mainstream, and locks him first into a duo (Parry/Jack) and then into a quartet (Parry/Lydia/Jack/Anne). Only at the end of the film is Parry seen "leading" people again, singing the same song but in an institutional setting, the hospital where he is recovering from his coma. When Parry led his ad hoc army in song at the film's beginning, their song is ragged and their role as vigilantes is extra-legal, the marginal defending the marginal. The song at the hospital is authorized by being institutionally contained, a song that indicates the beginning of the healing process and not a warning to vicious thugs lighting the homeless on fire. Parry has been brought back into the structures of society and power, but he has arguably lost a kind of personal power. One assumes that the homeless are still burning somewhere in the city, but the film ignores this possibility to celebrate the return of the normal as the defender of the marginal re-enters the center.

The film's engagement with madness and homelessness only becomes acute (rather than moderately whimsical) when Parry and Jack rescue a character simply identified as "Homeless Cabaret Singer" in the film's closing credits (Michael Jeter). For a character with no name, transvestite Homeless Cabaret Singer (HCS from now on) looms rather large: s/he is the second example of Parry rescuing someone as his assumed "profession" demands; his sudden appearance just as Jack is about to abandon the friends he's made for another shot at success drives him back to the comatose Parry's quest (although perhaps inadvertently); and he delivers one of the film's great comic moments, informing Lydia of her "win" in the video store's fake contest through the medium of a loud show tune at her workplace. An interpretation of the film that links it only to the Arthurian legend might see Kundry lurking in this char-acter: the female messenger of the Grail and Loathly Lady figure from Chrétien de Troyes, named in Wolfram von Eschenbach's version and the opera Wagner based upon it. The description of the equivalent figure in Chrétien, unnamed, focuses on a succession of animal images:

> They saw a damsel approaching on a tawny mule, holding a whip in her right hand. The damsel's hair was plaited in two twisted black pigtails; and if what is said and related in the book is true, there was never any creature so completely hideous, even in Hell. You have never seen iron as black as were her neck and hands, and yet that was the least part of her ugliness. For her eyes were two holes as small as those of a rat; her nose was like that of a monkey or cat and her lips like a donkey's or bullock's, whilst her teeth were so yellow that they looked like egg-yolk; and she was bearded like a billy-goat. She had a hump in the middle of her chest, and her spine was crooked-shaped. Her loins and shoulders were splendid for leading a dance! She had a lump on her back and hips twisted like two osiers: splendidly made for leading a jig! [Chrétien, *Perceval* 435].

Jeter's HCS is characterized by both feminine cabaret clothes and a noticeably bushy mus-tache—conflicting markers of gender which place the character in between traditional norms, matching the gendered symbolism found in Chrétien and subsequent versions. The parodic promise that the Lady will lead a dance occurs at a pivotal moment in the film, when HCS delivers a show-tune invitation to Lydia. Further, the Loathly Lady's role in the medieval text—symbolized by the small whip she carries—is to drive men to perfection and compas-sion, and thus to the Grail (Blumstein 160–164). Chrétien's Lady berates Perceval for his stupidity and silence at the Grail castle, a silence which condemns the Fisher King to con-tinued suffering. While HCS is not nearly as sarcastic or confident as Kundry, s/he is a mes-senger, twice (albeit inadvertently) driving the plot forward and Jack towards his destiny as Parry's savior, "the one" heralded by Parry's invisible little people.

HCS is also a means by which Parry's fair-mindedness can be revealed, his ability to see past the dichotomy of reality/fantasy. When he first hears HCS's cries for help, he spe-cifically avoids making a gender judgment: he claims only that he is thankful for an oppor-tunity to assist some "miserable male or female," a welcome contrast to the befuddlement of Lancelot faced with the "Damsel" Herbert in *Monty Python and the Holy Grail*. When HCS sings the show-stopping Video Stop invitation to Lydia, the scene is certainly played for comedic effect, but it ends on a serious note: the small figure of HCS, seen from a balcony above and framed between two yuppies, whose facial expressions are therefore more visible to us than that of HCS. The camera, for a moment, places us firmly with the affluent main-stream against the temporarily amusing underground. His big, boisterous song ends, and he is silent and small. Something similar occurs when Parry and Jack stare in the window at Lydia's attempt at eating dumplings (her Wednesday ritual), our view framed by the yuppie couple whose meal is thereby interrupted. When Jack nearly comes full circle towards the end of the film, before he decides to steal the Grail for Parry, we again see him in the stu-dio—noting that he is about the interview the stars of the failed sitcom he was originally supposed to be in. He is offered another sitcom, one intended to highlight the plight of the homeless, called *Home Free*; the project is a lighthearted look at three homeless characters who like being homeless, and who are "wacky but wise." His sudden unexpected revulsion to the project, combined with HCS's earlier demand for Jack's acknowledgment, is Jack's salvation. It may be problematic that the film has at times also suggested that the homeless are "wacky but wise," and that on some level they prefer their outside status; certainly, it does not seem at all clear that Parry is going to get a job and hold down a mortgage just because he drank from a cup. When HCS screams at Jack to recognize him, Jack's silence comes close to being damning; when he rushes out of the building to acknowledge HCS too late, he realizes the cost of his silence and inaugurates a plan to acquire the Grail for Parry.

An episode Blanch argues is "bizarre" might shed light on the film's complicated mediation of madness and social norms, that of the "Stockbroker Bum": "Formerly an affluent stockbroker, this man is now reduced to begging on the street and to engaging in imaginary conversations on a disconnected phone," conversations in which he bellows orders to sell stock until Parry gives him some money Jack has just tried to give him, at which point the man yells "Buy, buy, buy ... Fuck 'em all!" (130). Blanch accepts that this man was what he now only pretends to be, just as Osberg does. Perhaps they are right that the film makes this claim: Parry's madness is rooted in who he was before his trauma, in an adoption of what he studied as a new code for how he will live. But the film does not actually support that position with the Stockbroker Bum any more than it supports Parry's being a knight before his trauma (rather than simply studying them), or HCS's being a woman rather than merely playing one on stage. The scene involving the Stockbroker Bum invokes the world of finance with which the film is much concerned, but it does so parodically and subversively: the idea of buying and selling and the attachment to the dead telephone have no greater claim to the character's back story than Parry's insistence that his profession is the rescue of the miserable. However, Osberg asks an interesting question: "It is hard to know if his job has driven him mad, or if his job was itself a kind of madness" (214). If it is the former, it is the film's only example of the world of the yuppie causing madness, rather than that of the world being disrupted by a sudden explosion of unexpected violence. If it is the latter, it clearly does participate in the film's critique of the modern world of finance—but that remains true whether the Stockbroker Bum was a stockbroker or a teacher in his former life. It is an odd indicator that all commentators agree that the film is concerned with the disconnection of word and image, but still take the film's visual semiotics at face value.

Osberg's question is better directed to Jeter's HCS, because it can then illuminate the film's attitude to madness, reality and liberty (questions which help further place this film within Gilliam's overall *œuvre*). To paraphrase, then: "It is hard to know if performing in drag cabarets has driven him mad, or if singing in drag was itself a kind of madness." The two decades following Fisher King have seen a growing tolerance of various forms of gender play and for trans communities, and that might make it difficult for us to see what the film is saying about HCS. Clearly, the lifestyle of HCS is meant to explain his/her situation, and it appears to be somewhere on the dissociation spectrum, but s/he is kept out of the central male binary of Jack/Parry. The Iron John mythos has no final place for the androgynous, although the film is broadly sympathetic to the character on an individual level. Like Edwin, HCS disappears from the film, having fulfilled a necessary role in the progression of the protagonists.

There is a third Fisher King in the film: Carmichael, the old man whose grade-school Christmas pageant prize is Parry's Grail. Carmichael's life is saved when Jack breaks into his fortress-like house—it is actually an Armory on New York's Upper East Side—to steal the cup, finds him unconscious, and deliberately sets off the alarm to summon help. The viewer sees a *New York Post* headline which reads: "Accidental Suicide Thwarted by Night Prowler"—it is telling that we now get an image of a newspaper prior to its being reduced to floating paper, at a moment when it is needed to tie off a narrative line. The alarm line is predictably a bright red line across the front doors, which would be unremarkable in a film that did not also have a Red Knight riding violently around in it: in effect, Jack embraces the "red" to stop a trauma from happening, at which point the film begins to wind up its vision of madness. The red line of light is meant to protect Carmichael, and in fact does so, although not in the way he or its creators intended. The color that has thus far represented violence and death suddenly stands for life. It seems plausible to conclude that the film's real Fisher King is neither Parry nor Jack, but Carmichael, the only vaguely authoritative figure in the film, albeit one whose visual semiotics are suspect: a Grail that is not a Grail, a house disguised as a castle (or a castle which pretends to be a house). The most compelling point of contact between the film and its distant medieval source material might be architectural as well as thematic: like Jack, Perceval gave up hope and faith following his initial failure at the Grail castle (Chrétien, *Perceval* 456–458). Knowing that he cannot abandon Carmichael despite the fact he is committing a crime, Jack asks the right question: the ringing siren that summons assistance.

In turn, Parry can ask his "right question" after he drinks from the stolen Grail. He wakes up from his coma and remembers his wife in the scene following the theft of the Grail, asking Jack if he can begin to miss her. Whether this question is a sign that Parry is sane again is inconclusive: he still remembers this period in his life as a dream, and soon goes back to leading a chorus of the marginalized in a hospital rendition of "How About You" and running naked in the park (now with Jack participating). Parry will be easier for society to handle, which may indicate that his madness is simply less troubling than it was before. The film ends with a display of fireworks over New York, a vision no more likely to be real than that of the Red Knight. Gilliam's persistent theme—the power of the imagination—does not easily facilitate an answer to the question of sanity/insanity; what was once behavior associated with Parry's trauma now takes the benevolent form of embracing whimsy: as Stukator puts it, "Parry functions as Jack's mentor; through Parry Jack is initiated into play, imagination, and energy, and thus the means to heal his wounds" (217).

The resolution of the film's tensions occurs most directly in Jack's story, not Parry's. While Jack may or may not return to the world of the media following the film's climax, he will do so with his love for both Anne and Parry acknowledged as part of his new life. What on first glance appears to be happy symbolism—two men heal each other—is undermined by a few things. One is the previously-discussed dismissal of Edwin's pain and eventual fate, as well as the deaths of those fourteen people: are there not several Parrys potentially out there? Do only medievalists have the imaginative capacity to fall so far into trauma that they need ancient symbols to help them get out? If the film's message is that negative acts have unforeseen consequences, those consequences themselves must have consequences. The film's

Grail cannot heal everyone and everything, and indeed this failure that pretends to be resolution begins to point not to healing but to redirection of dissociative tendencies: we need our illusions to sustain us, like water from a cup.

A discussion thread the online film site IMDb asks whether Parry is sane at the end of the film. The answer is that the film does not really know nor care. If anything, Jack seems to have gone happily mad himself. Gilliam's entire *œuvre* has been dedicated to the problem of the individual eccentric struggling to survive in societies which are oppressive in one way or another, with the most common oppressive pattern being the disparity between haves and have-nots. *The Fisher King* ultimately posits that madness is perhaps inevitable, and beneficial if it adds whimsy to the world: and yet, the Red Knight is visually stunning. Something beautiful has come from the tragic series of events initiated by Jack and Edwin, and the fireworks explode over the city both to celebrate that fact and to forget those who have been lost along the way.

Works Cited

Blanch, Robert J. "The Fisher King in Gotham: New Age Spiritualism Meets the Grail Legend." In Harty, 123–140.

Blumstein, Andree Kahn. "The Structure and Function of the Cundrie Episodes in Wolfram's *Parzival*." *The German Quarterly* 51 (March 1978): 160–169.

Butler, Lisa D., and Oxana Palesh. "Spellbound: Dissociation in the Movies." *Journal of Trauma & Dissociation* 5.2 (2004): 61–87.

Chrétien de Troyes, *Arthurian Romances*. Trans. and ed. D. D. R. Owen. 1987; rpt. and rev. London: J. M. Dent, 1993.

Doob, Penelope B. R. *Nebuchadnezzar's Children: Conventions of Madness in Middle English Literature.* New Haven: Yale University Press, 1974.

Edwards, Elizabeth. *The Genesis of Narrative in Malory's* Morte Darthur. Cambridge, Eng.: D. S. Brewer, 2001.

Foucault, Michel. *Psychiatric Power: Lectures at the Collège de France, 1973–74*. Trans. Graham Burchell. New York: Picador, 2006.

Gilliam, Terry, dir. *The Fisher King*. TriStar Pictures, 1991.

Harty, Kevin J., ed. *King Arthur on Film: New Essays on Arthurian Cinema*. Jefferson, NC: McFarland, 1999.

Hertzberg, Hendrik. "Onward and Upward with the Arts: Naughty Bits." *New Yorker* 29 March 1976: 69–70.

Hughes, Jonathan. *Arthurian Myths and Alchemy: The Kingship of Edward IV.* Stroud, Gloucestershire: Sutton, 2002.

Klosowska, Anna. *Queer Love in the Middle Ages.* New York: Palgrave Macmillan, 2005.

Larsen, Darl. *Monty Python, Shakespeare and English Renaissance Drama.* Jefferson, NC: McFarland, 2003.

Lerer, Seth. *Chaucer and His Readers.* Princeton: Princeton University Press, 1993.

Malory, Thomas. *Works*. Ed. Eugène Vinaver. 2nd edition. Oxford: Oxford University Press, 1971.

Miller, Barbara D. "'Cinemagicians': Movie Merlins of the 1980s and 1990s." In Harty, 141–166.

Osberg, Richard H. "Pages Torn from the Book: Narrative Disintegration in Gilliam's *The Fisher King*." *Studies in Medievalism* 7 (1995): 194–224.

Osberg, Richard H., and Michael E. Crow. "Language Then and Language Now in Arthurian Film." In Harty, 39–66.

Pirie, Chris. "Gilliam the Snake Charmer." http://www.smart.co.uk/dreams/cpirie02.htm. Accessed 4 June 2013.

Rickey, Carrie. "Mercedes Ruehl Spiraling Toward Fame She Has Won a Tony and an Obie. Now, There's Talk of an Oscar for Her Work in 'The Fisher King.'" Philly.com. http://articles.philly.com/1991–

09–29/entertainment/25801864_1_anne-napolitano-mercedes-ruehl-roz-russell. Accessed 5 June 2013.

Rushton, Cory James. "The King's Stupor: Dealing with Royal Paralysis in Late Medieval England." In *Madness in Medieval Law and Custom*. Ed. Wendy J. Turner. Leiden: Brill, 2010.

Stubbs, Phil. "Dreams: The Fisher King." http://www.smart.co.uk/dreams/fkprod1.htm. Accessed 4 June 2013.

Stukator, Angela. "'Soft Males,' 'Flying Boys,' and 'White Knights': New Masculinity in *The Fisher King*." *Literature/Film Quarterly* 25.3 (1997): 214–221.

A Son, His Father, Some Nazis
and the Grail: Lucas and Spielberg's
Indiana Jones and the Last Crusade

Joseph M. Sullivan

While strolling along the beach during a Hawaiian vacation in May 1977, George Lucas and Steven Spielberg had a discussion that would result in one of the most successful collaborations in recent Hollywood history. Following Lucas's vision for a film project "based on the serials I loved when I was a kid: action movies set in exotic locales with a cliffhanger every second" (Taylor 104), the two men would go on in the course of the next twelve years to create the highly successful series of *Indiana Jones* films including 1981's *Indiana Jones and the Raiders of the Lost Ark*, 1984's *Indiana Jones and the Temple of Doom*, and the subject of this essay, a film in which the Holy Grail figures as a major element, 1989's *Indiana Jones and the Last Crusade*.[1]

While in the quarter century that has passed since the completion of the first three installments of the series,[2] *Indy I*—that is, *Raiders*—arguably has come to occupy the primary place in the public's imagination as the jewel in the series' crown; at the time of *The Last Crusade*'s release, a quite sizeable proportion of reviewers echoed sentiments similar to that of a reviewer for *The Times* of London who judged *Indy III* as "probably the best written and generally most accomplished of the series" (Robinson, "Good old-fashioned fun").

Absolutely central to the success both critically and financially of *The Last Crusade*—with the movie's opening-weekend receipts of $46.9 million, for example, setting a record for premiers (Baxter 348)—was its ingenious use of the Grail as its "MacGuffin," that is, as the device that drives the story. It will be the main purpose of this essay to demonstrate that Lucas and Spielberg employ their Grail primarily as a device that is not so important in and of itself. Rather, they use the Grail as a means-to-an-end, one whose attainment stands metaphorically for the film's most important theme, namely the quest of a son for, and reconciliation with, a distant father. I also will attempt to show how the filmmakers' inclusion of a highly developed father figure for Indiana Jones contributed to the success of the film.

Lucas and Spielberg's Grail

Like the cleverly constructed, entertaining, but ultimately superficial Indiana Jones character that Harrison Ford portrays, the Grail that shares center stage with him and his *Indy III* father, Dr. Henry Jones, Sr., is a quite appealing, cleverly constructed, if not particularly profound creation on the part of the filmmakers.

As the suave but traitorous American industrialist Walter Donovan explains to Indy when he first tries to recruit the hero to find the Grail, the vessel which Indy's father, a professor of medieval literature, has dedicated his life to studying is none other than "The chalice used by Christ during the Last Supper. The cup that caught His blood at the Crucifixion and was entrusted to Joseph of Arimathea."[3] At its most basic level, then, *Indy III*'s Grail, as a chalice associated with Joseph and the Passion, accords with what is perhaps the most widely known understanding of the Grail in popular culture, which in turn seems to have been first articulated by Robert de Boron in his early–thirteenth-century Old French *Le Roman du Graal.*

Past this point, however, George Lucas and Steven Spielberg's Grail departs from any definitively identifiable source. Thus, in Jeffrey Boam's screenplay, the Grail becomes the "Carpenter's Cup," with a golden and lustrous interior but a gray, dull, and thoroughly plain outer surface. Further, the filmmakers put the Grail in the care of an ancient knight, the last of three brothers who, during the First Crusade, rediscovered the Grail and dedicated their lives to its preservation. Under the old knight's watch, the Grail now resides deep inside a secluded cave-like Grail temple in the canyon of the Crescent Moon in the fictional present-day Republic of Hatay. Along with this True Grail, the temple is populated by a large number of False Grails, consisting of gold and silver chalices and a number of luminous serving plates.

The Grail's most important attribute in *The Last Crusade* is its ability to bestow eternal life. In this sense, it is akin to both the Grail of the first preserved medieval Grail romance, namely, Chrétien de Troyes' circa 1191 *Perceval, The Story of the Grail*, and even more clearly to the Middle High German retelling of Chrétien's *Perceval*, that is, Wolfram of Eschenbach's Middle High German masterpiece, *Parzival*, from about 1210. Thus in *Perceval*, the Fisher King's old father has been kept alive the past twelve years by a consecrated host he receives regularly from the Grail. And in Wolfram's *Parzival*, it is the Fisher King's grandfather and the first Grail knight, the ancient Titurel, who, because he gazes on the Grail stone, cannot die. Despite such similarity between these Perceval/Parzival romances and *The Last Crusade*, however, there is no indication that Chrétien or Wolfram or any other author of a medieval Grail romance directly influenced the filmmakers in the formulation of their own Grail. Instead, the decision to make the Grail a source of eternal life seems to have been a rather spur-of-the moment one that Lucas proposed to make the Grail idea more appealing to a reluctant Spielberg, who has remarked, "I had always associated it [i.e., the Grail] with Monty Python" (Freer 171) and "I didn't think that was a very exciting MacGuffin" (*Last Crusade* DVD Commentary). Thus Lucas, as Spielberg recollects, suggested: "Hey, why don't say, if you drink from the cup you have everlasting life. It's the fountain of youth." In Lucas's final formulation, then, *Indy III*'s Grail can bestow eternal life, but, as the old knight warns, "the False Grail will take it [i.e., life] from you."

As we eventually learn when Donovan, German archaeologist Dr. Elsa Schneider, Indy, and his father enter the Grail building, moreover, the Grail not only bestows eternal youth, but it also heals. When Donovan shoots his father, Indy saves Henry Sr. by pouring the water he has scooped into the Grail from a baptismal-like font into his father's mouth and directly onto his father's bullet wounds, thereby fully restoring the elder Jones to health.

While it took considerable time for the filmmakers, and especially Spielberg, to come around to using the Grail as the MacGuffin that would drive *Indy III*, the public's positive reception of the film, and of the Grail story at its heart, proved that hard-won choice to have been a good one. Indeed, we might observe that the Grail represented for Lucas, Spielberg, main screenwriter Boam, and Boam's collaborator in writing the script, Menno Meyjes, an ideal motif around which to base their story.[4] While the Grail is certainly one of the most known and attractive icons in the popular imagination, the public's knowledge of exactly what it looks like, what properties it has, and what it stands for symbolically is, arguably, quite ambiguous. Most viewers would come to *The Last Crusade*, therefore, with only a vague notion of the Grail as perhaps a chalice-like cup imbued with some mysterious aura. The filmmakers, as a result, would have a most elastic device that they could modify and augment as they wished, and upon which they could graph almost any story and larger theme they cared to—which is, of course, exactly what they did. More specifically, the filmmakers allowed the artifact to retreat into the background behind the larger story arc it supported, namely, the quest of a son for his father. As Lucas has expressed it: "The film is about a father and son finding one another, rather than going after some specific thing [i.e., the Grail]. They find the Grail in each other" (Woodward 1).

Additionally, in choosing the Grail as *Indy III*'s MacGuffin, the filmmakers selected a symbol particularly in tune with the contemporaneous state of American society and popular culture. The late 1980s and early 1990s saw, importantly, the sudden rise of that loose movement encompassing holistic healing, a revival of mysticism, and non-denominational spirituality known as New Age. The Grail, as vessel in the public imagination for vague notions of spirituality, timelessness, and regeneration thus epitomized many of the ideals that large portions of society and, contestably, potential members of the *Indy III* audience had begun to embrace so enthusiastically.[5] It is thus perhaps unsurprising that the Grail as metaphor for the healing of a son's relationship with his father found such resonance among the film's viewership.

The Grail in the Context of Other Artifacts in the Indy Cycle

Let us now turn our attention briefly to the use of artifacts in the *Indiana Jones* films and how *Indy III*'s Grail conforms to, and departs from, the typical contours of those objects. While each of the cycle's first three installments features a minor artifact that figures in the action before the main story begins—including a golden godhead idol in *Indy I*, the remains of Emperor Nurhachi in *Indy II*, and the Cross of Coronado in *Indy III*—a main artifact in each film actually serves as the picture's MacGuffin around which the central story revolves. Thus, just as the Grail provides a point of departure for the main narrative action in *The*

Last Crusade, so too do the Ark of the Covenant in *Raiders* and the Sankara Stones in *Temple of Doom*. A common property of each of these main artifacts, furthermore, is its connection with the Divine. For instance, just as the Sankara Stones are associated with Hinduism and the god Shiva and the Ark with the Hebrew God, the Grail is intimately connected to the Christian Jesus.

Common to all three primary artifacts of the *Indiana Jones* movies is their awesome power. Thus the artifacts, at least in *Indy II* and *III*, hold the potential to work tremendous good. In *The Temple of Doom*, for instance, the Sankara Stone held by an Indian village ensures the welfare of that community, which falls into poverty and chaos when the stone is taken from it. And in *The Last Crusade*, the Grail's main attribute is its ability to bestow everlasting life. Despite such substantial positive qualities, however, it is the artifacts' destructive powers that the films devote their time to illustrating. For instance, as Indy notes of the Ark in *Raiders*, the Bible speaks of that object "laying waste, leveling entire regions. An army which carries the Ark before it is invincible." Similarly, in *The Temple of Doom*, the evil Goddess "Kali Ma will rule the world" if the nefarious Thuggee cult succeeds in its sinister intent of bringing together all five Sankara Stones. And, finally, in *The Last Crusade*, Henry Jones, Sr., warns of the fearsome power the Grail would manifest in the hands of evildoers: "If it is captured by the Nazis, the armies of darkness will march over the face of the Earth."

In all three films, as well, the artifact works ultimately to destroy those who "seek secular gain, whether monetary profit, governmental dominance, or personal power" (Friedman 83). In *Temple*, for example, the Thuggee priest Mola Ram plunges to his death while trying to prevent one of the Sankara Stones from falling into a river and becoming irretrievably lost. And in *Raiders*, the Nazi villains who pursue the Ark are incinerated in spectacular fashion by the powers emitted from that artifact when it is opened toward the end of the film. Finally, in *Indy III*, the traitorous Donovan, selfishly pursuing at all costs eternal life, perishes after he drinks from a False Grail. We might note also that the artifacts function as objects of desire that typically elicit impure motives in both negative and more positive characters. For example, in *Raiders* and *Temple*, the mostly positive Indiana's search for the Ark and the Sankara Stones seems more motivated by the pursuit of fortune and glory than a moral responsibility to keep those items from falling into the wrong hands. However, with *The Last Crusade*, the filmmakers depart from this formula. While negative characters like the greedy Donovan are still motivated by evil intent, Indiana Jones, most importantly, is driven in his search for the Grail solely by his concern for others. Thus he only agrees to Donovan's offer that he undertake the search when, while visiting his kidnapped father's ransacked house, he glimpses a decades-old picture of himself as a child next to the older Jones. Indeed, Indiana's search from the beginning is not one for the Grail but quite literally one for his father, who has disappeared mysteriously while searching for Grail clues in Venice. As Susan Aronstein has noted, for Indy, "the search for the father and the search for the Grail are one and the same" (21). Thus, for instance, Indy informs one of his pursuers who asks why he seeks the Grail, "I didn't come for the Cup of Christ; I came to find my father."

Other characteristics of the Grail in *Indy III* are also typical of the primary artifacts from the other *Indy* films. Thus all the artifacts reside within protected sanctuaries. Just as the Grail, for instance, is maintained in a grotto-like temple,[6] the Sankara Stone that is looted from an Indian village in *Temple of Doom* had previously resided in a primitive shrine at the heart of that community. Similarly, the Ark has lain for centuries safe and undisturbed within the subterranean Well of Souls in the city of Tanis. Further, sacred and ancient texts provide the necessary clues to find and understand each of the artifacts. In *Indy I*, for instance, the Bible provides the primary information requisite to comprehending the nature of the Ark, and it is a long-forgotten model of Tanis, buried under centuries of sand in an underground map room, that pinpoints the exact location within that city of the Well of Souls. In like fashion, in *Indy II*, a scrap from an illuminated manuscript confirms for the hero that the artifact he will pursue is indeed a Sankara Stone. And, finally, in *Indy III*, an illuminated Old French codex compiled by a Franciscan friar discusses how the Grail came to rest where it currently lies, and two mid–twelfth-century sandstone tablets inscribed in Latin—one unearthed near Ankara, Turkey, by Donovan's engineers and one eventually found by Indy in the Venetian catacombs within the sarcophagus of one of the three brother knights who had found the Grail—hold the clues to where the Grail temple lies.

While the filmmakers' elaboration of the Grail, the Sankara Stones, and the Ark as well as the steps necessary to attain them seem to have succeeded in entertaining the audience and holding its attention—especially in the cases of *Indy I* and *Indy III*—their treatment of those artifacts is, nevertheless, uniformly quite superficial. As one *Last Crusade* reviewer noted, recalling also how shallow the exploration of the Ark in *Raiders* had been, "Also predictable is the film's [i.e., *Indy III*'s] simplistic treatment of themes from religion and myth" (Sterritt 11). Indeed, we may observe that the filmmakers touch on the origins and the possible religious and cultural significance of the Grail and their other artifacts only to the quite limited extent that such exploration of deeper meaning serves to drive the narrative action and entertain viewers.

The Bad Guys Audiences Love to Hate: The Nazis

With *Indy III*, we find Lucas and Spielberg reprising from *Raiders of the Lost Ark* as their most visible villains the Nazis, a group for which, at least at the time of *Indy III*'s release, there seems to have existed no societal taboo against stereotyping or vilifying.[7] In *The Last Crusade*'s depiction of its National Socialist characters, the filmmakers deploy many of the same general strategies they use to establish real or imagined national identity throughout the *Indiana Jones* cycle, with visual cues representing their most important tools. Thus the color palette of red, black, and white is visible whenever the filmmakers want to suggest Nazi presence. Not only is it the color combination of the uniforms of the SS officers who seek the Grail for the Third Reich, with their black uniforms adorned with prominent red-white-and-black armbands, but it is also the color palette of the many Nazi flags and pieces of regalia that the camera homes in on throughout the film, including the tail fins of the zeppelin—the iconic Nazi means of transportation *par excellence*—with which Indy and Henry Sr. make their escape from Berlin, "through wild Nazistan"[8] (Kilb 56), and into the Republic of Hatay. The weaponry of the German soldiers similarly leaves no doubt that they are Nazis. Thus Spielberg and Lucas equip them primarily with the P08 Luger pistols and flashy MP 40 "Schmeisser" submachine guns so stereotypical of Third Reich soldiers in 1940s Hollywood movies rather than with the more mundane rifles that were the standard weapons issue for most German soldiers from 1933 to 1945. While the filmmakers depart, therefore, to some degree from absolute fidelity to historical accuracy—for example, sometimes dressing their 1938 German soldiers in uniform items that did not appear until the war had actually commenced—we nevertheless see in the equipping and costuming of Nazi soldiers that tremendous attention to detail that is the hallmark of almost all films that Spielberg has directed, and which in his later films handling National Socialist Germany in a more serious manner, including especially *Schindler's List* (1993), would add historical credibility to his depiction of German soldiers.

The visual is similarly at work in the filmmakers' portrayal of German archaeologist Dr. Elsa Schneider. Played by tall, red-headed Alison Doody, Lucas and Spielberg not only had her speak with a German accent but also changed her hair color to blond (James, *The Advertiser*), thus transforming her visually into the Hollywood stereotype of Aryan womanhood.

Apart from Elsa Schneider, who in any case is not truly committed to the Nazi cause and thus does not fully embody the Nazi menace that is so central to the *Indy III* storyline, Nazi characters in *The Last Crusade* undergo no character development. They are, in fact, rather one-dimensional, comic-strip–like figures that conform, once again, to a Hollywood stereotype of, in the words of Henry Jones, Sr., the "goose-stepping moron." Indeed, SS Colonel Vogel, the Nazi heavy of *The Last Crusade*, like his counterpart in *Raiders*, the leather-trench-coat–wearing Gestapo agent Toht, cuts a menacing but ridiculous figure. Thus both men are petty in their love for cruelty, with Colonel Vogel, for instance, at one point slapping Jones Sr. repeatedly with his stereotypically Nazi black leather gloves. Moreover, with their rather creepy screen voices, both Nazi characters come across in their vocalizations as mincing and wormy. Finally, and as if to suggest visually that Colonel Vogel is a man of towering import in his mind alone, the filmmakers show him early on, during Indy's freeing of his father from an Austrian castle, standing side-by-side with Elsa Schneider and appearing a full head shorter than she, a woman.

In *The Last Crusade*, then, as in *Raiders* before it, Nazi villains appeal to the "near–90s taste of turning Nazis into pulp-comic baddies" (Clark 1D). Indeed, reviewers at the time *Indy III* appeared recognized that the filmmakers intended their Nazis simply to represent generic "bad guys" (Cullen, *Hobart Mercury*), to appear "nasty" (James, *The Advertiser*), and to be "good for a laugh ... as the height of sneering evil" (Partridge, *Courier-Mail*). In other words, the filmmakers chose not to explore the complexity of the actual historical Nazi evil with their own, cartoonish film–Nazis but rather to let them stand in for a kind of general, vague badness to contrast with the inherent goodness of the Grail. As Indy explains to Elsa at a Nazi rally in Berlin—which he attends to recover his father's Grail diary, a detailed record of Henry Jones, Sr.'s Grail research—the Nazis "are the enemy of everything the Grail stands for."

At that same Berlin Nazi Party rally, the filmmakers put the Nazis truly on stage. Replete with martial music, black-white-and-red swastika flags, marching troops, brown-shirted SA members, a dais upon which sit Hitler, Göring, Himmler, and Goebbels, and even a book-burning, the sequence is, in its visual opulence, as impressive as the chorus sequence in a Shanghai nightclub that had opened *Indy III*'s predecessor, *Temple of Doom*. In the midst of the rally, Indy, having just retaken his father's Grail diary from Elsa, bumps dumbfoundedly into none other than Adolf Hitler himself. Der Führer, evidently the ultimate media star in the fictional world of *Indy III* and in a moment that conforms to recent cinema's propensity to highlight the "lighter side of fascism,"[9] takes the diary from Indiana's hands and personally autographs it.

While a very small proportion of reviewers objected to the nonchalant way in which the film presented the Nazis and twentieth-century Europe's most maniacal leader—with, for instance, *The Jerusalem Post* criticizing this "totally gratuitous appearance by Der Fuehrer" and deeming it "particularly inexcusable to use his presence simply to deliver a lame joke" (Ben-David, "Raiders of the Old Scripts")—what is even more noteworthy is that the overwhelming majority of reviewers found nothing objectionable in the filmmakers' presentation of this scene or of Nazi characters anywhere in *The Last Crusade*. Obviously, the filmmakers had calculated correctly in assuming that few among their audience would object either to them lampooning the Nazis or even to them making the Nazi leader a vehicle to elicit laughter. In a larger sense, the success of the filmmakers' gamble points to the fact that, by the 1980s, the Nazis had simply become a very safe group to criticize and, indeed, even to make fun of, with little chance of offending a sizeable portion of the potential audience. As Spielberg has noted, "It was always fun to pick on the Nazis, because you've sort of got a get-out-of-jail-free card when the Nazis were the villains" (*Last Crusade* DVD Commentary).

A Nazi Grail?

Given the amount of time the filmmakers allow Nazi characters to appear on screen and the sizeable role they allot the Nazis to stand for a kind of generic evil in *The Last Crusade*, it is perhaps surprising that they did not associate the Grail itself and the search to find it closer with the Nazis. While, with *Raiders of the Lost Ark*, the filmmakers made such a connection between the Nazis and the Ark—with a representative of the U.S. Army intelligence agency announcing that "the Nazis have had teams of archaeologists running all over the world looking for religious artifacts" and that Hitler "is obsessed with the occult"—*Indy III* conspicuously contains no such reference to Hitler's desire to find one of the world's great religious artifacts. The fact that Hitler and members of his inner circle, in particular SS chief Heinrich Himmler, were actually engaged in searching for the Grail and establishing a fellowship of blood around it has become fairly well known in popular culture in the last decade-and-a-half, especially since the broadcast of British historian Michael Wood's 1999 television documentary *Hitler's Search for the Holy Grail*.[10] However, at the time the story was developed for *The Last Crusade*, the Nazis' interest in the Grail was not generally known among the broad public. In any case, even if Lucas, Spielberg, or screenwriter Boam had in the late 1980s any idea of the National Socialists' very real interest in the Grail—for which there seems to be no indication in anything they have said about the film since—they evidently chose not to exploit that interest in any meaningful way for *Indy III*, foregoing the opportunity to present a Nazi Grail.[11]

A Villain, a Rival, a Son and a Father

While the Nazis may represent the embodiment of true evil in *The Last Crusade*, they are not, collectively, the film's ultimate villain, a role that is instead fulfilled by British actor Julian Glover's Walter Donovan character. In making the rich, cultured American industrialist Indiana's primary enemy at the expense of the Nazis, the filmmakers followed a formula that they had previously employed in *Raiders of the Lost Ark*. As Lucas notes for the whole series, "We worked really hard to create great villains" (*Last Crusade* DVD Commentary), and for both *Raiders* and *Last Crusade*, that meant going with two types of villains. "What the Nazis do," according to *Raiders* screenwriter Lawrence Kasdan, "is they're an all-purpose backup" to the main villain (*Last Crusade* DVD Commentary). The more important villain, which Spielberg terms the "champagne-villain" (*Last Crusade* DVD Commentary) and who also represents Indiana's main enemy in *Indy I* and *Indy III*, is characterized by his urbanity and intelligence. In *Raiders*, rival archaeologist René Belloq—a polyglot master of the Native-American language Hovitos, English, German, and his own French—fills that role, and in *Last Crusade*, Donovan. That the refined, polished Donovan, in his lust for the Grail, chooses to collaborate with the Nazis—and, as Indiana expresses it, to become "a Nazi Stooge"—serves to illustrate just how corrupted his morality has become.

In the end, it is Donovan's greed that gets the best of him and indicts his character. Intent on securing for himself everlasting life, he drinks, based on its gaudy opulence, from a False Grail that he believes is the True Grail. Declaring it "the cup of the King of Kings," the water Donovan drinks from it causes his death. In similar fashion to *Raiders'* Toht, whose face melts away quite spectacularly when he beholds the Ark, Donovan's eyes bulge, his facial features writhe, and he ages instantly in a sequence that was technically trailblazing at the time, and which took the Lucas Light and Sound Company over three months to bring to the screen (Kaplan 9).

While the unscrupulous American Donovan is Indiana's true enemy in *Crusade*, the role of his rival falls to a woman and a German, the archaeologist Elsa Schneider. Although her blondness and Teutonic accent mark her as a German, Elsa is only half-committed to the Nazis for whom she works. Thus, when we see her at the party rally in Berlin, Elsa appears visibly crestfallen and disturbed by the seductively evil pageantry she has just witnessed. And when Indy confronts Elsa there and takes the Grail diary from her, she offers no resistance and remarks tellingly, "I believed in the Grail, not the swastika." Indeed, Elsa engages with the Nazis only to forward her own career as an archaeologist. In putting her ambition before political scruple, Elsa is, in fact, clearly intended as a mirror-figure for Indy, who also—especially in the first two *Indiana Jones* installments—is motivated in his own search for artifacts by less-than-always-fully-honorable reasons, including career ambition and monetary gain.

In her own career ambition, intelligence, and sexual prowess—this "real Mata Hari," in

Spielberg's words (*Last Crusade* DVD Commentary), seduces both Henry Jr. and Henry Sr.—Elsa is not only a cleverly drawn counterpart to Indiana but also a true departure from the female figures of the two earlier *Indiana Jones* movies. As many critics and reviewers have noted of the female leads up to *Indy III*, "Women have been given short shrift in the boy's own world of the *Indy* trilogy" (Fuller 31). Indeed, from Karen Allen's role as Indiana's female sidekick and erstwhile love interest, Marion, in *Raiders* to the annoying "screeching wimpette of a heroine" (Sutton 40) Willy Scott, whom Kate Capshaw portrayed in *Temple of Doom*, the female figures before Doody's Elsa Schneider character contributed little to the arc of the story.[12] With Elsa, however, the filmmakers created a figure not only who in the closeness of her personality to Indiana served to illuminate his own ambivalent character but also who was interesting and heavily involved in the story in her own right.

If Elsa has a negative side, she is only slightly darker than her mirror-figure, Indiana, has been throughout the series. Indeed, her death trying to fish the Grail out of the crevice she herself then falls into is almost repeated exactly by Indy, who gives up trying to retrieve the Grail from that crevice only when his father pleads with him, "Indiana, let it go." Thus Indy learns that the career ambition that characterizes Elsa and that had marked him up to now throughout the entire cycle should not rule his actions. That realization, however, coming as it does at the end of the last movie of the original *Indiana Jones* trilogy, has been a long time coming for this very imperfect hero.

Indeed, up to this point in *Indy III* and throughout both *Indy I* and *II*, the Indiana Jones character had been anything but an ideal hero, a fact that often has eluded audiences, reviewers, and critics who have tended to see in the larger-than-life Jones a character far more perfect and exemplary of idealized American values than the filmmakers intended him to appear. As George Lucas has commented, from the very beginning on that Hawaiian beach where he first pitched his idea to Spielberg, he imagined "Indiana Jones as this kind of fallen archaeologist" (*Raiders* DVD Commentary). And of the Indiana who actually materialized out of that original vision and strode the screen in all three *Indiana Jones* films of the 1980s, Lucas has observed: "Indiana has never been a particularly moral person.... He has a very nefarious side to him" (Woodward 1). Indeed, Lester D. Friedman is certainly correct in his conclusion that "Indiana Jones is an ineffective and largely unsuccessful figure, one not particularly well suited to hoist the banner of American manhood triumphantly aloft" (113).

In *The Last Crusade*, while Indy does in fact triumph in his quest to find the Grail, it is perhaps indicative of their intention to represent their hero as imperfect that the filmmakers do not closely align his personality with that of a knight. The closest the filmmakers come to doing so is when the old knight guarding the Grail explains to Indy how he came to be in the Grail temple: "I was chosen because I was the bravest, the most worthy. The honor was mine until another came to challenge me to single combat." Acknowledging that Indy is that individual, he then hands his sword "to you [i.e., Indy] who vanquished me." Indiana, however, gives no indication that he intends to become the knight-guardian of the Grail. And, indeed, he even tries to remove the cup from the Grail sanctuary, despite the fact that the old knight has told him that is not permissible to take the Grail past the "Great Seal" near the entry to the sanctuary. In the end, it is only the impassioned words of his father that convince a wavering Indy to leave the Grail to rest in the ruins of the sanctuary built expressively for it.[13]

Not only are Henry Sr.'s words instrumental in saving his son's life and in thereby helping Indy in what was then this final film of the series to overcome his excessive ambitions to retrieve artifacts at nearly any cost,[14] but also the elder Jones's presence is responsible for giving the entire film a depth and audience appeal that it otherwise certainly would not have had. Indeed, along with the Grail and, arguably, the pre-credit prequel that portrays Indy's youth, the presence of Indiana's father is among the three items that give *The Last Crusade* its unique character among the first three films of the *Indiana Jones* cycle, and which led to the film's critical and financial success.

Part of the appeal to the audience certainly lay in the fact that the father's strained relationship to his son as an adolescent—as depicted in the pre-credit prequel—provided a backstory to Indiana's own story, allowing the audience the pleasure of discovering and decoding how Indiana got to be the way he is an adult, including his love for learning and his broken idealism. But in a larger sense, what registered most with *Indy III*'s audience was the human element that the father-son relationship brought to a series that, in its first two

Grail Knights medieval and modern, Robert Eddison (left) and Harrison Ford as Indiana Jones in Steven Spielberg's 1989 film *Indiana Jones and the Last Crusade.*

installments and following the conventions of the "B-movie adventure serial format," had "focus[ed] on outward physical actions (especially violence) rather than the inner life of the characters" (Buckland 132). As the reviewer for the Australian *Sunday Tasmanian* remarked, "The scenes between Ford and Connery give *The Last Crusade* the most heart of the trilogy" (Stuart, "Review"), and as a reviewer for *USA Today* observed, in contrast to the first two films, *Indy III* "turns out to be humanistic and benign" (Clark 1D).

The choice specifically of Sean Connery to play Indiana's father also proved key to the film's popularity among audiences. Legendary *New York Times* movie reviewer Vincent Canby captured the sentiment of a majority of his colleagues when he remarked that for the movie's success "[t]he secret ingredient is Sean Connery" (15). But while North American reviewers were quite enthusiastic about Connery, it was especially their overseas counterparts who valued his performance, with, for instance, Sydney's *The Sun Herald* typical in observing that putting Connery in the role of Henry Jones, Sr., was "the casting coup of the century" (Lowing 118). While Spielberg and Lucas have never said anything that would indicate they cast Connery in order to help sell *Indy III* abroad, it seems reasonable to assume that overseas marketability, at a time in the late 1980s when Hollywood was just starting to think about producing films for a truly global cinema market,[15] might have been a factor in their selecting Connery. As *The New York Times* noted, "Sean Connery is a good actor to Americans, but a superstar to the rest of the world" (Harmetz, "Movies Look Abroad" 13). And that the film did, in fact, earn much more overseas ($297 million) than domestically ($197 million) undoubtedly had at least something to do with Connery's star power among foreign audiences.[16]

Although Connery ultimately proved an inspired casting decision, he was interestingly not an automatic choice to play the father. In fact, George Lucas envisioned Indiana's dad as an older individual than Connery and more of a retiring "scholar like Joe [i.e., Joseph] Campbell" (Woodward 1), a role he thought best played by an actor in the mold of John Houseman (Freer 173). It was Spielberg, however, who proposed Connery, after having been particularly impressed by his Oscar-winning performance (for best actor in a supporting role) as Jim Malone in 1987's *The Untouchables* (Smith 180 and Cullen, "Review"). Lucas at first objected, recalling later that "I thought he [i.e., Connery] was too formidable a figure for the character as he was written" (Woodward 1). He eventually relented, however, after Spielberg reminded him that, upon that beach in 1977 where they had first discussed the *Indiana Jones* project, a James Bond–type character was their original vision for the hero who would go on to be played by Harrison Ford. That the original movie–Bond, Sean Connery, might now play in a film series inspired by the James Bond movies was too inviting an opportunity to pass up. As Spielberg remembers telling Lucas, with the casting of Connery as the elder Jones, "James Bond [i.e., Sean Connery] really is Indiana Jones' father" (*Last Crusade* DVD Commentary).

Connery's casting also would prove critical for a major expansion in the scope of the father's part. When he received his script, Connery was reportedly "furious about the erosion of his part," thinking the father's role too limited and his personality too forgiving (Baxter 337). As Connery has explained, he envisioned the role not as Lucas's scholarly bookworm, but as "a Sir Richard Burton idea, someone who would have been indifferent to his son growing up" (Freer 172). Needless to say, in an exceptional case of filmmakers allowing their actors major input into story development, Lucas and Spielberg accepted Connery's demands, with Spielberg calling in his friend, scriptwriter Tom Stoppard of *Shakespeare in Love*-fame to help with a major rewrite of Connery's part (Baxter 337). Stoppard at the time received only $120,000 (Dubner 229) for what would be an uncredited screenwriting job (Smith 180). However, when *Indiana Jones III* eventually turned out to be a financial blockbuster, Spielberg—certainly realizing how critical the rewritten part of Indy's father had been to the success of the movie—rewarded Stoppard with a million-dollar "thank-you bonus" (Dubner 229).

The more developed Henry Jones, Sr., who finally made it to the screen, and who in the opinion of many reviewers at the time "steals the film from the movie's adventurer hero" (Cullen, *Courier-Mail*), is fundamental to making the Indiana character seem more human than had the relatively one-dimensional action hero of *Indy I and II*. Connery's bespectacled and bearded, "tweedy, academic, mildly befuddled Dad" (James, "Indiana Jones" C15) had been, as he is portrayed in the prequel that opens the film, a distant and detached parent in Indy's youth.[17] As the younger Jones reminds his father over a drink during their zeppelin-escape from Germany, when Indy was a boy, "We never talked." That Indiana would now agree to Donovan's offer to search for the Grail not in order to find the Grail itself but rather because looking for it might allow him to find this most imperfect, unloving father is a clear indication that the roguish and self-serving Indiana has a true moral compass and a more profound personality than that hinted at in the previous two films.[18] The greater gravity and participation of the father in his role as reimagined by Connery and rewritten by Stoppard also work, arguably, to emphasize the meaning of the quest for the Grail in *The Last Crusade*, namely, as a metaphor for the search for the father by the son.

In associating the Grail with the reunification of father and son, the filmmakers stumble upon a connection between Grail and family that is at the very heart of many medieval Grail romances. Thus in Chrétien de Troyes' *Perceval*, the eponymous hero who seeks the Grail is both the maternal nephew of the old Fisher King as well as related to many of the figures most instrumental to directing him to the Grail and making him a more perfect knight. It is especially, however, in the Middle High German tradition of Arthurian romance that genealogy becomes so central to the Grail story. Thus when *Perceval* is reworked into medieval German at the beginning of the thirteenth century in the *Parzival* of Wolfram of Eschenbach, that *romancier* greatly expands the genealogical focus of Chrétien's *Perceval* to make the story, in essence, one that is primarily about family, and one in which finding the Grail is almost synonymous with reconnecting with close relatives. Thus Wolfram extends the kinship network of the hero to the other characters, making, for instance, the Grail Maiden the hero's aunt. Further, Wolfram even adds a prequel describing the lives of the hero's parents and illuminating how they, and Parzival, are related both to the family of the Grail keepers and to Arthur's kinship circle. And telling for the connection in German romance of the Grail to family, in the wake of *Parzival*, is Albrecht's *Younger Titurel* (circa 1270), an immensely popular text in the German Middle Ages that was written as a prequel to *Parzival* and which describes the origins of the family that came to be the keepers of the Grail. While there is no indication that Lucas, Spielberg, or their scriptwriter, Jeffrey Boam, were familiar with the propensity of medieval Grail romance to focus on family, it is nevertheless intriguing that both they and the writers of medieval Grail romance so intimately associate the Grail and family to produce compellingly entertaining narratives.

Conclusions

In medieval Arthurian romance, the attainment of the Grail metaphorically signifies that the hero seeking the Grail has achieved a state of ideal spiritual knighthood. In George Lucas and Steven Spielberg's Grail film, *The Last Crusade*, the filmmakers also imbue their own Grail with a metaphorical meaning that far outweighs its literal importance as a physical object. The quest for the Grail becomes symbolic for the spiritual quest of the hero, Indiana Jones, for Henry Jones, Sr., that is, of the son for the father. And the attainment of that Grail at the end of the quest metaphorically stands for the son and the father finding each other, reuniting, and reconciling.

Given that "its parts snap together with precise dry cunning" (White 10)—that is, *The Last Crusade* seamlessly combines a father-son story, the motif of the Grail, and several innovative story sequences including a prequel that turns the *Indiana Jones* series into a true narrative cycle—the doubt in George Lucas's words when he thought back years later on the development of the film is striking: "I thought we'd just barely got by in *Indy III* because the MacGuffin [i.e., the Grail] had always been the problem" (McBride 522). Needless to say, Lucas's fears proved unwarranted. Indeed, the filmmakers' highly original presentation of the Grail in *The Last Crusade* and its use to tell the film's larger story of a father and son's discovery of understanding for each other earned the picture a measure of popular and critical acclaim far greater than the vast majority of movies from the last several decades featuring medieval motifs.

Notes

1. Lucas and Spielberg have told the story of their Hawaiian beach discussion in full or in part many times over the years. The most comprehensive and best-contextualized description of that meeting is probably that by *The New York Times*' Richard B. Woodward, "Meanwhile, Back at the Ranch," 2.1.

2. The filmmakers ultimately would go on also to make an *Indy IV*, *The Kingdom of the Crystal Skull*, in 2008.

3. All quotations from the *Indiana Jones* films and references to DVD commentaries are from Paramount Home Entertainment's *Indiana Jones, The Complete Adventure Collection* box-set from 2008.

4. Officially, Menno Meyjes received "story" credit along with George Lucas, but his greatest contribution to the film was his work with Boam on the script (Eisenberg 47).

5. For a contemporaneous report on the birth of the New Age movement about the time of *The Last Crusade*'s release, and for the Grail's place in at least one New Age self-help program's curriculum, see Goldman's 1989 *New York Times*' piece, "Searching for the Holy Grail at an Adult Healing Camp," B1.

6. Itself housed within an imposing edifice, specifically the first-century–CE Nabatean Treasury Building, with its dramatic reddish façade cut directly into the face of a high rock, in Petra in present-day Jordan.

7. Indeed, it was certainly in part to avoid the charges of racial callousness that had dogged them especially after the release of *Temple of Doom* that, in *The Last Crusade*, we find the filmmakers avoiding the portrayal of people of color as negative characters and returning to Caucasians to fill such roles.

8. "durchs wilde Nazistan."

9. This characterization is from Shreve 108.

10. On the National Socialists' search for the Grail and its place in their ideology, see also Harty, "Arnold Fanck's 1926 Film *Der Heilige Berg*," 230–233.

11. Martin B. Shichtman, "Whom Does the Grail Serve?" 284, even goes so far as to assert that "Spielberg ... transforms the Holy Grail into a weapon to be used ... in the war against Nazism." Among the critical articles that suggest a possible link between the Grail in *Indy III* and the interest of the National Socialists for the Grail is that by Brown and Boughton, "The Grail Quest as Illumination," 15.

12. On the ineffectuality of the heroines of especially the first two *Indy* films, see, for instance, the thoughtful treatment of the first three *Indy* films by Biskind 130–135.

13. For an alternative view holding that Indy is, in fact, a knight, see Aronstein 3 and, more recently, Huse 245

14. Ford would, of course, reprise his role as Indiana Jones in 2008's *Kingdom of the Crystal Skull*.

15. For a contemporaneous report on Hollywood's growing acknowledgement in the late 1980s of the profits to be made by producing films that also would play well internationally, see, for instance, Stevenson, "Hollywood Takes Global Stage," 1.

16. Box-office figures are from Wasser 143.

17. Given Spielberg's aversion to aligning *Indy III* with anything resembling *Monty Python and the Holy Grail* (dir. Terry Gilliam and Terry Jones 1975)—see, for example, Freer 171—the resemblance of Connery's fusty, Victorian Henry Jones, Sr. to the pedantic historian of the Python film must be regarded as a happy accident. Connery's involvement in medieval film also includes his appearance as Robin in *Robin and Marian* (dir. Richard Lester 1976), as the Green Knight in *Sword of the Valiant* (dir. Stephen Weeks 1983), and as King Arthur in *First Knight* (dir. Jerry Zucker 1995).

18. The best treatment of the father-son dynamic in *Indy III* is that in Aronstein 19–25.

Works Cited

Aronstein, Susan. "'Not Exactly a Knight': Arthurian Narrative and Recuperative Politics in the *Indiana Jones* Trilogy." *Cinema Journal* 34 (Summer 1995): 3–30.

Baxter, John. *The Unauthorized Biography: Steven Spielberg*. London: HarperCollins, 1996.

Ben-David, Calev. "Raiders of the Old Scripts." *Jerusalem Post* 8 September 1989. Accessed on the Web through LexisNexis Academic.

Biskind, Peter. "Blockbuster: *The Last Crusade*." In *Seeing Through Movies*. Ed. Mark Crispin Miller. New York: Pantheon Books, 1990.

Brown, Christine, and Lynne C. Boughton. "The Grail Quest as Illumination." *Journal of Interdisciplinary Studies* 9.1–2 (1997): 39–62.

Buckland, Warren. *Directed by Steven Spielberg: Poetics of the Contemporary Hollywood Blockbuster*. New York: Continuum, 2006.

Canby, Vincent. "Spielberg's Elixir Shows Signs of Mature Magic." *New York Times* 18 June 1989: 2, 15.

Clark, Mike. "*Indiana 3*: Raiders of a Father-Son Lark." *USA Today* 24 May 1989: 1D.

Cullen, J. "From James Bond to Big Daddy." *Courier-Mail* (Brisbane) 20 May 1989. Accessed on the Web through LexisNexis Academic.

Cullen, Jenny. Review of *Indiana Jones and the Last Crusade*. *Hobart Mercury* 31 May 1989. Accessed on the Web through LexisNexis Academic.

Dubner, Stephen J. "Steven the Good." In *Steven Spielberg: Interviews*. Ed. Lester D. Friedman and Brent Notbohm. Jackson: University Press of Mississippi, 2000.

Eisenberg, Adam. "Father, Son, and Holy Grail." *Cinefex* 40 (November 1989): 46–67.

Freer, Ian. *The Complete Spielberg*. London: Virgin Publishing, 2001.

Friedman, Lester D. *Citizen Spielberg*. Urbana: University of Illinois Press, 2006.

Fuller, Graham. "Keeping Up with the Joneses: Alison Doody Gells Graham Fuller About the Boy's Own World of Indiana Jones." *Independent* (London) 23 June 1989: 31.

Goldman, Ari L. "Searching for the Holy Grail at an Adult Healing Camp." *New York Times* 21 August 1989: B1.

Harmetz, Aljean. "Movies Look Abroad for Profits." *New York Times* 17 December 1988: 1, 13.

Harty, Kevin J. "Arnold Fanck's 1926 Film *Der Heilige Berg* and the Nazi Quest for the Holy Grail." In

Romance and Rhetoric: Essays in Honour of Dhira B. Mahoney. Ed. Georgiana Donavin and Anita Obermeier. Turnhout, Belgium: Brepols, 2010.

Huse, Swantje. *Zum Bild wird hier der Text: Parzival und der Gral im Film: Monty Python and the Holy Grail, Perceval le Gallois, Indiana Jones, The Fisher King.* Munich: Martin Meidenbauer, 2011.

Indiana Jones and the Last Crusade. Dir. Steven Spielberg. Prods. George Lucas and Frank Marshall. 1989. DVD rerelease as part of the *Indiana Jones, The Complete Adventure Collection* box-set. Paramount Home Entertainment, 2008.

Indiana Jones and the Raiders of the Lost Ark. Dir. Steven Spielberg. Prods. George Lucas and Howard Kazanjian. 1981. DVD rerelease as part of the *Indiana Jones, The Complete Adventure Collection* box-set. Paramount Home Entertainment, 2008.

Indiana Jones and the Temple of Doom. Dir. Steven Spielberg. Prods. George Lucas and Frank Marshall. 1984. DVD rerelease as part of the *Indiana Jones, The Complete Adventure Collection* box-set. Paramount Home Entertainment, 2008.

James, Caryn. "Indiana Jones in Pursuit of Dad and Grail." *New York Times* 24 May 1989: C15.

James, Stan. "The Last Crusade for Harrison Ford." *Advertiser* (Adelaide) 8 December 1988. Accessed on the Web through LexisNexis Academic.

Kaplan, David. "Secret Lair of the Jedi, the Grail and Green Slimers." *New York Times* 2 July 1989: 2, 9.

Kilb, Andreas. "Ein Greenhorn wird erwachsen: Steven Spielbergs Film *Indiana Jones und der letzte Kreuzzug*: Der schöne Abgang eines Serienhelden." *Die Zeit* 15 September 1989: Feuilleton 55–56.

Lowing, Rob. "That's My Boy—All Action!" *Sun Herald* (Sydney) 11 June 1989: 118.

McBride, Joseph. *Steven Spielberg: A Biography.* 2nd ed. Jackson: University Press of Mississippi, 2010.

Partidge, D. "Indiana's Back to His Best." *Courier-Mail* (Brisbane) 10 June 1989. Accessed on the Web through LexisNexis Academic.

Robinson, David. "Good old-fashioned fun." *The Times of London* 29 June 1989. Accessed on the Web through LexisNexis Academic.

Shichtman, Martin B. "Whom Does the Grail Serve? Wagner, Spielberg, and the Jewish Issue of Appropriation." In *The Arthurian Revival, Essays on Form, Tradition, and Transformation.* Ed. Debra N. Mancoff. New York: Garland, 1992.

Shreve, Adam. "'Buenos Noches, Mein Führer': A Look at Nazism in Popular Culture." *Journal of Popular Culture* 35 (Spring 2002): 103–112.

Smith, Jim. *George Lucas.* London: Virgin Books, 2003.

Sterritt, David. "Grand Exit for Indiana Jones." *The Christian Science Monitor* 13 June 1989: 11.

Stevenson, Richard W. "Hollywood Takes to the Global Stage." *New York Times* 16 April 1989: 3, 1.

Stuart, Diwell. Review of *Indiana Jones and the Last Crusade. Sunday Tasmanian.* Accessed on the Web through LexisNexis Academic.

Sutton, Martin. "*Indiana Jones and the Last Crusade.*" *Films and Filming* 417 (July 1989): 40–41.

Taylor, Philip M. *Steven Spielberg: The Man, His Movies, and Their Meaning.* 3rd ed. New York: Continuum, 1999.

Wasser, Frederick. *Steven Spielberg's America.* Cambridge, UK: Polity Press, 2010.

White, Armond. "Keeping Up With the Joneses." *Film Comment* 25 (July-August 1989): 9–11.

Woodward, Richard B. "Meanwhile, Back at the Ranch." *New York Times* 21 May 1989: 2, 1.

A Grail or a Mirage? Searching the Wasteland of *The Road Warrior*

Paul B. Sturtevant

This essay examines what at first may seem an unlikely candidate for inclusion within the canon of metaphorical or allegorical versions, or adaptations, of the Grail story: George Miller's 1982 film, *Mad Max 2: The Road Warrior*. There is little to suggest that the filmmakers set out to create a Grail film, and perhaps even less to suggest that its audience would view it in that light. Having said that, is it possible to discuss *The Road Warrior* as a Grail film, and, if so, does doing so offer up any productive insights about the film, the time in which it was made, or our understanding of the Grail's place in modern popular culture? To answer the question, this essay will explore the film's setting, archetypes, and historical context in an attempt to see not only whether the Grail can be found here, but, if it can, whether finding it is a valuable exercise.

The Road Warrior *as Myth*

A Campbellian or Jungian approach to the "Grail" content in *The Road Warrior* would de-emphasize the contribution of the filmmakers. Instead, it would focus on the universality of the mythological and archetypal figures present. It is perhaps ironic, then, that George Miller views *Mad Max*, and approached making *The Road Warrior*, this way. As he explained in an interview:

> In Japan they called it [*Mad Max*] a samurai movie and said, "You must know Kurosawa." I'd never heard of Kurosawa. In—in France they said, "Oh it's a western on wheels." In Scandinavia they said "He's a Viking." And basically I began to realise that somehow there was something else going on there and that was the realisation that there is a collective unconsciousness going on. That there's a mythology out there and basically *Mad Max* was a kind of a weird Australian version of that. A kind of road warrior. And so that led us to Joseph Campbell and once you, once Campbell, opened those doors of perception into storytelling I suddenly became ... forgot about cinema all together and basically became a storyteller.... [Max] was indeed a mythological figure, you know, a mini-version of one. He's not—he's not a great hero but he has that, something like that is nascent in him. And it was ... so it was a little bit more self-conscious in *Mad Max 2*. Not following it, you know, religiously—the hero myth. But it was an understanding that that was what was at foot [Byrnes, Interview: George Miller].

If Miller is to be taken at face value, it seems that any Grail content in *The Road Warrior* may not have been placed there by the filmmakers in a conscious attempt to create a neo–Arthurian legend in the outback, but to create a story roughly inspired by the "monomyth" of the hero's journey outlined by Campbell in *The Hero with a Thousand Faces*. We as medievalists may be projecting our own expertise and desires onto the film in the same way that Miller described the Japanese, French and Scandinavians having done so when viewing *Mad Max*—hooking it into our own intellectual schematic frameworks (Anderson 418–419). That said, it does not mean that the Grail is not there. What elements present in the film can be viewed as Grail-types—whether they were placed there intentionally, or arose as common expressions of our collective cultural unconscious?

The Wasteland

The most apparent Arthurian aspect of *The Road Warrior* is its setting. While the Australian outback is not known for its hospitability in the best of times, the film renders it into a desert junkyard of biblical, mythological proportions. Arch-villain Humungus commands the virtuous settlers to whom he has laid siege, "Look around you. This is the valley of death," referencing Psalm 23. At the same time, the film implies that this Wasteland is not necessarily endless—Humungus says to the settlers that "you plan to take your gasoline out of the Wasteland." So, one of the principal ways in which this Wasteland differs from the Arthurian is that the chief objective (at least of the settlers) is to escape the Wasteland, rather than to heal it. This Wasteland is irrevocably so; no question, Quest, or Grail can change it. It echoes Merlin's prophesy from *Historia Regum Britanniae*: "Arripiet mortalitas populum cunctasque nationes euacuabit. Residui natale solum deserent et exteras culturas seminabunt. (Death will seize the populace and all nations will be purged. The surviving will desert the places of their birth and they will plant in foreign lands)" [75].

The apocalypse that renders the world into Max's postdiluvian one is never well-defined. The opening of *The Road Warrior* gives the viewer the only window into the past: a voice-over recounts what little is known over vignettes of the first *Mad Max* intercut with documentary footage from World War II, the UN, and rioting:

> My life fades, the vision dims. All that remains are memories. I remember a time of chaos, ruined dreams, this wasted land. But most of all, I remember The Road Warrior: the man we called "Max." To understand who he was you have to go back to another time, when the world was powered by the black fuel, and the desert sprouted great cities of pipe and steel. Gone now, swept away. For reasons long forgotten, two mighty warrior tribes went to war and touched off a blaze which engulfed them all. Without fuel, they were nothing. They built a house of straw. The thundering machines sputtered and stopped. Their leaders talked and talked and talked. But nothing could stem the avalanche. Their world crumbled. The cities exploded. A whirlwind of looting, a firestorm of fear, men began to feed on men. On the roads it was a white line nightmare. Only those mobile enough to scavenge, brutal enough to pillage would survive. The gangs took over the highways, ready to wage war for a tank of juice. And in this maelstrom of decay, ordinary men were battered and smashed. Men like Max: the warrior Max. In the roar of an engine, he lost everything, and became a shell of a man; a burnt out, desolate man; a man haunted by the demons of his past; a man who wandered out into the Wasteland. And it was here, in this blighted place, that he learned to live again.

This opening establishes *Mad Max II* as a film steeped in, and thus a product of, Cold War paranoia. That said, the conflict that ignited the world seems of little consequence to the world in which Max lives; the two tribes of the old world order no longer exist and play no part in the action. The only relevant remnant of the conflict is that which caused their downfall and that which defines Max's desert. The junkyard tarmac of Max's outback is defined by a lack of fuel. This defining characteristic is emphasized when, after the first scene in which we see Max defeat a pair of raiders, his first move is to collect the dirty fuel leaking from his opponent's upturned vehicle in any container he can find—a helmet, a piece of scrap metal, his hands. Clearly, Max lives within the Wasteland of the Arthurian legends.

The chief cause of Max's desert being turned to waste is not magical—there does not seem to be a specific dolorous blow which rendered the land thus. Society has simply imploded not "with a nuclear bang but with a long, drawn-out whimper" (Shapiro 174), and the film's description of its Wasteland corresponds with that of the wasted Grail kingdom presented either by Chrétien de Troyes and his continuators, or in *Perlesvaus* (see Chrétien 55 and Bryant 18).

The chief features of these lands are rampant, senseless warfare caused by the destruction of feudal and social bonds resulting from a breakdown of leadership. As Barber describes it, "There is no hint of magic, merely the stark reality of a land left prey to marauders" (20). *The Road Warrior* certainly presents itself in this fashion: the opening scene (after the introductory montage) thrusts us into this world. We come upon Max *in medias res* doing "battle without any real cause" with a group of bikers across the blasted highways of the Australian outback.

That said, as Shapiro notes, despite the *Mad Max* series not being "bomb films," they are regularly interpreted this way by audiences and scholars: "Many scholars seem intent on reading into the trilogy nuclear themes which simply do not exist" (175). Such readings are probably the result of a combination of the Wasteland and the post-apocalyptic aspects of its setting; the bomb is such a potent figure in post-apocalyptic fiction that any desert therein bears the implication that that it was created by nuclear fire. So, Max inhabits a Wasteland that might seem familiar to Chrétien or his medieval audiences—and to us. Unlike the Fisher King's Wasteland, which is tied to the fate of the ruler, the Wasteland in *The Road Warrior* has no apparent cause, nor any apparent solution. But crucially, it cannot be healed, only escaped. As such, is this Wasteland sufficiently Arthurian—or are all Wastelands, by definition, Arthurian?

The Grail(s)

But where does the Grail lie within this Wasteland? Perhaps unsurprisingly, the Grail is not easily found—there are three (and perhaps more which I have not considered) candidates for the Grail in this film: the Grail-as-fuel, the Grail-as-civilization, and the conspicuously-absent Grail.

The most obvious reading of the film is that fuel represents the Grail. It is the lynchpin without which society has crumbled. Its tantalizingly infrequent presence provides the inciting motivation for Max's quest (as the Grail does when appearing and disappearing from Arthur's court in *Le Morte Darthur*). If we view Max as a knight errant, his Quest is to feed his hungry "horse." This comment is perhaps a flippant way of viewing the film, but embedded within it is a deeper critique of Western society. Fuel in *The Road Warrior* does not represent energy, warmth or light, but mobility—the ability to keep moving towards and away. Of course, we do not know what or whom Max is fleeing from or pursuing (nor does, it seems, Max), but his role as wanderer requires him to keep moving, seeking, and thus consuming. Within this context, petrol is rendered into the water of life. The refinery—and in particular its fuel tanker—may be viewed as a Grail-type. On a very surface level, the tanker is a vessel which holds the promise of a near-infinite amount of sustaining "juice." But instead of providing eternal sustenance (as in the Grails of Wolfram or Chrétien), Max's cup always runneth on empty.

When Max is first told by the Gyro Captain of a fortified city resplendent with fuel, it does sound like a Grail castle. When he sees it, it has energy to spare: it shines with an abundance of electric lights, the burning of excess gas, and the flicker of defensive flamethrowers. It pierces the otherwise inky night of the desert outback like Bertilak's shining castle in *Sir Gawain and the Green Knight* that "schemered and schon thurgh the schyre okez" (180). But instead of the actual Grail castles Corbenic or the Castle Adventurous, inside which wonders never cease, this castle is under siege, such as the one in the kingdom of Zazamanc that the knight-errant Gahmuret encounters in Wolfram von Eschenbach's *Parzival* (7–14). For the inhabitants of the castle in *The Road Warrior*, mobility implies safety and the possibility of exit from Humungus' Wasteland. Pappagallo, the leader of the settlers sees it as their only hope of escape: "But remember. Remember one thing. That is more than just a tanker of gas. That is our lifeline to a place beyond that vermin on machines.... But the first step ... defend the fuel." And so, if fuel is to be the film's Grail, Max undergoes a series of trials to attain it—first retrieving a dying man for the settlers, then retrieving a truck that can haul the tanker. But Max rejects possession of the Grail itself; when the settlers ask him to drive the tanker, he takes his fuel payment and leaves. Ultimately, he does drive the truck (thus taking possession of the Grail), but only after he has been defeated by the marauders, his car destroyed and his dog killed. However, after he has killed the marauders, and the Grail-truck is upturned off the road, Max finds that it carries only an empty promise: sand instead of fuel. The real fuel had been loaded into oil drums carried in the settlers' cars. His Grail is ultimately a false one. He then wanders into the desert, no longer pursuing fuel, broken, and on foot.

In this interpretation, Max's world, like much of contemporary western (particularly, but not exclusively, Australian and North American) culture, has fetishized mobility. Our engines have rendered us addicts; like Max, we will kill for mobility and would die without it. This observation is particularly potent when viewed from an historical framework; the film was produced in the immediate aftermath of the 1973 Oil Crisis and 1979 Energy Crisis (Yergin 570–594). The filmmakers—and their audiences—had thus seen a hint of the chaos which would result when the global oil reserves ran dry. This specter of a post-peak oil world haunts us perhaps even more now than at the release of the film; on the one hand, there are those echoing Sarah Palin's mantra "drill, baby, drill," who view oil as a Grail which should be sought at all costs irrespective of ecological or personal damage. On the other, environmentalists and scientists seek a new technological Grail—perhaps cold fusion, perhaps water splitting, perhaps something else entirely—which would permit our society to maintain its current consumption without the side-effects of the unending pursuit of oil (Sofge "MIT Fights"; Foley "New Water-Splitting System"). Time can only tell which, if any, of these Grails are real.

But fuel- or tanker-as–Grail is only one possible interpretation of the film. Another valid interpretation might be that civilization and community—as represented by the survivors in the refinery—is the real Grail. Such a reading sets up a contrast between Max's pursuit of the "earthly Grail," fuel, and his rejection of the "heavenly Grail," civilization. While it may seem that Max's rescue of the wounded settler evidences the compassion that was central to Perceval's failure to achieve the Grail in Chrétien and Wolfram's versions, but Max quickly shows his true nature by telling the man begging to be saved: "Save it. I'm just here for the gasoline." He only reconsiders when the desperate man offers "As much as you like. Just take me back there." Perhaps such an ethic is the real origin of the Wasteland—it is not a lack of fuel that has destroyed civilization, but simply a lack of civility and compassion. Furthermore, this interpretation would fit neatly within the structure of an archetypal "quest for redemption," since Max, as will be discussed below, clearly begins the film as a broken, nihilistic man.

The settlers offer Max a place in their new civilization (resonating with the Biblical Exodus or the Mormon journeys across the United States) in exchange for his driving the tanker, in the following exchange:

PAPPAGALLO: Look, I don't have time for long speeches. I want you to drive the tanker.

MAX: Sorry. We had a contract. I kept my part of the bargain.

PAPPAGALLO: We'll make a new contract.

MAX: I've got all I need here.

PAPPAGALLO: You don't have a future. I could offer you that. Rebuild our lives. Buy a ticket for 2,000 miles.

THE CURMUDGEON: You have to come, sonny. This is where we're going. Paradise! 2,000 miles from here. Fresh water, plenty of sunshine. Nothing to do but breed.

MAX: No thanks.

Pappagallo then asks Max to explain why he is so wounded, and why he rejects their offer. But Max is no King Pelles, and the questions bounce off Max's armor. Pappagallo continues:

What is it with you? What are you looking for? Come on, Max, everyone's looking for something. You happy out there, are you? Eh? Wandering, one day blurring into another? You're a scavenger, Max. You're a maggot. Do you know that? You're living off the corpse of the old world. Tell me your story, Max. What burned you out, huh? Kill one man too many? See too many people die? Lose some family? ... Do you think you're the only one that's suffered? We've all been through it in here, but we haven't given up. We're still human beings with dignity. But you, you're out there with the garbage. You're nothing!

So Max is offered the Grail of civilization, but turns it down—or is incapable of accepting it—because of his past. When Max is then returned to the refinery (after he loses everything and is gravely wounded by the marauders), he takes up the job of driving the truck by simply, enigmatically, stating:

> MAX: If it's all the same to you, I'll drive that tanker.
> PAPPAGALLO: The offer is closed. Too late for deals.
> MAX: No deals. I want to drive the truck.
> PAPPAGALLO: Why? Why the big change of heart?
> MAX: Believe me, I haven't got a choice.

The last line is puzzling; there is no reason to believe Max, in his wounded state, could not ride with one of the settlers. His motivation—why doesn't he have a choice?—is ambiguous. Is it a result of a newfound sense of nobility, or, perhaps, more convincingly, a desire—echoing the final act of the first film—to exact vengeance upon those who wronged him?

For either reason, the ending of the film also remains problematic—and calls into question the validity of viewing the civilization as the Grail. For all their civility, the settlers are happy to use Max as an unwitting decoy in order to allow themselves to escape, as Pappagallo instructs:

> Now, at this point, that's all they want: the tanker. So they'll come straight after us. So we'll use that to punch our way out which will give all of you a very, very good chance. Now, don't hesitate! Once you're outside there, split up and go as hard as you can. Now, 200 miles to the north there's a place with a bridge called Powder River. That's our rendezvous. Give us till sunset. If we haven't made it by then, keep going.

We do not know whether the settlers expected Max to survive the assaults by the marauders, but they clearly did not trust that he would, or else the tanker would not have been filled with sand. As a result, it seems even the offer of a chance to rejoin civilization—which, the viewer is told by the narrator at the film's close, was re-established by the settlers who founded the "Great Northern Tribe"—was a sham. The narrator (whom we are told was the leader of this Great Northern Tribe) concludes the film by saying "And the Road Warrior? That was the last we ever saw of him. He lives now only in my memories." The film implies that the narrator was the feral boy who aided Max in the climactic battle. The Gyro Captain, whose gyrocopter was wrecked in the battle, is also shown to escape. But if the Feral Kid and Gyro Captain were rescued by the settlers, why not Max?

It remains ambiguous whether the settlers made an offer after the battle for Max to join their society and he refused, or whether he disappeared—or they simply left him—to wander the Wasteland. Perhaps he found the deception of his supposedly civilized friends too much to bear. In either instance, if we are to view civilization as the Grail, it is, for Max, either a false Grail, or an entirely elusive one. Despite the initial monologue's claim that "And it was here, in this blighted place, that he learned to live again," Max does not seem especially redeemed. In fact, if anything, his brush with civilization has left him worse off.

A third interpretive option exists. It is entirely possible that this film, like T.S. Eliot's *The Waste Land*, contains a Wasteland without a Grail. *The Road Warrior* is a post-apocalyptic film. Such classification places it outside the purview of the Grail; as a supreme focus of lay Christian piety, the Grail is, by definition, a pre-apocalyptic artifact. But in this film, the apocalypse has come and gone. This apocalypse is a distinctly secular one, without the pageantry demanded by John's Revelation. God and Christ are only notable in this film in their complete absence: no characters are outwardly religious; there are no religious symbols of any kind; and the words *God* and *Jesus* are only voiced as epithets. The problematic nature of both of the first two analyses of *The Road Warrior* would give some credence to this pessimistic view, where all the supposed Grails are, in fact, false. Any Grail, any goal sought to solve the problems of this world (whether fuel, civilization or safety) will, by definition, be an imperfect solution. Such a realization may have caused the film's questing knight to take such a nihilistic act—as Max seems to do at the close of the film—and reject these imperfect Grails altogether. It seems to him the quest is more appealing than the Grails he finds at the end of it. Perhaps, then, *The Road Warrior* simply is not a Grail film; a quest film, certainly, but not necessarily a film in which the quest is not a quest for a Grail. But, in order to see whether the Grail is conspicuously absent or simply so, it would be best to explore further contextual elements that might reveal whether there really is a Grail-shaped hole in this film.

Wasteland Knight(s?)

A chief ingredient in any Grail quest is the questor, and, in this film, Max is the obvious candidate. That said, if Max is a questing knight, he is hardly an ideal one. At the end of the original *Mad Max*, Max's wife and son are killed by a motorcycle gang. Having already resigned his commission as a policeman (readily a kind of latter-day knight), Max turns vigilante, steals a souped-up police car, and systematically hunts down, tortures and murders every gang member even remotely responsible for the death of his family. That done, he wanders into the wastes with nothing left to live for.

The conclusion to the first film clearly sets up Max's description in the introduction of *The Road Warrior*: "In the roar of an engine, he lost everything, and became a shell of a man; a burnt out, desolate man; a man haunted by the demons of his past; a man who wandered out into the Wasteland." While the Arthurian canon is replete with imperfect knights, it is rare to find one so nihilistic and broken. Perhaps only Perceval's situation, at the end of Chrétien's *Le Conte du Graal*, relates closely to Max's: "Perceval ... had lost his memory to such a degree that he no longer remembered God.... That's not to say that he stopped seeking deeds of chivalry: he went in search of strange, hard and terrible adventures" (72).

But unlike Perceval, Max does not attain redemption. And Max is not a Perceval-figure in any other way; he has no youthful innocence, no battle with a Red Knight, no regrets for the death of his mother. Max makes a poor Lancelot-figure as well, though Lancelot is also a sinful knight and is generally renowned for his martial prowess, just as Max is. Max is wounded and wears an improvised leg brace through the film—but he is no Fisher King. In fact, it is very difficult to pair Max with any Arthurian figure, because, in large part, Max reveals very little about himself. Unlike the typically-loquacious knights of medieval romance, Mel Gibson only has sixteen lines throughout the film, which does allow Max to stand as an archetypal hero—an empty sign, with meaning that can be imbued by the viewer. Instead of a Gawain-type, a Perceval-type, a Galahad-type or a Lancelot-type, perhaps he is simply Sir Max.

Sir Max makes a peculiar romance hero, seeming to belong as much to the samurai or

Western traditions as to the medieval. But, as explained by Miller, perhaps he truly belongs to none—or to all. He is an archetypal lone wanderer, and his appearance, wearing tattered Police leathers in all black, designates him as a figure more a part of the Wasteland than of the city. His character is also morally ambiguous: he is as quiet, gruff and mysterious as the Ronin in *Yojimbo* (1961) or in Clint Eastwood's Man with No Name in Leone's *Dollars* trilogy. He never speaks of his past, and seems only to have two desires: fuel and vengeance. After the tanker is destroyed and his vengeance is achieved, Max has no moral epiphany or redemptive moment. He simply wanders into the Wasteland with even less than when the film began.

And while this neo-medieval knight uses no sword, he does carry a weapon with magical properties that sets him apart: a rare sawed-off shotgun. In a world that has reverted to medieval weaponry, the threat presented by Max's working gun is profound; by simply unsheathing it, he is able to scare off a pair of raiders in the opening scene. The threat of its power is also sufficient to keep the Gyro Captain compliant. But, unlike the omnipresent firearms in the Western, where every pistol is loaded and waiting for an itchy finger, or the swords of Arthurian films always ready to do battle, Max's weapon presents an empty threat: he has no ammunition (which has also become a rare commodity in this world defined by lack). He only receives a handful of working shotgun shells upon finally volunteering to drive the tanker in the final act. Max crashes the tanker, in part, because he is unable to reload his gun. Humungus is presented as a worthy adversary to Max for a similar reason; he is armed with a scoped Smith & Wesson Model 29 revolver that he keeps in an ornamental case decorated with a large Prussian *Totenkopf.* Their climactic duel is not fought with swords on the battle-

Mel Gibson as the eponymous hero and potential Grail Knight in George Miller's 1982 film *The Road Warrior.*

field or guns at high noon, but with cars—Max crashes the tanker into the Humungus' car head-on, ultimately destroying both vehicles. In this moment, a game of automotive chicken is fused with a medieval joust.

Just as Max does not correspond with a Grail hero, neither do any of the other characters in *The Road Warrior*. The Gyro Captain, for example, may have resonances with Perceval, insofar that his is the only truly redemptive story. When the audience is introduced to him, he is even more morally-debased than Max—not only a Wasteland scavenger, but a thief (closely associated with the neatly venomous snakes he keeps as pets) who survives by setting traps for others and stealing their possessions once they are dead. By the end of the film, he has not only rejoined civilization by joining the settlers, but also enters into a hetero-normative relationship with one of them and becomes their leader. Is his assuming the mantle of Grail-leadership after a period of amorality in the wilderness enough to make him a Parzival-figure (insofar as Parzival becomes the Grail king at the conclusion of Wolfram's version)? But he also represents one of the trials Max faces on his quest for fuel, and is, according to a Campbellian interpretation, the "Herald," providing Max with his "call to adventure" when he leads Max to the refinery. In fact, Campbell's assertion that "the herald or announcer of the adventure *is often dark, loathly, or terrifying*, judged evil by the world; yet if one could follow, the way would be opened through the walls of day into the dark where jewels glow" seems fitting (44). Continuing a Campbellian analysis, as the film progresses, the Gyro Captain can also be viewed as Max's "Supernatural Aide" (57). His flying machine makes him a man with seemingly-magical powers in this junkyard world. He assists Max in battle from above on two occasions, and rescues Max after he fails his "road of trials" once he rejects the settlers' offer to drive the tanker and is subsequently run off the road—though this episode could equally be interpreted as a "Refusal of Call," or submission to "Temptation" (Campbell 49, 81), depending on whether Max's "quest" is to procure fuel or to drive the tanker.

Similarly, the Feral Kid, whom Max briefly adopts (or, perhaps, who briefly adopts Max), can arguably bear an Arthurian interpretation. Perhaps, *he* is Perceval—the Arthurian feral child who grew up with no knowledge of knighthood, the world, and courtly behavior. Both dress in rags, and both characters use missile weapons to kill a superior foe. Perceval uses javelins to kill the Red Knight, whereas the Feral Kid uses a sharpened boomerang to attack Wez—who dodges, and, as a result, the Feral Kid kills the Golden Youth instead. The Feral Kid is the only person to whom Max shows even a brief moment of compassion by giving him a working music-box mechanism. And the Feral Kid becomes the film's narrator and, ultimately, leader of the Great Northern Tribe—taking on the mantle of the Grail King. But now we have three potential—and not wholly satisfactory—Perceval figures. It is clear that any resonances with the Arthurian legends will be fragmentary and jumbled and can change as the film progresses.

Similarly, Pappagallo and the remainder of the settlers are also only fragmentally, tentatively resonant with the Arthurian legends. Perhaps Pappagallo is a Fisher King. He is the guardian of the Grail (whatever it is), is shot in the leg with an arrow part of the way through the film (though his injury is temporary rather than magical, and has no bearing on the state of the Wasteland), and dies in the finale to make way for a new keeper of the Grail. If the settlers are to be a Grail court, they are a peculiar one—a paraplegic, mumbling "Mechanic" (perhaps another Fisher King?), a helmeted "Curmudgeon," a "Warrior Woman" (who could be viewed as a Grail maiden, but only because of her gender), and a small group of uncredited background warriors. The Arthurian metaphor seems not to extend far enough to encompass all the characters here.

Similarly so with the bikers Max opposes. The simple problem is that in Arthurian Grail stories, the obstacle to achieving the quest for the Grail is typically either spiritual or personal—typically a lack of piety, as in the *Lancelot-Grail Cycle* or in *Le Morte Darthur*, or a lack of courtesy and maturity as in the Vulgate or *Parzival*. Such stories do not generally feature monsters, an army, or even other knights who must be defeated in order to attain the Grail. The only suitably-impressive enemy defeated by the Grail knights is the dragon defeated by Lancelot in the tomb, and this episode is largely incidental to the quest for the Grail (Mahoney 39). This is not to say that there is nothing notable about Humungus and his band, just that they do not fit very well into a Grail context.

A Historicist View: A Post-Apocalyptic Dark Age

Instead of relating to the history and popular perceptions of the Grail, a more fruitful interpretive model for the marauders and settlers may lie in the popular perceptions of the Fall of Rome. *The Road Warrior* presents a vision of the world where, after the collapse of civilization, remnants of civil society struggle to survive when beset by barbarians at the gate. As such, the film draws heavily upon the history—or at least the popular understandings—of the world after the Fall of the Roman Empire. The presence of the Fall of the Roman Empire in a post-apocalyptic 1980s action film reinforces Bowersock's claim that Western culture sees the Fall of Rome as a shadow looming over of all of our cultural failures: "we have been obsessed with the fall: it has been valued as an archetype for every perceived decline and, hence, as a symbol of our own fears" (31).

The Road Warrior presents a dual-vision of the dystopic future: on the one hand, the survivors within the walls of the refinery represent the remnants of civilization and uphold (relatively) conservative social values. On the other hand, the marauders represent the worst possible excesses of humanity—and specifically masculinity—unleashed from socio-sexual mores and taboos. The dichotomy between the two groups could not be starker; in broadly Freudian terms, the raiders represent humanity's latent id and the survivors its superego. This dichotomy is based upon socially-conservative ideology and sexual anxiety that is intended to resonate with a (predominantly) heterosexual (predominantly) male action-film target audience of 1981. Humungus and his men embody male sexuality and aggression without social restraints. They howl and gibber as they rape and murder their victims while clad in a pastiche of hyper-masculine signs: punk hairdos, biker leathers, football pads, and S&M bondage–wear (all in black). Humungus himself, the apex predator and idealized figure of this society, is clad only in a leather bikini, bondage harness and metal mask (which, at once, resembles both a hockey mask and the grille of a car). As a result, his costume bears visual resonances with Frank Frazetta's influential 1966–1973 paperback-cover adaptations of *Conan the Barbarian* (Bond, Winiewicz, and Steven 2008). The muscle-bound figure of Humungus (provided by Kjell Nilsson, a Swedish Olympic weightlifter) is thus wholly on display, and seems designed to evoke homosexual desire—and thus anxiety—in the gazing male audience. This homosexual anxiety is not incidental, as homosexual references are rife within the film: the Humongous' chief lieutenant Wez is in a homosexual master/slave relationship with the blonde who shares his motorcycle, one of the raiders drives a pink 1958 Chrysler DeSoto (and sports a beard dyed pink), and Humungus refers to groups of his army as "gayboy-berserkers" and "smegma crazies." Women are almost completely absent from this society; in spite of this absence, or perhaps because of it, taboo sex is shot through every facet of the marauders' society. The threat presented by the barbarian siege is not only a fear of these men forcefully penetrating the walls of the compound, but also a fear of homosexual rape.

This "barbarians-as-hypermasculine-rapists" subtext is, perhaps surprisingly, one way in which the film's medievalism becomes apparent. The perceptions of barbarians in this fashion can be traced back to the Fall of Rome itself, as Thompson notes: "the literate Roman of the later empire saw them [the Barbarians] as invaders and destroyers: they fought, plundered, burned, raped and killed—nothing more" (231). Moreover, though more recent scholars of late antiquity are quick to dispel these perceptions, there has been a strand within the popular and academic historiography of the Fall of Rome that views the event partially through the lens of gender and sexuality. Gibbon's *The History of the Decline and Fall of the Roman Empire* views the fall of Rome as, in part, a byproduct of the effeminization of Roman warrior society where "effeminate luxury, which infected the manner of courts and cities, had instilled a secret and destructive poison into the camps of the legions" (III 129). By contrast, he describes the Germanic invaders in masculine terms, such as when "the fierce giants of the north broke in [and] restored a *manly* spirit of freedom; and after the revolution of ten centuries, freedom became the happy parent of taste and science" [my emphasis] (I 83).

There has been a national difference based upon the interpretations of barbarians as noble or ignoble savages, "German and English historians in particular," such as Gibbon, "have been fond of picturing the barbarians as sweeping away a tired, effete and decadent Mediterranean civilisation and replacing it with a more virile, martial, Nordic one.... French and Italian historians, on the other hand, have tended to see the barbarians as a bad thing destroying a living civilization, inducing a barbaric Dark Age" (Halsall 35–36). Indeed, the academically-outmoded (but still very much part of the popular conception of the medieval world) notion of the "Dark Ages" following the fall of Rome to Germanic "barbarian hordes" (Sturtevant 123–130) is predicated on the Franco-Italian model. The barbarians at the gate in *The Road Warrior* thus incorporate aspects of each model; the barbarians are both savage and masculine, virile and deviant: punk-rock Visigoths in buttless chaps.

The occupants of the refinery, by contrast, represent the last remnants of virtue in a blasted world. They are a bastion, not only of civilization, but also specifically of hetero-normative civilization. Their clothing, though ragged, is concealing, a combination of natural-browns and gleaming cliché-whites. Their society includes women, but is, surprisingly for an action film (and in contrast with the marauders), chaste: there is no love-interest for Max in this civilization—only one for the Gyro Captain. In addition, their society functions collaboratively in contrast to the autocratic barbarians. Their leader, Pappagallo, describes their difference with outsiders to Max: "We've all been through it in here. But we haven't given up. We're still human beings, with dignity." Such framing of the conflict—between dignity and indignity, between humanity and inhumanity—infuses the struggle for vanishing resources with a moral and existential component: one which an audience in 1981 (as well as one today) might understand.

Conclusions

Where then does this discussion leave us? *The Road Warrior* does seem to bear some Grail resonances, particularly if one is to interpret the film with an allegorical-kaleidoscopic mode, where references are fragmentary and can (and do) shift from moment to moment. There is certainly a Wasteland in the film. The Grail itself is somewhat more ambiguous. Either Max's Grail is the fuel in the tanker, which he entirely fails to achieve as sand spills out of the wreckage; or Max's Grail is civilization, which he entirely fails to achieve as he walks into the desert at the end; or there are only false Grails here; or *The Road Warrior* is simply not a Grail film. Max's status as a Grail knight is ambiguous, not fitting very well the role of any of the questors with which Arthurian scholars are familiar. And one may get tantalizing glimpses of Grail-types in other characters—the Gyro Captain, Pappagallo, or the Feral Kid. But those glimpses are fleeting and require intimate knowledge of Grail types and tropes. Without an exegesis of the film like the one done in this essay, such fleeting connections might never be made.

Does this mode of analyzing *The Road Warrior* have any value? I am uncertain. If one wishes to see the Grail here, it can be found. This position might support the case that the Grail can be found in even some unlikely places within our culture, and that its universality represents yet another example of the enduring legacy of the Middle Ages within contemporary culture. However, if one wishes for it not to be here, such a view is also defensible. It is reasonable to argue that the universality of Grail-types is a byproduct of its elevation—both in the cultural consciousness and even in popular parlance—of the Holy Grail (as in The Holy Grail of…) as a universal icon for a desirable but difficult-to-achieve solution to a significant problem. One could also argue—supported by Miller himself—that a Campbellian analysis bears more ready fruit.

Then, is there nothing for a scholar of medievalism to say about *The Road Warrior*? I do not believe this statement to be true. In films of the post-apocalyptic subgenre, medieval narratives and themes are (perhaps surprisingly) commonplace. A world defined by lack—of food, of technology, of energy, of people, of civilization—lends itself easily to quest narratives—whether Grail quests or ones more banal. In this world, one needs not go to the questing forest to find adventure; the questing forest has engulfed the world. Furthermore, these specific lacks correspond neatly with a popular perception of the Middle Ages as an era defined (partially) by barbarism, filth, and violence (Sturtevant 150–156).

It is easy, therefore, to find medieval resonances dotted through the post-apocalyptic cinemascape. *The Book of Eli* (2010) centers on the quest of a man braving the post-apocalyptic Wild West to deliver the last copy of the Bible into the safekeeping of the new monastery at Alcatraz Island. In *The Postman* (1997), a lone survivor of the apocalypse wanders the Wasteland on a quest to deliver mail from before the apocalypse (and ends up raising an army inspired, in part, by his quotations from *Henry V*). In *Waterworld* (1995), the hero wanders a flooded landscape, fleeing bandits and hopping from island castle to floating city in the search for a New World on dry land. Even video games have been influenced by Max's medieval-infused world; the award-winning *Fallout* game series depicts a lone wanderer scouring the post-nuclear punk-junkyard deserts in search of a terraforming device that will heal the Wasteland. Why do each of these contain aspects of the medieval? Why do we conceive of a collapse in society as a return to the Middle Ages rather than to any other historical epoch? Why do we see ourselves bombed back, not to the Stone Age, but to the Middle Ages?

Part of the answer must be that each of these pop-culture iterations owes a debt to *The Road Warrior*. Not only do many owe their existence to the critical and financial successes of this film, but many draw aesthetic and narrative elements from it. *The Road Warrior* is certainly a quest film, set in a world that is on the verge of re-collapsing into a new Dark Ages replete with junk cars, punk hairdos, and homosexual rape. And while *The Road Warrior* is by no means straightforwardly medieval, its medievalisms have been copied by many others in its genre, and remain influential to this day. And it is for this reason that *Road Warrior*, while perhaps not a traditional Grail film, should still attract careful attention from scholars of medievalism.

Note

Special thanks to Andrew B. R. Elliott for his thoughts on and revisions to this essay.

Works Cited

Anderson, Richard C. "The Notion of Schemata and the Educational Enterprise: General Discussion of the Conference." In *Schooling and the Acquisition of Knowledge*. Ed. Richard C. Anderson, Rand J. Spiro, and William Edward Montague. Hillsdale, NJ: Lawrence Erlbaum, 1977.

Barber, Richard. *The Holy Grail: Imagination and Belief*. Cambridge: Harvard University Press, 2004.

Bond, James A., et al. *The Definitive Frazetta Reference*. [N.p.], New Jersey: Vanguard Productions, 2008.

Bowersock, Glen W. "The Vanishing Paradigm of the Fall of Rome." *Bulletin of the American Academy of Arts and Sciences* 49.8 (1 May 1996): 29–43.

Bryant, Nigel, trans. *The High Book of the Grail: A Translation of the Thirteenth Century Romance of Perlesvaus*. Cambridge, Eng.: D. S. Brewer, 2007.

Byrnes, Paul. "Interview: George Miller." *Australian Screen Online, National Film and Sound Archive*. http://aso.gov.au/people/George_Miller_1/interview/. Accessed 11 August 2013.

Campbell, Joseph. *The Hero with a Thousand Faces*. 3rd ed. Novato, CA: New World Library, 2008.

Chrétien de Troyes. *Perceval: The Story of the Grail*. Trans. Nigel Bryant. New Edition. Cambridge, Eng.: D. S. Brewer, 2006.

Foley, James. "New Water-Splitting System Could Be 'Holy Grail' of Clean, Alternative Energy Revolution." *Nature World News*. 2 August 2013 http://www.natureworldnews.com/articles/3301/20130802/new-water-splitting-system-holy-Grail-clean-alternative-energy-revolution.htm. Accessed 12 August 2013.

Geoffrey of Monmouth. *The Historia Regum Britannie of Geoffrey of Monmouth*. (Vol. I. Bern, Burger-bibliothek, MS. 568.) Ed. Neil Wright. Cambridge, Eng.: Boydell & Brewer, 1985.

Gibbon, Edward. *The History of the Decline and Fall of the Roman Empire.* New York: Harper & Brothers, 1876–1879.

Halsall, Guy. "The Barbarian Invasions." In *The New Cambridge Medieval History: Volume 1, c.500–c.700.* Ed. Paul Fouracre. Cambridge: Cambridge University Press, 2005.

Mahoney, Dhira B., ed. *The Grail: A Casebook.* New York: Garland, 2000.

Miller, George, dir. *Mad Max 2: The Road Warrior.* Warner Bros., 1982.

Shapiro, Jerome F. *Atomic Bomb Cinema: The Apocalyptic Imagination on Film.* London: Routledge, 2013.

Sofge, Erik. "MIT Fights for Clean Power With Holy Grail of Fusion in Reach." *Popular Mechanics.* 1 October 2009. http://www.popularmechanics.com/science/4251982. Accessed 12 August 2013.

Sturtevant, Paul. *Based on a True History? The Impact of Popular "Medieval Film" on the Public Understanding of the Middle Ages.* Ph.D. diss. The University of Leeds, 2010.

Thompson, E. A. *Romans and Barbarians: The Decline of the Western Empire.* Madison: University of Wisconsin Press, 1982.

Winny, James, ed. *Sir Gawain and the Green Knight.* Orchard Park, NY: Broadview Press, 1992.

Wolfram von Eschenbach. *Parzival.* Ed. Andre Lefevre. New York: Continuum, 1991.

Yergin, Daniel. *The Prize: The Epic Quest for Oil, Money & Power.* New York: Simon & Schuster, 2011.

The Grail as Symbolic Quest
in Tarkovsky's *Stalker*

Andrew B. R. Elliott

At first glance, Andrei Tarkovsky's 1979 film *Stalker*, like a number of other films discussed in this collection of essays, would seem to be a perfect fit as a kind of allegorical Grail film. The story of three men on a Quest for a supernatural goal matches both a Vulgate and a Malorian model of the Grail. Their boarding of a tiny vessel that mysteriously carries them across a gulf into a secluded and isolated area, set apart from the banality of modern life, resembles various descriptions of questors' travels across mysterious waters to an unnamed land. The obstacles and barriers that assail the three questors seem to require the sorts of exegetical interpretation that nearby monks and hermits such as Nacien might offer to our Grail heroes. The free interflow between dreams and waking life infuses the whole Quest with a sense of oneiric, ethereal and, above all, supernatural forces; these forces control and guide their actions, with the result that actions in the liminal dream world have as much significance as those in waking life, which recalls the extended dream sequences of Malory's Grail heroes. The use of fragmented, but interconnected, images and motifs like the wolf, falling water, or lingering close-ups of the Stalker all reflect Hatto's identification of the legend as a composite assortment of fragments rather than a canonical text (7).

Closer analysis of the film further reveals moments, as this essay will demonstrate, in which specific elements of the familiar Grail legends seem to emerge from the shadowy underworld of the Zone. Snapshots and key sequences of the film seem to reveal a deep and intimate knowledge of the intricacies of the Grail legends or of medieval literary tropes, such as a long, six-minute take in which the three men sit hunched in total silence on a railway trolley which transports them almost autonomously through the militarized zone and into the Wasteland of the Zone itself, like the Miraculous Ship of the *Queste del Saint Graal* which appears without crew in the harbor and plays such a key role in transporting the Grail heroes along their way without their guidance. Likewise, the various talismans (nuts tied to a handkerchief, waterfalls, the roaming animals that appear at key narrative moments as though to point the way through the forest ahead) and the disembodied voice which admonishes the non-believer seem to map neatly onto our conceptions of the Grail, and its surrounding legends and its various prohibitive or exhortative inscriptions. Likewise, the conception of the Room not as a magical object, but as a space of introspection, fits the idea of an allegorical Quest as in *La Queste del Saint Graal*. In this way, the search for an object leads ultimately to the Self in a moment of self-reflexivity suggesting, as Mahoney points out, that the Grail on some occasions "connotes not the goal of the search, but the search itself, the Quest that drives men (for it is traditionally men who search) unstintingly" (1). It is no surprise, then, that in his extraordinary study of the film, Geoff Dyer describes the Stalker's destination, the Room, as "the Holiest of Grails" (155).

And yet, paradoxically, one of the first things to be said about the film is that it most definitely—and defiantly—is *not* a Grail film. Tarkovsky's fascination with literature and books often extends into his films such as *Andrei Rublev*, and *Stalker* might seem, on the surface, to be no exception. His hero in this film, the eponymous Stalker, is accompanied by a Writer and a Professor, and one glimpse of a bookshelf heaving with well-thumbed volumes reflects Tarkovsky's own literary tastes, as he himself admits.[1] Such erudition might then suggest an awareness of medieval Grail lore. However, for anyone familiar with Tarkovsky's *oeuvre*, *Stalker* cannot unproblematically be understood as an adaptation of a literary text, since his remarkable book, *Sculpting in Time*, makes it clear that he views cinema as an art form completely separate from literature, and one with markedly different aims and objectives. Despite such surface similarities to the Grail legend, Tarkovsky's film is clearly not a textual adaptation of a Grail legend in the same way as Rohmer's *Perceval le Gallois* is a direct adaptation of Chrétien. Nor is it even the kind of loose adaptation which saw *Le Mort le roi Artu* become Bresson's *Lancelot du lac*. The absence of easily identifiable, one-to-one parallels with the Grail legend means that it is not even a free adaptation of the matter of Britain like Romero's *Knightriders* or Levinson's *The Natural*.

In fact, not only is the film not an adaptation of medieval Grail legends, it is not even in fact a true adaptation of *Roadside Picnic* by the Strugatsky brothers, the book on which it is putatively based. The original novel begins with a clear premise (as does *Stalker* in its opening credits) that the Zone was created by the visit to Earth of a passing alien craft. However, in the novel, the Zone's mystery is the subject of scientific curiosity, and the narrative is told from the perspective of the protagonist, Red Schuhart, an employee of the Institute created to investigate the Zone, who leads a shadowy existence between his legally-sanctioned, scientific excursions into the Zone and his twilight forays as a Stalker. Tarkovsky's film eliminates the ambivalence of the novel's hero, and focuses all of its attention instead on the Stalker's illegal incursions and the concomitant search for truth and self-knowledge that his Quests engender. As such, what might be better described as a kind of science fiction frontier-myth (Schuhart's excursions into the Zone are, initially, for purely financial gain, destined to supplement his official income) becomes in the hands of Tarkovsky an allegorical, deeply mysterious and enigmatic tale of the search for self-knowledge.

The numerous discrepancies between the book and the film, in fact, caused no less a figure than Fredric Jameson to condemn the film as an obscurantist and "lugubrious religious Fable" (92). Discussing this unsuccessful adaptation, he laments that the science-fiction elements of the novel have been replaced by a messianic subtext full of allegories and dominated by the "drearily suffering Christ-like solemnity of the protagonist" (92). It is true that there was no conscious attempt at fidelity or realism in the transition from page to screen, leading Griffin and Waldron to describe the film as "only tenuously linked to the ... novel" (257), a fact which even Tarkovsky himself recognized in his acknowledgement that it shares only two words—the *Zone* and *Stalker*—with the original (Guerra).

Even when trying to situate the film within a wider genre or within a definable *oeuvre*, *Stalker* poses problems in classification. As a director, Tarkovsky was noted for his rejection of categorizations, and he steadfastly refused to be labeled a historical filmmaker after his earlier foray into the medieval world, *Andrei Rublev*. Indeed, in a 1981 interview with Ian Christie, he explicitly rejected the idea of cinematic genres entirely, claiming that "I do not believe that the cinema has genres—the cinema is itself a genre. Once we start talking about genre, we are dealing with a systematization resulting from the cinema as a commercial enterprise" (66). Such a claim, however, is in fact borne out by a closer analysis of the film. Griffin and Waldron describe the film as science-fiction noir—though, in fact, it is the novel and not the film which more easily fits the requirements of noir with its "characteristic feature [of] the 'curious depopulation of space,' which means that 'spaces have been emptied of desire'" (265).

Stalker resists genre by adducing and embracing elements from a host of other genres. There is the Western journey with its laconic cowboy leader and its permeable frontier, its lawmen and its wilderness juxtaposed against the homestead. There are staple sci-fi tropes in its bland, industrial setting and in the suggestion of alien interference in the creation of the Zone in the first place. There is the buddy film, mixed with the road movie, in which three very different personalities reluctantly join forces to achieve their goal. There is also, in the detective subplot, a hint of traditional film noir (revealed also in its use of black and white outside of the Zone), alongside a sense of melodrama recalling the films of Yasujiro Ozu in its domestic relationships. Others desperate for a cinematic parallel might even read into the "final mission" theme an extended allegory of the military movie that underpins films as disparate as *The Seven Samurai*, *The Magnificent Seven*, *Apocalypse Now*, or *Rambo: First Blood Part II*, and that have been reinserted into Dark Age films such as *King Arthur* or *The Eagle*. In all of these cases, the film's heroes break through the border in order to save a group of trapped people. The difference in *Stalker* might be that this time they are *metaphorically* trapped, transforming their rescue into a metaphysical battle with their own doubts and fears.

However, none of these genres provides a perfect fit, and *Stalker* does seem actively to resist generic compartmentalization. The most honest thing to be said about the film is that, as well as not being a Grail film, *Stalker* is not really a genre film of any kind at all, but it is instead a powerful and difficult exploration of the human condition. In Tarkovsky's own words, "my objective is to create my own world and these images we create mean nothing more than the images which they are.... If my account is allegorical, that is not my intention—there is no ulterior motive to reveal a hidden meaning" (Christie 67).

In addition to the problems of applying any kind of generic categorizations to the film, a secondary problem arises with the director's unwillingness to accept symbolic interpretations of his films. As Dyer observes, "Tarkovsky has always been opposed to symbolic readings of the images in his film" (13), making it very difficult to try to read into his Grail film any kind of neat allegorical subtext. In a brief aside in his *Sculpting in Time*, the filmmaker openly rebuffs any such attempts to deconstruct the film's symbolism:

> People have often asked me what the Zone is, and what it symbolises, and have put forward wild conjectures on the subject. I'm reduced to a state of fury and despair by such Questions. *The Zone doesn't symbolise anything, any more than anything else does in my films: the zone is a zone,* it's life, and as he makes his way across it a man may break down or he may come through. Whether he comes through or not depends on his own self-respect, and his capacity to distinguish between what matters and what is merely passing [200].[2]

Such resistance means that it is difficult, if not impossible, to detect hidden meanings and intertextual references retrospectively in a film that aimed to

> mark out that essentially human thing that cannot be dissolved or broken down, that forms like a crystal in the soul of each of us and constitutes its great worth. And even though outwardly their journey seems to end in fiasco, in fact each of the protagonists acquires something of inestimable value: faith. He becomes aware in himself of what is most important of all; and that most important thing is alive in every person [Tarkovsky 199].

Such was his vehement opposition to symbolic readings that not only did Tarkovsky refuse to accept the possibility of allegory, but he also (deliberately) introduced ambiguities in various interviews discussing his films by suggesting that different interpretations are simultaneously possible. Speaking to Guerra, for example, he suggests that "the spectators should doubt not only the existence of other stalkers, but also the existence of the forbidden Zone. Perhaps even the place where wishes are realized is only a myth. Or a joke. Or perhaps it is only a fantasy of our protagonist. For the public this remains a mystery." Likewise, Tarkovsky admits to Aldo Tassone that, in his own Quest for open-endedness, he even removed objects present in the source novel from his film where they might attract too simple an interpretation:

> In the original novel by the Strugatsky brothers ... there was a place where desires were fulfilled. But this was represented by a gold orb. There was a golden orb, for whatever reason. However, in the Strugatsky story, the desires were truly fulfilled, whereas in the script this remains a mystery. You don't know whether this is true or whether it's the Stalker's fantasy. For me as the author of the film, either choice is OK. It seems to me that it's just as well if it's all part of his fantasy— that would not affect the main point at all [55].

Nevertheless, despite Tarkovsky's protestations and rejection of allegory, a viewing of the film by anyone acquainted with aspects of the Grail legends leads to a striking feeling of familiarity and of continuity with recurring elements of the Quest theme. Tarkovsky's shift of emphasis away from the *object* of the search, instead focusing on the *Quest itself*, reflects the frequent use of the "Holy Grail [as] a standard symbol [...] for an object of search far off, mysterious and out of reach." (Mahoney 1) In this respect, the film works in much the same ways as certain other updated versions of the Grail story do in popular adaptations, in replacing the Grail with something else, and in extirpating the whole Quest from its religious context. Such freedom, as with Gilliam's *The Fisher King*, allows for an allegorical reading that interprets the Grail not as an object, but that sees the Grail symbolically as a potent icon of wider searches for meaning.

It is this last aspect of the Grail which, I will argue below, underpins Tarkovsky's "Grail film"; it is a view of the Grail not as a Christian, nor even a religious, icon, but one according to which Emma Jung and Marie-Louise von Franz recast the Grail as a universal symbol of legend:

In nearly all mythologies there is a miraculous vessel. Sometimes it dispenses youth and life, at other times it possesses the power of healing, and occasionally, as with the mead cauldron of the Nordic Ymir, inspiring strength and wisdom are to be found in it [150].

To begin with, the motif of the Quest reflects a number of metaphorical readings. The Quest theme in *Stalker* begins in the opening scene with, appropriately, the image of the Stalker rooted in his daily life in the mundane world, a world with which he is visibly ill at ease. The film opens with a long credit sequence rolling over a backdrop of an almost empty, dirty bar in which the three protagonists will later be seen drinking before setting out on the Quest (is this a Soviet Camelot awaiting "marvelous adventures"?). Immediately after the credits, however, the initial disruption of time becomes apparent as the camera switches to the protagonist lying in bed with his wife—though it is not immediately apparent whether the scene is taking place at the same time as the men await him in the bar (as the principles of parallel editing would suggest), or whether we have already jumped backwards through time, and the scene takes place before the action to which we have already been introduced. The initial unbroken shot lasts a full minute, introducing the long, lingering shots that characterize the film as a whole.

Starting with an establishing shot that begins outside of the house, the camera slowly zooms in through the window to reveal a small iron-framed bed. The sequence then switches to a fragmented overhead shot of the whole family lying in bed: beginning on the right of the bed, the frame is filled with a close-up of a glass of water shuddering across an iron bed-side table accompanied by the noise of an oncoming train, whose proximity is suggested by incessant rattle of the creaky old house. Following the same direction of the train, the camera then pans left to reveal a close-up of a sleeping woman facing the wall, yet, rather than following her gaze, the camera continues to pan slowly, inexorably, away from the woman, to frame a young girl lying in the opposite direction, then a long, empty gap, before settling on a close-up of our protagonist, the Stalker, who lies awake and looks back across the bed at this sleeping family. As the sound of *La Marseillaise* played on a crackly radio reaches a crescendo, the whistling of the train, the gush of the steam, the rattling of the house and a number of unseen men's cries merge into one roar, yet the camera pans relentlessly back across the sleeping women who are undisturbed by the banging, shouting and clattering train, eventually settling on the table which rattles quietly once more as the train moves off into the distance, leaving a silence punctuated solely by a relentless dripping of water.

In a further disruption of time and space, the camera cuts awkwardly back to the establishing shot to reveal the Stalker rising from the bed, already wearing a sweater and socks. He leans across to take a watch from the headboard, dresses silently, and walks out of the shot past his wife, at which point—rather than following him—the camera holds its frame on the bed for a few unnatural seconds during which no one in the bed stirs.

Suddenly, unexpectedly, the Stalker reappears in front of the camera, whereupon the camera tracks back out the way it came in as he passes through the doors and half-closes them behind him, again leaving the shot to the right. Once again lingering for a few awkward seconds, the wife can be seen through the doors stirring and rising herself. As the camera finally cuts to another angle (it must be remembered here that, at almost 10 minutes into the film, we are still only on the fourth cut), we hear the first words of the film, spoken by the wife who asks abruptly (along with the audience, perhaps), "Why did you take my watch?"

As mysterious and disorienting as this sequence might appear for an introductory scene (which, in keeping with the mystery of the remainder of the film, in fact introduces nothing in terms of the plot), on subsequent viewings it becomes apparent that the introduction to the routines and domestic life of the Stalker and his family already contains everything necessary to understand what is to come. The sadness and poverty of the house underscore a fundamental longing and dissatisfaction with the world, prompting the desire for "adventures" beyond the purely material realm, and the search for something mystical and mysterious. Longing and lack of fulfillment can be read into the Stalker's insomnia; his poverty and misery (and hence aspiration) are suggested by the house's poor state of repair, the leaks, the grubbiness, and its proximity to the railway. The Stalker's obsession with time and his lack of regard for his wife and child can be understood by his casual theft of the family's only watch, coupled with the fact that, rather than explain himself to his wife, he makes no response at all but continues noisily washing himself off-camera. As in the Grail myths, the scene makes it clear that something is missing from their terrestrial existence, a lack that spurs the Stalker on to pursue adventures in the service of something greater, imparting a sense of inevitability to the Quest.

Perhaps more important than the narrative and the dialogue, however, is the aesthetic itself, which is punctuated by long, slow moving pans, tracks and zooms that combine space and time in a disorientating and unnatural way. Tarkovsky describes his vision for this aesthetic in terms of a deliberate temporal disorientation:

> [I]n *Stalker* I wanted there to be no time lapse between the shots. I wanted time and its passing to be revealed, to have their existence, within each frame; for the articulations between the shots to be the continuation of the action and nothing more, to involve no dislocation of time, not to function as a mechanism for selecting and dramatically organising the material—I wanted it to be as if the whole film had been made in a single shot [*Sculpting in Time* 193–194].

As Dyer describes it, "*Stalker* is a literal journey that is also a journey into cinematic space and—in tandem—into time" (46). Tarkovsky's refusal to interrupt each carefully constructed sequence thus feeds into his unique directorial style, which uses the passage of time as a means of exploring space that, when broken up, reflects an unrealistic (or for Tarkovsky an anti-realistic) depiction of the correlation between time, space, and memory. For him, as with Bazin, editing is a way of distorting reality by the unnatural dissection of continuously lived experience as mere fragments of a greater whole, and thus cuts should only occur in order to support the overall aesthetic value instead of offering support for the narrative meaning. As Tarkovsky writes in *Sculpting in Time*, "assembly, editing, disturbs the passage of time, interrupts it and simultaneously gives it something new. The distortion of time can be a means of giving it rhythmical expression" (121). As such, the isolation of the film's characters in space becomes anchored to a slow movement in time that emphasizes not the objects of the Quest, but the Quest itself. Such a conception—though not intended as such by Tarkovsky—offers further parallels with the Grail Quest as the ultimate fusion of time, movement, and space. As Baumgartner puts it, the Grail Quest represents an "ultimate adventure," a "moment that brings narrative, temporal and spatial closure all in one" (108–109).

Alexander Kaidanovsky as the title character in Andrei Tarkovsky's 1979 film *Stalker* (Pacific Film Archive).

It is this question of the separation from the mundane world that thus underpins our ability to read *Stalker* as a Grail Quest in all but name, since it reflects one of the key elements of the Grail Quest in particular, namely the desire to achieve something spiritual. All three of our "Grail knights" (that is, the Stalker himself, as well as the Professor and the Writer) are incomplete, acknowledging that something is missing from their everyday lives. The Writer is a cynic who is tired of a life without mystery—we are here in the realm of a Camelot without adventure, here transposed onto a relentlessly logical Soviet milieu. It is precisely this absence of mystery that provokes the Writer to go on the Quest in the first place: we first encounter him midway through a speech ascribing his rejection of the modern world to its absence of spirituality. The Writer goes on to dismiss all terrestrial mystery as simply a tyranny of logic, including the Bermuda Triangle, claiming that, by contrast, "to live in the Middle Ages was interesting. Every home had its house-spirit and every church had its God." By reframing the Middle Ages as a period characterized by mystery in which life was not controlled by rationalism and scientific logic, the Writer thus stands in contradistinction to the Professor, who comes to represent science that systematically undermines the supernatural.

However, the rigorous application of science and logic by no means makes life any more fulfilling for his fellow passenger, the Professor. Despite his faith in reason, the film slowly reveals that the Professor's confidence in truth is purely professional; in his private life, his ability to hide behind scientific truth as a formidable ally make him a coward in interpersonal relations and unable to stand up to his colleague, a competitor not only for advancement but also for his place in the marital bed. He thus emerges as a kind of Lancelot *manqué*, one who has risen to the top of an earthly existence, but one who is disbarred from achieving the new Quest for the Grail which takes place on the spiritual realm. As a consequence of his logical rationalism, towards the end of the film the Professor's true intentions in visiting the Zone are revealed not to be self-fulfillment, but rather to blow up the Zone to prevent its falling into the wrong hands. Thus, like Lancelot peering through the doorway at the sacred rite of the Grail Mass but condemned to misunderstand it, the Professor is doomed not to understand the mysteries of the spiritual realm; instead of throwing off the shackles of Reason, he hopes to extend the laws of science and reason into the Zone itself, thereby transforming a magical realm into an extension of the drab monotones of the real world lying beyond its borders.[3] These two companions thus share—albeit for very different reasons—the Stalker's longing for fulfillment that underpins their collective Quest.

In all three cases, then, the questors enter the Zone itself not necessarily to seek an object, to but to find the parts of themselves that were missing outside of the Zone; it is not a Quest for an object, but a step towards self-improvement. Such a Quest thus moves us away from the realm of legend as derived from the matter of Britain, and into the domain of myth, here universalized as a pattern which Campbell classifies the "nuclear unit of the monomyth: separation, initiation, return" (23). Following this pattern, the questors consciously leave the world outside the Zone on the grounds of a central lack (separation). They are then introduced to a new kind of world that requires the acquisition of new skills or a new mindset (the initiation into the "rules" of the Zone), and then they must return to the normal world in order to redeem it (the return, which in fact sees all three questors return to the status quo).

The opening scene outlined above already contains an early separation from a trinity of the family, both literally in terms of the Stalker's attempt to sneak out of the house and metaphorically in the visual separation of the Stalker from his family by squeezing him into the corners of the frames. In leaving the house to begin his Quest, the Stalker experiences a kind of self-actualization, abandoning in the process his wife and child in the pursuit of a higher ideal. In response, his wife collapses to the floor much like Perceval's mother when her son departs, writhing in a physical manifestation of a more spiritual—or at least psychological—pain. This image is familiar; Tarkovsky returns to it in a number of his films, in which female protagonists suffer from hysterical fits. From Adelaide (Susan Fleetwood) in *Sacrifice* (1986) to Hari (Natalya Bondarchuk) in *Solaris* (1972), the recurrent images of hysterical women overpowered by emotional outbursts prompt Sheehan to suggest that it is a staple trope demonstrating the "sexist parameters of Tarkovsky's psychology," which persistently conflates wives with mothers (200–201).

As a potential Grail film, the scene of the male questor leaving his family, and the heart-wrenching pain that his departure inflicts on them, is also by no means unfamiliar, and, as a staple trope in the Quest, it forms a recognizable motif that cannot be ascribed to the "sexist psychology" of one writer-director in particular, but instead infuses the Grail myths with a masculine exclusivity. In this male-dominated Quest, the separation from the mundane is marked as much by the absence of women as it is by the presence of men. Accordingly, the bar where the men meet, the empty warehouses in which they hide, the military barriers to the Zone as well as, notably, the Zone itself are all exclusively male spaces, even if not explicitly gendered as such. The exclusivity of the Zone as a site of *male* questing is later made explicit when the Writer arrives at the scene with a female companion in tow. The Stalker's visibly angry reaction is, nevertheless, ambiguous. While it is clear that the woman is not to join them on their Quest, the reasons why are carefully kept quiet with the Stalker barely speaking to the woman except to say "go," upon which she insults the Writer, gets back into her car, and drives away, leaving the menfolk to begin their Quest.

Such exclusion, however, is certainly not foreign to the world of the Grail, in which female characters play a complex and ambivalent role as both perilous obstacles and embodiments of diabolic temptation (as we see with the Writer's female companion below) as well as essential helpers in the Quest (like Perceval's sister or the Stalker's wife), who sustain and support the Grail knights, and without whom the Grail cannot be achieved. The male-oriented domain of the Zone thus offers a reflection of this complex role of femininity— while the three knights do not encounter any women while inside the Zone, the Stalker's family are the central pillars which allow him to go into the Zone in the first place, and re-accommodate him once he returns. The hysterical fit suffered by the Stalker's wife is thus, like the sorrow of Perceval's mother, a physical manifestation of the pain that the Quest causes his family; less temporary, however, is the effect that the Stalker's activities have on their disabled daughter, nicknamed "Monkey," who seemingly is born without legs and must be carried everywhere. In this sense, the daughter becomes a maimed Fisher King to be "cured" by the Stalker. However, Tarkovsky's ambiguity once again strikes here to prevent us from drawing any clear-cut conclusions about the child. In the novel, her disability is explained as a wider phenomenon that afflicts all offspring of the Stalkers (and which leads to an emotionally-charged scene in which Red Schuhart's pregnant girlfriend must decide whether to keep the child, knowing of the probability of birth defects). In Tarkovsky's film, however, the general spirit of post-apocalyptic destruction points to more earthly causes, most obviously nuclear radiation—here, Chelyabinsk in 1957, though today the film's more obvious associations with Chernobyl would be anachronistic given that the disaster would not take place until 1986.[4]

From the moment they leave the bar, then, the "Quest" of the three characters once again looks oddly familiar to anyone acquainted with the Grail legends. The image of the three questors on the railway trolley recalls certain manuscript illustrations[5] as they sit hunched over, facing outwards, relinquishing control to the Stalker, or Fate, or the Zone itself as it drags them in. As the noisy machine gun fire fades out, and the scene slowly segues from black and white to color, the trolley/boat takes them away from the battles against earthly, human foes (in this case the machine-gun fire of the sentries) and over water to a new environment, which is no less hostile, but characterized by lush, verdant forests populated by invisible, natural forces. The inexorable passage of the trolley suggests a degree of inevitability that is also characteristic of the Grail seekers' Quests, in which the knights have no control over their itinerary but must submit meekly. Here we might mention the mysterious ship which awaits Malory's Grail knights; in the same way as the ship carries away the best of Camelot, so too is *Stalker*'s trolley neither driven nor controlled by the Questors. That this was, in fact, a conscious change made by Tarkovsky himself can be seen by a comparison with *Roadside Picnic*, in which excursions to the Zone show none of these signs of inevitability, but are instead conducted using a kind of hovercraft that is steered and controlled by one of Red Schuhart's crew following his instructions. The inevitability of Tarkovsky's film is further underscored by a later scene in which the Professor turns back to retrace his steps, only to find himself once again joining the others at a point further along their journey. By denying the Questors any agency in the Zone, then, Tarkovsky makes the Zone a much more active, and mysteriously supernatural, force than the Zone of the Strugatsky brothers' novel. This active agency in turn nudges *Stalker* away from science fiction, and closer to the Grail's magical realm, suggesting that turns and deviations are futile: there is only one real itinerary, and it is not determined by human will.

Such resigned fatalism, curiously, makes the trio into surprisingly competent Grail knights, albeit in a very Soviet and constrained way. In *Roadside Picnic*, the Zone is essentially the result of a "comfort break" by the aliens (hence the title); by contrast, the post-apocalyptic, dystopian world of *Stalker* is ravaged by something nuclear, something radioactive, which continues to exert power long after the departure of the extra-terrestrials. In this case, then, we are not dealing with a Terre Gaste in which nothing will grow—there are forests and foliage aplenty here—but rather one which few are willing to enter, perhaps recalling Tennyson's waste fens, rather than Eliot's Waste Land. Upon realizing that the Zone is more powerful than they are, the three entrust themselves to Fate, relinquish control and bravely (or naïvely) enter in search of their goal. There are, as in Malory, three who make it to the Room and who, in a way, achieve their Quest, although (again like Malory) not all of them are successful in achieving their Grail which does not take them into a new, spiritual realm but which restores them by allowing them to return to their original milieu. Whether their return means that they have achieved the Grail or not, however, is, as might be expected by this stage, left deliberately ambiguous.

The use of color—or its absence—is another notable way in which the mundane world is separated from that of the Zone, and one which is likewise introduced in the opening sequence. The entire scene is shot neither in color nor in black and white, but is infused by a muddy brown suffused with shadows and key lighting cutting across the bed at haphazard angles, creating a crisscross of shadows and light, separating swathes of the screen, leaving each character isolated in mid- or long-shots to emphasize their isolation and the absence of spirituality in the world outside the Zone. This conscious use of black and white is explained as an attempt by Tarkovsky to escape the casual association of color with realism, which he describes as

> a bad period in terms of aesthetics. Filming in color is regarded as getting as close as possible to reality. But I look on color as a blind alley. Every art form tries to arrive at truth and seeks to form a generalization. Using color is related to how one perceives the real world. Filming a scene in color involves organizing and structuring a frame, realizing that all the world enclosed in this frame is in color and making the audience aware of this. The advantage of black and white is that it is extremely expressive and it doesn't distract the audience's attention [Mitchell 77].

Thus, Tarkovsky's decision to use monochrome to depict the "real" world creates a subtle dialectic between realism and the realistic, on the grounds that "viewers like colored pictures, but strangely enough I believe that color can be much less realistic than black and white" (Christie 69). Even here, however, Tarkovsky refuses to commit to such a strict dialectic between realism and unreality as seen in films as varied as *The Wizard of Oz*, *The Purple Rose of Cairo* or *Pleasantville*, claiming that "the Zone is a diseased area, abandoned: certainly there's an unreality about it. The use of color could well mean that it's unreal," before adding in typical ambiguous style, "...but I don't know for sure" (Strick 71).

Having anchored his reality in a kind of Brechtian alienation, then, the unreality of the Zone creates the kind of *unheimlich* ideal that suggests otherworldliness; for the Zone, "the ideal is concerned with things that do not exist in our own world as we know it, but it reminds us of what ought to exist on the spiritual plane" (Tarkovsky 238). Just as the color is ambiguous, so too is the monochrome a compromise between true black-and-white and a sepia tinge that creates a unique, aged, muddy palette rather than the crisp chiaroscuro of the Italian neorealists which he admired. As Dyer eloquently describes it, "even to describe the black-and-white of *Stalker* as black-and-white is to tint what we're seeing with an inappropriate suggestion of the rainbow. Technically this concentrated sepia was achieved by filming in color and printing in black-and-white. The result is a kind of sub-monochrome" (8). Tarkovsky's use of color thus serves to distinguish between the banal grays and browns of life outside the Zone and, by contrast, uses the bright, vivid hues as a means of demarcating the Zone as a place alive with lush greens, deep browns and vibrant reds, which for our purposes it is tempting to read as a greater attunement to spirituality and an awakening of the senses. Interestingly, though almost certainly by chance, such a chromatic scheme also finds echoes in Grail literature, such as Christine Poulson's analysis of the use of color by Victorian artists depicting the Grail Quest as means of emphasizing the heightened sensuality of the realm of the Grail (148–153; see also 27).

Nevertheless, the emphasis on this separation—as with the explosion of color that marks the finale of *Andrei Rublev*—allows us to understand the Zone and, therefore, the Quest of the three men as a whole, as a search for something missing outside of the Zone, whose discovery promises to enrich the non-magical world of reality. By extension, such a reading suggests that the Room represents (in true Grail style) those qualities, values, or elements missing from everyday existence that require a spiritual, and not material, Quest for absolution. This removal of a material dimension explains in part Tarkovsky's excision of objects like the golden orb of *Roadside Picnic*, since the absence of a specific object to be acquired on the Quest not only increases ambiguity about interpretation, but also forestalls any purely material explanations or objectives, shifting the Quest onto the spiritual plane. Such a separation thus initiates a third theme; that of faith and magic, here interpreted as a generic, laic belief in something lacking in the world around us.

As in any Grail story worth its salt, the faith of the three questors here is continually tested, and the "knights" are besieged by obstacles and tests that can only be overcome by faith both in the Quest as a whole and in magical objects as talismans. From the moment the trio enters the Zone, their path takes no straight lines, but, instead, follows an indirect course to avoid unseen traps and, quite literally, pitfalls. The course is marked out by some very post-industrial talismans, signposts, and walkways symptomatic of a post-apocalyptic Wasteland: nuts tied to strips of white cloth which are thrown arbitrarily into the Zone by the Stalker; burnt out shells of cars, tanks and machinery; the claustrophobic tunnel of a silo; and the overgrown frontage of a brick-built factory. At one point, when the Writer steps off the route marked out by the Stalker, he is beaten back by a deep, disembodied voice booming out of the forest, in a scene which brings the natural world to life so that—like the color scheme mentioned above—the whole seems somehow *too* green, *too* perfect and therefore, paradoxically, *unnatural*. Throughout their itinerary, they are besieged by apparitions of one sort or another, and haunted by dreams which require exegesis and interpretations.

Not unlike medieval knights embarking on the search for the Grail, the trio finds that even the arms and weapons drawn from outside the Zone are ineffective against the supernatural foes faced inside the Zone. In the same vein as Galahad's sword with the prohibition engraved upon its hilt, the arms that the Writer and Professor introduce to the Zone threaten to do more harm than good when in the wrong hands. The Writer brings along a revolver, which in a desert-like ante-room becomes the subject of a dispute with the Stalker on the grounds that there is no predicting what the forces of the Zone will do to a questor carrying such a weapon. The Professor's backpack, as we have seen, does not contain the scientific instruments that he claims it does, but instead a thermal bomb which he intends to detonate inside the Room. However, in the final scenes, as the Stalker is incapacitated by a sort of existentialist terror in which he questions his own motivations and belief in the Zone, it is not the arms that protect the questors, but the simple act of belief in the Stalker, which means that none of the three ultimately needs to enter the Room to achieve his individual Grail.

It is in this sense that it is the search which the Stalker, Professor and Writer undertake which becomes the Grail itself. Though Tarkovsky initially entertained the alternative title *The Room of Desires*, the change of title is significant, as on closer examination of the film we see that it is not the Grail/Room itself which is sought, but the fact of going on the Quest itself which offers the tempting restorative powers exerted by the Zone. This change suggests that the agent of change is not material (a Grail as object), but the one who brings about the Quest in the first place. Thus the spirituality is transposed from the Room onto the Stalker himself. What matters more than anything is not that the three questors *achieve* the Grail by finding and entering the room, but rather its reverse. As Tarkovsky himself states, "what's important is that the two travellers *don't* enter the room," since "in that room it isn't one's desires that are fulfilled but *rather a hidden vision lying deep within the heart of each person*. These are true desires, which correspond to one's interior world" (Tassone 55; emphasis added).

In this allegorical reading of the Quest, then, we might find material that is inadvertently much closer to the spirit of the Grail legends than many other, more deliberate, adaptations of the Grail, since it is not the Grail as *object* or *goal* that fulfills the person, but instead the act of going on the Quest itself. Such an allegorical reading allows us to understand that the very act of entering the Zone is an expression of the Writer and Professor's faith and belief in the Stalker, for whom the act of guiding the trio offers him the faith of people who believe in something—irrespective of what that something might actually be.

As such, like many versions of the Grail, the significance of the Quest lies not in the discovery of the Grail, but in the act of questing itself.

Tarkovsky's rejection of the supernatural within the Zone leads us to the realization that the lack was not an *externalized* one to be remedied by faith, magic or the supernatural, but was, instead, a flaw rooted deep within the human soul, in this case the reason for their hesitation to enter the Zone in the first place. Consequently, the internalization of magic turns the legend on its head, by using its unique sense of spirituality as a means to extirpate the Quest from its religious trappings. Without magic or God, the questors are instead required to believe in themselves and in the Stalker's version of the story: for Tarkovsky, "it is always through spiritual crisis that healing occurs.... This, too, is what *Stalker* is about: the hero goes through moments of despair when his faith is shaken; but every time he comes to a renewed sense of vocation to serve people who have lost their hopes and illusions" (Tarkovsky 193). Such a laic and mundane interpretation of the Grail Quest thus resolves the "three unities of time, space, and action" (Tarkovsky 193) by negating the effects of action, and eliding space into time. After the three enter into the Zone, they immediately get lost and embark upon a period of aimless wandering whose duration is deliberately ambiguous and unspecified. With the rejection of a supernatural element to their Quest, however, what is deliberately left unclear is whether the Professor has found a shortcut, or whether the Stalker has taken them in circles (and thus we wonder whether he has in fact been doing so throughout their journey, and whether in turn his doing so is deliberate).

As they meander for well over a third of the screen time, however, the real message of this non-spiritual Grail Quest begins to emerge, revealing that it is not the space which must be negotiated (and thus it does not really *matter* whether or not they have been going round in circles) but rather, like Purgatory or Lancelot's 24-day illness, that it is the time which must be spent inside the Zone that matters. The important detail is not where they go once inside (and hence it matters little whether their magical trolley will return), but that they spend sufficient time there to divest themselves of their old personalities, and that enough doubt is introduced to overcome their reliance on the logic of the world outside. The circuitous route thus reinterprets the spatially-dominated Quest as a temporal one while, at the same time, retaining the sense of a journey of self-discovery. As Tarkovsky admits: "in fact this isn't a trip but a conversation in which the characters discover who they are" (Tassone 60).

As a consequence, the fact that, even by the film's close, the trio never actually achieve the Grail, hesitating on the threshold of the room itself for fear of discovering their real personalities, does not necessarily translate to failure of the Quest but instead calls into question the credibility of the Quest in the first place. As such, the ambiguity of the film suddenly falls into place as one of the only truly spiritual aspects of a relentlessly logical film, since it matters little whether they find the Room or not, nor even does it matter whether the Room exists or is merely a figure of the Stalker's imagination: "the existence, in the Zone, of the 'room' in which wishes are realized, serves only as a pretext to discover the personalities of the three protagonists of the film" (Guerra). Thus not only can we find in *Stalker* a neat parallel with a number of core elements of the Grail story (the absence of women, the infusion of a higher power, the oneiric overlap between reality and fantasy, and the importance of belief in the higher power), but we also find that the complex subtext of the Quest, which abnegates any kind of object in favor of an introspective self–Questioning, maps neatly onto many of the more abstract interpretations of the Grail legend.

Ending on such a mystical note, then, returns us back to the beginning of this essay, forcing us once again to broach a fundamental paradox which underpins Tarkovsky's difficult film. If, as I have argued, *Stalker* can be easily be read as an allegorical Grail Quest, but Tarkovsky's vehement rejection of allegorical readings prevents us from doing so, then which of the two is the correct or preferred reading? Or perhaps we might fall back on a Barthesian idea of the "Death of the Author" (1977) to suggest that Tarkovsky's beliefs do not matter, in which case we solve one problem only to face new questions about *our own* ability and authority to decode the film as a Grail film. Perhaps the only way out of such a hermeneutic impasse is to suggest that, even if it is not consciously intended as a Grail film, it is possible that *Stalker* reflects a sufficient number of elements of the Grail legend to suggest that it is nevertheless informed by the global appeal of Quest motifs. In this way, we might see the Grail as sufficiently embedded into the collective imaginations of modern culture to find itself reflected unwittingly in all kinds of searches for mysterious objects and experiences, or even in the search itself. Such a question is thus best answered by viewing it not as an either/or dichotomy, but rather by suggesting that the two ideas both spring from the same roots, namely the human Quest for truth itself. For Tarkovsky, the duty of the filmmaker is to use art to unlock truths about life in itself:

> The life principle itself is unique. The artist therefore tries to grasp that principle and make it incarnate, new each time; and each time he hopes, though in vain, to achieve an exhaustive image of the Truth of human existence. The quality of beauty is in the truth of life [Tarkovsky 104].

As such, then, the coincidence of *Stalker*'s parallels with the Grail legends need not be wholly coincidental nor yet wholly intentional, but instead reflect the ideals of the artist— be it a Grail romancier or a Soviet filmmaker—to examine the self. As Norris J. Lacy terms it, "the Grail can be anything or nothing, a holy object or a hoax; the Quest can be a sacred enterprise that gives meaning to life or it can be a pointless exercise or an absurd waste of time and humanity" (11). Whatever the Grail might represent in its individual iteration, the durability of the legend can be traced to the importance of the Quest, rather than the goal, since as the Stalker shows, it is the Quest which reveals an "image of the truth of human existence."[6]

Notes

1. In the 1979 Nostalghia.com interview with Tonino Guerra, Tarkovsky admits to identifying with the Stalker as a cultured man: "despite being an outlaw, he is much more cultured, educated, and intelligent, in the film, than the writer or the scientist, who nevertheless, as characters, express the very idea of intelligence, science, education. From the very beginning I had the urge to make a bookshelf stuffed full of books appear, suddenly, in the film. And it appears in the film's finale, in a scenography that is entirely inappropriate for such an object. I would like to have such a bookshelf in my home. I've never had such a bookshelf. And I would like to have it in the same disorder in which the Stalker keeps his." Likewise, in the same interview, the director recognizes that these are common tropes to which he returns again and again in his films.

2. Emphasis added. See also a similar diatribe against symbolism and interpretation of his films in Christie 71.

3. Were I particularly zealous in a search to apply metaphors, I might be tempted to call the Professor's actions an allegory of Enlightenment reason that seeks to destroy the mystical, mysterious elements of the Middle Ages.

4. The issue of radiation and industrial contamination, however, is one with sad repercussions beyond the film. Having been shot on location at an abandoned electrical generation plant in Estonia, the sound recordist Vladimir Sharun later claimed that a nearby chemical plant poured toxins downstream, to which he attributes the death from cancer of Tarkovsky, his wife Larissa, and actor Anatoly Solonitsyn. See http://people.ucalgary.ca/~tstronds/nostalghia.com/TheTopics/Norton.html for a full description. In a further curious twist, *S.T.A.L.K.E.R.*, a recent video game franchise (2007–2009) and film (2011), see the idea of an exclusion Zone woven back into the story of Chernobyl, and the eponymous stalkers are here sent back into the Zone to contain nuclear mutants.

5. Such as, for example, one illustration from the Lancelot Cycle, Bod. MS. Douce 215, which frames the three Grail Knights in a boat as they seek the Grail. The image can be accessed through the online Bodleian collections at http://bodley30.bodley.ox.ac.uk:8180/luna/servlet/detail/ODLodl~1~1~40847~ 123985:Lancelot-Cycle,-Branches–3,-4,-5—f?qvq=w4s:/what/MS. percent20Douce percent20215/; lc:ODLodl~29~29,ODLodl~7~7,ODLodl~6~6,ODLodl~14~14,ODLodl~8~8,ODLodl~23~23, ODLodl~1~1,ODLodl~24~24&mi=113&trs=117, last accessed 31 July 2013.

6. I am grateful to Kevin J. Harty and Paul B. Sturtevant for their helpful discussions with me about this chapter and its ideas, and for reading through earlier drafts of the essay.

Works Cited

Barthes, Roland. "The Death of the Author." In *Image, Music, Text*. London: Fontana, 1977.

Baumgartner, Emmanuèle. "The *Queste del Saint Graal*: Semblance to Veraie Semblance." In *A Companion to the Lancelot-Grail Cycle*. Ed. Carol Dover. Cambridge, Eng.: D. S. Brewer, 2003.

Campbell, Joseph. *The Hero with a Thousand Faces*. Novato, CA: New World Library, 2008.

Christie, Ian. "Against Interpretation: An Interview with Andrei Tarkovsky (1981)." In *Andrei Tarkovsky: Interviews*. Ed. John Gianvito. Jackson: University of Mississippi Press, 2006.

Dyer, Geoff. *Zona: A Book About a Film About a Journey to a Room*. Edinburgh: Canongate, 2012.

Griffin, Michael J., and Dara Waldron. "Across Time and Space: The Utopian Impulses of Andrei Tarkovsky's *Stalker*." In *Exploring the Utopian Impulse: Essays on Utopian Thought and Practice*. Ed. Michael J. Griffin and Tom Moylan. New York: Peter Lang, 2007.

Guerra, Tonino. "Tarkovsky at the Mirror: A Conversation between Andrei Tarkovsky and Tonino Guerra." Trans. David Stringari. Available at Nostalghia.com: http://people.ucalgary.ca/~tstronds/nostalghia. com/TheTopics/Tarkovsky_Guerra–1979.html. Accessed 21 May 2013. The original interview appeared in *Panorama* 676 (3 April 1979): 160–161, 164, 166, 169–170.

Hatto, A. T. "Foreword to Wolfram von Eschenbach." *Parzival*. Harmondsworth: Penguin, 1980.

Jameson, Fredric. *The Geopolitical Aesthetic: Cinema and Space in the World System*. Bloomington: Indiana University Press, 1995.

Jung, Emma, and Marie-Louise von Franz. "The Central Symbol of the Legend: The Grail as Vessel." In *The Grail: A Casebook*. Ed. Dhira B. Mahoney. New York: Garland, 2000.

Lacy, Norris J., ed. *The Grail, The Quest, and the World of Arthur*. Cambridge, Eng.: D. S. Brewer, 2008.

Mahoney, Dhira B., ed. *The Grail: A Casebook*. New York: Garland, 2000.

Mitchell, Tony. "Tarkovsky in Italy." In *Andrei Tarkovsky: Interviews*. Ed. John Gianvito. Jackson: University of Mississippi Press, 2006.

Poulson, Christine. *The Quest for the Grail: Arthurian Legend in British Art 1840–1920*. Manchester: Manchester University Press, 1999.

Sheehan, Thomas W. "The Production of a Woman in Andrei Tarkovsky's *The Sacrifice*." *Women and Performance: A Journal of Feminist Theory* 9.2 (1997): 199–210.

Strick, Phillip. "Tarkovsky's Translations." In *Andrei Tarkovsky: Interviews*. Ed. John Gianvito. Jackson: University of Mississippi Press, 2006.

Tarkovsky, Andrei. *Sculpting in Time*. Trans. Kitty Hunter-Blair. Austin: University of Texas Press, 1986.

The Waterboy and Swamp Chivalry: A Grail Knight for American Teens

Laurie A. Finke and *Martin B. Shichtman*

What are the roots that clutch, what branches grow
Out of this stony rubbish?—T. S. Eliot, The Waste Land

At the conclusion of Barry Levinson's *The Natural* (1984), outfielder Roy Hobbs, sick, beaten, corruptible but not corrupted, strikes a blow to save the New York Knights baseball franchise for Pop Fisher. It has been a dry season for the Knights, but Hobbs delivers salvation. As lightning and thunder threaten to end the game prematurely, Hobbs sends a fly ball into the lights, his walk-off homerun clinching a championship for the team. Hobbs circles the bases and rain begins to fall, not real rain, but a downpour of light, emanating from exploding stadium lights. This mythic moment, Levinson's cinematic heightening of the Grail knight's "releasing of the waters," so different from the strikeout that concludes Bernard Malamud's novel, provides, we believe, the intertext for Adam Sandler's *The Waterboy* (Frank Coraci, 1998), a comedy written by Sandler and Tim Herlihy. If *The Natural* draws upon medieval Grail narratives—a baseball team called the Knights, with Roy Hobbs as its greatest knight and redeemer, Wonderboy as Excalibur, Pop Fisher as the wounded Fisher King—to elevate the game of baseball to a heroic trial of mythic proportions, *The Waterboy* uses the very same set of parallels to poke fun at the self-importance of films that mystify sports, inflating them into near religious experiences by connecting them to mythic themes. In the move from Wonderboy to Waterboy, from baseball to "fooseball," viewers in the know—cynical viewers[1]—can recognize the absurdity of such posturing even as we ultimately indulge in its consolations. While this essay documents narrative and visual parallels between *The Waterboy* and Chrétien's Grail romance, *Le Conte du Graal*, exploring the humorous effect created by the juxtapositions, we have a larger point to make. What, we ask, is at stake in the transfer of the mysteries associated with the Grail and Fisher King to sports like baseball and football?

The formulas of the sports film, at some level, lend themselves to themes of the Grail myth, doubling many motifs central to the romance genre. The sports film is built around a hero as an outsider, a fair unknown who must prove himself, usually by saving a failing franchise in the midst of a losing streak, a "dry spell." *The Natural*, for instance, hammers home its parallels to Grail Wastelands with its dusty diamonds and dried up water fountains. Sports films frequently explore the linkages between generations, especially between fathers and sons, a recurrent motif in Grail legends as well. In doing so, like Grail romances, they explore the assemblage of beliefs, values, desires, and practices that constitute masculinity in a given culture. Because sports is a domain in the contemporary world in which manhood can be definitively demonstrated, the genre of sports film provides a space in the contemporary world for men to elevate masculinity to a virtually mythopoetic status while indulging in nostalgia, sentimentality, melodrama, and even nationalism. If the sports film is to achieve its lofty aims of healing the rifts between fathers and sons and conferring masculinity, it must somehow elevate what are, after all, children's games, pastimes, to something weightier, to a metaphysical or ethical system capable of overcoming the corruption and cynicism of modern life. Online fans of the film make this point repetitively in their commentaries: "*The Natural* is a film that gives glory and magic back to the game of baseball" (YouTube),[2] "If you dislike this, you dislike America" (http://www.youtube.com/watch?v=54–6yimtjtA), "A wonderful, magical fairy tale, and morality play; ... It is a story about faith, good and evil, right and wrong, fathers and sons," and "This is mythical. This is not realistic" (IMDb; http://www.imdb.com/title/tt0087781/reviews? ref_=tt_urv). Our argument in this essay, then, is two-pronged. In the first part, we ask how a reading of *The Waterboy* might enhance our understanding of Chrétien's Grail romance, drawing attention specifically to its humor; in the second, we ask how the Grail mythology serves to elevate sports films like *The Waterboy* to the level of myth, examining specifically the ways in which the ending of *The Waterboy* recuperates sports as mythology even in the face of the film's humorous debunking of the myth.

If anyone ever knew what the Grail "really" was meant to be, by the late twentieth-century its meaning had shrunk to designate some obscure object of desire; perhaps this was always the case. Deleuze and Guattari's notion of desiring-assemblage might be a useful concept for understanding the techniques through which sports films adapt Grail mythologies, themselves desiring-assemblages, to lionize and inflate games into epic contests that can carry grand themes about heroic masculinity, the relationships between fathers and sons, and even the health of the nation. Admittedly a bit clunky, the term desiring-assemblage does have the advantage of calling attention to the argument that desire is never a "'natural' nor a 'spontaneous' determination" (Deleuze, "Desire and Pleasure"). Rather, as Deleuze insists elsewhere, "desire only exists when assembled or machined. You cannot grasp or conceive of a desire outside a determinate assemblage, on a plane which is not pre-existent but which must itself be constructed.... In retrospect every assemblage expresses and creates a desire by constructing the plane which makes it possible and, by making it possible, brings it about ... *[Desire] is constructivist, not at all spontaneist*" (Dialogues 96). Beginning with this take on desire, let us try to unpack what kind of desiring-assemblage the Grail represents in both its medieval romance and its modern cinematic contexts, most specifically in the context of the sports film.

We begin with the desiring-assemblage first outlined by Jessie L. Weston in her largely discredited, but nevertheless influential, 1920 book, *From Ritual to Romance*, in which Weston traces a line of filiation from the Aryan god Indra to the Grail Knight of Arthurian myth, suggesting that both fulfill a task of reviving the Wasteland by "freeing the waters." Weston writes:

> It is not necessary here to enter into a discussion as to the original conception of Indra, and the place occupied by him in the early Aryan Pantheon, whether he was originally regarded as a god of war, or a god of weather; what is important for our purpose is the fact that it is Indra to whom a disproportionate number of the hymns of the Rig-Veda are addressed, that it is from him that the much desired boon of rain and abundant water is besought, and the feat which above all others redounded to his praise, and is ceaselessly glorified both by the god himself, and his grateful worshippers, is precisely the feat by which the Grail heroes, Gawain and Perceval, rejoiced the hearts of a suffering folk, i.e., the restoration of the rivers to their channels, the "Freeing of the Waters" [26].

Weston believed that Grail legends were mythopoetic in the sense that their origins could be traced to a common Eurasian mythology associated with Nature cults that linked the maturation of the hero—especially his sexual potency—to the fertility of the land. The desiring-assemblage of Aryan fertility cults that she proposes creates a network that links war, weather, sexual potency, agriculture, and water, as the hero must overcome his initial ignorance, learn what it means to be a man through a series of trials, so that, finally, his sexual potency frees the waters that will restore the Wasteland.[3]

From Ritual to Romance describes parallels to these adventures in several Grail romances. "The task of the Grail hero," Weston writes, "is in this special respect no mere literary invention, but a heritage from the achievements of the prehistoric heroes of the Aryan race" (29–30). Without subscribing to Weston's Frazierian interpretation of the Grail,[4] we note that her analysis links medieval Grail romances to what Derrida in *The Gift of Death* calls "orgiastic mysteries." Where Weston insists on a continuity between the ancient world and the Middle Ages, Derrida's reading of the relation between nature cults and Christianity stresses rupture; he sees at work in Christian mysticism the psychoanalytic processes of repression and incorporation rather than derivation (*Gift of Death* 11). The mysteries Weston describes do not come down unchanged to the Middle Ages; rather they become part of an entirely new desiring-assemblage. According to Deleuze:

> Feudalism ... is an assemblage that puts into play new relations with animals (the horse), with the earth, with deterritorialisation (the battle of knights, the Crusade), with women (knightly love), etc. Completely mad assemblages, but always historically assignable. I would say for my part that desire circulates in this assemblage of heterogeneities, in this sort of "symbiosis": desire is but one with a given assemblage, a co-functioning ["Desire and Pleasure"].

The piece of that chivalric desiring-assemblage that Deleuze misses is precisely what Derrida means by the *mysterium tremendum*, "the experience of being transfixed or possessed by the unseen gaze of a mysterious and inaccessible wholly other" (Goldman), which he sees as the return of the repressed in Christian rationalism.[5] The Grail is the focal point that connects chivalry to the experience Derrida describes:

> The dissymmetry of the gaze, this disproportion that relates me, in whatever concerns me, to a gaze that I don't see and that remains secret from me although it commands me, is the terrifying dreadful, tremendous mystery that ... is manifested in Christian mystery.[6]

The Grail elevates chivalric experience—courtly love, knightly combat—in some ineffable way. The experience becomes tied to something more, something mystical, beautiful, perfect.

The Grail fills the mundane with an unspeakable promise of transcendence. Little surprise, then, that by the thirteenth century the Grail has morphed into the device that delivers the mystery of transubstantiation, has morphed into the chalice of the Last Super into which Joseph of Arimathea collected Christ's blood and which he had with him when he arrived in Britain in AD 63.

Interestingly, the desiring-assemblage of modern baseball repeats in a new key many of the elements from Weston's mythic one; it brings war, weather, sexual potency, agriculture, and fathers and sons together with the assemblage of sports in a modern capitalist society: stadiums, concessions, signage, souvenirs, jumbotrons, contracts, media. For a culture in which sports heroes have become tarnished through greed, cheating, and sexual transgression, films like *The Natural* provide the surplus of the Grail, retrieving, somehow, a sacrality remembered but that never was—or, as Terence Mann offers in *Field of Dreams*, "they'll watch the game and it'll be as if they dipped themselves in magic waters. The memories will be so thick they'll have to brush them away from their faces. People will come." If baseball indulges nostalgia for pastoral sentimentality, football recalls the excitement of anarchic violence, the arena rather than the field of dreams. For this reason, football does not lend itself as easily to the same mystifications so common to baseball films, perhaps why Sandler chose football as a vehicle to satirize the romance of sport. The spectacle of football—especially its violence—is so extreme that it threatens to overwhelm the *mysterium tremendum* of the Grail. The expectation of baseball's heroes is a kind of introverted self-confidence. Football demands displays of ostentatious hypermasculinity. At least part of *The Waterboy*'s humor resides in the tension between its hero's inarticulate ability to "open a can of whoop-ass" on those who stand in his way and the elevated, mystical promise of the Grail romance. This tension returns us to the medieval romance with a greater appreciation of its comic potential.

Grail romances—whether they are about chivalry or sports—require the presence of a pure fool (Wagner's *der reine Tor*), someone untouched by the corruption and cynicism that have infected the desiring-assemblage (whether that assemblage is chivalry or sports) who will redeem the Wasteland. Chrétien's *Le Conte du Graal* demonstrates that, for a culture soaked in that corruption, the pure fool would appear ludicrous, ridiculous, out of place. A reader's initial response to him might range from amused dismissal to contempt and abuse. *The Waterboy* encourages us to appreciate the subtle humor of *Le Conte du Graal*, which opens with a sustained comic riff, a full-blown stand-up send-up on the ways of the Welsh, and one Welshman in particular, Perceval. A backwoods ignoramus, abandoned by his father to be raised by an overprotective, overbearing mother who has intentionally kept him from the desiring-assemblage of chivalric contestation, Perceval dresses poorly, fights inappropriately, and is, to put it mildly, a catastrophe with the ladies. He is, in other words, the pure fool. Chrétien descends to the level of slapstick in detailing Perceval's first meeting with a group of Arthurian knights. At first, Perceval believes he has encountered malevolent forces: "By my soul, my lady mother spoke truth to me when she told me that devils are the most hideous things in the world" (375). Perceval's mother has adopted a program of religious negative reinforcement to keep her boy in line. But Perceval's attitude is changed once he takes a closer look:

When he had a clear view of them once they had emerged from the woods, and when he saw the glittering hauberks and the bright gleaming helmet and the lances and shields, which he had never seen before, and saw the white and the scarlet shining in the sunlight and all that gold, sky-blue and silver, he was charmed and delighted and exclaimed: "Ah, God, have mercy on me! These are angels I see here. Now I have really committed a great sin and have just done very wrong to say they were devils. My mother wasn't telling stories when she told me angels were the most beautiful creatures there are, apart from God who is the most beautiful of all...." Throwing himself at once to the ground, he recited the whole of his creed and those prayers he knew which his mother had taught him [375–376].[7]

The joke depends, of course, on ethnic stereotyping: what fools these Welshmen be. But not just fools. Perceval is so backward, the land he inhabits so remote from anything resembling civilization, that he can be raised with an ignorance of knighthood so profound that he mistakes the knights first for devils and then for angels. The Welsh are primitive backwoodsmen who have no court, and consequently no social existence; they are little more than animals: "be certain beyond a doubt that all Welshmen are, by nature, more stupid than grazing cattle," sneers one of the knights (377).

Even worse than animals, they are mama's boys. Perceval's mother has sequestered him in the remotest parts of Wales, ferociously protecting him from any knowledge of the world, especially of the knighthood that killed both his father and brothers. Perceval invokes his mother's wisdom almost like a mantra. The Welsh, Chrétien suggests, are emasculated, infantilized imbeciles so cut off from the trappings of civilized life—the glittering court of his patron, Count Philip of Flanders, for instance, in which Chrétien amuses an aristocratic elite—that they cannot help but behave badly. Chrétien's courtly audience is invited to laugh at the distance between Philip's wealthy and sophisticated court and Perceval's backwoods idiocy. As he gazes on Arthur's knights in awe, Perceval offers little to recommend him as an incarnation of the messianic figure, the transcendental waterboy Weston describes above. On his journey to Arthur's court, this bumpkin oafishly steals a ring, food, and a kiss from a maiden he finds sleeping in a tent, mistakes Yvonet's armor for his skin, and has to be taught how to dress himself. He is a comic savage, a spear thrower, who cannot even imagine chivalric combat. He is a clown. How can it be that this moron will ultimately surpass all other knights in chivalric aptitude? How can it be that he will heal the Fisher King and deliver the Wasteland?

The Waterboy offers a somewhat warped slant on the humor of this pure fool. Bobby Boucher, the film's eponymous hero lives, as Janet Maslin of the *New York Times* notes, in "happy idiot mode." In the stereotypical world of none-to-bright, southern jocks, Sandler's Bobby is even more backwards and backwoods, a swamp dweller; he lives in a house that resembles a Joe's Crabshack restaurant and subsists on a steady diet of alligators, snakes, and squirrels. He has been raised by an overprotective and overbearing mother, Mama Boucher (played by Kathy Bates), who has denied him both a formal education and, much more important to the film's concept, the kind of masculine self-definition associated with the game she repeatedly refers to as "the fooseball." She insists, "My boy is all I got left"; "My boy is too delicate to be playing fooseball"; she remarks (not incorrectly) that football players are a "bunch of overgrown monsters manhandling each other." Mama Boucher calls to mind Perceval's mother in bringing the wrath of hell down upon her easily intimidated son. She tells him "girls are the devil" and tries to scare away a potential girlfriend, Vicki Vallencourt (Fairuza Balk)—to whom she refers as trailer camp trash—by telling her of Bobby's smelly feet, his Deputy Dawg pajamas—Vicki responds, "I find Deputy Dawg very, very sexy"—and his urine stained sheets. But the point, of course, is that, like Perceval, Bobby must get beyond the narrow existence his mother has constructed for him, must fulfill his destiny of "freeing the waters." Could we expect anything less from a waterboy?

The Waterboy sets up its parallels with the Perceval mythology from its opening shots. A tracking camera passing across swamps sets the location and introduces the film's theme of water. The camera tracks back and up to reveal a football stadium; the ensuing montage establishes the desiring-assemblage of big time college football. The virility of the football players is established by a series of shots of men as they run, throw, and tackle during practice. Their prowess is validated by the presence of Lynn Swann, sportscaster and former professional football player, who suggests that the Louisiana University Cougars are on track for yet another "championship trophy." These men are fashioned, as the knights in the opening of the *Conte du Graal* are, as representatives of hegemonic masculinity, the culture's dominant form of masculinity against which all other forms must subordinate themselves.[8] The Waterboy's introduction provides a stark contrast, even as it participates in the assemblage. Boucher enters sporting a water tank on his back complete with cups, pumps, hoses, gauges, and the motto, "Keep it Clean, Keep it Cold," on the back. He can barely walk under the weight of his equipment. However skillful he is at what he has learned (water), he is a joke, as comically incongruous as Perceval with his javelin. His awkwardness exists to certify the players' hypermasculinity through the abuse they heap on him.

Like the Grail stories that serve as its pretext, *The Waterboy* explores fantasies of class mobility within a hypermasculine warrior society—with an American twist. At the heart of Grail narratives—and the Grail's desiring-assemblage—is the certainty that nobility will always announce itself. Perceval is a "pure fool," raised in isolation without paternal guidance. He suffers continual humiliation for his ignorance and his effeminacy—and within the texts' semiotic of masculine exchange, these may well be the same thing. But a dream of aristocratic origin permeates the narrative. Limitations of nurture—the geographical remoteness of Wales and the excessive and detrimental influences of his mother—are insufficient to overcome heredity; genealogy will out. Perceval, the son of a great knight, is destined to surpass his father.

The Waterboy morphs this medieval ideology of aristocratic certainty into a fantasy of late–twentieth-century capitalist radical individualism. Bobby Boucher is a not-so-Fair Unknown, a geographically marginalized, home-schooled idiot whose mother has taught him that alligators are aggressive because they have many teeth but are unable to brush them. He wears leisure suits that come in colors found nowhere in nature. Challenged by a stutter and, as Roger Ebert of the *Chicago Sun Times* notes, "a lisp, a whine, a nasal grating and an accent that nobody in Louisiana actually has," Boucher is a wimp, a nebbish, a schlemiel who triumphs to become not only a football star, but also an accomplished college student. At the film's conclusion, after passing a high-school equivalency examination that, we are told, none of his college teammates could handle, he is offered an opportunity to turn professional, but turns it down to stay in school. Managing years of pent-up hostility towards those who have treated him miserably, Boucher is transformed into a linebacker, a position that requires both intelligence—he must be able to read offenses—and brutality. He is transformed not because of aristocratic birth or middle-class entitlement but as an exemplar of American myths of rural virtue and common sense that promise upward mobility. We turn now to a consideration of the "cruel optimism" embedded in that promise.[9]

Early on in their narratives both Grail knight and Waterboy are subjected to acts of violence performed as kinds of theater. They are humiliated for the amusement of an audience of the initiated, warriors who have successfully engaged in hypermasculine contestation. Perceval is mocked by the Arthurian knights, who misread his innocence as mental defect. The football players greet Boucher's arrival on the field with jeers: "Here comes the shit ass." When he is hit by a football, the players laugh hysterically as he falls down under the weight of his equipment. He receives a note in his suggestion box, "Eat shit and kill yourself, signed Everybody." Finally a crowd of large players converges on him to punch, kick, and otherwise torment him while he's down. The opening scene contrasts Boucher's unappreciated technical know-how with the highly valued physical prowess of the football player. The familiar contrast between jock and nerd is set up in a few shots. In both cases, the nerd, the "wise fool," puts up with, and even participates in, his abuse because of his desire to be included in hegemonic masculinity.

In this opening scene, Boucher is fired from his job as waterboy for the Cougars because he proves too much of a distraction for the football players whose hazing of Boucher diverts them from practice. Indeed, both the football players and the medieval knights take their masculine identity, fashion themselves as men, by mistreating those whom they define as less than men, those who become effeminized through staged acts of brutality and humiliation. The socio-economic, psycho-sexual theater that is played out in these narratives suggests Slavoj Žižek's discussion in *The Metastases of Enjoyment* of "the way a male hysterical 'sadist' justifies his beating of a woman.... What we encounter here is a kind of loop in which the (mis)perceived effect of the brutal act upon the victim retroactively legitimizes the act" (*The Metastases of Enjoyment* 93). Pleasure is derived, at least in part, through public displays of dominance, through demonstration of social and sexual superiority.

These scenes that subject our waterboys to ritualistic humiliation, however, are coordinated within a masochistic, not a sadistic, narrative; those who dominate are set up for their own humiliation so that our heroes can emerge triumphant, can restore the Wasteland. Žižek argues, following Deleuze, that there is an asymmetry between sadism and masochism. "In sadism we encounter direct negation, violent destruction and tormenting, whereas in masochism negation assumes the form of disavowal—that is, of feigning, of an 'as if' which suspends reality" (91). Žižek describes how the logic of heterosexual love "defines the parameters within which the two sexes relate to each other" (89). We want to resituate psychoanalytic discussions of masochism in which acts of cruelty are staged for the gaze of the cold and distant Lady of Courtly Love to the realm of the homosocial, to the affective relations between men, to describe a masochistic theater of homosocial bonding staged for a wider audience of men. The contestations among men are, we would argue, erotically charged; the power they contest is always thoroughly imbued with sexuality, even as, or especially when, that sexual charge is being most violently denied. The tactics involved in such contests nearly always require a kind of secondary gendering in which the winners, through acts of physical or intellectual violence mark the losers, the less powerful, as "women," opening up the field to the possibility of a sexualized theatre of homosocial sadomasochistic cruelty. In the Grail narratives and *The Waterboy*, such scenes are played for laughs, a kind of degrading minstrel show—despite hints that the victims may seek retribution, may "open a can of whoopass."

We designate as homosocial masochism forms of sexualized abuse theatrically performed for an audience of other men. This approach to the Perceval myth was suggested to us by the work on masochism by Theodor Reik, one of Freud's early disciples, who in the 1940s began using the term "social masochism" (a more neutral expression of Freud's "moral masochism"[10]) to designate forms of abasement that have no obvious relation to sexuality, and by David Savran's materialist analysis of male masochism in *Taking It Like a Man*, which explores the role of masochism in creating modern ideas about masculinity. Homosocial masochism reinforces hegemonic masculinity by creating a class of men who function as "women" in all-male structures. Initiations offer one example of the form, in which individuals temporarily engage in masochistic and effeminizing acts. Those rites and rituals used to initiate a group of men into a brotherhood—whether a fraternity, a football team, or an army—separate the initiates from their day-to-day lives to create a liminal space that transforms them into a particular type of man, worthy of being incorporated into a hegemonic masculinity defined as fraternal. This hegemonic masculinity, however, also requires subordinated forms of masculinity—men who will always be permanently excluded from the club, from the team, from the fraternity.

At the beginning of *Waterboy* and *Perceval*, our waterboys appear to belong to this second excluded class of men. Masochism, however, destabilizes simplistic oppositions between pain and pleasure, active and passive, male and female, inside and outside. Perceval and Boucher are not the passive recipients of others' violent abuse that they first appear to be. They actively formulate their own positions in these performances differently from those who abuse them. Our two heroes are, to some extent, willing participants, "masochists," whose enthusiasm for their suffering turns the tables on their tormentors, in effect both lowering the tormentors' social status and in turn effeminizing those who would effeminize them. They construct a different kind of theater, in which the submissive plays the masculine part and domination becomes the effeminized role. Žižek writes: "Masochism ... is made to the measure of the victim (the servant in the masochistic relationship) who initiates contact with the Master (woman), authorizing her to humiliate him in any way she considers appropriate (within the terms defined by the contract) and binding himself to act 'according to the whims of the sovereign lady.' ... It is the servant, therefore, who writes the screenplay—that is, who actually pulls the strings and dictates the activity of the woman [*dominatrix*]: he stages his own servitude" (*The Metastases of Enjoyment* 91–92), as Sandler has written the screenplay of his own humiliation and eventual triumph.

From the perspective of filmmaking, Žižek's appropriation of the metaphors of performance, of the "screenplay," is revealing. *The Waterboy* plays out the connections Deleuze articulates among masochism, contract, and ritual. Sandler himself wrote the screenplay (in collaboration with Tim Herlihy), allowing him to stage his own theater of homosocial masochism. By willingly adopting the position of the abused and subservient, Sandler's idiot male masochist recasts his sadistic male tormentors into the role of the Woman who performs a script written by the victim. Although Boucher suffers the humiliations, it is his tormentors who ultimately become the buffoons. After demonstrating his unexpected ability to "open a can of whoopass" on anyone who angers him, Boucher is told by his coach, "You're a war-

Adam Sandler as the Perceval-like Bobby Boucher in Frank Coraci's 1998 film *The Waterboy*.

rior." He is admired and befriended by the beautiful, and not so beautiful, people who once shunned him. As one character proclaims, Boucher is "an inspiration to all of us who weren't born handsome, charming, or cool." Through some unexplained, even mystical, intervention, Boucher is able to marshal violence in a way that sets him above even the most hypermasculine of men.

Boucher becomes a late twentieth-century desiring-assemblage: the below-average Joe who is revealed to be exceptional, the perfect hero for George Bush's America. The waterboy pulls the strings, writing the script of his encounters. The drama of socio-economic/sexual reversal is complete—and nervous laughter transformed into the laughter of relief. Far from disturbing hegemonic masculinity, then, *The Waterboy* reinforces it by creating the fantasy (however cruel) that any man—even the most inept and idiotic—can be initiated into it.

This relief is ironically accompanied by ostentatious displays of masculinity as Perceval and Boucher join and ultimately dominate the ranks of the initiated "warrior" class. The "freeing of the waters," coincides with the waterboys' coming of age, which is represented partially in the healing of the Fisher King and the restoration of the Wasteland. The Fisher King of Grail narratives lies stricken with a thigh wound; in Chrétien, Perceval's mother informs him that his father "was wounded through the thigh and physically maimed," his lands "devastated" (380). This injury, this metaphoric castration, renders the Fisher King helpless to perform his roles either as a man or as a monarch. The land reflects the king's state of disrepair and has turned to waste. The Fisher King of *The Waterboy* is Coach Klein (played by Henry Winkler), who oversees South Central Louisiana State University's Mud Dawgs' football program. His team has lost 41 games in a row, has not, in fact, won a game since 1994. Klein once was a contender for the coaching position at more respectable Louisiana University, but, because he was a coward, he lost the job to the detestable Red Beaulieu (played by Jerry Reed), the coach who fired Bobby Boucher at the film's beginning. As Coach Klein puts it, "Red took my playbook and my manhood." His emasculinization is emphasized with sledgehammer symbolism in flashback, as he wears a pair of women's pumps while making the call to his grandmother to complain about the missed coaching opportunity.

At South Central, Coach Klein is surrounded by decay; it is a parched Wasteland (no small feat in Louisiana). It is, we think, no accident, that his team, and the school it represents, are designated South Central. For the L.A. screenwriters of *The Waterboy*, the phrase "South Central" holds particular resonances. South Central is one of Los Angeles' scenes of urban blight, itself a kind of Wasteland. Mud Dawg Stadium has large patches of brown grass on its playing field. The sportscasters' booth has ceiling stains from rain damage. The cheerleaders and mascot engage in drinking games and perform their functions halfheartedly in an alcoholic haze. There are almost no fans in the stadium. Even the water in the team's cooler has gone disgustingly stagnant, an affront to Boucher's occupational pride. When Bobby Boucher enters Coach Klein's office looking for a job, he offers more than just clean water; he offers the prospect of redemption.

The curing of the Fisher King restores the Wasteland. In the case of South Central Louisiana University, the healing process occurs at the Bourbon Bowl, during which Bobby Boucher, only just emancipated from his mother, nearly single-handedly produces a victory over the previously unbeaten Cougars. The game is played in a gleaming stadium, the Mud Dawgs' cheerleaders sobered with good, strong coffee brought by Mama Boucher, conforming to a more traditionally acceptable femininity. As Bobby performs masculine heroics on the field, Vicki Vallencourt assumes the feminized role of providing water for the players. In case movie fans miss the symbolism here, the sportscasters announce that Bobby has "gone from waterboy to savior." At the game's conclusion, Boucher proudly proclaims, "Coach Klein, you got your manhood."

The heteronormativity required by the desiring-assemblage that is hegemonic masculinity is played out across two interrelated fields that are explored both by Grail romances and sports films: romantic love and the relation to the father. Romance and paternity (taking the father's place) are the rewards that follow from the hero's prowess and potency. Both Perceval and Boucher encounter love on their way to apotheosis, and their love may in itself offer a kind of apotheosis. Perceval's love, particularly as it is portrayed by Wolfram Von Eschenbach, offers a glimpse at courtly transcendence in its absolute perfection. *The Waterboy*, in a more perfunctory, even vulgar, manner, concludes with a wedding and the promise that Boucher, a 31-year-old virgin, is about to make quick progress towards becoming a man by demonstrating the sexual potency required of a waterboy, of a Grail knight; he is encouraged by a member of the heckling crowd, "you can do it; you can do it all night long."

However, it is the relationship with the father, and not the love relationship, that, in the sports film, becomes the occasion for sentimentality and melodrama. *The Natural* and *Field of Dreams*, like the Grail romances on which they are based, are both "inextricably tied up with the search for the 'proper' relation to the absent [that is, dead] father" (Finke and Shichtman 25). Because in both films and romances the hero's father is dead as the narrative begins, he is free to pursue substitute fathers with whom he need not compete, smoothing over Oedipal conflicts. The sudden appearance at *The Waterboy's* end of the father Boucher thought was dead[11] provides a twist on the conventional reconciliation of father and son that especially marks baseball films. Sandler brings back Boucher's father only to discard him. The Oedipal drama is played for laughs. Boucher's mother runs interference between him and the long-lost father who has returned just in time to share in his son's good fortune. Sandler's film, then, rejects genealogy as a mechanism for success, offering a fantasy of the autonomous individual's ability to impact the world, a new paradigm for initiation and for demonstrations of prowess.

Adam Sandler once "wisecracked that he became a multimillionaire despite being neither handsome nor talented" (O'Hehir). With *The Waterboy*, Sandler looks to deconstruct the misty-eyed mythologies evoked by films like *Field of Dreams* and *The Natural*—with their pretty-boy heroes. He suggests that the desiring-assemblage of chivalry, of the Grail story, can be made to work for the plain, for the untalented—just so long as we don't take it too seriously. But, even though *The Waterboy* makes fun of Grail mythologies, of mythologies that fashion Western masculinity, it ultimately reinscribes them in the end, in an optimism that may be crueler than the original abuse. Sandler's comic turn on the *mysterium tremendum* of the Holy Grail reinscribes within its comedy the same feelings of awe, satiation, and pleasure it pokes fun at. Yes, it is a stupid movie. Still, hegemonic masculinity, though reconfigured, is restored; heteronormative love is asserted; the Wasteland is saved. The waters flow again, affirming life, affirming that the way things are is the way they should be.

Notes

We are indebted to Susan Aronstein, Hannah Markley, and Kevin J. Harty for comments on earlier drafts of this essay.

1. We are following here Slavoj Žižek's definition of contemporary ideology as cynicism: "I know this comparison is absurd and overinflated but still I am moved by it"; see the discussion in *Sublime Object of Ideology*, pp. 29 ff.

2. Posted by "Templar Returns"; see YouTube, http://www.youtube.com/watch?v=54-6yimtjtA (accessed August 3, 2013).

3. We note here that this desiring-assemblage is entirely Weston's creation without suggesting that it corresponds to the desires of ancient peoples to which we have no direct access. We would argue, however, that this desiring-assemblage does figure prominently as an intertext in the assemblage created by films like *The Natural* and *Field of Dreams* and that it finds its way into *The Waterboy*.

4. Weston was heavily influenced by the Scottish anthropologist James Frazier's *Golden Bough* (1890–1900).

5. Goldman suggests that Derrida is arguing in *Gift of Death* that Christianity *derives* from the orgiastic (a claim Derrida never makes). Goldman's historicist (and, we believe, ultimately rationalizing) analysis of Derrida's text ignores the psychoanalytic apparatus of incorporation and repression central to Derrida's unpacking of the uncanniness of the Christian *mysterium tremendum*. Derrida states that Platonism *incorporates*, in the psychoanalytic sense, the orgiastic mysteries and that Christianity subsequently represses Platonism (which had already incorporated the mysteries; see p. 11). This psychoanalytic model is harder to refute than the argument from derivation (Goldman's and Weston's arguments) because Christianity can of course consciously repudiate the orgiastic, as Goldman argues, while still repressing and hence incorporating it into the *mysterium tremendum*.

6. *Monty Python and the Holy Grail* makes fun of this mystical experience of "a gaze that I don't see" in its Grail scene. "Oh don't grovel," says the cartoon God appearing to Arthur in the clouds, "and don't apologize. Every time I try to talk to someone it's 'sorry this' and 'forgive me that', and 'I'm not worthy.'"

7. On knighthood as a Deleuzoguattarian assemblage of "human, animal, objects, and intensities" a fusion of horse, man, armor, and weapons into a single "identity machine," see Cohen 46.

8. We use this term following R. W. Connell to designate the dominant form of masculinity within a given gender hierarchy, another kind of desiring-assemblage. In most Western societies hegemonic masculinity is associated with a complex that includes whiteness, heterosexuality, competition, and aggression. While contemporary sports introduces some racial complications into this mix, the Louisiana Cougars in this film are a remarkably white lot (Connell and Messerschmidt, *Masculinities* 830).

9. Examples of rural virtue run through American literature and film; think *Huckleberry Finn* or *Mr. Smith Goes to Washington*. The term "cruel optimism" is Lauren Berlant's; it suggests that our desires are often obstacles to our flourishing. Her understanding of desire parallels Deleuze and Guattari's: "when we talk about an object of desire, we are really talking about a cluster of promises we want someone or something to make to us and make possible for us." "Cruel optimism is the condition of maintaining an attachment to a significantly problematic object."

10. See "The Economic Problem in Masochism."

11. His mother had told him that his father died of dehydration in the Sahara while serving in the Peace Corps.

Works Cited

Berlant, Lauren. *Cruel Otimism*. Durham: Duke University Press, 2011.
Chrétien de Troyes. *Arthurian Romances*. Ed. and trans. D. D. R. Owens. London: J. R. Dent and Sons, 1987.

Cohen, Jeffrey Jerome. *Medieval Identity Machines*. Medieval Cultures vol. 35. Minneapolis: University of Minnesota Press, 2003.

Connell, R. W. *Masculinities*. Berkeley: University of California Press, 1995.

_____, and James Messerschmidt. "Hegemonic Masculinity: Rethinking the Concept." *Gender and Society* 19 (2005): 829–859.

Deleuze, Gilles. "Desire and Pleasure." Trans. Melissa McMahon. Web. http://www.artdes.monash.edu.au/globe/delfou.html Accessed 3 August 2013; originally published as "Désir et plaisir," *Magazine littéraire* 325 (October 1994): 59–65.

Deleuze, Gilles, and Claire Parnet. *Dialogues II*. Trans. Hugh Tomlinson and Barbara Habberjam. New York: Columbia University Press, 2007.

Deleuze, Gilles, and Leopold von Sacher-Masoch, *Masochism: Coldness and Cruelty & Venus in Furs*. Trans. Jean McNeil. New York: Zone Books, 1971.

Derrida, Jacques. *The Gift of Death*. Trans. David Wills. 2nd edition. Chicago: University of Chicago Press, 2008.

Ebert, Roger. "Review of the Waterboy." *Chicago Sun Times*. November 6, 1998. http://rogerebert.suntimes.com/apps/pbcs.dll/article?AID=/19981106/REVIEWS/811060304/1023. Accessed 29 May 2010.

Finke, Laurie, and Martin B. Shichtman. "Who's Your Daddy? New Age Grails." *Arthuriana* 19 (2009): 25–33.

Freud, Sigmund. "The Economic Problem in Masochism." In *General Psychological Theory*. Ed. Philip Rieff. Trans. James Strachey. New York: Collier, 1963.

Goldman, Peter. "Christian Mystery and Responsibility: Gnosticism in Derrida's *The Gift of Death*." *Anthropoetics* 4.1 (1998). http://www.anthropoetics.ucla.edu/ap0401/pg_DERR.htm. Accessed 3 August 2013.

Maslin, Janet. "Review of *The Waterboy*." *New York Times* 6 November 1998. http://movies.nytimes.com/movie/review?res=9A00E3D9173EF935A35752C1A96E958260. Accessed 29 May 2010.

O'Hehir, Andrew. "Review of *The Waterboy*." *Sight and Sound*. http://old.bfi.org.uk/sightandsound/review/114. Accessed 6 June 2013.

Reik, Theodor. *Masochism in Modern Man*. Trans. Margaret H. Beigel and Gertrud M. Kurth. New York: Farrar, Straus, 1941.

Savran, David. *Taking It Like a Man: White Masculinity, Masochism, and Contemporary American Culture*. Princeton: Princeton University Press, 1998.

Stewart, Suzanne R. *Sublime Surrender: Male Masochism at the Fin-De-Siècle*. Ithaca: Cornell University Press, 1998.

The Waterboy. Dir. Frank Coraci. Per. Adam Sandler. Walt Disney Video. 1998 (DVD 1999).

Weston, Jessie. *From Ritual to Romance*. Gloucester, MA.: Peter Smith, 1957.

Žižek, Slavoj. "*The Metastases of Enjoyment: Six Essays on Women and Causality*. London: Verso, 1994.

_____. *That Sublime Object of Ideology*. London: Verso, 1989.

Holy Grail, Schlocky Grail

David W. Marshall

In the medieval Grail legends recounted in both the *Queste del Saint Graal* and *Le Morte Darthur*, King Arthur laments the effects of the Grail vision. Upon hearing Gawain's pronouncement that he will undertake a Quest to find the Grail, Arthur expresses dismay that his fellowship of knights will never again come together about the Round Table. What follows are a series of adventures that confirm Arthur's premonition. While Gawain returns having found no adventures, while Lancelot struggles to overcome his sin and is redeemed by constrained encounters with the Grail, while Perceval and Bors are both tested and perfected, and while Galahad maintains his purity of heart and action, the perfection of the Round Table is forever destroyed. A tension results between the restorative powers of the Grail, or the refining of individual worth, and the rending of the collective Arthurian community to which it appears.

In many of the Grail legends, the Grail possesses powers to restore those who encounter it, figures such as the Fisher/Wounded King or the knights named above—films such as Lon Cheney's *The Light of Faith* (a re-edited version of *The Light in the Dark*) and John Boorman's Jessie Weston-inspired *Excalibur* hinge upon this theme. While concerns with the dismantling of the Round Table surface in a film like *Excalibur* or images of the Grail as taker-of-life exist in *Indiana Jones and the Last Crusade* exist, four recent B-films develop negative aspects of the Grail and the Quest for it, moving beyond the cynicism John Christopher Kleis attributes to Syberberg's *Parsifal*,[1] to emphasize the Grail as potentially destructive. To be sure, even in the medieval tales the Grail had destructive properties. As noted above, Arthur laments the impact that the Grail Quest will have on the Round Table, and those not worthy to experience the Grail are killed or wounded. But these films emphasize the destructive implication of the Grail and Grail-Quests on individual identity and self-determination. Florian Baxmeyer's *Code of the Templars* focuses on the dissolution of the nuclear family as a result of the Grail, while Lance Catania's *Cup of My Blood* makes the Grail the cause of a bloody series of conflicts and turns it into means for calling down the angelic armies of God to engage in an apocalyptic war. The Grail for Justin Galland's *Rosencrantz & Guildenstern Are Undead* becomes the instrument for destroying a vampire's sensual life and returning him to an unfulfilling existence. Only Jonathan Frakes' *The Librarian: Curse of the Judas Chalice* offers an optimistic resolution to the destructive potential of Grails and their Quests. These B-films together suggest that the Grail contributes as much to creating the Wasteland as to curing it and, as a result, suggest a cultural ambivalence about the value of Grail Quests.

Code of the Templars: *Replacing the Grail with Romance*

Produced for German television, Florian Baxmeyer's *Code of the Templars* (*Das Blut der Templer* [2004]) draws extensively from Wolfram von Eschenbach's *Parzival*. The film follows a boy named David (Mirko Lang), who is the illegitimate son of two special houses: the Knights Templar, whose head, Robert von Metz (Harald Krassnitzer), is his father, and the Priory of Sion, led by his mother Lucrezia de Saintclair (Catherine H. Flemming). Taken from Lucrezia by Robert and raised in a monastery, David, ignorant of his heritage, discovers that he has special abilities and, like Parzival, that he is heir to the Temple Master.[2] David soon learns that Robert protects the Grail, while Lucrezia seeks to find it for the powers it stands to bestow on those who possess the *Sang Real*. The blood of Christ flows through both houses, each descending from the nine Templars who found the Grail beneath the Temple Mount, and David's blood reunites them. The *Sang Real* bestows prolonged life, great strength, and rapid healing. As the two sides go to war, David is pulled between them but seeks his own path. With girlfriend Stella (Alicja Bachleda) by his side, David works with Quentin (Peter Franke), the monk who raised him, to beat his mother and Uncle Ares (Oliver Masucci) to the Grail only to be overtaken outside the Grail chamber. In a final duel David defeats Ares, but gives way to his mother, who activates the Grail (a large stone object patterned on Wolfram's version), to her own doom.

But where Wolfram's tale maintains an interest in the Grail Quest as spiritual journey, *Code of the Templars* swerves towards a non-spiritual Quest, one that locates the Grail as center of a tense conspiracy in which David comes of age. That conspiracy owes more to Dan Brown's *The Da Vinci Code* than to anything medieval, but the degree of emphasis put on the character's descent from Christ distinguishes *Code of the Templars*. While Brown focuses his plot around the secret descendants of Christ and Mary Madgalen, *Code of the Templars* uses the same premise to explain the supernatural powers of the Templars and Priors (an invulnerability like Connor McCloud's and Ramirez's in *Highlander*), and then quickly glosses over it to the Grail-as-object.[3] The blood line split between rivals, the *Sang Real* that enervates the Templars and Priors, is empowered blood, but little more. Even as Lucrezia unlocks the Grail's power in the final scenes, its association with the materiality of blood receives emphasis through the visual motif of the vertical, striated lines of a genetic sequence. The motif appears on the Temple Master's sword and by the Grail Chamber's lock, and is stamped in the middle of the Grail's basin, tying it to science more than to miraculous spirituality. Even after the Grail reverts from the shape of a wobbly red blood cell from which Lucrezia drinks to its metallic stone form (with a beam of light firing out of it), that potential miracle goes unremarked. The Grail of *Code of the Templars* is an object stripped of religious significance and spiritual implications. Instead, it functions as an object around which two social ideologies from which David must choose, emerge.

Baxmeyer develops Templars' and Priors' ideologies through each side's relationship to the Grail. The virtues of tradition and service characterize David's father and his Templars. In either conservative suits and overcoats or brown leather armor that recalls the stereotypes of medieval knights, they kneel to prayer before their castle's altar and among the tombs of their predecessors. Around them the past accrues in layers of architecture, sculpture, inscription, and ornament while they speak mirthlessly of brotherhood, tradition, and obligation. The Templars live in the past, looking backward in time to preserve the ancient Grail as an inert and useless relic. With blind devotion, they live to serve a fruitless cause. In contrast, Lucrezia's Priors occupy spaces featuring the clean, linear sophistication of modern architecture, with interiors spare in a modern fusion of East Asian and medieval furnishings. The Priors' compound starts history from their own moment, eschewing the past and looking, instead, towards their own future as dictated by the immortality they seek. That goal structures, too, their relationships. Ares speaks to Shareef (Rene Ifrah) condescendingly as an Arab and a slave. Lucrezia even demotes Ares, her brother, to taking orders from the slave Shareef when it suits her purposes, then dismisses him altogether. Where the Templars, David's paternal line, demand utter sacrifice to tradition, duty, brotherhood, and service, the Priors, his maternal line, represent an ego-centric will-to-power.

With this division of mother and father, Baxmeyer constructs a Wasteland in which the nuclear family is at odds in both personal strife and ideological conflict. As Howard R. Bloch observes, the Arthurian court, a center of order, is "marked ... by the integration of something resembling the nuclear family within the lococentric community"(266) and sets that order in opposition to the chaos of the Wasteland. But in *Code of the Templars*, David is presented with untenable options: a sullen father whose adherence to his order nearly led him in the opening scene to kill his own infant son and a sociopathic mother whose obsession with immortality and power causes her to prey on those closest to her to advance a megalomaniacal goal.[4]

If the Wasteland in *Code of the Templars* revolves around the fractured nuclear family, then the restoration of the family, not the Grail, becomes the cure, with newly formed female and male figures to assume a properly ordered union. In place of the pursuit of either duty or power, Baxmeyer privileges the ideals of romantic and courtly love.[5] In his scenes with Stella, David demonstrates chivalric service to his beloved while accepting the nurturing affection she offers in return. Such service appears in his earliest interactions with Stella at the party, where the bully Frank sits like a king enthroned among drunken revelers. In his irritation over David's presence, Frank shoves Stella, eliciting David's defense of her. At the end of the night, David explains to Stella that, the fight and his resulting wound notwithstanding, the night was good because it was spent with her. In this sequence, David occupies the role of the lady's champion, enduring hardship for her love and earning her favor in the process. The scene invokes the aristocratic behaviors of medieval courtly culture and elevates David above the crass scene over which Frank appears to be king. In the process, David elevates Stella as the object of his love.[6] His embracing of courtly love begins a rejection of either service to, or yearning for, the Grail. He thereby asserts his own interests in a self-determined life oriented to romantic desire. En route to thwarting his mother, David undertakes the Quest of the courtly lover, with Stella's love, like the wisdom of Perceval's sister guiding Perceval and Bors, enabling David to progress in his Quest.[7]

This privileging of the romantic Quest finds its clearest expression in the film's final scenes. Having killed his uncle and having seen his mother succumb to the power of the unlocked Grail, David declines the power the Grail can give him, tacitly rejecting all that drove his mother. Instead, he re-seals the Grail chamber, leaving the broken Temple Master's sword locked within, effectively renouncing his role as Temple Master. In the last shot, Quentin walks before David and Stella, who follow him out of the Roman catacombs holding hands. The final image, then, is one of lovers walking in union behind the religious figure who leads them out of a lifeless world. The Wasteland of the divided family sees a restoration of unity.

In *Code of the Templars*, the Grail becomes an image not of life-giving power or even of a noble spiritual pursuit. Rather, the Grail becomes the source of conflict and strife that compels David to emerge as a Grail knight not in spiritual terms, not by embracing the relic, but by rejecting it. The de-spiritualized emphasis on Grail-as-object sets *Code of the Templars* apart from the various medieval Grail stories (including Woforam's *Parzival*) and overthrows their spiritual emphasis. The film's focus on genetic family ties encoded within blood renders the Grail a magical object that, in practical terms, associates it with vague notions of worldly power, the pursuit of which fractures the bonds that the genetic code creates. Baxmeyer's film concludes with the feel-good affirmation of a self-determined life of religiously-guided romantic love that carries the couple through and out of a Wasteland of death. *Code of the Templars* thereby depicts a story of families riven by desires and asserts a return to chivalric romance as its own conservative solution.

Cup of My Blood: *The Apocalyptic Grail Knight*

Like *Code of the Templars*, Lance Catania's *Cup of My Blood* (2005) draws its narrative tension and conflict from conspiracy-theory books and films like *The Da Vinci Code*, but taps a variety of the traditional images associated with the Grail tradition. Taking its inspiration from psychological horror films, Catania's low-budget, independently produced film follows the redemption and return to faith of photographer Jack Fender (Daniel Patrick Sullivan). Broken by his wife Tina's suicide, Jack functions as a type for Chrétien's wounded king, occupying his time shooting photographs for Sparky's (Roger Anderson) pornographic website, 2nd Cuming, and resisting his agent Alex's push to return to more respectable forms of art. When he comes into possession of the Grail, he learns he is the foreordained protector, akin to Galahad in the *Queste* and *Morte*, though lacking Galahad's purity. Instead, Jack must grow into his role, similar to the way Chrétien's Perceval must. Jack's maturation begins when he discovers 2nd Cuming conceals a second website dedicated to the apocalyptic second coming of Christ and the Holy Grail, operated by the seemingly paranoid Nibbles (Circus-Szalewski) and Scooter (Quiana Whittler). While hiding the Grail, grisly phantoms haunt Jack, but his artistic inspiration returns after a night of passion with the young Iona (Janina Gavankar). The Grail, however, is a key to calling and commanding the angels of the apocalypse, and brings with it earthly strife. Alex and his henchmen resort to violence to possess it. Iona reveals herself to be a centuries-old demonic succubus who desires to forestall the apocalypse. Sparky and his mumbling albino thug priest, Limpy (Laurence Skorniak), desire the Grail for its power. All fail in a violent and bloody conclusion that leaves Jack shot through one eye but resolved to protect the Grail.

The juxtaposition of the Holy Grail, religious iconography, and pornography in the film makes for an odd combination, one that draws to mind Alcuin of York's concern over the reading of heroic tales in the holy spaces of Anglo-Saxon monasteries, prompting him to ask, "What has Ingeld to do with Christ?" The full-frontal nudity of Sparky's pornographic "2nd Cuming" website conceals Nibbles' predispensationalist website full of pictures of Jesus, the Holy Grail, and manuscript illuminations of the Final Battle. If Alcuin of York's question about the relationship between Ingeld and Christ was fitting, then certainly we are justified in asking of *Cup of My Blood*: What has hooha to do with holiness?

Cup of My Blood's interest in End of Times events taps predispensationalist theologies such as that of J.F. Rutherford and popularized by Tim LeHaye's *Left Behind* series.[8] As a result, this Wasteland is distinct from the medieval images described by Bloch, who explains, "the Arthurian Wasteland is always geographically situated; it is a landscape and a relation of men to their environment that is characterized by depopulation, the infertility of nature, the failure of agriculture, and a crisis of kingship and of political order" (257). Catania constructs an urban, apocalyptic Wasteland of rusted metal overpasses and city streets, its "depopulation" conveyed through establishing shots of streets void of people or cars. The *mise-en-scène* of the interior shots locates Jack within that world as one of its victims. Shadows dominate the scenes and a death-hued green tone washes out the colors, affecting an eerie mood, as if the setting in which Jack moves is itself dead. That emptiness and lifelessness contrast dramatically with the brief occasional shots of Jack's memories of Tina. In those shots, rich colors fill his apartment. Deep purple walls, bright white light and warm skin tones accent smiles and laughter to convey a life of love and human connection that have been transformed into Jack's sallow loneliness. When Alex or Sparky do enter his spaces, their conversations are taut with disagreement, so that the death-hued tones that close in those scenes accentuate the lack of affection and further locate Jack in a Wasteland of tenuous human connection. The Wasteland for Catania emerges as human isolation and, where people come together, an unsettling anxiety. It is, to use Angus J. Kennedy's description of *Perlesvaus*, "not so much a geographical location as a dark country of the soul into which, through sin or blindness, man is ever-likely to stay" (233). If the Grail narrative seeks to remedy the Wasteland, then in *Cup of My Blood* the object in need of remedy is not the setting, but the psycho-emotional state of the protagonist.

To effect that reform, *Cup of My Blood* deploys a system of signification similar to the typological readings that advance the narrative of the *Queste*. But the film shifts the *Queste*'s typological reading to a related hermeneutic that seems to reference Neo-Platonic forms. This Neo-Platonic economy of perception provides a frame in which to understand the association of the pornographic "2nd Cuming" and its religious shadow site, "2nd Coming." Søren Kierkegaard's works develop this notion in terms remarkably relevant to this strange collocation of imagery. According to William McDonald, Kierkegaard, throughout his works, parodies the Platonic ideal of *eros* (sexual love) as a material act that directs the lover towards a greater love of the divine. For Plato, *eros* elevates the lover to selfless love that directs the heart to love of the divine. One love overlaps the other, as it were, so that sexual love enables the lover to "climb the ladder of *eros*" towards the greater object of love (60–90). In other words, the hiding of the religious site behind the sexual understands that desire for the sexual is desire for the spiritual not yet perfected. Thus, "2nd Cuming" enacts a substitute until the heart is ready for "2nd Coming."

In *Cup of My Blood*, the Gothic theme of hiddenness establishes this economy of perception through physical signifiers that, in carnal terms, conceal, but also point to, a spiritual reality that transcends the material. Not unlike Laurence N. deLooze's sense of the *Queste del Saint Graal* as offering two competing signifiers and "two systems ... [of] diametrically opposed readings" (239), the film's movement between the physical and the abstract, the material and the spiritual, assumes a Neo-Platonic character. Sparky begins to point to this economy when he explains to Jack the distinction between Jack's earlier erotic art photographs and the pornography that he shoots now: "Erotica is softer, lets the imagination fill in the blanks. Pornography celebrates the explicitness of detail." Sparky suggests that pornography presents the fullness of the female form, while Jack's erotica leaves parts of the female form mysterious. While this description might be taken to mean that pornography reveals the real in its fullness, the film's interest in the hidden and the spiritual belies the idea, given its Neo-Platonic bent. The abstraction that occurs in the imaginative engagement with the erotic assumes a greater reality, because it approximates the form (in the Neo-Platonic sense) of the female body. Erotica's ability to instigate desire for the imagined directs the desiring heart towards an abstract object of desire and/or love.

In the narrative trajectory of Jack's return to faith, we do see this principle enacted, but with a decidedly Kierkegaardian turn. Still mourning Tina's suicide, Jack has avoided sexual relationships, that is until he meets the sultry young Iona at the pool.[9] As their relationship continues, Jack's artistic inspiration sparks to life around the beauty of the female form and the sacredness of religious artifacts such as rosaries, ceremonial incense burners, and relief sculptures of Jesus. Three times in the film they engage in sex, with each of the three times becoming more and more animalistic, even violent. In the final sex scene, Jack's eyes remain closed as he twists and contorts beneath Iona. A second woman (whom we have seen lurking throughout the film) joins them without Jack's realizing. She and Iona speak of finding the Grail, and the second woman encourages Iona to kill Jack then. The implication in terms of the Platonic ideal of *eros* is that sexual love absolutely does not elevate the heart towards the divine, but, as Kierkegaard argues, becomes a parody that entraps the lover in selfish, self-satisfying but destructive love. Iona and Jack's lovemaking is a greedy love that holds the potential for Jack's ruin, not his salvation. In McDonald's Kierkegaardian terms, it establishes "an emphatic distinction between sensuous self-love (*eros*) and divinely given, selfless Christian love (*agape*)" (89), demonstrated in flashback scenes to Jack's bedroom banter with Tina and his caring for her in the depths of her depression.

Agape replaces *eros* in the final bloody sequence in which the various people in Jack's life attempt to claim the Grail. In the clutter of competing interests, Iona reveals herself to be a demonic figure who leads Jack to his moment of greatest weakness, a confrontation with Tina's suicide and a sense of culpability that drives him nearly to hand her the Grail. In that moment, Nibbles explains that Jack is the protector, to which Jack asks: "Why me of all people?" Just before Nibbles is killed by Iona, he replies, "To show you his love and forgiveness. His grace...." Jack demonstrates an internalizing of that message in his final confrontation with Sparky, when he hands Sparky a gun, leaving himself unarmed. While the gesture may appear to be the last, suicidal act of a tormented man, Sparky's response suggests otherwise: "You've magically recovered your lost faith, Jack. Is it strong enough to stop a bullet?" Jack's handing Sparky the gun enacts the selflessness of Jack's love of the divine, not brought through *eros*, but by means of the divine initiation of love named by Nibbles. Jack abandons his own desires and cedes his will to God. Though Sparky shoots him through the eye, that moment signals Jack's becoming the Grail Knight, a redeemed protector for the sacred object of divine apocalypse, capable of surviving the wound and re-securing the Grail.[10]

Given Jack's growth into that role and the rejuvenation of the psychological Wasteland, we might expect the wasted setting to resolve itself, but Catania's apocalyptic framework prevents such a resolution. When a bandaged Jack finds Sparky and one of his porn models dead, the camera lingers over an open Bible, with the dead girl's cracked, gray fingers pointing to 2 Chronicles 32: 4–7,[11] which describe the preparations of Judah for war and Judah's faith in God's protection. The verses, juxtaposed with Jack's entry to reclaim the Grail, imply the coming Armageddon and Jack's role as a leader within it.[12] While chosen or foreordained, like Galahad, the Grail Knight here is not one who pursues the Grail for spiritual ends, but a figure sanctified in a divine love (*agape*) that enables him to commit violence in defense of the Grail. *Cup of My Blood* thus inverts the spatial metaphors of the spirit seen in the Galahad Quest narratives. Where Galahad retreats from the world and receives a vision of the Grail's full signification prior to an ascent from the world, Jack must mire himself in the violence of the world to preserve the relic that will call divine destruction upon the earth.[13] Despite that spatial inversion, *Cup of My Blood* adopts a conservative position not far removed from the *Queste* and the *Morte*: rejection of worldly pursuits and the selfish love of *eros* (akin to Perceval's tests in Malory's *Morte*) in favor of spiritual values, though unlike those texts, determined by an extreme predispensationalist perspective.

The Librarian: Curse of the Judas Chalice: *Quest for Quest's Sake*

Jonathan Frakes' *The Librarian: Curse of the Judas Chalice* (2008) takes up questions related to the tension between self-determination and destined service that I have argued structure both *Code of the Templars* and *Cup of My Blood*. Embracing the former's optimism and the latter's emphasis on service, the film explores the dialectic between individual desires and communitarian commitments. Turner Network Television's (TNT) third installment of the successful *Librarian* TV movie trilogy, *The Judas Chalice*, puts protagonist Flynn Carsen (Noah Wylie), a librarian who secures and protects historical relics for the Metropolitan Library, into a Quest narrative similar to that described by Elspeth Kennedy in her study of failure in Grail legends. Chastised for overspending in the successful completion of another adventure, Flynn laments the demise of another relationship, distraught over what life as a librarian has taken from him. That dismay sends Flynn on "a second journey leading to a revindication of the knight's reputation, rediscovery of himself, redemption from his former fault through the new adventures he has undertaken, and the attainment of a greater understanding through his experience" (Kennedy 283)—in the film, a journey that turns out to be a vacation to New Orleans. There Flynn meets jazz singer Simone, who rushes him away from gun-toting thugs with talk of the Judas Chalice, a magical cup forged from Judas' thirty pieces of silver. "The Holy Grail for vampires," as Flynn describes it, the Chalice endows vampires with ultimate speed and strength and revivifies their dead victims. The thugs prove to be former KGB agents intent on returning Russia to greatness by creating an undead army led by Vlad Dracula, whom they do not know is living as the historian Professor Lazlo (Bruce Davison). With the occasional guidance of Judson (Bob Newhart), support from cabbie Andre (Werner Richmond) and Professor Lazlo, and repeated help from Simone, Flynn races from Capuchin churches in the French Quarter, through raised-crypt cemeteries, and, finally, to pirate Jean Lafitte's wrecked ship to secure the chalice. On the way, he complains about narrowly-escaped dangers, falls in love with Simone despite her own vampirism, and delivers the Chalice to the library a changed man.

Within this context, the Judas Chalice functions as an anti–Grail (the Holy Grail itself is kept in the collections of the Metropolitan Library, along with Excalibur and a unicorn) and occupies one half of the larger moral dichotomy of the film's world. In its implicit opposition of Holy Grail/Judas Chalice, the film presents a Manichean opposition between good and evil that structures two distinct systems of human sociality. Both cups enervate life, with the Grail restoring vigor to the wounded king and the Chalice revivifying dead vampires; both cups also restore strength. The Grail supports spiritual vigor while the Chalice provides, as noted above, ultimate strength and speed to vampires. Despite those parallels, the Chalice operates as a parody of the Grail on two counts: first, it emphasizes the material over the spiritual, restoring un-death and bestowing physical superiority rather than focusing on matters of the spirit; second, and related to the first, the Chalice promises dominance by the few (the strong) over the many, whereas the Grail, if we follow the narratives of the *Queste* and the *Morte*, derives from resisting worldly forces in favor of harmonious camaraderie in service to spiritual transcendence.

The film, thus, establishes an antithesis between predatory worldly domination and human sociality for virtuous ends. And yet, Frakes seems to blur that opposition by juxtaposing the villains and the Library as sharing similar qualities. Former KGB agent and Russian Minister of Defense Sergei Kubichek (Dikran Tulaine) endeavors to return Russia to a dominant world status by preying on opponents with an army of vampires, and Professor Lazlo/Vlad Dracula simply desires his own return to predatory superiority by feeding from humans. Tied as it is to the vampire and the draining of blood from victims, the Chalice invokes traditional associations with blood-sucking and the stealing of life. In the early scenes, however, Flynn accuses the Library of having a similar effect. Exasperated by the loss of his girlfriend and the sacrifices the Library has demanded of him, Flynn shouts, "This place is sucking the life out of me." While working at the level of metaphor, the line implies that the Library, just like a vampire, drains Flynn of life, depriving him of those things that make life enjoyable. Flynn rattles off a list of missed occasions and lost romances he associates with the relics he has collected for the Library. To some extent, that emphasis on worldly desires and indi-

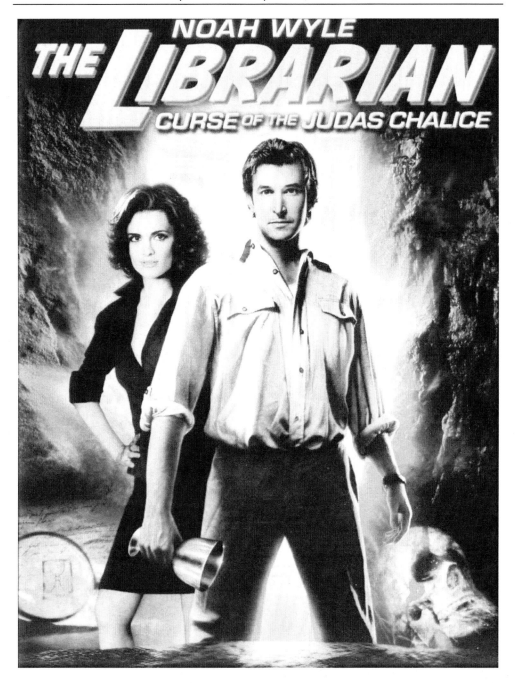

Advertisement for Jonathan Frakes' *The Librarian: Curse of the Judas Chalice*.

vidual interests shifts Flynn towards the villains in valuing the material world and one's satisfaction with it over the nobler pursuits represented by the Library. Frakes initiates Flynn's Quest from this point, a place of limited perspective that fails to perceive the differences between vampires and the Library. The narrative, then, is a Quest in which Flynn arrives at a rightly ordered understanding of the Library, its mission, and his own place within it.

The dichotomy of Grail/Chalice structures not just the moral framework of the film, as noted above, but also the opposition of the Library and the combined villains of Kubichek and Vlad Dracula. If the Chalice orients towards extreme physicality, then we find in the villains a similar inclination to material interests. Most simply, Vlad Dracula, even in his guise as Professor Lazlo, seeks the Chalice to imbue himself with his former vitality and physical superiority. The Russian operatives, however, are similarly focused on material concerns. Kubichek, lamenting Russia's decline in a post–Soviet era, aspires to return his country to global dominance with an army of vampires capable of the physical domination exemplified by Vlad Dracula. In so far as the film locates Kubichek in an obsessive focus on the material situation of the here-and-now, he aligns with the medieval Grail legends' Lady of the Black Ship, who tempts Perceval with the physical delights of wine and sex. His nefarious plan centers not just on use but on control of bodies to advance a vision of the world in which his own sinister force overcomes and literally swallows its opposition. Kubichek's longing for Communist might emerges in an inverted moral view that paints the Soviet dogma as one of vicious and tyrannical deprivation of human life and freedoms, much like the image of the Nazis in Spielberg's *Indiana Jones and the Last Crusade*.

The Library, then, occupies the opposite moral pole, but, despite the Grail/Chalice dichotomy, the Grail does not receive description or explanation. Frakes simply leaves it as a vague indicator of goodness. Flynn, therefore, must discern the function of the Library. In the medieval Grail legends, Gawain's misperception of the Grail Quest as yet another pursuit of worldly honor yields no adventures and prevents him from achieving any success. Discernment of the Library's mission, the fullness of the good it represents, becomes the true end of Flynn's Quest. The film reveals the mission in a painting of "the Library's eternal battle against evil." In that painting, four mounted warriors, whom Flynn describes as "knights," ride over three demonic figures. In the center of the painting, the foremost knight bears a shield emblazoned with a white tree, which Flynn identifies as the Tree of Knowledge. Simone explains that he is Yahudah (Hebrew for "Judson," according to Flynn), the scholar and greatest librarian of all, responsible for building the library. The painting and Simone's explanation of it draw together several strands that percolate throughout the film: the opposition of good and evil conveyed by the Grail/Chalice dichotomy, the preoccupation with Flynn's many advanced degrees, and the role of the library in preserving "relics." Knight, scholar, and librarian, Yahuda stands as warrior, devotee to learning, and preserver of knowledge in a nexus that defines virtue as a humanist pursuit of knowledge.

If evil in Frakes' film is the tyrannical deprivation of life and freedom, then good emerges as a defense of social freedoms that are rooted in enlightened humanist values of sociality. The film thus promotes what has, in the years after the September 11 attacks, become a cliché: freedom is not free. Flynn's egocentric moaning about lost romantic relationships and his complaints about a life lived escaping danger in the early scenes run counter to that ethos. His whining asserts a radical individuality that ignores the contingency of individual freedom on responsibilities to a larger community.[14] Andre and his myriad "cousins," who come from a variety of ethnic backgrounds, illustrate this ideal, one that entails mutual interdependence and interpersonal responsibility. *The Librarian: Curse of the Judas Chalice* draws Flynn's development to a close, then, around his realization that the freedoms deriving from humanist values require defense, and that defense requires sacrifice. While the Quest, as a means of defense, carries destructive potential, it also assures the continued possibility individual freedoms that make meaningful relationships possible. Frakes handles the destructive effects of the Grail by offering a vision of balance between self-determination, as in *Code of the Templars*, and utter sacrifice to service, as in *Cup of My Blood*. Justin Galland's *Rosencrantz and Guildenstern Are Undead* pushes away from this balance and attempts a move similar to *Code of the Templars*. As we shall see, it ends in a far more cynical place.

Rosencrantz and Guildenstern Are Undead: *The Grail's Shallow Emptiness*

Unlike the preceding films, Galland's *Rosencrantz and Guildenstern Are Undead* (2009) focuses not on the Holy Grail, but on vampirism and Julian Marsh's (Jake Hoffman) directing a bizarre, vampire-themed production of *Hamlet*. After breaking up with his girlfriend, Julian languishes in the doldrums, living in a spare room in his father's medical office and bedding a different woman every night, while his beloved Anna (Devon Aoki) has moved on and is now dating suspected mobster Bobby Bianchi (Ralph Macchio). When his father threatens to kick him out, Julian is forced to take a job directing the strangest version of *Hamlet* anyone has seen. Purporting to tell the true story of Hamlet, the play involves a blood-sucking Horatio turning Hamlet into a vampire, who goes on to locate and sip from the Holy Grail, thereby curing himself and receiving prolonged life. Julian listlessly directs the play, fails to prevent Anna from taking the role of Ophelia, and jealously (but impotently) tries to keep her from dating the theatre owner, writer, and chief vampire, Theo Horace (John Ventimiglia). Enter the secretive society Rosicrucian and Goldenstone, whose representatives warn Vince (Kris Lemche), Julian's Hamlet and best friend, that the play is a nefarious plot by a coven of vampires to feed on both the cast and audience. After Vince mysteriously dies, Julian learns of the vampire plot, assumes the role of Hamlet and fails to protect Anna from becoming a vampire herself. Only the Grail can save her, so Julian follows through with the production in vain hope of meeting the real Hamlet and securing the Grail—and with it, Anna's soul. When Hamlet does arrive, Rosicrucian and Goldenstone grab the Grail, and Julian is left with a choice: stake Anna or join her.

The New York in which Galland sets *Rosencrantz & Guildenstern Are Undead* is a Wasteland of consumerism that causes shallow human relationships. I do not mean to suggest that Galland's film fills the screen with commodity obsession, but rather that, when we leave the medical office or the theatre, the dominant imagery tends towards images of consumption that will have obvious implications for the vampire tale. Bobby Bianchi becomes the lodestar around which the idea revolves. Bobby's first appearance features him in his penthouse apartment revealing a brand-new product, The Germ-O-Whack. Little more than a small black squirt gun filled with hand sanitizer, Bobby invests the product with excessive value, promoting the need it fills for men to keep clean in a manly way. A reporter's and Julian's discernment belies the value Bobby ascribes to the fetishized squirt gun and reveals the commodity to be empty of actual value. But Bobby's insistence on the significance of the Germ-O-Whack defines the world of the film as one in which, to quote Marketing Consultant Victor Lebows, a "promotional campaign ... has no guarantee of success, yet it may contribute to the general pressure by which wants are stimulated and maintained" (8). My point here is that *Rosencrantz & Guildenstern Are Undead* sets its characters in a New York driven by consumption, but presents its characters as always only experiencing want. The reporter's and Julian's rejection of the Germ-O-Whack's ascribed value may frustrate Bobby's attempt to instigate feelings of want, but, as characters in the consumerist world of the film, all the film's characters are driven by wants.

As a result, human relationships in Galland's film appear largely empty. The clueless disregard Bobby demonstrates for everyone around him evinces a reduction of everything, including people, to use-value. For example, when Anna discovers Bobby has been filming their love-making, she storms out saying, "I'm leaving you." Bobby calls after her, "If you're going out, can you bring me back some soy milk?" Anna's identity as person becomes commodified as provider of comforts, including sex and soy milk. Julian's womanizing amounts to the same revaluing of the other. The opening scene, in which he wakes next to an anonymous bedmate and she exits hostilely from the room, establishes this theme in direct correspondence to the revaluing of the woman as sexual toy. Additionally, the competition to consume before others can do so disrupts human relationships. It develops in Julian's jealous conversations about and with Anna, as well as when Vince highlights Julian's failures as a boyfriend, and when Julian goes to a night club where women seem interested only in Theo. The consumerist culture of the film causes the characters to "[value] 'stuff' over people, competition over cooperation, and the individual over the group" (Levine, par. 21). Galland thus defines the world of the film as one of narcissistically consuming both objects and people with a resulting dis-integration of community. The ego-centric clambering after individual wants reduces interactions between the characters to struggles for acquisition, possession, or defense of the objects of those desires.

Within this Wasteland, Julian occupies dual roles as wounded king and Questing Grail Knight. The film establishes the first of those roles, the wounded king, through Julian's literally living in a doctor's office, which suggests a chronic ailment. Julian's wound manifests itself in Hoffman's almost affectless, monotone portrayal of Julian as a disinterested, sleeping director, a near stereotypical image of disaffected young adults. Julian, as wounded king, suffers from the psychological impotence of depression. Rather than Perceval seeking to restore the wounded king, Julian must restore himself. As a Questing Knight, Julian pursues the Grail to save his beloved, despite the unrequited nature of his affection. He eschews other women as the plot develops, focused solely on Anna and protecting or, after Theo "turns" her, restoring her to a human state. Julian's character development elevates his desires away from the narcissistic consumption that marks him in the early part of the film towards a less selfish affection for Anna. Galland's film thereby locates Julian within the courtly idea, in which love ennobles the lover. Julian's Grail Quest does not seek the Grail for the narcissistic impulses of commodity fetishism. It is a tool for healing his beloved.

But those associated with the Grail render that tool little more than an empty cup. In the Rosicrucians and Goldenstone DVD that Charlotte gives to Julian, the voiceover's historical exposition of Hamlet and Horatio's (the film's Theo) struggle ends by explaining that their anticipated showdown will give "our society a chance at long last to gain possession of the Holy Grail." No reason is given for possessing the Grail. Our sense is that Rosicrucians and Goldenstone seek the Grail as pure fetish, devoid of any but imaginatively ascribed value. In the final scenes, Hamlet's (Joey Kern) appearance goes further, to suggest the Grail is no cure, but a new curse. A smiling, blonde golden-boy, Hamlet panders to the crowd with juvenile humor and simplistic critiques of the play's performances. He insults Theo saying, "The only one you should despise is whomever dresses you. My God, Horatio, for reals." In response to Theo's retort that he has "the vitality and energy of a custard," Hamlet quips, "That's what you get when you have a great workout routine and you stick to it." Hamlet's retorts revolve around superficialities like clothing and the fitness culture, while he plays to the audience in a display of ego that encapsulates the problems of Galland's particular image of the Wasteland. The portrayal of Hamlet makes a return to the human world of commodity consumption decidedly unattractive.

The inversion of the Grail's moral associations emerges in full force as a result of Hamlet's arrival on the scene. While, throughout the last act of *Rosencrantz & Guildenstern Are Undead*, we have sympathized with Julian and his Quest to return Anna to human form, Hamlet's appearance refocuses attention on what a return to human life actually means. As a result, Theo and his vampiric lifestyle appears no worse an option. As he explains in the lines of the play, "One should only eat what one hungers for. That is my philosophy." (To which Vince's Hamlet replies, "There are more things in heaven and earth than are dreamt of in your philosophy.") Theo's line distinguishes between types of consumption by implying a difference between actual hungers and fabricated wants. Actual desires for Theo are sensual. In an acting exercise, he becomes entirely lost in miming the devouring of an apple, slurping at the imaginary fruit and licking its juices from his hand and wrists. Contrast that enjoyment with Bobby Bianchi's struggle to induce desire for his Germ-O-Whack, to invest it with value that nobody sees. Theo's way encourages bodily appetites and their satisfaction in lieu of subscribing to the imaginary values of economic materialism.

As a vampire, Anna encourages Julian to join her with those very desires. Julian enters her dressing room to stake her, telling her that she is undead, but she interrupts him after *un-* and substitutes "-believably attracted to you" for *-dead*. She plays on his desire for her and tempts him with the possibility of spending eternity with her as a vampire. The Quest for the Grail having failed, proven in the process to result in a return to the Wasteland, Julian abandons the Quest to adopt the hedonistic life Theo represented. In the final scene (titled "Breakfast is Tiffany"), the film ends as it began, Julian, in his bed with another woman, answering the phone when Anna calls. This time he does not lie about the woman but awaits Anna and Vince to join him for breakfast. Anna's final line voices the complete rejection of Grail-oriented values: "...a vampire doesn't need to save her soul when she has a soulmate." Galland ends his film, therefore, with a total inversion of the structures that define human relations in consumer culture by turning the Grail into the ultimate fetish and associating it with simply a return to, rather than a curing of, the Wasteland. The Grail becomes just another Germ-O-Whack, an unnecessary sanitizer overinvested with meaning and value it does not actually possess.

The inversion enacted by Galland's trio of new vampires ultimately does not hold. The feel-good end of the romantic Quest achieved tries to assert a valuing of love over all other desires, but Anna's final line and the final shot of Julian unsettle that inversion. In that shot, Julian's eyes glow and fangs grow as he prepares to devour the young blonde girl in his bed. They may have rediscovered their love for one another, but, in the process, they have become predatory consumers. In Theo's showdown with Hamlet, he argues, "A vampire is the most graceful, majestic and powerful of creatures," but, within the desire-driven competition of the film's consumer culture, Theo's remarks simply turn these new young vampires into apex predators. As Fred Botting has observed in his examination of the Anne Rice's vampires, "the vampire is more than an 'observer of the marketplace,' he is absorbed in its operations" (24). Being so absorbed in the operations of the market, of consuming people, Galland locates the trio as commodity narcissists. Robert Cluley and Stephen Dunne argue that commodity narcissists "consume to harm others and, consequently, elevate [themselves] over them" (260), while failing to allow knowledge of their aggression to guide their behavior away from it. The new trio of vampires in *Rosencrantz & Guildenstern Are Undead* takes this theory to an extreme. If Julian's problem in the beginning of the film was an inability to compete effectively, then his life as a vampire enables him to escape the pressures of that world by dominating it.

Replacing Compromise with Debate

I have argued that each of these films problematizes the traditional image of the Grail and the Quest with which it is associated. In the medieval legends, the Grail functions as a sacred relic of spiritual redemption and the Quest as a process of purification that prepares one for a life in its service. The films I have discussed disrupt that simple relationship between Grail as object of the Quest and the Quest as means of obtaining its benefits. All four emphasize the destructive effects of the Grail (or Chalice) and the Quest to acquire it: the Grail and its pursuit tear away at individual desires. But two distinct patterns emerge that differentiate the films from one another. First, *Code of the Templars* and *Rosencrantz & Guildenstern Are Undead* parallel and then supersede the Grail Quest with the romantic Quest. In both, the Grail itself is rejected as inhibiting a more fulfilling existence as an earthly being able to delight in the desires of romantic love. Second, *Cup of My Blood* and *The Librarian: Curse of the Judas Chalice* emphasize the Manichean struggle of good and evil as the larger frame in which both the Grail and the Quest operate; they are parts of that larger whole. In each, the protagonist must sacrifice individual desires in lieu of service to a greater community and cause.

Like a fractal, these four films manifest collectively the central tension that each takes up individually: the tension between self-determination and communitarian contingency. The films suggest that the struggle between independence and sociality preoccupies our own cultural moment in much the same way it preoccupied Arthur as he lamented the demise of his collective as his knights individually pursued the Grail. The terms of the Quest, however, seem to have changed. In the Grail stories told in both the *Queste* and the *Morte*, attainment of the Grail results in spiritual bliss. The perfect knight, the virgin knight, and the chaste knight devote themselves to the Grail's service, with Galahad ascending to Heaven upon full revelation of the Grail, Perceval dying in that service, and only Bors returning to Camelot to relate the full story. Even Lancelot's incomplete Quest and partial vision yield deeper spiritual insight and penitence. But in the terms of popular culture's B-films, the spiritual virtues of the Grail Quest evaporate in lieu of competing ideals of worldly fulfillment, with the result that Arthur's terms are inverted. Dedication to community requires embracing the Quest (even if not focused on the Grail), whereas the commitment to the individual's pursuits depends on its rejection. Lacking the imprimatur of religion, however, we are left to a debate rather than embrace Arthur's compromise of a depleted community.

Notes

1. Kleis examines the way in which Syberberg's film meditates on the loss of the Grail spirit in Wagner's opera and on the loss of good works. See "The Arthurian Dilemma: Syberberg's *Parsifal*," especially 118–119.

2. In *Parzival*, the naïve young knight Quests after the Grail only to discover that he descends from and is named as one of the Templiesen, or Grail Knights. Despite the unlikelihood that Wolfram intended to refer to the Templars, his use of "Templiesen" has spurred a popular tradition of association, which the film follows, between the Templars and the Grail. See Richard Barber, *The Holy Grail: Imagination and Belief* 179. Barber discusses at some length the association of the Templars with the Grail (306–311).

3. The film confuses the idea of Christ having produced children when Brother Quentin, in his explanation to David, notes that the original Templars were known as the "siblings" of Christ, because the same blood flowed in their veins. While *Code of the Templars* depends on that line of descent to justify the abilities of the Templars and Priors, it seems to want to blur that connection.

4. The film implies that David was conceived deceptively, which seems to play on the conception story of Galahad, with Pelles soliciting the help of the sorceress Dame Brusen to enchant and disguise Elaine as Guinevere for the purpose of conceiving the future Grail knight. See Malory's treatment in *Malory: Complete Works*. Eugene Vinaver, ed., 477–506. In "How to Handle a Woman, or Morgan at the Movies," Maureen Fries discusses Morgana's conception of Mordred, observing that she raises Mordred "as avenger of the family feud" (77). Both Boorman's Mordred and Basmeyer's David greet their mother's death with little concern, Mordred actually being the instrument of Morgana's death. While David does come to her side in her failing moments, he shows little grief, indicative of the fullness of his rejection of Lucrezia's priorities.

5. My use of the term "courtly love" here and below are decidedly vague, drawing on a general sense of modernity's clichéd images of courtly love and benefitting from the fuzziness produced by Joachim Bumke's analysis of the multiplicity of its forms (see *Courtly Culture: Literature and Society in the High Middle Ages* 360–392).

6. James Schultz explains that courtly lovers fall in love with courtly behaviors, labeling the idea *aristophilia*. We see a similar privileging of such behaviors, though in a decidedly modern way, in the party scene in *Code of the Templars*. See *Courtly Love, the Love of Courtliness, and the History of Sexuality* 79–100.

7. Janina Traxler argues that the Grail Quest succeeds theologically because of the guidance and actions of Perceval's sister. See "Dying to Get to Sarras: Perceval's Sister and the Grail Quest" 261–278. Susan Aronstein's "Rewriting Perceval's Sister: Eucharistic Vision and the Typological Destiny in the *Queste del Saint Graal*" argues to the contrary, that Perceval's sister fails, ultimately, to satisfy the demands of her role by allowing her blood-letting.

8. See, for example, J. F. Rutherford's *Deliverance*, originally published in 1926, in which Rutherford describes his vision of the end times, involving a war against the Antichrist, out of which believers are saved. The sixteen book *Left Behind* series, by Tim LaHaye and Jerry B. Jenkins, draws on the predispensationalist theologies to which works like Rutherford's have contributed. In the series, the Tribulation Force battles against the Antichrist Nicolae Carpathias' Global Community.

9. Iona seems to derive from the tradition of fey women described by Myra Olstead as contributory to the women of the Arthurian legends, associated with water, "sensitive to slights, protective towards their chosen heroes, skilled in magic, and aggressive in matters of love and war." See "Lancelot at the Grail Castle," *Folklore* 50.

10. The film never clarifies if, or to what extent, Sparky and Nibbles are working together, but, whether they are or not, leaves the impression that they have different interests even if common efforts.

11. "They gathered a large group of people who blocked all the springs and the stream that flowed through the land. 'Why should the kings of Assyria come and find plenty of water?' they said. Then he worked hard repairing all the broken sections of the wall and building towers on it. He built another wall outside that one and reinforced the terraces of the City of David. He also made large numbers of weapons and shields. He appointed military officers over the people and assembled them before him in the square at the city gate and encouraged them with these words: 'Be strong and courageous. Do not be afraid or discouraged because of the king of Assyria and the vast army with him, for there is a greater power with us than with him.'"

12. The same principle applies to the film's discourse around its setting. The diegetic world that surrounds the settings inscribes Catania's film with immanent Old Testament wrath and violence that does not appear in physical, material terms (at least not until Jack fully assumes his role as Grail Protector). But Nibbles draws our attention to the vague apocalyptic happenings signified in normal perceptions of the world. He explains their significance as a sort of prophet figure parallel to the hermits who provide commentary on *senefiance* in the medieval Grail stories.

13. Jack, in the closing voiceover, explains, "Sparky warned me about all the horrible things I'd have to do to keep it safe. Maybe I am the guy for the job." The film seems to offer up Jack as someone like the crusaders, inspired by the cult of warrior saints, who legitimated the violence committed in the name of a holy Quest or pilgrimage. See James B. MacGregor, "Negotiating Knightly Piety: The Cult of the Warrior-Saints in the West, ca. 1070–ca. 1200" 342–345.

14. I invoke here Lee Patterson, who describes the distinction between medieval and modern notions of subjectivity in similar terms. Where modern individuality is conceived in terms of radical individuality, medieval subjectivity emerged as a dialogical synthesis of individual and community. See *Chaucer and the Subject of History* 1–13.

Works Cited

Aronstein, Susan. "Rewriting Perceval's Sister: Eucharistic Vision and the Typological Destiny in the *Queste del Saint Graal.*" *Women's Studies* 21 (1992): 211–230.

Barber, Richard. *The Holy Grail: Imagination and Belief.* Cambridge: Harvard University Press, 2004.

Bloch, Howard R. "Wasteland and Round Table: The Historical Significance of Myths of Dearth and Plenty in Old French Romance." *New Literary History* 11.2 (Winter 1980): 255–276.

Botting, Fred. "Hypocrite Vampire...." *Gothic Studies* 9.1 (May 2007):16–34.

Bumke, Joachim. *Courtly Culture: Literature and Society in the High Middle Ages.* Berkeley: University of California Press, 1991.

Cluley, Robert and Stephen Dunne. "From Commodity Fetishism to Commodity Narcissism." *Marketing Theory* 12.3 (December 2012): 251–265.

Code of the Templars. Dr. Florian Baxmeyer. Genius Entertainment, 2004.

Cup of My Blood. Dir. Lance Catania. X Ray Productions, 2005.

de Looze, Laurence N. "A Story of Interpretations: The *Queste del Saint Graal* as Metaliterature." In *The Grail: A Casebook.* Ed. Dhira B. Mahoney. New York: Garland, 2000.

Excalibur. Dir. John Boorman. Orion Pictures, 1981.

Fries, Maureen. "How to Handle a Woman, or Morgan at the Movies." In *King Arthur on Film: New Essays on Arthurian Cinema.* Ed. Kevin J. Harty. Jefferson, N.C.: McFarland, 1999.

Kennedy, Angus J. "Punishment in the *Perlesvaus*: the Theme of the Waste Land." In *The Grail: A Casebook.* Ed. Dhira B. Mahoney. New York: Garland 2000.

Kennedy, Elspeth. "Failure in Arthurian Romance." In *The Grail: A Casebook.* Ed. Dhira B. Mahoney. New York: Garland, 2000.

Kleis, John Christopher. "The Arthurian Dilemma: Syberberg's *Parsifal.*" In *King Arthur on Film: New Essays on Arthurian Cinema.* Ed. Kevin J. Harty. Jefferson, N.C.: McFarland, 1999.

LaHaye, Tim, and Jerry B. Jenkins. *Left Behind: A Novel of the Earth's Last Days*. Carol Stream, IL: Tyndale House Publishers, 1995.

Lebow, Victor. "Price Competition in 1955." *Journal of Retailing* 31.1 (Spring 1955): 5–10.

Levine, Madeline. "Challenging the Culture of Affluence." *Independent School* Fall 2007. http://www.nais.org/Magazines-Newsletters/ISMagazine/Pages/Challenging-the-Culture-of-Affluence–150274.aspx.

The Librarian: Curse of the Judas Curse. Dir. Peter Winther. Dean Devlin, Electric Entertainment, 2008.

The Light in the Dark (The Light of Faith). Dir. Clarence Brown. Hope Hampton Productions, Vitagraph Company of America, 1922.

MacGregor, James B. "Negotiating Knightly Piety: The Cult of the Warrior-Saints in the West, ca. 1070-ca. 1200." *Church History* 73.2 (June 2004): 317–345.

Malory, Sir Thomas. *The Works of Sir Thomas Malory*. Ed. Eugène Vinaver and P.J.C. Field. 3rd ed. 3 vols. Oxford: Clarendon Press, 1990.

McDonald, William. "Love In Kierkegaard's *Symposia*." *Minerva: A Journal of Philosophy* 7 (2003): 60–93.

Olstead, Myra. "Lancelot at the Grail Castle." *Folklore* 76.1 (Spring 1965): 48–57.

Queste del San Graal. Ed. E. Willingham. Turnhout: Brepols Publishers, 2012.

Rosencrantz & Guildenstern Are Undead. Dir. Jordan Galland. C Plus Pictures, 2009.

Rutherford, J.F. *Deliverance*. Brooklyn: International Bible Students Association, 1926.

Schultz, James A. *Courtly Love, the Love of Courtliness, and the History of Sexuality*. Chicago: University of Chicago Press, 2006.

Traxler, Janina. "Dying to Get to Sarras: Perceval's Sister and the Grail Quest." In *The Grail: A Casebook*. Ed. Dhira B. Mahoney. New York: Garland, 2000.

About the Contributors

Susan **Aronstein**, a professor of English at the University of Wyoming, is the author of *Hollywood Knights: Arthurian Cinema and the Politics of Nostalgia* (2005) and *An Introduction to British Arthurian Narrative* (2012), as well as the coeditor of *The Disney Middle Ages: A Fairy Tale and Fantasy Past* (2012).

Alan **Baragona** is a professor emeritus at Virginia Military Institute. He has written on Arthurian legend, Chaucer, medieval drama, Shakespeare, and baseball literature. He is a founding member of the Chaucer MetaPage and creator of the *Arthuriana* Pedagogy Pages. He also performs with the Towneley Players, an academic theater group that performs and records staged readings of medieval theater for the Chaucer Studio.

Raeleen **Chai-Elsholz**, an independent scholar and technical translator, researches hagiographical texts from Anglo-Saxon England and the late ancient Latin West. She also researches and publishes on various eighteenth-century ecclesiastical topics and personalities. She is a member of the board of directors of the International Medieval Society based in Paris, France.

Andrew B. R. **Elliott** is a senior lecturer in media and cultural studies at the University of Lincoln, UK, where he teaches history, film, and television. His research focuses on the representation of history, particularly the Middle Ages, in modern media, including film, television and video games. He is the author of *Remaking the Middle Ages* (2010), editor of *The Return of the Epic Film: Genre, Aesthetics and History in the 21st Century* (2014), and co-editor of *Playing with the Past: Digital Games and the Simulation of History* (2013).

Jean-Marc **Elsholz** has published in *Positif* and is completing his doctoral thesis in the Art History and Film Studies Department of the Université Panthéon-Sorbonne (Paris I). His thesis investigates how the visual underpins and nourishes a narrative plane that is specific to film, and it examines some of the consequences on film analysis and art history of identifying this kind of narrative, with particular attention to the reciprocal relationships and contributions between cinema and other visual arts.

Laurie A. **Finke** is a professor of women's and gender studies at Kenyon College. With Martin Shichtman, she has co-authored *Cinematic Illuminations: The Middle Ages on Film* (2009), *King Arthur and the Myth of History* (2004), and numerous articles on medieval literature and culture. Their book *Medieval Texts and Contemporary Readers* (1987) was the first collection of essays to provide a systematic representation of the diversity of contemporary critical debate about the nature of discourse and that debate's relevance to the study of medieval literature.

Joan Tasker **Grimbert** is a professor emerita of French and medieval studies at the Catholic University of America in Washington, D.C. She has published extensively on Arthurian literature and film and has authored, edited, or co-edited six books. Her previous film essays have focused on

Rohmer's *Perceval le Gallois*, Delannoy and Cocteau's *L'Éternel retour*, Gunlaugsson's *Shadow of the Raven*, and Truffaut's *Femme d'à-côté*. She is immediate past president of the North American Branch of the International Arthurian Society.

Kevin J. **Harty,** a professor and chair of English at La Salle University in Philadelphia, is a past president of the North American Branch of the International Arthurian Society and book review editor for *Arthuriana*, the branch's quarterly scholarly journal. The editor or author of books on the Middle Ages, Chaucer, King Arthur and film, he has also published essays on film treatments of Robin Hood, Joan of Arc, El Cid and King Arthur, as well as on Malory, on Chaucer, and on other literary and cultural topics.

James **Jesson** is an assistant professor of English at La Salle University. He studies twentieth-century drama and radio plays, and he has published essays on radio drama by Orson Welles and Samuel Beckett.

David W. **Marshall** is an associate professor of English at California State University, San Bernardino, where he specializes in medieval literature, medievalism, and literary adaptation. His edited collection, *Mass Market Medieval* (2007), explores the breadth of medievalism in popular culture. Additionally, he has published articles on the use of medieval dragon legends in Young Earth Creationism, as well as on cinematic depictions of the Vikings, on recent film adaptations of *Beowulf* and on the fourteenth-century John Ball letters.

Christine M. **Neufeld** is a professor of literature at Eastern Michigan University, where she teaches courses in medieval literature, cultural studies and theory. While specializing in late medieval antifeminist satire, the literary history of witchcraft and magic and theories of sound, she has also published numerous articles on medievalism in film. She is also the managing editor of *The Once and Future Classroom*, a journal published by the Consortium for the Teaching of the Middle Ages.

Cory James **Rushton** is an associate professor of English at St. Francis Xavier University in Nova Scotia, Canada. He is co-editor of *The Companion to Medieval Popular Romance* and has also co-edited two books on zombies and culture (both 2011). He has published articles on historical conspiracy theories in which the Grail comes to Nova Scotia, on miscegenation in Tolkien and Pratchett, and several articles and chapters on various aspects of Thomas Malory's *Morte Darthur*.

Jon **Sherman** is an assistant professor at Northern Michigan University where he teaches German language and medieval literature. His research interests lie primarily in medieval German, and to a lesser degree medieval Scandinavian, literature. He has published on the 13th-century Arthurian romance *Wigalois* and on the detective fiction of Austrian novelist Wolf Haas.

Martin B. **Shichtman** is a professor of English and director of Jewish studies at Eastern Michigan University. With Laurie A. Finke, he has co-authored *Cinematic Illuminations: The Middle Ages on Film* (2009), *King Arthur and the Myth of History* (2004), and numerous articles on medieval literature and culture. Their book *Medieval Texts and Contemporary Readers* (1987) was the first collection of essays to provide a systematic representation of the diversity of contemporary critical debate about the nature of discourse and that debate's relevance to the study of medieval literature.

Paul B. **Sturtevant** is a program and museum evaluator with the Smithsonian Institution in Washington, D.C., as well as managing editor of *Curator: The Museum Journal*. His scholarship focuses on using empirical research methods to explore the popular understanding of the Middle Ages. He has previously published essays on the public influence of medieval historical and fantasy films.

Joseph M. **Sullivan** is an associate professor of German in the Department of Modern Languages, Literatures, and Linguistics at the University of Oklahoma. His research is comparative in nature and spans several national cultures and Arthuriana past and present. He is translating the thirteenth-century Middle High German romance *Wigamur* into English.

K. S. **Whetter** is a professor of English at Acadia University in Nova Scotia. His Arthurian publications include the monograph *Understanding Genre and Medieval Romance* (2008), as well as the essay collections *Re-Viewing Le Morte Darthur: Texts and Contexts, Characters and Themes* (co-edited with Raluca L. Radulescu, 2005), and *The Arthurian Way of Death: The English Tradition* (co-edited with Karen Cherewatuk, 2009).

Index